Projecting **Beirut**

Projecting **Beirut**

Episodes in the Construction and Reconstruction of a Modern City

Edited by Peter G. Rowe
and Hashim Sarkis

Prestel

Munich · London · New York

Contents

Acknowledgments

Books like this do not materialize without significant support. We would first like to express our sincere gratitude to the Arab Bank plc for their generous sponsorship, which made this publication possible.

This volume grew out of a conference, which was held at the Graduate School of Design at Harvard University on April 11 and 12, 1997. To the conference organizing committee we owe a special debt of gratitude, particularly to Farès el-Dahdah, Rodolphe el-Khoury, Joumana Ghandour Atallah, Oussama Kabbani, Samir Khalaf, and Jad Tabet. Also, without the kind support of such coorganizers as the René Moawad Foundation and Deputy Nayla Mouawad, the Center for Behavioral Research at the American University of Beirut, Solidere – the Lebanese Company for the Development and Reconstruction of the Beirut Central District – the Order of Engineers and Architects of Beirut, and its president, Assem Salam, this conference could not have taken place nor this volume prepared.

Scholarship of this kind requires archival support. To this end we would like to thank a number of different institutions, including the Constantinos Doxiadis Archives, the Aga Khan Trust for Culture, the Oscar Niemeyer Foundation, Solidere, and the Francis Loeb Library here at Harvard. Research work was ably carried out by Zeina Misk, Ayman Zahreddine, Lillian Kuri, Markus Schaefer, Thomas Doxiadis, and Allen Sayegh.

Finally, staff support is an essential ingredient in such an undertaking. We would like to express our sincere thanks to Maria Moran and Celia Slattery here at the Harvard Graduate School of Design.

Introduction: Projecting Beirut

by

Peter G. Rowe and Hashim Sarkis

As the title suggests, this book deals with two specific periods in the urban development of Beirut. The first coincides with the Welfare State, roughly from the late 1950s until the late 1960s, and the second with the contemporary period following the Civil War. These two periods were chosen for a variety of reasons, not the least of which is the useful comparative perspective which can be gained about modes and styles of planning, urban design, and architecture. Ironically, perhaps, many of the buildings constructed during the Welfare State are now being reconstructed or replaced during the present postwar era. In fact, when one speaks of reconstruction nowadays in Beirut, one must be clear about the fact that it is taking place largely against the backdrop of the relatively expansive social, economic, and physical investment of prior regimes and not *de novo*. Indeed, in this regard, Beirut provides an important and interesting case study of the general phenomena of urban development and city building elsewhere in the world. Moreover, both periods represent happier and more progressive times for Beirut, so often depicted these days in a state of ruin, beset by civil strife and desperation.

Another reason for focusing on an episodic presentation of modern Beirut's history is to reflect directly and accurately the process by which cities seem to grow and develop – a process which, after all, is more likely to be spasmodic in its spatio-temporal trajectory than continuous. As history often tells us, there are likely to be periods of intensive development, followed just as frequently by times of retrenchment and even reversal of a prior period's perceived excesses and gains. Although far more catastrophic than most, Beirut's modern history is no different than that of many other cities in various parts of the world. Even before the establishment of the Lebanese Republic in 1943, there were periods of technological advancement and modernization, for instance, followed by less productive interludes in urban progress, sometimes despite the best efforts of those in power and authority. On other occasions, such as during World Wars I and II, as well as during pan-Arab movements in later years, outside forces came to bear on Beirut, changing the direction of its political history and influencing both the form and fabric of the city.

A third reason for choosing these two periods is inextricably bound up – by contrast to these generalizations – with Beirut's uniqueness as a place, and the idea of a pluralist, multiconfessional city. Certainly during modern times, Beirut's image as a city of strong character emerged onto the world scene, notably during President Shihab's term in office between 1958 and 1964, again, like today, after a period of civil strife. It is also the impression of the city that is now foremost in many people's minds during the present reconstruction of Beirut, together with the well-remembered images of this once prosperous Mediterranean city before the Civil War in 1975. In fact, architecturally and urbanistically speaking, many of the projects from the period of the Welfare State form a heritage which can be proudly and productively built upon today, during the current period of reconstruction.

To be sure, there are also asymmetries and dissimilarities between the two periods as well, which only make for interesting comparisons and discussions. First, in keeping with the times, the Welfare State was commensurate with strong public sector involvement in all matters of building, public works, and civic projects. By contrast, today belongs to an era of privatization or, at the very least, of public-private joint ventures that might otherwise have been public projects. This trend is quite conspicuous, for example, in the development and then redevelopment of Beirut's Central Business District, as well as other districts to both the north and the south of the city. In a corollary fashion, these two periods also allow useful contrasts to be drawn between two quite different attitudes or stances toward town planning and city building. The Welfare State was a time of big plans, comprehensive concepts, and infrastructure improvements on a very large scale. By contrast, the postwar period of today is one of specific projects – sometimes large, perhaps, but actual projects rather than plans, nevertheless. In this sense, both periods reflect the fashions and practical exigencies of their respective eras. As many are aware, the unbounded confidence with which modernism was regarded

as a point of departure for city building has both waxed and waned. Today, if anything, the comprehensiveness and assumed certainty or exactitude of earlier modern city-building processes is likely to be highly contested and often disregarded altogether.

Finally, territory is a very important issue in Beirut these days, whereas during the era of the Welfare State it was not quite so important or so clearly differentiated. Probably precisely because today it is so difficult to address socio-political issues directly, urban space and its remaking tend to define much of the contemporary dialogue various people in Beirut have about themselves and their world. Put more simply, urban space – including its production, transformation, use, and symbolic deployment – matters a great deal, unlike the more open and robust discourse which could take place in earlier, less exhausted eras. To a large extent, when estranged family members living in the same house finally turn to one another, it is often the furnishings and other spatial accoutrements of their joint occupation which are the liveliest topics of conversation.

Episodes of Construction and Reconstruction

In most accounts of modern Lebanon, the Shihab era of 1958 to 1967 is referred to as the 'good times,' the flowering of the Welfare State. Nevertheless, like most episodes in a nation's history, the record we have of this period has been defined very much by what went before it and by what came afterwards. The history of modern Lebanon, according to

Salibi, may be said to have begun in 1918 with the French occupation.[1] In Allenby's division of the Levant after World War I, the British maintained Palestine, the Arabs occupied the Syrian interior, and the French were ceded Lebanon and coastal Syria. The state of Greater Lebanon was created in 1920 under the French Mandate, governed by a high commissioner, and from then on France gradually devolved power and self-determination to the Lebanese people under its tutelage. In 1926 the Lebanese Constitutional Republic was established, giving the ›Lebanese more control over internal affairs while reserving control over external matters and a right of veto for France, a power which could effectively dissolve the national legislature. Naturally enough, the nationalists, who had been gaining in strength off and on since 1861, and the Lebanese *Mutasarrifiyya* objected to this potential interference and pushed for further autonomy. During World War II the French Vichy Government lost its hold on the region. Lebanese independence was proclaimed in 1941, resulting, finally, in the founding of the present Lebanese Republic and the election of President Khoury with the Mandate's termination in 1943.

The liberal economic policies adopted under Bishara Khoury resulted in a substantial increase in foreign exchange and trade. These practices were particularly conspicuous in the Middle East, especially given the abundance of restrictive trade policies elsewhere. It was a laissez-faire period in which merchants prospered. Although attempts were made to modernize the country's administration, many of Khoury's efforts in this regard were thwarted by family and sectarian interests. Clientelism continued, as it had since feudal times in many sectors, organized for the most part along confessional lines. Khoury stood for reelection in 1947 and succeeded against strong challenges from Pierre Eddeh, the son of one of the early nationalists, Emile Eddeh, and Kamal Jumblatt, the Druze leader and the founder of the Progressive Socialist Party. Earlier on, in 1945, Lebanon had also joined the League of Arab States as a founding member, although outside Arab influences on the fledgling nation were soon to play a significant role.

Camille Chamoun succeeded Khoury in 1952 and continued where his predecessor had left off by further encouraging the movement of foreign capital to Lebanon with the guarantee of bank security. Shortly thereafter, Beirut, Lebanon's capital, unequivocally became the leading banking center in the Middle East. As time went on Chamoun alienated many earlier supporters, although his regime also fell victim to outside pressures. Between 1953 and 1954, Gamal Abdul-Nasser began to take over the Egyptian revolutionary movement, declaring a pan-Arab state of affairs. In 1956 he nationalized the Suez Canal, drawing France, Britain, and Israel into the fray on the opposing side. Chamoun, a Christian, did not, however, break ties with France, Britain, or Israel over the canal in spite of strong Arab urging and more general participation by Lebanon in Arab affairs. Matters deteriorated further when, in 1957, Chamoun and the Lebanese government accepted the Eisenhower Doctrine, under which the United States could use armed force at the request of a state in the Middle East against signs of communist aggression. Predictably, Egypt strongly objected to this arrangement and began posing an even greater threat to Lebanon and others with, together with Syria, the 1958 formation of the United Arab Republic. Disaffection among Lebanon's confessional groups, especially the Muslims less favored by the clientelist system, erupted into armed violence and demonstrations. By mid-year full-scale armed insurrection had broken out. As head of the army, General Fuad Shihab refused to crush the insurrection but rather stopped it from spreading and protected the country from outside aggression. On July 15, the American 6th Fleet and a Marine contingent were sent into Beirut, although the Lebanese Muslim rebellion continued. Finally, later that month Shihab resigned his rank in the army and succeeded Chamoun as the nation's president, thus ending what most history books refer to as the 'Crisis of 1958.'[2]

Somewhat aloof and patrician, Fuad Shihab proved to be an effective leader in many respects. First, he quickly ensured that the Muslims would have a larger and fairer share of government positions. Second, he set out to placate Lebanon's neighbors and to reduce outside Muslim resentment of the state. Third, he paid particular attention to economically depressed areas in the country and began all manner of social service improvements and public works. However, in spite of his best efforts and disdain for personal interest, Shihab was only able to carry out limited reform of Lebanon's old system of *zaim* (patron-client) relationships. Still, the powerful clans or *zu'ama*, representing different sectarian clientele, operated in the rough and tumble of political life – as a government of men rather than of laws, as

one historian put it.[3] Avoiding both Khoury's manipulation of the *zu'ama* grand coalition and Chamoun's confrontation with it, Shihab sought to sidestep the *ancien régime* through his own network of functionaries in order to press on with Lebanon's modernization. In particular he used the *Deuxième Bureau* of military intelligence, together with many new appointments to a burgeoning bureaucracy in what became known as Shihabism – a combination of mild étatism, security service influences within a civilian regime, and a strong drive toward social welfare.[4]

In addition to the policies cited previously, Shihab's Welfare State made a strong commitment to the 1943 National Pact, involving markedly increased government expenditure, the funding of a central bank to gain more control and leverage over the economy, the creation of numerous new agencies staffed by competent technocrats, and a substantial diversion of public spending, as implied earlier, in the direction of public works, education, health, and social welfare. The increased government expenditure rose quickly from about 11 percent of the Gross National Product to 25 percent by 1964, roughly equivalent to that of the social democracies of Europe.[5] If nothing else, the creation of a central bank for the first time in 1964 began to reverse the laissez-faire practices of the merchant republic of Khoury and Chamoun. New agencies were created for planning, statistics, regional development, medical dispensation, and social security. Although costing less in terms of a percentage of the Gross National Product thanks to a rapidly expanding economy, government expenditures doubled between 1958 and

Fig. 1. View of the old souks with the Azzariyeh Building in the background, 1958

1964. There was a 425 percent increase in public works, with about eight to ten projects announced each year, compared to about two per year during the Chamoun regime. Also, an almost equally intensive development occurred in education.[6] Although he survived an attempted coup d'état in 1961, Shihab decided not to seek reelection in 1964 and was succeeded by Charles Helou.

Helou continued the Shihabist policy of investing in Lebanon's infrastructure and in social reform. He also remained open to other Arab states and influences, allowing, for instance, the training of Palestine Liberation Organization forces within Lebanon. The general welfare of the Lebanese also continued to improve. The Gross Domestic Product per capita in 1960, for instance, was only U.S. $370, almost doubling to $660 per capita by 1971, again in stark contrast to

neighboring states like Turkey with $340 per capita, Syria with $290, and even oil-rich Iraq with $370 per capita.[7] Nevertheless, Lebanon remained a relatively poor country, with around 50 percent of the labor force still in agriculture, although producing only around 9 to 10 percent of the Gross Domestic Product, compared to around 70 percent for services or the tertiary sector, with only 30 percent of the labor force. Although there was some sharp improvement in industrial development and industry's share of Gross Domestic Product during Shihab's regime to about 20 percent of the nation's total, little further improvement was made during the subsequent years, all the way up into the early 1970s.[8]

The war of 1967 with Israel was seen as crushing and humiliating to Arab causes. Also, between 1969 and 1970, there was a

Fig. 2. Aerial photograph of downtown Beirut, 1996

rather sharp increase in the outbreak of civil conflicts in Lebanon as the dualism created in the Lebanese administration by having organizations like the *Deuxième Bureau* operate alongside conventional government organizations began to unravel. There was also the Intra Bank crisis of 1967, threatening for the first time the financial structure of Lebanon. Palestinian military operations began on Lebanese soil in 1968, and intensified in 1970 after the Black September episode in nearby Jordan. In short, the events between 1967 and 1970 made it clear that many of the nation's wounds had not healed and that it remained vulnerable to outside influences. Perhaps not surprisingly the Shihabist regime came to a definite end in 1970 with the election of President Franjieh, who immediately purged the *Deuxième Bureau* of Shihab and Helou

loyalists, replacing it with his own people. This regime, however, floundered badly, losing control of security and declaring martial law in 1972. Clashes between the Palestine Liberation Organization and the Lebanese army broke out in 1973, Israel became increasingly alarmed by the inability of Lebanon to control the Palestinian militias, and the nation headed toward full-scale civil war.

Throughout this first episode of nation building, Beirut, as the largest city in Lebanon and its capital from one regime to the next, continued to gain and, by and large, to prosper. With the establishment of the French High Commission in Beirut at the beginning of the Mandate in 1920, many modern services like electricity and water supply were installed, along with an extensive paving of streets and ordered parceling out of land for development purposes. According to a League of Nations estimate, the population of Beirut in 1926 stood at 118,070, rising quickly to 179,370 by 1932. Major building projects of the modern era began in the 1920s and particularly the 1930s with the Place de l'Etoile in 1930, and also the rather revolutionary Hotel St. Georges by Antoine Tabet in the same year. In 1932 the Danger Plan was produced by a French planning consultant, although ultimately it was never approved by the government. Nevertheless, new building laws were enacted in 1933 regulating set-back requirements, sanitary requirements, ventilation requirements, and so on. The beginning of the Lebanese Republic was ushered in by the first of Michel Ecochard's two master plans for Beirut in 1943, presenting the first comprehensive study of land use and a zoning proposal which separated future industry, business, commerce, and residential development. This plan did not succeed immediately. However, it was adopted much later by the Egli Report in 1950 and as the primary basis for the master plan of 1952. Under Shihab centralized planning intensified. In 1963 the General Directorate of Urban Planning was created, together with the Higher Council for Urban Planning, concerned mainly with developments in Beirut, which was by now very much the largest urban area in the country. In 1964, Ecochard produced his second plan – the *Plan Directeur de Beyrouth et des Banlieues* – including proposals going well beyond the city proper, although many of these parts of the plan were subsequently neglected. By 1970, Beirut's population stood at about 1 million persons, representing about 45 percent of the na-

tion's population in roughly 2 percent of the land area. Because of this density, plans were developed to decentralize the burgeoning metropolitan area from about 1973 onwards.[9]

In 1990, after the cessation of hostilities which had continued largely unabated since 1975, the episodic character of Lebanon's socio-political life continued, and with it Beirut's process of urban development. The Taif Agreement of 1989 adjusted and reconfirmed the power-sharing among various confessional groups, establishing a formula for Lebanese governance and the eventual withdrawal of Syrian forces responsible for creating the peace. Tragically, René Moawad was assassinated only three weeks after becoming president, and was succeeded by Elias Hrawi. Nevertheless, in the new formulation of governmental authority it was Prime Minister Rafik Hariri who quickly assumed most of the power and leadership. A Saudi national, although with roots in Sidon to the south of Beirut, al-Hariri took office in 1992 and quickly became committed to restoration and the maintenance of political stability.

By contrast to the former times of the Shihab regime, the reconstruction of Beirut is not proceeding, so far anyway, according to a grand plan or metropolitan vision, but rather by occasional references to general studies like the Bechtel Recovery Plan of 1992 and the Metropolitan Schéma Directeur of 1986. Instead efforts are being concentrated, strategically, one suspects, on smaller project areas within the city. Most conspicuous among these are probably the Beirut Central Business District under the auspices of the private development company Solidere; Elisar to the south, toward the airport, a project which is under governmental jurisdiction; and Linord, along the coast to the north of Beirut proper, which is proceeding as a joint venture. The new master plan for the Central Business District dating from 1991 was conceived by Henri Eddeh of the Dar al-Handasah Group. Administration of the overall project in turn also remains in private hands by legislative decree in the form of Solidere, a real estate company specially created to administer reconstruction of the central area, even though approval must eventually go through the Higher Council of Urban Planning. In fact, all three projects follow substantially different processes of implementation, ranging from public and private sponsorship to a build-operate-and-transfer setup in the case of Linord.

None of this is particularly out of the ordinary in other parts of the world today. The much heralded recent public improvements in Barcelona, for instance, took the form of projects rather than plans, deliberately eschewing the totalizing effects of master planning strategies in favor of specific local responses.[10] Privatization of what would otherwise have been public projects, as mentioned earlier, has been on the rise for some time in both the United States and Europe, and turnkey joint-venture projects are pushing ahead in a number of parts of the developing world, such as China, in an attempt to get the job done more rapidly and efficiently. The issue of local context has arisen in Beirut, just as it has recently in many other parts of the world, resulting in a much stronger movement in favor of historic preservation and cultural conservation than

probably would ever have been imaginable at a policy level during the heyday of modern planning efforts. This is particularly important in Beirut where at least the remnants of an Eastern Mediterranean tradition are clearly in view from both modern and pre-modern periods. What the future holds for planning, urban design, and architecture in Beirut remains to be seen. So far, however, it is quite unlike earlier periods, especially the 'good years' of the Welfare State. Yet, just as there was during that time, there is a striking similarity today between what is happening in Beirut and what is occurring in other parts of the world.

A Brief Outline of the Book

The geographic scope of this book includes both the city and suburbs of Beirut. Relatively early on in its modern urban history, Beirut began to exhibit what would become its characteristic form of development: a concentration of commercial and business functions in and around its historic center surrounded by residential neighborhoods, whose densities decrease with increasing distance from the center. Areas along the magnificent coast, often with views back toward the mountains, also became prime sites for real estate development. In spite of attempts by Ecochard and others to zone areas of the city for different uses, Beirut remained a collection of mixed-use communities, often with very high degrees of social cohesion and local autonomy. With a current population of about 1.5 million people, the metropolitan area of Beirut extends well up the northern coast toward Byblos, south beyond the airport in the direction of Sidon, and well out into the hinterland toward the interior, primarily along the old roads to the east and to Damascus. One geographic effect of the Civil War has been a separating of communities, largely along confessional lines, adding to the metropolitan sprawl and also removing them from the traditional nexus of commerce by means of a polycentric form of development. The geographic scope of the book also covers projects of varying size, from large metropolitan plans to individual buildings. Throughout, however, the emphasis is on the urban and architectural contributions of these projects to the physical conformation of Beirut.

The book begins, logically enough, with the presentation of some aspects of urban history and archaeology. Following a short introductory text by Nasser Rabbat, this section contains three chapters. The first, by Helen Sader, deals with recent archaeological discoveries and their contribution to an overall assessment of Beirut's history. The second, by Jens Hanssen, sets the stage for later discussions of the modern period, with an appraisal of Beirut's urban history in the late nineteenth and early twentieth centuries. The third, by Farès el-Dahdah, takes a more contemporary and theoretical turn by broadening the question of criteria for historical preservation from various periods and thus from various cultural points of view. Indeed, in the face of many recent archaeological finds and the mass destruction of many historical buildings, especially in Beirut's Central District, the question of what to preserve and reconstruct, as well as how to integrate this sense of history and antiquity into contemporary development, has become a pressing issue.

The second section of the book deals directly with the modern architecture and planning of Beirut, principally during the Shihabist regime, but more generally between 1943 and 1970. After an introduction by Michael Hays, the first chapter, by Jad Tabet, presents an overview of Beirut's modern architecture, including the work of foreign architects such as Alvar Aalto, Alfred Roth, Oscar Niemeyer, Paul Rudolph, and Edward Durrell Stone, as well as the work of local architects such as Antoine Tabet, Farid Trad, Pierre el-Khoury, Pierre Nehmeh, Wassek Adib, and George Rayes. This is followed by a chapter by Marlène Ghorayeb concerning the plans of Michel Ecochard, which provided the broad framework for Beirut's modern development, followed, in turn, by a chapter by Assem Salam concerning the role of the public sector during the Shihabist era in guiding and shaping the built environment.

After a brief introduction by Peter Rowe, the third section begins with two overviews presenting the socio-economic framework for the reconstruction of Beirut. The first, by Samir Khalaf, deals with aspects of the urban sociology of Beirut and, in particular, the question of identity and its spatial implications in the postwar reoccupation and construction of the city. The second, by Freddie Baz, provides an empirical perspective and interpretation of the macroeconomic factors shaping Beirut's present and future development, an essential aspect of the city's reconstruction. Finally, the third chapter, by Mona Harb el-Kak, describes social, economic, public policy, and environmental issues relevant to a specific area of Beirut, in this case the southern suburbs and their contention with the Elisar master plan.

The fourth section of the book, concerning the postwar planning of Beirut, is also composed of three chapters. After a brief introduction by Rodolphe el-Khoury, the first, by Hashim Sarkis, describes the current Schéma Directeur, or master plan for Beirut, including its historical roots and the technical attitudes behind its formation. The second, by Joumana Ghandour Atallah, concerns the plans for the northern suburban development of Beirut and, in particular, Linord and the projects of Dar al-Handasah and Ricardo Bofill. The third, by Angus Gavin, covers the extensive redevelopment of Beirut's Central Business District, initially under the plan of Dar al-Handasah and then under Solidere. Of particular importance here, in Gavin's contribution, are the urban design principles and procedures being applied to that area today.

Following Jorge Silvetti's introductory comments, Oussama Kabbani begins the fifth section of the book surveying the recent building developments and proposals for Beirut's city center and the manner in which they interpret the urban design guidelines established for the area. This is followed by Rodolphe el-Khoury's reflections on the predicament and opportunities confronting the reconstruction of the city center. In a final chapter, Rafael Moneo's presentation of the souks project, a culturally significant and extensive aspect of Beirut's contemporary urban renewal program, is made.

The final section of the book includes two essays. The first, by the co-editors of this volume, Peter Rowe and Hashim Sarkis, draws together some conclusions regarding the topics raised in earlier sections. In particular, three questions are addressed concerning the issues of architectural style, the concept of pluralism and an open city, and the matter of heritage, respectively. The second chapter, by H.E. Ghassan Tuéni, outlines a vision for the urban future of Beirut, now that the hostilities of the Civil War have come to an end.

Notes

1. K.S. Salibi, *The Modern History of Lebanon* (New York: Caravan Books, 1977).
2. Ibid., p. 259 and William W. Harris, *Faces of Lebanon: Sects, Wars and Global Extensions* (Princeton: Markus Wiener Publishers, 1997), p. 147.
3. D.C. Gordon, *Lebanon: The Fragmented Nation* (London: Croon Helm, 1980), p. 101.
4. Harris, *Faces of Lebanon*, p. 150.
5. Ibid., p. 147 and B.J. Odeh, *Lebanon: Dynamics of Conflict, A Modern Political History* (London: Zed Books Ltd., 1985), p. 62.
6. C. Winslow, *Lebanon: War and Politics in a Fragmented Society* (New York: Routledge, 1996), p. 132.
7. Gordon, *Lebanon: The Fragmented Nation*, p. 70.
8. Odeh, *Lebanon: Dynamics of Conflict*, p. 77.
9. S. Khalaf and P.S. Khoury, eds., *Recovering Beirut: Urban Design and Postwar Reconstruction* (New York: E.J. Brill, 1993), appendix.
10. P.G. Rowe, *Civic Realism* (Cambridge, Mass.: MIT Press, 1997).

Section One
The Urban History and Archaeology of Beirut

The Interplay of History and Archaeology in Beirut

by
Nasser Rabbat

History and archaeology are usually thought of as sister fields, albeit with a considerable age difference. One is old, learned, and established; the other is young, dirty-footed, and empirical. History, having endured many contortions from its Greek root *historie,* "to know by inquiry," has settled on the dignified though disputed definition as "the study of and writing about the past." To that end, history displays a formidable array of techniques, most of them text-based and text-derived (though many events of the past were initially orally preserved). Identifying, investigating, classifying, analyzing, evaluating, and synthesizing the written records of the past have thus been the mainstay of the historian's craft. He or she is aided in that task by the evidence of artifacts, monuments, inscriptions, and whatever else belongs to the same period, when such materials are available; this 'whatever' constitutes the context of the event under study, or at least preserves its memory in tangible and interpretable form.

Archaeology pursues another way to study the past. Its method can be summa-rized as the systematic collection and analy-sis of material evidence. Since its inception in the late eighteenth century as a scientific endeavor with its own rules and boundaries, archaeology has been honing its tools speci-fically to reconstruct the 'real' or 'tangible' (i.e., physical) context of the place under study in a prescribed time. Through digging, measuring, comparing, and classifying, archaeology has always depended on the objects to tell their history: pottery shards, luxury and common items, tombs, buildings, and entire settlements. They tell it as narra-tive through their stratification and in con-text through their comparative attributes vis à vis one another or other objects in other places and other times.

This object-oriented method is some-times the only way available for unveiling the past, since the bulk of history went by unnoticed by those who lived it and enjoyed or suffered it, but never recorded it in text either because they did not know how or be-cause they did not care to. But, whenever history was recorded and preserved, a cru-cial question emerged time and again. How do we treat historical texts in relation to the evidence of the excavated artifacts? Some archaeologists use the texts only as another piece of evidence, which may or may not be admitted in the telling of the story depending on how they measure up to the artifactual evidence, which, to them, reigns supreme in the narration of the past. Others, as is the case, for example, with biblical archaeologists, privilege a set of texts – biblical and para-biblical – and search for archaeological confirmation of their contents. But in critical reconstructions of the past, it is not the veracity of one form of evidence against another that forms the paramount concern. It is instead the interplay of text and context, or of history and archaeology, which usually yields the most fascinating readings and interpretations: conflicting, confirming, modifying, and even at times unsettling, but always enriching and informing – and, perhaps, closer to reality than history or archaeology alone.

This is primarily why – in my opinion – the large-scale archaeological excavations in Beirut (almost 100,000 square meters covered so far of a possible total of 900,000 square meters) – and the massive restoration of selected monuments of its recent past – ought to be so meaningful both for the citizens of the city, of Lebanon, and for the history of the world. For the Berutis and the Lebanese, these excavations supplement, clarify, and fill some of the gaps in the city history which they inherited from their parents or read in school books and national tracts. The various archaeological finds would, one by one, illuminate and enliven specific, distinctive moments of that history and verify some of its junctures. A

segment of a glacis that once encircled the Iron Age Phoenician settlement would indicate not only the antiquity of *Beruta* and its relatively small size, but would also evoke the care devoted to ensuring its defensibility from land invaders when all its attention was focused on the sea. The brick arcades that once formed the infrastructure of a Roman *therma* (bath), designed for the circulation of hot air, would symbolize the important status of *Colonia Julia Augusta Felix Berytus* and the sophisticated urban life of its citizens. A row of mosaic-paved Byzantine shops, complete with inscribed Greek letters indicating their number, would suggest commerce in the life of the ancient city and bring to life the luxurious setting where commercial as well as cultural exchange once thrived (although the search for the great fourth-century law school continues). A solitary Mamluk *zawiya* would conjure up an entirely different way of life, devotional and secluded, which was once the norm in the *thaghr* of al-Imam al-Uza'i and his Muslim successors, a way of life that is today almost totally absent from the hustle and bustle of the modern metropolis. An Ottoman silk workshop, with its plastered basins and cisterns, would distill in one site the entire economic basis of the pre-modern city. And a modern building, pockmarked with bullet holes, but still standing in the souk area after seventeen years of fierce civil conflict, would provide a poignant reminder of the buoyant 'Paris of the Orient,' and, one might hope, of the futility of war.

These and other visible and tangible relics of the past would together form a thread for the Berutis of a living, pulsating history of their city and its tribulations and glories.

In the not-so-distant future, when the new downtown of Solidere with its tall buildings and wide, tree-lined boulevards is completed and the face of postwar Beirut is totally remade, these remains, both underground and above, restored and reconstructed, will constitute more than historical landmarks for the Berutis strolling amidst them. They will form corporeal anchors for the contemporary, ultra-modern city that tie it to its rich and varied history and articulate the specificities of its character formed and reformed over time. They will indeed become what Pierre Nora has termed a *lieux de mémoire* (realm of memory), and the city as a whole in its new garb will cease to be a *milieu de mémoire,* or an environment for memory.

For the rest of us, the excavations offer, in addition to their often remarkable archaeological finds, intellectual and procedural challenges and, obviously, rewards and guidance for future studies and analyses of large-scale urban archaeological projects and the theoretical, practical, political, economic, and cultural problems they are bound to encounter. On the historical and scholarly level, we have here a rare opportunity to examine an ancient city which has been continuously occupied if unevenly developed since its founding in the third millennium B.C.E. Beirut is a city that has seen good days and bad, and survived them all while absorbing their exploits and showing their traces on its layered face. Thus far, the history of the city has been woven primarily from textual fragments found in ancient Phoenician, Greek, and Latin, medieval Arabic and Crusader texts, as well as later documents and the material frag-

ments that have serendipitously been brought to light during the building booms of the first half of the twentieth century. The archaeological material that has been steadily turning up in the last seven years of digging, sifting, and arranging will better allow us to reconstruct the episodes of Beirut's urban and architectural history – and the history of its surroundings near and far – uninterruptedly from its earliest days as a small Canaanite settlement to its recent climb to prominence as the major commercial city of the Eastern Mediterranean.

An urban archaeology project of this magnitude is rare, especially in a living and historically rich city such as Beirut. Its feasibility itself, it has to be remembered, was occasioned by the destruction left after years of senseless civil war. Nor is this an unusual *raison d'être* for comparable projects in the past, especially in Germany after World War II. It is almost always a tragedy, a violent rupture in the normal life of a city, that bares its substructures and brings its past nearer to the surface along with rubble generated by the calamity. Planners, developers, and officials almost always rush to cover the exposed entrails with new buildings and new boulevards, perhaps in an attempt to counter the psychological effects of ruin and devastation on the citizens coming out of recent trauma, but perhaps for other political or financial gains as well. To them, the traces of the past are valuable only insofar as they fulfill a tangible, contemporary value, be it nationalistic, artistic, or economic.

To the historians and the archaeologists, and to all those concerned with questions of culture, heritage, and art, archaeological excavations and historical buildings carry meanings of a different order. They literally represent culture and history, both individually and in their totality, regardless of their economic or mythologizing national value to economists and politicians. Therefore, they should be uncovered, studied, and preserved, both as single objects and as ensembles of objects, or as buildings or remains of buildings or even as entire cities. Moreover, they should ideally be preserved *in situ*. In most examples of urban archaeology, this means the surrender of very lucrative real estate to unprofitable land use either permanently, in the form of museums and archaeological parks, or for the duration of excavations and restoration projects. In this scenario, a clash of cultures and of values will inevitably ensue between the 'managers of the heritage' (to borrow an expression from Helen Sader) and the managers of the urban environment, even if we suppose, unrealistically, that no other agendas animate either side.

The excavators in Beirut – as well as the restorers of venerable buildings in the souk area – have had to negotiate a precarious and not altogether blameless position in the interstices between the interests of the land managers and the demands of the heritage advocates. From my talks with several people involved in the Beirut project, it became clear that a great deal of realism and maneuverability was needed at every stage of the process.

Significant sites had literally to be snatched from the claws of bulldozers by persuasive assertions about their historical, national, or artistic value, and sometimes through acts of daring defiance, while others have been lost despite the best efforts of would-be saviors. Architecturally important buildings were saved through the same kinds of intervention, rationalizing, and challenging, but other, equally important examples have been demolished for a host of adverse reasons. There are lessons to be learned from the experiences and perseverance of the archaeologists and restorers over the last seven years, and mistakes to be avoided. But, most importantly, there are visible results – objects, buildings or fragments of buildings, drawings, and texts – to be appreciated and further studied and integrated into the continuous telling and retelling of the urban and architectural history of Beirut.

Ancient Beirut:
Urban Growth in the Light of Recent Excavations

by
Helen Sader

Until 1993 Beirut was not considered to be one of Lebanon's major archaeological attractions. The city, for one, did not enjoy in antiquity the fame and wealth of other ancient coastal settlements like Sidon, Tyre, or Byblos. Although impressive structures had been uncovered on several occasions since the beginning of the twentieth century, no visible remains were left standing to bear witness to the city's long and at times glorious past. The reason simply is that ancient Beirut was and still is the victim of its location. Indeed, it is situated on the site of the modern central district of the capital, the most coveted and expensive parcel of land in Lebanon.

It is precisely this downtown area that witnessed the most terrible and destructive episodes of the Lebanese war. When the mines and earthworks were removed, the Lebanese were horrified at the sight of collapsed and burnt buildings, of broken sewers, and heaps of rubbish and garbage. The reconstruction of the devastated center of the capital was given top priority by the Lebanese administration and the planned reconstruction scheme soon became, in all its aspects, the most controversial project of postwar Lebanon.[1]

The reconstruction operation launched a destruction frenzy in the city center and an army of bulldozers threatened both modern and ancient remains. In this struggle, the balance of power was tilted against archaeology. A Department of Antiquities official summed up the situation by openly asking whether the outcome of the forthcoming reconstruction project would simply be "une destruction de l'histoire."[2]

The Beirut Archaeological Project

Concerning the archaeological aspects of the reconstruction project, one expected the planners and the responsible authorities to secure a harmonious coexistence and coordination between the reconstruction and the archaeological operations, and to help reduce the apparent incompatibility of interests between developers on the one hand and managers of cultural heritage on the other. This was by no means impossible since many model patterns of cooperation were already available from the various experiences of European countries which were faced with similar problems of urban archaeology after World War II. Instead, the original reconstruction design just ignored the problem and failed to devise an appropriate long-term strategy for the archaeology of Beirut. This was an unjustifiable omission on the part of the planners, for this district is known since the 1920s to have yielded important monumental archaeological remains such as the Roman forum and basilica, to mention only a very few.

1. *The 1993 Agreement (LEB/92/008: Réhabilitation de la Direction Générale des Antiquités et Soutien à la Reconstruction du Centre-Ville de Beyrouth)*

Under very strong media pressure and growing criticism on the part of the archaeologists, as well as public opinion, it became obvious that bulldozers and developers could not have their way and that excavations in Beirut were inevitable. Consequently, a one-year agreement concerning the archaeology of Beirut was signed in April 1993 by the Council of Development and Reconstruction (CDR) and UNESCO, and later ratified by the United Nations Development Program (UNDP). It divided the archaeological operations into three phases: soundings, extensive excavations, and rescue excavations. It also stipulated that the first two phases were to be financed by the Hariri Foundation and the UNDP, and placed the project under the auspices of UNESCO, which was responsible for the management, organization, and coordination of the excavations. This international institution also acted as a consultant and advisor to the Lebanese Directorate General of Antiquities (DGA) for all technical and scientific matters. The Directorate General of Antiquities was responsible for the supervision and control of the archaeological operations. A committee presided over by the CDR representative coordinated archaeological and reconstruction operations.

Although this agreement clearly stated the objectives of the project, as well as its technical and scientific aspects, it failed to achieve its goals. The first reason for this failure was that the agreement clearly minimized the role of the Directorate General of Antiquities, under whose auspices the excavations were taking place. The DGA is the only institution invested by the present and still valid 1933 antiquities law with the right to plan, organize, and control any archaeological activity in Lebanon whether or not this is stipulated in an agreement. So, to engage in a complex and lengthy project in Beirut with a devastated and understaffed Department of Antiquities seriously jeopardized the project's chances of success from the start. The second reason is the *mala fide* that was and still prevails in the relations between the heritage managers and the developers who failed to establish proper and honest cooperation. Finally, UNESCO has a large share of responsibility for this failure because its management was unable to meet the challenges of the Beirut archaeological operations. For instance, this agreement gave the archaeological project its first impetus and local archaeologists, in small numbers, were invited to start immediately without further preparation and without a minimum number of trained and qualified field specialists. Four sites were opened in the first year: south and north of Martyrs' Square, north of the Rivoli building, and north of the Maronite Cathedral of St. George.

2. *The Archaeological Project Since 1994*

When all the money given by the Hariri Foundation and the UNDP had been spent, no new funds were available and the excavations had to stop. This crisis then led to an emergency solution in order to break the deadlock on the archaeological project.

Fig. 1. Area expropriated by Solidere where excavations are taking place

Confronted with both the financial and the technical impotence of the DGA, which according to the previous agreement had to be rehabilitated, Solidere, the real estate company in charge of the reconstruction of Beirut's center, decided to fund the rescue excavations (fig. 1). In fact, the company realized that if it did not want its massive infrastructure projects to be delayed, it would have to pay all the rescue operations in these areas to free them from archaeological constraints.

In this second phase of the archaeological project, Solidere, the DGA, and UNESCO were directly involved without any written agreement regulating this new alliance. The parties agreed to deal with the archaeology on a case by case basis, and for each new site to be opened. Solidere renewed its commitment to pay, the DGA issued the dig permit, and UNESCO's role was restricted to that of a consultant for the scientific aspect of the excavations. An ambiguous situation, unfair and dangerous for the archaeology, resulted from this agreement. On the one hand, a private company clearly backed by the government, with business oriented administrators and lucrative aims in mind, acted as the main interlocutor of the archae-ologists. The Council of Development and Reconstruction, in turn, implicitly delegated its prerogatives concerning the archaeology of Beirut. On the other hand, the main heri-tage manager, the Department of Antiqui-ties, a state institution legally responsible for the archaeology but still deprived of its means, was unable to assume its responsi-bilities. The fact that Solidere controlled the funds led certain archaeologists to deal directly with the real estate company with-out involving the DGA. All the archaeological work on the infrastructure, for example, was done without the written consent of the DGA. It became, effectively, a bilateral agreement between Solidere and the archae-ologist in charge. The constant pressure exercised by the developers to excavate the archaeological remains and to remove them as quickly as possible led to many abuses and errors, sometimes resulting in legal prosecution.

But in spite of all these and other diffi-culties, archaeological work progressed because an international appeal for cooper-ation had been made by both the Ministry of Culture and Higher Education and UNESCO. French, British, German, Italian, Dutch, and Czech teams participated in the excavations alongside their Lebanese colleagues from Lebanese and American universities. Be-tween 1994 and July 1997, over 100 new sites were added to the first four. Beirut's past slowly emerged from the ruins and the ancient city gradually unveiled itself.

Ancient Beirut Reveals Itself

In Beirut, the surface area under recon-struction, and where ancient remains are to be expected, is roughly 700,000 square meters in scope. It is the largest urban site being excavated in the world. This area extends between the Fuad Shihab Ring to the south, the Kantari-Fakhreddin Street to the west, Avenue des Français and Harbor Street to the north, and Georges Haddad Avenue to the east. It coincides with the area expropriated by Solidere, which is to be rebuilt according to a master plan prepared by Dar al-Handasah and approved by the Lebanese parliament.

The site of ancient Beirut is one and indivisible. The fifteen local and foreign teams have excavated different sectors of one and the same settlement, and some 90,000 square meters have already been explored. The sites were numbered accord-ing to a simple chronological order: 1 being the first and 107 the last site to be opened in June of 1997. All the information re-trieved from these excavations, and more to come, will have to be put together to recon-struct a complete picture of Beirut's past. To fit this vast amount of information, so var-iously collected and recorded, into one archival system will certainly be a difficult task for the Department of Antiquities. Work on this has already begun with the elabora-tion of an archaeological plan for the entire central district on which the main archaeo-logical features are represented according to their respective historical periods. This plan is currently being drawn up for the DGA in Germany, and is being funded by the German Ministry of Foreign Affairs (fig. 2).

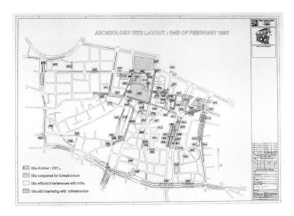

Fig. 2. Location of excavated sites in the Beirut Central District as of March 1, 1997

1. Excavations in Beirut before 1993

The excavations which first started in 1993 were not the first archaeological operations to take place in central Beirut. Since the early years of the twentieth century under the French Mandate, fortuitous discoveries were made (mainly between 1916 and 1928) during building or public works activities. However, no systematic publication of these excavations was ever made.[3] The first attempts to map out some of these uncovered remains were made by Du Mesnil du Buisson, who produced two plans of Beirut: Beirut in the sixth century A.D.[4] and a plan of the city's Ottoman fortifications.[5] The first large-scale excavations in the center of Beirut took place between 1941 and 1947, in and around Place de l'Etoile or Parliament Square. They were supervised and partly published by Jean Lauffray,[6] who was also able to collect archival material from the Department of Antiquities and most of the unpublished information on previous excavations from his French colleagues and predecessors: "J'eus la bonne fortune de découvrir dans les dossiers du Service des Antiquités, des renseignements inédits et de me voir confier par le R.P.R. Mouterde, par M.M. Virolleaud, Lanore et P.E. Guigues des notes prises pendant les fouilles mêmes."[7] His plan of Roman Beirut based on this collected evidence and on his own excavations remained, until 1993, the primary if not only document upon which modern archaeologists could rely. But Lauffray was only interested in the architecture and consequently all the other finds were never recorded, studied, or published. New features of the Roman city, namely the Roman bath near the Serail and the Roman road on Parliament Square[8] were excavated by the DGA in the 1950s and 1960s and were used by Lauffray to revise his plan.[9]

In 1954, a major discovery was made north of Martyrs' Square[10]: Middle and Late Bronze Age tombs were found on Beirut cadastral plot 289 according to recently published records of the late Roger Saidah, a DGA archaeologist.[11] This plot corresponds to the site of the modern Byblos building. The first tomb was emptied by the developer ("Saeb Bey eut l'amabilité de recueillir les pièces de céramique trouvées dans cette tombe et de m'aviser de la découverte")[12] and the remaining three were excavated by the DGA. Nothing was said about the other destroyed structures on this and neighboring plots. Recent excavations, however, have clearly shown that the construction of the Byblos and other modern buildings in this area completely obliterated the intra muros settlement of pre-Hellenistic Beirut and cut the Bronze and Iron Age stone fortifications (fig. 3). Unfortunately, no record of these remains has been preserved. The discovery of these tombs, together with

Fig. 3. Example of modern destruction of ancient remains: sewage pipes laid in the 1960s cutting a Bronze Age wall

the material collected in 1969 by Roger Saidah, were clear evidence for the location of the ancient tell of Beirut. Saidah says clearly that his planned excavation of this area, identified as plots 237/238, "will probably be the last opportunity for archaeologists to study the history of the pre-Roman city."[13] The Department of Antiquities' planned excavations never took place; this area is currently being excavated by the American University of Beirut (AUB) museum team.

In 1977, the Directorate General of Antiquities and the French Archaeological Institute, IFAPO, undertook excavations in the partly destroyed Central District of Beirut. The French team excavated a site next to the municipal building and discovered an important Byzantine house with a

gold treasure hidden in a jar.[14] The Lebanese excavations took place on Parliament Square, among the Greek Orthodox, Greek Catholic, and Maronite churches, as well as under the Nuriyyeh church and in Souk Sursock, but they were never published.[15] The plans of the excavated remains will be integrated in the above mentioned general archaeological plan. The last excavation, before the beginning of the present Beirut project, was a very short campaign made by a Japanese team in the 1980s north of Martyrs' Square. They apparently found remains of a prehistoric settlement, but their excavation findings still await publication.

To sum up, and contrary to what has often been claimed, intensive archaeological work was done in Beirut's center long before 1993. It yielded substantial information on the Roman and Byzantine city and enough evidence to locate the pre-Hellenistic settlement. But apparently neither the Mandate authorities nor the Lebanese government was interested in preserving the archaeological heritage of Beirut, and their policy was to remove the archaeological structures systematically with little or no record of the operation. The most important Roman and Byzantine public buildings had been uncovered throughout these decades, but they were sacrificed to the city's urban planning and development. The worst part of this archaeological phase is that most of these discoveries were not understood and never will be for lack of proper archives. The whole of the pre-Hellenistic city has been obliterated without leaving a trace either in situ or in the records. The only relics of almost seventy years of intermittent excavations left standing are the Roman bath below the Serail, Roman columns on Parliament Square, now covered by the al-Abd clock, and the so-called Daraj al Arbaïn columns.

2. *The Urban Growth of Beirut: Recent Excavations*

This was the situation of the archaeological record of Beirut before the beginning of the excavations in November 1993. The new finds have contributed to a better understanding of the city's settlement history, its topography, and urban growth in various historical periods. Although a final analysis and an interpretation of the results are not yet available, preliminary reports published in the new DGA journal, the *Bulletin d'Archéologie et d'Architecture Libanaises*, volumes 1 (1996) and 2 (1997), as well as information presented by excavation direc-

tors in public lectures,[16] popular journals (*Al Kulliyah* 1993 and 1995, *Archéologie et Patrimoine*, volumes 2 [1995] and 3 [1996], *Archéologia*, volume 316 [1995], *Archaeology*, July–August [1996], *l'Année du Patrimoine* [1996–97], *National Museum News*, volumes 1 [1995], 2 [1995], 3 [1996], and 5 [1997], and *Urban Archaeology '94: Beirut. Excavations of the Souk Area*), and the media allow at present a tentative reconstruction of the most prominent features of Beirut's past.

Human presence in Beirut's center is attested to since Late Palaeolithic times, that is, starting around 50,000 B.C.[17] Neither the settlement, which was never discovered, nor all the lithic finds were found *in situ*. It seems, however, that the site was probably located in the northeastern part of the city center in the immediate surroundings of the ancient tell, because most of the retrieved flints were collected from this area (BEY 028, 030, and 034). Other prehistoric finds come from the German excavations on Debbas Square (BEY 048).

The oldest urban settlement of Beirut was found northeast of Martyrs' Square. The area where the pre-Hellenistic city is located, the so-called ancient tell, was preserved almost intact until 1920 (Plan de Beyrouth au 5000e Service Géographique de l'Armée, July 1920). It was located outside the walls of the Medieval and Ottoman city and was covered by a Muslim cemetery. This cemetery was removed before World War I by the Ottomans, and the area was left intact and free of modern constructions. The exact contours and location of the ancient settlement were clear, but the Mandate authorities and later the DGA never took the necessary measures to protect and investigate it. The first destruction took place in the 1950s and the 1960s with the construction of modern high-rise buildings with very deep foundations (Rivoli parcel 139, Byblos parcel 289, as well as other buildings, mainly parcels 391, 1390, 1399, 1389, and 249; plan 1/2000- Feuille K4-h4) and with the laying of new streets and sewers (Cadmus Street, Byblos Street, and Azmi Bey Street) (fig. 4). These building operations cut very deeply into the archaeological strata, and the destruction they caused became evident during recent excavations. They are also largely responsible for the loss of the *intra muros* settlement of the Bronze and Iron Ages. Ironically, most of the damage caused to the 5,000-year-old archaeological remains dates back to the last fifty years. The rescue excavations begun in 1993 are salvaging what has been spared from the destruction.

The ancient tell was excavated in four different sites (BEY 003, 013, 020, and 032)[18] and it clearly appeared to have been settled for the first time in the Early Bronze Age. The excavations yielded a series of successive city walls dating to the third, second, and first millennia B.C. The most interesting features of these fortifications are the well-built Middle Bronze Age wall and gate as well as the impressive Iron Age glacis with the staircase leading up to the city (figs. 5 and 6). These successive city walls gave us the exact extension of the fortified pre-Hellenistic settlement, which did not exceed three hectares. It was located on a rocky promontory overlooking the harbor, and in the first millennium, a paved street probably linked the harbor to the citadel. The domestic quarters inside the walls have not been preserved and were obliterated by modern constructions.

The settlement remained confined within its walls until the sixth century B.C. During the Persian period, the city of Beirut witnessed its first urban growth and developed outside its city walls. Evidence for this lower city was found north of Martyrs' Square (BEY 002),[19] on Weygand Street (BEY 028,[20] BEY 031, and BEY 045), on the site of former Souk Ayyass (BEY 010),[21] and along Avenue des Français (BEY 018).[22] Most interesting is the evidence for an orthogonal urban grid with houses

Fig. 4. Cadastral plan showing modern buildings and streets built on top of the pre-Hellenistic settlement; Cadmus and Azmi Bey Streets follow the Bronze and Iron Age fortification walls almost exactly

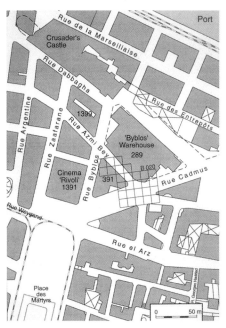

Fig. 5. Middle Bronze Age city gate BEY 003

Fig. 6. Iron Age sloping wall, or glacis, uncovered in areas BEY 013 and 020

arranged along the streets which came from the residential quarter in the Souk Ayyass area. This discovery strongly suggests that the later Hellenistic grid system might have been an extension of the earlier Iron Age urban layout. The limits of the Late Iron Age city are indicated by the necropolis. Rock-cut tombs were found on Avenue des Français and earth burials were uncovered south of Weygand Street. Phoenician Beirut consisted of an upper fortified city on a promontory, a lower city which developed on the plain at the foot of the citadel and around the harbor, and a necropolis bordering the residential area (fig. 7).

The ceramic and other small finds clearly indicate trade connections with Egypt, Crete, Greece, and Cyprus going back at least to the late third millennium B.C. These archaeological discoveries complemented the sparse information provided by the ancient Near Eastern texts which had left large gaps in the city's early history.[23] The earliest mention of Beirut dates indeed to the fourteenth and thirteenth centuries B.C., at least one millennium after the establish-

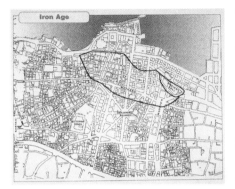

Fig. 7. Map showing the extension of Phoenician Beirut: stronghold and lower city

ment of the first urban settlement. According to the Amarna correspondence[24] and the Ugaritic texts,[25] the city was, in the Late Bronze Age, the capital of a small independent kingdom whose King Ammunira was Egypt's loyal vassal. The city was called *Biruta* meaning 'wells.'[26] Many centuries later, the annals of the Assyrian king Asarhaddon[27] mention *Biru* once as one of Sidon's fortified cities which were included in the new province of Kar Asarhaddon. Because of the scarcity of written documentation, the opinion prevailed that Beirut was an insignificant settlement in the pre-Hellenistic period. The recent archaeological evidence demonstrates that Beirut was an important center on the Lebanese coast and was able to grow and develop intensive trade with the Eastern Mediterranean.

The city's urban expansion which started in the sixth and fifth centuries B.C. witnessed a new impetus under the successors of Alexander the Great (third to second centuries B.C.). The city came under Seleucid rule and was renamed Laodikea by Antiochus IV. The old citadel was not abandoned. On the contrary, its fortifications were rebuilt on top of the older Phoenician glacis and the foundations of two of its eastern towers have been excavated. The Hellenistic lower city was larger than the Phoenician city and extended as far south as Amir Bashir Street and as far east as Georges Haddad Avenue. In the southern sector of the souks area (BEY 006), the earliest occupation is dated to the Hellenistic period and regular patterns of streets organized on a grid plan were found there: "From the various observations an irregular but orthogonal street grid can be reconstructed."[28]

Very little is still preserved of the Hellenistic city, because most of its structures have either been obliterated or reused in the later Roman buildings. There is, however, ample evidence for trade connections attested to in the presence of large numbers of stamped Rhodian jars, lamps, coins, and hundreds of complete or fragmentary pottery vessels. Beirut's prosperous trade in the Hellenistic period is also evidenced by the foundation of a Berytian trade colony on the island of Delos.[29] An interesting find suggests the existence of a Hellenistic temple of Astarte. It is a marble plate fragment found in Foch Street (BEY 019) that bears a Phoenician inscription dedicating it to the goddess.[30]

Recent excavations also yielded additional information on Roman Beirut which complemented and at times modified the above mentioned Lauffray plan. In Roman times, the center of the city moved to the west, to the modern Place de l'Etoile area, and for the first time the ancient tell lost its significance as the fortified center of Beirut. The city witnessed an unprecedented growth which certainly may be linked with the new status it received from the Roman emperor. Berytus recovered its old name and in 14 B.C. became a Roman colony, the *Colonia Julia Augusta Felix Berytus*, and as such received all the privileges and public buildings of a Roman city. The abundant textual material related to the history of Roman Beirut provided substantial information on the city's major religious and public buildings, but the problem of their location and of the city's urban layout and extension remained to be solved by archaeological investigations.

Lauffray had correctly pointed out the fact that the relief of Beirut made it impossible for the Romans to adopt one system of orthogonal streets: "Le relief naturel ... et peut-être des vestiges urbains antérieurs avaient obligé l'urbaniste romain à utiliser plusieurs quadrillages d'orientations légèrement différentes."[31] He also suggested that the Roman urban layout survived until the early twentieth century,[32] an assumption recently reassessed and confirmed by Michael Davie.[33] The *insulae*, or apartment blocks, delimited by Lauffray's partly reconstructed urban layout were 120 meters by 45 meters in size.[34] The French architect believed that the main east-west axis, or *decumanus,* followed the orientation of Weygand Street and continued past Bab Idriss,[35] and that the north-south axis, or *cardo*, was to

be resituated on old Souk al-Haddadin and Souk al-Najjarin.[36] This latter information was modified by the recent discovery of a sixteen-meter-wide north-south street bordered by porticoes and running west of the Maronite cathedral, which is believed to be the main *cardo* of Beirut (BEY 004).[37] Archaeological work on Weygand Street did not yield decisive evidence for its identification with the *decumanus* of the Roman city. This axis turns toward the souks area and does not continue its straight orientation toward Bab Idriss as expected and as claimed by Lauffray. The solution to this problem will have to await further study and discussion.

Most of the Roman public buildings found in and around Parliament Square were already known to Lauffray. Marble arches and underground galleries of the western forum were recently found under the Banco di Roma building (BEY 009).[38] A late Roman bath was discovered south of Weygand Street (BEY 045). This second Roman bath was reported by Lauffray on his first plan on the basis of observations recorded by previous scholars.[39] The main bulk of new information on Roman Beirut was provided by the excavation of the former souks area[40] which had not been previously investigated. The results complemented the Lauffray plan by adding a whole new quarter of the Roman city where commercial, industrial, and residential units have been uncovered. These excavations also showed that "the Roman colony was established at Beirut without leading to any significant alteration of the Hellenistic town plan."[41] With the exception of some shops and houses found east of the municipal building,[42] previous excavations had mainly concentrated on public and official buildings. Recent archaeological work largely contributes to a better understanding of the commercial and residential areas as well as of the street and sewage network of Roman Beirut.

The limits of the urban settlement are indicated by its necropolis, which developed at the fringe of the residential area. The nineteenth- and later twentieth-century discoveries of stone and lead coffins on the hill of Ashrafiyyé had pointed out the eastern limits of Roman Beirut.[43] Recent archaeological work on Kantari and Rue de l'Armée uncovered another Roman cemetery showing the western extension of Berytus.[44] It is also worth noting that during the Roman period the city developed its first suburban quarters, in Uzai and Jnah, where villas have been found.[45]

Beirut continued to prosper in the Byzantine period and the city owed its fame to the law school founded there in the early third century A.D.[46] No evidence for this building has been found during the recent excavations. All the excavated sites in downtown Beirut have yielded Byzantine remains, as the extension of the Byzantine city covered all the area presently under reconstruction. The most significant and most recently uncovered urban features from this period are a paved street bordered by shops northeast of Martyrs' Square (BEY 028)[47] and industrial areas on Avenue Georges Haddad and north of Martyrs' Square (BEY 002),[48] where potters' workshops and glass factories were found. A building with a rock-cut apse and mosaics was found in the southern sector of the souks area and was first interpreted as a small church. It is now said to be a

house. A portico with fourteen preserved mosaic-paved shops numbered with Greek letters was found south of the souks area (BEY 006).[49] Large residential villas, some of them with mosaic pavements bearing Greek inscriptions,[50] have also been uncovered in this district. The previous urban topography was respected[51] and the commercial and residential character of the Roman-period souks area was preserved during Byzantine times. Other mosaic pavements indicating domestic quarters have also been found in Banks Street. Very little evidence for the earthquake that destroyed the city in 551 is attested to and it seems that the destruction was not as dramatic as described in ancient sources. Coins of Maurice and Constans II found in the souks area indicate that the city resumed its activity almost immediately after the disaster.[52] The fortifications of the Roman-Byzantine city, if there were any, have not been found.

The early Islamic period is still very badly documented, in spite of the new excavations. Apart from scattered finds such as pottery shards and lamps, no valuable information was brought to light concerning Omayyad and Abbasid Beirut. After the destruction of the law school and its transfer to Sidon, Beirut seems to have progressively lost its importance. For half a millennium, the city is hardly mentioned in texts, and the archaeological evidence does not fill the gap left by the written sources concerning its extension and urban layout.

We are better informed about Crusader and Mamluk Beirut. The Crusaders rebuilt the city's fortification, parts of which are well known from nineteenth-century photographs and paintings. These are the castle

Fig. 8. The Crusader Cathedral of St. John, now the Great, or Omari, Mosque

built on a promontory near the ancient tell and two towers erected on an islet to protect the harbor. They were destroyed at the end of the nineteenth century by the Ottomans who wanted to enlarge the harbor. Recent excavations have uncovered the foundations of the castle together with a vaulted room and a cistern northwest of the tell. Concerning the city's extension, a ditch of the western medieval fortification wall was found parallel to Patriarch Hoayeck Street and gives us the western limit of the settlement.[53] One of the watch towers, the famous Burj, was also found southeast of Martyrs' Square and was probably situated outside the city wall.

The Mamluks did not enlarge the city and the fortifications described by Salih ibn Yehia,[54] our only source for that period, certainly follow the line of the Crusader walls. Apart from the medieval ditch, no substantial evidence related to the city's urban planning and extension during that period was yielded by the recent excavations. The center of the medieval city seems to have focused on the main Crusader

Cathedral of St. John, later transformed into Beirut's Great Mosque by the Mamluks (fig. 8). Worth mentioning is the discovery of an industrial zone in the souks area where pottery kilns and a pottery dump have been found together with evidence of a glass industry. No new buildings have been discovered, and with the exception of Ibn Iraq's partly preserved *ribat* at the entrance of Souk al-Tawileh, the Mamluks do not seem to have attempted rebuilding the city (fig. 9).

The status of Beirut changed under Ottoman rule and the city gained some importance after the seventeenth century. There is enough textual and archaeological evidence to reconstruct, with fair certainty, its extension and internal structure. The city wall had seven different gates and encompassed the area between Martyrs' Square to the east, Amir Bashir Street to the south, Bab Idriss to the west, and the harbor to the north. The grid pattern of the Ottoman city coincided with the Roman urban layout, but the land occupation seems to have changed radically. The economic center of the city moved from the north to the south of Weygand Street. Recent archaeological evidence has clearly shown that the modern souks, where the Roman and Byzantine economic center was found, were abandoned after the medieval period and remained free from occupation until the nineteenth century. The Ottoman souks occupied the center of the fortified settlement, where the Roman public buildings were found. These Ottoman souks were also surrounded by several mosques and churches. At the eastern edge of the city Fakhreddin II built his famous palace, described by various travelers. Remains of the irrigation network feeding its beautiful gardens have been found on Martyrs' Square (BEY 069).[55] Also uncovered were the foundations of the small Ottoman *serail* built in 1879 and destroyed in the 1940s (fig. 10). The main cemetery of Ottoman Beirut lay northeast of Martyrs' Square and prevented the expansion of the city in that direction.

Another interesting discovery was that of the quay of the Ottoman harbor at the northern edge of the souks area (BEY 007). Except for Khan Antoun Bey, no clear evidence was found for the multitude of *khans* and *zawiyas* known from the textual sources. The Ottoman sewage system, as well as the vaulted basements of houses and shops, appeared in almost all the excavated sites. It was at the end of the nineteenth century that Beirut started expanding beyond its walls, mainly to the west, and when it received the status of capital of modern Lebanon, it grew to occupy the entire peninsula known as Ras Beirut.

Fig. 9. The surviving Mamluk *ribat* of Ibn Iraq, located south of the former souks area

Fig. 10. Foundations of the small Ottoman *serial* uncovered at the northern edge of Martyrs' Square

The Future of the Beirut Archaeological Project

More information about Beirut's urban and economic history will have to await the final publication of the vast amount of material amassed during the last four years, as well as the new material to be excavated in the future. Archaeological work in Beirut is far from being completed. Only 10 percent of the area has been excavated and, for many years to come, the ancient city will continue to surface.

This raises the question of future archaeological work in Beirut. Infrastructure operations are almost completed, but Solidere is selling parcels of land which will eventually be developed. Just who is going to excavate these large areas potentially brimming with archaeological finds remains a compelling question, and exactly who is going to pay for the archaeological operations remains

uncertain. All the problems that the archaeology of Beirut was facing four years ago are still as acute as ever. The Department of Antiquities, for instance, is still unable to take over the archaeological work in downtown Beirut. The funds are not available and no full-time Lebanese archaeological teams are available for rapid intervention. As a result of this situation, many archaeological remains are now being removed without proper excavation and, tragically, there is no solution in sight. The concerned parties seem to have accepted this reality and they will not try to find solutions as long as major crises can be avoided.

Because of these unsolved problems, the Beirut archaeological project has lost its impetus and is slowly dying out. It is perhaps normal that in the years following a long and destructive war, the preservation of the cultural heritage comes last on any list of government priorities. The problem, though, is that the preservation of the cultural heritage is a national and not a private concern. It can only be achieved if the public authorities are well-intentioned and have a clear policy in this regard. Moreover, such a policy can only be implemented if institutions concerned are properly rehabilitated and equipped and guided by up-to-date regulations. In this regard, the archaeology of Beirut can only hope for genuine official concern and a rapid rehabilitation of the Department of Antiquities.

Notes

1. N. Beyhum, A. Salam, and J. Tabet, eds., *Beyrouth: Construire l'Avenir, Reconstruire le Passé?* (Beirut: Urban Research Institute Files, 1994).

2. S. Hakimian, "Beyrouth: L'Histoire d'une destruction ou les destructions de l'histoire?" in *Beyrouth: Construire l'Avenir, Reconstruire le Passé?*, eds. N. Beyhum, A. Salam, and J. Tabet (Beirut: Urban Research Institute Files, 1994), pp. 17–29.

3. J. Lauffray, "Forums et Monuments de Béryte (à suivre)," *Bulletin du Musée de Beyrouth* 7, 1944–45, pp. 13–80.

4. P. Collinet, *Histoire de l'Ecole de Droit de Beyrouth* (Paris: Recueil Sirey, 1925), plan.

5. Comte du Mesnil du Buisson, "Les anciennes défenses de Beyrouth," *Syria* 2, 1921, fig. 3.

6. Lauffray, "Forums et Monuments de Béryte (à suivre)," pp. 13–80.

7. Ibid., p. 15.

8. R. Saidah, "Archaeology in the Lebanon," *Berytus* 18, 1968–69, pp. 119–41.

9. J. Lauffray, "Beyrouth. Archéologie et Histoire, époques greco-romaines. I- Période hellénistique et Haut Empire Romain," *Aufstieg und Niedergang der römischen Welt* 8, 1977, pp. 135–63.

10. M. Chéhab, "Chronique," *Bulletin du Musée de Beyrouth* 12, 1955, pp. 50–51.

11. R. Saidah, "Beirut in the Bronze Age: The Kharji Tombs," *Berytus* 41, 1993, pp. 137–86.

12. Chéhab, "Chronique," p. 51.

13. Saidah, "Archaeology in the Lebanon," p. 139.

14. C. and J.D. Forest, "Fouilles à la Municipalité de Beyrouth," 1977, *Syria* 59, 1982, pp. 1–15; F. Turquety-Pariset, "Fouilles de la Municipalité de Beyrouth," 1977, les objets, *Syria* 59, 1982, pp. 27–76.

15. S. Hakimian, *Matériaux pour une histoire de Beyrouth depuis les origines jusqu'à l'époque des Croisades, Mémoire de D.E.A. en Histoire (option Archéologie)* (Beirut: Université Saint Joseph, 1992), p. 10.

16. H. Sader, "Cycles de conférences sur les fouilles de Beyrouth," *National Museum News* 2, 1995, pp. 12–13.

17. M. Heinz and K. Bartl, "Beirut: City Excavations 1995," *Bulletin d'Archéologie et d'Architecture Libanaises* 2, 1997; H. Curvers and B. Stuart, "BEY 032: Preliminary Report," *Bulletin d'Archéologie et d'Architecture Libanaises* 2, 1997. In press.

18. U. Finkbeiner and H. Sader, "BEY 020: Preliminary Report on the 1995–1996 Seasons," L. Badre, "BEY 003: Preliminary Report," N. Karam, "BEY 013: Rapport préliminaire," Curvers and Stuart, "BEY 032: Preliminary Report," *Bulletin d'Archéologie et d'Architecture Libanaises* 2, 1997. In press.

19. C. Aubert, "BEY 002: Rapport préliminaire," *Bulletin d'Archéologie et d'Architecture Libanaises* 1, 1996, pp. 60–85.

20. Curvers and Stuart, "BEY 032: Preliminary Report."

21. H. Sayegh, "BEY 010: Les Souks, Secteur nord/est," *Bulletin d'Archéologie et d'Architecture Libanaises* 1, 1996, pp. 235–70.

22. Curvers and Stuart, "BEY 032: Preliminary Report."

23. W.A. Ward, "Ancient Beirut," in *Beirut – Crossroads of Cultures* (Beirut: Librairie du Liban, 1972), pp. 14–42; Finkbeiner and Sader, "BEY 020: Preliminary Report on the 1995–1996 Seasons."

24. W.L. Moran, *Les Lettres d'El Amarna. Correspondance diplomatique du Pharaon* (Paris: Les Editions du Cerf, 1987), pp. 136–38, 141, 143.

25. D. Arnaud, *Textes syriens de l'Age du Bronze Récent* (Barcelona: Ausa, 1991), pp. 219–20; C. Virolleaud, *Palais Royal d'Ougarit* II, Paris, 1957, pp. 18–19.

26. S. Wild, "Libanesische Ortsnamen. Typologie und Deutung," *Beiruter Texte und Studien* 9 (Wiesbaden: Steiner, 1973), p. 122.

27. R. Borger, "Die Inschriften Asarhaddons Königs von Assyrien," *Archiv für Orientforschung*, vol. 9 (Biblioverlag, 1967).

28. D. Perring and others, "BEY 006: 1994–1995 the Souks Area," *Bulletin d'Archéologie et d'Architecture Libanaises* 1, 1996, p. 190.

29. G. Picard, "Observations sur la société des poséidoniastes de Bérytos et sur son histoire," *Bulletin de Correspondance Hellénique* 44, 1920, pp. 236–311.

30. H. Sader, "Phoenician Inscriptions from Beirut," in *Denkschrift William A.Ward*, ed. L. Leskoe, 1997. In press.

31. Lauffray, "Forums et Monuments de Béryte (à suivre)," p. 20; R. Mouterde and J. Lauffray, *Beyrouth, ville romaine. Histoire et Monuments* (Beirut: Villes Libanaises, Directorate General of Antiquities publications, 1952), pp. 25–27.

32. Lauffray, "Forums et Monuments de Béryte (à suivre)," pp. 19–20.

33. M. Davie, "Trois cartes inédites de Beyrouth," *Annales de Géographie de l'Université Saint Joseph* 5, 1984, pp. 37–82; "Maps and the historical topography of Beirut," *Berytus* 35, 1987, pp. 141–64.

34. Lauffray, "Forums et Monuments de Béryte (à suivre)," p. 76.

35. Ibid., p. 19 and note 1, p. 25; Mouterde and Lauffray, *Beyrouth, ville romaine. Histoire et Monuments*, p. 28.

36. Lauffray, "Forums et Monuments de Béryte (à suivre)," p. 75 and pl. I.

37. M. Saghiye, "BEY 001 and 004 Preliminary Report," *Bulletin d'Archéologie et d'Architecture Libanaises* 1, 1996, pp. 42–43, 48.

38. P. Marquis and R. Tarazi, "BEY 009: L'Immeuble de la Banco di Roma," *Bulletin d'Archéologie et d'Architecture Libanaises* 1, 1996, pp. 148–76.

39. Lauffray, "Forums et Monuments de Béryte (à suivre)," p. 26ff.

40. Perring and others, "BEY 006: 1994–1995 the Souks Area," pp. 176–207.

41. Ibid., p. 191.

42. Mouterde and Lauffray, *Beyrouth, ville romaine. Histoire et Monuments*, pp. 16–17

43. N. Jidéjian, *Beyrouth à travers les Ages* (Beirut: Dar el Machreq, 1993), pp. 1–3.

44. Curvers and Stuart, "BEY 032: Preliminary Report."

45. Mouterde and Lauffray, *Beyrouth, ville romaine. Histoire et Monuments,* p. 38.

46. P. Collinet, *Histoire de l'Ecole de Droit de Beyrouth* (Paris: Recueil Sirey, 1925), pp. 16–20.

47. Curvers and Stuart, "BEY 032: Preliminary Report."

48. C. Aubert, "BEY 002: Rapport préliminaire."

49. Perring and others, "BEY 006: 1994–1995 the Souks Area," p. 191ff.

50. F. Alpi, "BEY 006: La mosaïque inscrite," *Bulletin d'Archéologie et d'Architecture Libanaises* 1, 1996, pp. 215–18.

51. Perring and others, "BEY 006: 1994–1995 the Souks Area," p. 192.

52. K. Butcher, "BEY 006: The Coins," *Bulletin d'Archéologie et d'Architecture Libanaises* 1, 1996, p. 210.

53. P. Mongne, "BEY 008 bis. Zone des Souks. Dégagement du fossé médiéval," *Bulletin d'Archéologie et d'Architecture Libanaises* 1, 1996, pp. 270–93.

54. F. Hours and K. Salibi, *Salih Ibn Yahya. Tarih Bayrut, Récits des anciens de la famille de Buhtur B. Ali, Emir du Gharb de Beyrouth* (Beirut: Dar el Machreq, 1969).

55. J. Bouzek, "BEY 069: Sondage A," *Bulletin d'Archéologie et d'Architecture Libanaises* 1, 1996, pp. 135–47.

"Your Beirut Is on My Desk"
Ottomanizing Beirut under Sultan Abdülhamid II (1876–1909)

by

Jens Hanssen

It is very tempting to project the history of a city's physical development back in time and measure an epoch by virtue of its contribution to the city's present shape. However, such an approach is bound to disregard those historical epochs which have ostensibly left no or few physical traces on the 'modern' city. Furthermore, an approach set out to trace lineages of a 'modern city' is dependent on present definitions of modernity and does not capture the extent to which the population of a given age perceives urban transformation.

The fact that Ottoman Beirut was taken over by a European colonial power after World War I stigmatized its urban development in the late nineteenth century as traditional, morose, and chaotic. During the Mandate period, French urban planners and Orientalists came to Lebanon and Syria to study the urban histories, and characterized the cities by virtue of what they apparently lacked in comparison to ideal-typical European cities. The eminent French urban historian André Raymond goes as far as to argue that "this tendency was all the more natural as French colonization willingly represented itself as reestablishing the Roman 'imperium' after an interval of some fifteen centuries."[1] The profound physical transformation of the landscape of Beirut during the

French Mandate period, with its ideational antecedent in the colonial notions of the Oriental city, triumphantly monopolized the definition of modernity vis à vis the constructed backwardness of the previous order under the 'Turkish tyranny.' The Place d'Etoile and the clock tower at its center symbolized, maybe most persuasively, colonial representation of rupture between French and Ottoman rule.[2] One could quickly come to the conclusion that newly independent Lebanon saw a perpetuation of the French discourse of discontinuation with Lebanon's Ottoman past, whether in adaptation or rejection of French urbanist principles. But even in early independent Lebanon there were certain voices advocating an appreciation of Beirut's pre-Mandate urban profile and turning the idiom of 'the traditional' into 'the original.'

A seemingly trifling episode surrounding the removal of the Ottoman fountain on Riadh al-Solh Square, formerly Sahat al-Sur, in 1957 may serve as an illuminating example of the interpretive nature of continuity and discontinuity in Beirut's modern urban history (fig. 1). In a letter to the popular historical journal *al-Awraq al-Lubnaniyya* in March 1957, a subscriber complained bitterly about the lack of concern of what he called the French-influenced municipal

Fig. 1. Assour Square showing the Hamidiyya Fountain

Fig. 2. Map of Beirut during the reign of Abdülhamid showing the major public institutions

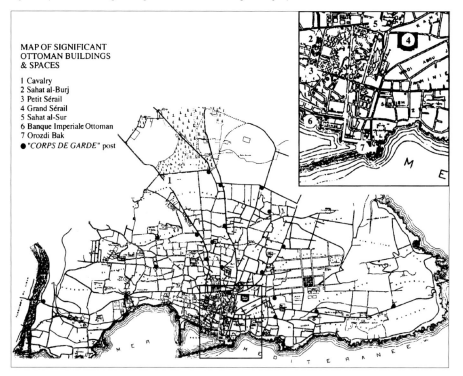

MAP OF SIGNIFICANT
OTTOMAN BUILDINGS
& SPACES

1 Cavalry
2 Sahat al-Burj
3 Petit Sérail
4 Grand Sérail
5 Sahat al-Sur
6 Banque Imperiale Ottoman
7 Orozdi Bak
● "CORPS DE GARDE" post

council for the "impressive oriental monument which was ornamented in the most beautiful artistic engravings and with splendid Arabic calligraphy." Cynically, he continues, "we should be grateful that they dismembered its construction stone by stone and transferred it to the Sanayeh Garden, which rescued the fountain from destruction, and that they did not sell it at a public auction as they did with the stones of the Petit Serail seven years ago!"[3] The recent reconstruction of the Grand Serail generated similar polemics when a third floor was added to the original two, the roof acquired gables, and the courtyard was reduced in size to suit the residential needs of the prime minister.[4]

The fact that all three constructions – the fountain, the Sanayeh Garden, and the Petit Serail – were built during the reign of Sultan Abdülhamid II (1876–1909) (the fourth, the Grand Serail, dates back to the 1850s) may serve as a point of departure for this essay on Beirut's late Ottoman urban history (fig. 2). The essay is premised on Raymond's notion that "a city, that is to say a geographical concentration of a large population, can only subsist or develop within a system of coherent relations between its society and the space in which it expands."[5] In the case of late Ottoman Beirut, this system consisted of multilayered dynamics between agents of change. On the one hand it involved both legal and physical regularization of urban space through legal directives and new modes of organization and certain technologies, like the distribution of *corps de garde* posts or the tramway. In turn, these agents generated new patterns of spatial imagination. On the other hand, the system conjured up the reaction – at times, indeed, the resistance – of Beirut's population to these agents, through strikes and boycotts.

These dynamics were by no means marked by a clear-cut imperial versus local antagonism, but rather they developed in the context of reciprocal interactions on the imperial, regional, and local levels. Within this context, the creation of the province of Beirut in 1888 marked the convergence of all three levels in Beirut as the province's capital (fig. 3). As such, the term 'Ottomanization' attempts to capture the

Fig. 3. View of
Beirut looking east,
ca. 1880

historical process by which the evolving modernization around the turn of the nineteenth century drew the city of Beirut ever closer into the orbit of Ottoman state power.

The Imperial Level: Inventing Ottomanism and the *Tanzimat* City

In the latter half of the nineteenth century, the Ottoman Empire underwent a series of reforms, the *Tanzimat*, which had a great impact on the relations between the political center in Istanbul and the Ottoman provinces. By the time Abdülhamid II became the Ottoman sultan on September 1, 1876, the transformation of the capital Istanbul and other cities of the empire conforming to European models had already become one of the most tangible manifestations of Ottoman centralization in the wake of the *Tanzimat*. The loss of the Balkan territories in 1878 meant that the administration of the Arab provinces assumed increased importance for the Ottoman government in Istanbul. The first municipal administration had been set up in Pera, Istanbul, in 1856 to oversee the implementation of new construction laws, directives of street alignment, and safety and hygiene regulations.[6] The Pera municipal district served as a model for Beirut which received its first municipal institution in 1868, which according to Perthuis, a prominent French entrepreneur of Beirut, "a été presque entièrement copié sur celui de Pera: il fixe la composition de la commission ainsi que ses attributions qui sont limitées à la voierie à jour, la voierie souterraine, les embellissements de la ville, la police des denrées alimentaires, celle des lieux publics et à tout ces qui touche la santé et la salubrité publique."[7]

However, it was during the last quarter of the nineteenth century, and particularly after it became a provincial capital in 1888, that Beirut witnessed a systematic and pervasive implementation of Ottoman urban management. The term 'urban management' here denotes a system of city administration and, by extension, a consciousness and a will. In the *Tanzimat* cities, urban management, as will be seen in the course of this essay, involved laws and regulations, their enforcement, and the establishment of municipal, commercial, and health councils. As such the term captures the dynamic process between internal and external factors that shape the urban environment. It also stands in contrast to the term 'urban planning' of Haussmannian dimensions, which conjures up images of external impositions on the urban fabric and local society.[8]

The assertion of imperial power in Ottoman cities was driven by Abdülhamid's own interpretation of post-*Tanzimat* Ottomanism that strove to maintain social cohesion and imperial control. Moreover, Ottoman centralization coincided with the general tendencies during the 'Age of Empire' to create regularity, uniformity, and efficiency in urban space and time in rapidly growing cities. "The thrust of the age was to affirm the reality of private time against that of a single public time and to define its nature as heterogeneous, fluid, and reversible. That affirmation also reflected some major economic, social, and political changes of this period. As the economy in every country centralized, people clustered in cities, and political bureaucracies and governmental power grew, the wireless, the telephone, and railroad timetables necessitated a universal time system to coordinate life in the modern world."[9]

Threatened by European intervention in economic, political, and cultural spheres, there was a growing realization among the late nineteenth-century Ottoman rulers that in order to free the Ottoman Empire from its inferior position in relation to Western powers, they needed to reinvent their *raison d'état*. The new concept of Ottomanism here meant to unite all peoples of the empire, regardless of their confessional, ethnic, or geographical origin under the leadership of the sultan. Redefining the *raison d'état* was by no means confined to the nineteenth-century Ottomans. As in the cases of the Russian and Austrian empires, Ottoman 'official nationalism' meant that the person of the monarch, Abdülhamid II, came to be directly identified with state power, but this also had risks because now the monarch became directly responsible for the failures of the system.[10]

The reinvented, late nineteenth-century concept of the sultanate had many of the trappings of a nineteenth-century European monarchy: the invention of the throne, the reinvention of official music, such as the 'Ottoman March,' the 'Hamidiyye March,' or the 'Oriental Overture'[11]; the emergence of the theme of an Ottoman national flag; or the invention of commemorative iconography, i.e., the lavishing of Ottoman citizens with medallions for their service.[12] All these tokens served as "symbols of the renewed emphasis on royal power and ceremonial."[13] The joint impact of these symbols created a new public image and a new legitimacy of the modern Ottoman state based on the reinvention of a specifically Ottoman history and tradition. In doing so, the Ottoman government under Abdülhamid II took recourse to the ages of Sultan Suleyman the Magnificent (r. 1520–1566), or Ahmet III (r. 1703–1730), as an idealized past which was epitomized by the architectural masterpieces of the classical era under the architect Sinan (1490–1588) and by the Tulip Era (ca. 1700–1730). The architecture of these periods still distinguishes Istanbul's urban fabric today as a constant reminder of past Ottoman splendor. In a way then, public construction in late nineteenth-century Ottoman cities was also an attempt to match – or re-create – these ages in a modern context.

The material culture of the expanding cities of the Ottoman Empire was a very suitable platform on which the Ottoman imperial government practiced its 'new public image.' The management of urban space and time became an important vehicle to demonstrate convincingly this image of a modern Ottoman state. Throughout the Ottoman Empire, commemorative rituals were rehearsed at the opening ceremonies of public constructions. Within this rhythm of commemorative rituals two dates recurred almost religiously: January 9, the Sultan's birthday, and September 1, the anniversary of his accession to the 'Ottoman throne.' As in other cities of the empire, the numerous public buildings, barracks, hospitals, schools, and *serail*s in Beirut were not only responding to practical necessity. Through the magnificence of the buildings' dimensions, the amplitude of their lines, the uniformity of their design, the functional effect of their decorative elements, they confirmed the power of the state and provided visual and physical evidence of Ottoman claims to modernity. As such the management of urban space engendered not just physical changes in the built environment, but also filled urban space and time with new socio-political meaning.

The Regional Level:
The 'Capitalization' of Beirut

The administrative geography of Beirut within the Ottoman context shifted according to the tides of regional politics. The town reported to the immediate administrative superiors in Damascus, Sidon, or Acre, or was tributary to independent local potentates in these cities. Although the Ottoman Empire regained nominal control over Beirut after the Egyptian army was ousted from Syria in 1840, its authority was soon eroded by unrest in the mixed districts of the dual *qaimaqamat* regime in Mount Lebanon. While the Ottoman political center in Istanbul remained distant in terms of law enforcement, administrative hierarchy, and economic clout, European commercial expansion – especially the silk trade with Mount Lebanon – propelled Beirut into the orbit of the Euro-centered world economy.[14] Diplomatic representations, foreign investors, and missionaries settled in Beirut. They turned it into a city which passively (if we are to believe the literature) facilitated the accumulation of wealth, a process which was only magnified during and after the Crimean War (1853–1856).

When the Sublime Porte dispatched a military expedition to Beirut to investigate the atrocities of the 1860 civil wars in Mount Lebanon and Damascus, Grand Vizier Fuad Pasha made the Grand Serail his headquarters. The dispatch of one of the highest ranking Ottoman statesmen to visit the region since the Ottoman conquest in 1516 was not only a clear signal to the local population of the seriousness with which the Porte viewed the matter. The central location of the Ottoman military mission compared to the distant encampment of the French army in Beirut's pine forest gave Fuad Pasha a clear symbolic and structural advantage to establish stability and trust within a new Ottoman political framework, over the heads of the French military leadership.[15] It was in the Grand Serail that the plans for a new Ottoman order in Mount Lebanon and *bilad al-sham* (i.e., geographic Syria) took shape. The creation of the *Mutasarrifiyya* of Mount Lebanon as a system of shared rights and responsibilities not only heralded what Akarli termed 'the long peace.'[16] It also institutionalized a centripetal process of integration that tied the Ottoman provinces ever closer to Istanbul. The governor, a non-local Christian Ottoman, was appointed by the Sublime Porte and reported directly to the grand vizier in Istanbul. The innovations in telecommunication and transportation that swept the Middle East at the time nurtured this process of integration.

Beirut's phenomenal growth in the second half of the nineteenth century has been well documented in recent years.[17] Although Beirut continued to prosper economically and culturally, the notables of the city felt that they had lost out against Damascus under the administrative reshuffle of the Ottoman Empire, the city Fuad Pasha was in fact most concerned about during his mission. With the promulgation of the new provincial law in 1864, Beirut lost its privileged status as the seat of government of the province of Saida and was annexed to the province of Damascus.[18] Between 1864 and 1888 scores of petitions by Beiruti notables and religious dignitaries, the most prominent among whom was perhaps the Greek Catholic Patriarch Gregorius, were sent to the Porte to beg the Sultan to turn Beirut into a provincial capital.[19] When the Beirutis finally got their way, the British consul in Beirut, Eyres, commented that establishing Ottoman governmental institutions in Beirut would render obsolete the time consuming and costly trips to Damascus, where political elites "had no sympathy with the affairs of their neighbors [in Beirut] separated from them by a chain of mountains, and whose interests are entirely different if not antagonistic to the agriculturally based Damascus."[20] In any event, making Beirut a provincial capital was a purely Ottoman decision, surprising both the French and British consuls in Beirut. For the burgeoning commercial bourgeoisie of Beirut, however, access to central authorities was essential to cultivate the friendship and goodwill of the Ottoman governor and the senior officials.

The Ottoman decision in favor of Beirut expanded the city's political power far beyond the confines of geographical, confessional, or familial ties with Mount Lebanon.[21] As provincial capital, Beirut ruled over the sub-provinces, *Mutasarrifiyya*s or *sanjaq*s, of Tripoli and Lataqiyye in the north, and Acre and Nablus in the south.[22] The creation of the province, or *vilayet* – in Arabic, *wilaya* – of Beirut was by no means just an administrative adjustment by the Ottomans. The merchants and politicians of the coastal towns had to come to make their representations in rivaling Beirut in order to press their cases. On the fiscal level, most of the annual provincial revenues first went to the treasury in Beirut before being redistributed.

In terms of Beirut's position in the Ottoman Empire, the 'capitalization' was primarily an indication that, to the Beiruti notables, inviting central Ottoman authority was not deemed too high a price for upgrading Beirut administratively. Second, the fact that Beiruti notables should address their complaints directly to the Sublime Porte brought the local politics of Beirut closer to the Ottoman center. The struggle for the creation of the new *vilayet* with Beirut as its capital marked the convergence of two trajectories that determined Beirut's political relationship with Istanbul. It was an expression of a larger dual process in which Beirut became 'Ottomanized,' i.e., tied more closely to imperial politics at the Ottoman center, and in which Istanbul became 'localized,' i.e., involved more directly in the local politics of Beirut.

At the heart of this dual process stood four Malhame brothers, members of a Maronite family from Beirut, who were protégés of Abdülhamid II and rose to prominent positions in the Ottoman administration. Originally local notables with considerable wealth and land in Mount Lebanon, they were drawn in to Ottoman institutions by merit and political fortune. Salim and Najib, the two eldest brothers, received administrative training in Istanbul and spoke Ottoman and Arabic, as well as French and English. They held residences both in Istanbul and Beirut and systematically took their turn in commuting so as to ensure that they were close to political developments in the two cities. In 1893, Salim Pasha Malhame became the first *wazir* (or in English, vizier) of the newly formed Ottoman Ministry of Forests, Mines, and Agriculture. Najib Pasha also gained the rank of vizier in the Ministry of Public Works in 1908. He owed his previous post as a chief of the secret police to the fact that he had uncovered an assassination attempt on the Sultan's life.[23] In 1888, Philipp Malhame acted as the general director of the Public Debt Administration in Syria before becoming a senator, while Habib Malhame was a councillor of state. Two other brothers were listed in the 1908 Ottoman Yearbook of the *Vilayet* of Beirut as directors of the Ottoman Tobacco Regie in Janina and Jerusalem.[24] At home and in cooperation with their relatives, the Moutrans, the Malhames were involved in the concession business related to the port and land transactions.[25] Although the extent of the Malhames' involvement with the Porte was unusual, it nevertheless gives a sense of how close Beirut was to the Ottoman center of power during Abdülhamid's reign. When the CUP came to power in 1908, Salim Malhame was exiled only to return to Beirut and to Lebanese politics during the French Mandate period.

For a long time, the Beirutis had coveted infrastructural projects and public works. However, they only came to fruition after Beirut became a provincial capital, as the city's new status after the administrative upgrade provided the investment security to attract financial capital, both foreign and local: after decades of haggling over the enlargement of the harbor, an imperial concession was granted in 1889, and the construction of the port was completed in 1893. The idea for this project had gone back to 1863 when Perthuis' 'Compagnie Imperiale Ottomane des Diligences' had completed the new Beirut-Damascus road.[26] It had been taken up by the first municipal council in 1868, but again was quickly aborted due to lack of financing.[27] When in 1879 Midhat Pasha, the *vali* of Syria, raised the issue again, according to one source, the value of land property in Beirut rose by 40 percent.[28]

Reflecting the interdependent effects of both growing maritime trade and the construction boom in Beirut, a taller lighthouse was built in Manara in 1889, because "newly built houses had obstructed the view from the port to the lighthouse."[29] In a similar vein, the concession to build the Damascus railway with Beirut as the *tête de la ligne* was finally granted to Hassan Beyhum in 1891, while the construction – completed in 1895 – was carried out and financed by another of Perthuis' companies. Both the new port and railway line gave Beirut an edge over the rivaling port cities in capturing the trade of the hinterland, a regional hegemony the city maintained until well into the twentieth century.

The Local Level: Beirut's Changing Urban Fabric

In the 1840s, mosques, castles, and fortification towers still marked the medieval silhouette of Beirut. To journeymen and fishermen arriving in Beirut from the mountain and the sea, respectively, the city was optically dominated by Burj al-Mina and Burj al-Musalla on the northern, coastal side, Burj Umm Dabbous and Burj al-Jedid in the southwest, and in the southeast the Burj al-Kashaf, whose solid construction had succumbed to bombardment by the British fleet in 1840.[30] Above the twenty-meter-high city walls the minarets of the mosques, for example the ʿUmari, al-Amir Munzir, and al-Amir Mansur ʿAsaf, towered conspicuously.[31] Two sandy open spaces – Sahat al-Sur and Sahat al-Burj – lay between the city and surrounding orchards which were later remembered to have functioned as playing fields for the inhabitants.[32] While economic life thrived in the many *khan*s and souks of intramural Beirut, political life converged around the Serail, a legacy – like most of the military and religious edifices – of the period of the Druze ruler Fakhr al-Din II (r. 1593–1633). Situated just outside the eastern flank of the city wall, it functioned as the local magistrate's court and comprised the administrative services, the military rank, and the judiciary.[33]

The first physical manifestations of Ottoman reassertion of control over Beirut date to the 1850s. The infantry barracks, or the Grand Serail, as the building was later called, was completed in 1853, and commanded a majestic ridge above the roofs of the old city. The construction was the architectural expression of the new Ottoman military organization, the *nizam al-Jedid*, or 'new order,' at the time. Both in terms of its lofty location and austere facade, it was in fact a smaller version of the Selimiyye Barracks in Haydar Pasha, Istanbul, which

had also been completed in 1853.[34] The two expansive floors spread well over eighty meters on the elongated side, easily making it Beirut's largest building in living memory. Its arcaded porticus, protruding on the eastern facade, was flanked by two symmetrical wings regularly structured by three rows of sixteen small, identical windows. The building appeared conspicuously to inspect from an imperial distance – seemingly incorruptible – the bustle on Sahat al-Sur and the old city, and from afar, overlooked the port and the Mediterranean Sea. It functioned as a topographic reminder of who was in power in the city. The emphasis was on the building's imposing order, whose monumentality was amplified when in 1861 the similar but smaller structure of the military hospital emerged alongside the Grand Serail.

Within two generations the urban profile of Beirut was to change dramatically from what it had been in 1840. The impressive skyline that appeared on the Kantari hilltop, the joint visual effect of the barracks, the military hospital, and, conspicuously in between, the Ottoman clock tower, erased all traces of the Burj Umm Dabbous and Burj al-Jedid of old. Likewise, the old castle and seaside fortification towers gave way to the exigencies of maritime trade, being replaced by long straight jetties and rectilinear quays in the harbor. The city walls disappeared, and by the 1880s most of the seven gates passed into the city's memory merely as points of geographical reference. The height of the minarets was rivaled by the church and school towers that cropped up on the hills of the expanding city to mark physically the upsurging religious, educational, and cultural activities of Beirut.

In the 1890s the regional service of the Tramway Libanais started to operate. It eventually connected Tripoli and Sidon infrastructurally to Beirut. In 1898, a Belgian company, which in 1889 was the first to provide streets in Beirut with gas lighting,[35] obtained permission to build the city's 'electric' tramway.[36] It was inaugurated with great pomp on the Sultan's birthday on January 9, 1907. When the network was opened to the public in 1909, many streets had been aligned, paved, and widened alongside the rails. Initially, the Beirutis reacted to the tramway with the same fear and superstition that people in Europe had earlier directed at the first railways. But soon the tramway became such a popular means of transportation in Beirut that the guild of coachers, who until then had conducted the mainstay of public transportation in Beirut, saw their livelihood threatened and began to mobilize resistance against their new rivals.

Five lines were opened with end stops at the pine forest, Nahr Beirut, the lighthouse, and the port. Thus inner city distances were traveled more quickly and demanded less effort. Moreover, at least in theory, the introduction of scheduled transport service regulated the organization of time in Beirut more rigidly. In practice, however, the system of timetables and stops was undermined by passengers who stopped the carriages midway and forced them to wait for them to embark and disembark. The new dimensions of geographical mobility of Beirut's population caused considerable strain on public security in Beirut. There were incidents of highjacking carriages and boycotts by passengers.[37] Occasionally, tramway pas-

sengers molested the passing pedestrians, or a passing tramway was attacked by agitated coffeehouse guests along the lines.[38]

The tramway did indeed become an arena as well as an instrument for mobilizing labor and public protest. The workers of the company staged a series of strikes that left the city without light for several nights to press for higher wages and job security.[39] A decision in 1909 by the company to raise the fare was received by an organized boycott of passengers. Those Beirutis who chose to ignore the boycott were jeered by the crowd.[40] As much as such popular unrest and civil disobedience was driven by economic deprivation, it also signified resistance to intrusion by external agencies into people's organization of private life. The familiar entities of time and space were breaking down and being replaced by less proximate, homogenizing ones which obeyed larger external rhythms.[41] Some families, who happened to live on the tramway line, suddenly found themselves exposed to journeying crowds, and – as a passive form of protest against the imposition of an external rhythm by the tramway – moved out of their houses toward infrastructurally more remote areas of the city.[42]

As a capital city Beirut increasingly determined the social, economic, and political development in the region and itself became a powerful agent of the centralizing rhythm of the Ottoman state. Beirut changed from performing as the much quoted commercial entrepôt of the 'Syrian' and 'Lebanese' hinterland to impose itself economically, politically, socially, and culturally on the region. Beirut in the late nineteenth century became in many ways what Braudel called "the 'dominant city' which, while not strictly possessing a character of its own [because it is functionally part of a much greater spatial realm], nevertheless imparts certain characteristics to its spheres of influence, or reflects in a distinctive manner the societal structures and the mentalities of the regions which it serves."[43]

The joint impact of the above infrastructural changes in Beirut was part and parcel of a general shift in the center of gravity of economic activities to the extent that the sustenance of the urban space gradually became the driving force of economic development, while the silk-related role of the city gradually retreated.[44] The parallel shift of Beirut's center of gravity away from the port function to a city with its own distinct rhythms, culminating in its 'capitalization,' was very much reflected by the distribution of the consulates. While the French consulate stayed in Khan Antoun Bey, the British consulate and other diplomatic missions settled in Ashraffiyyeh and in Zukak al-Blat or Kantari after the turn of the century.

The construction boom in Beirut also, necessarily, became the focal point of the provincial populations seeking work. Formerly, seasonal workers connected with the silk industry would migrate from the mountain to the outskirts of the city, only to return to their villages off season. Job opportunities in the construction sector, among others, enticed workers to settle more permanently in what became the suburbs of Beirut, especially around Mazra't al-Arab. But more distant Jnah was also affected and eventually became the subject of international land speculation. The workmen from the Shouf, Metn, and Jnah had the advantage that it lay on the administrative border between the *Vilayet* of Beirut and the *Mutasarrifiyya* of Mount Lebanon, thus evading the jurisdiction of the *vilayet*, while at the same time being close to work opportunities in Beirut.[45]

Spatial Regularization and Spatial Imagination: "Your Beirut Is on My Desk"[46]

The expansion and diversification of Beirut's urban space since the 1880s coincided with – and was probably causally linked to – the promulgation of new standardized construction laws and directives for urban management in the wake of the *Tanzimat*. These applied to Istanbul and the provinces alike. The laws were revised and amended throughout the 1860s and 1870s, but it was not until 1885 that they constituted an enforced, reliable, and binding source of reference. In 1896, the Beiruti municipal engineer Amin 'Abd al-Nur translated and edited the Ottoman construction law "hoping that this service will promote public works, enable the municipal departments to carry out their business, and make the property owners aware what their rights and duties are."[47]

In its first part, the construction law determined the imperial, provincial, and municipal levels of competence. It regulated the width of streets, dividing them into five categories. At the beginning of each street a plate on a wall was to specify its width. One Beiruti editor summed up semi-scientifically the underlying objective of the law: "Widening the streets should not be limited to passageways and crossings, but it is necessary to consider streets as agencies for health improvement. It is well known that the distance of buildings from each other leaves space for the purification of air, disperses the bad smell, and enables the light and the heat of the sun to penetrate the cells and thereby prevent them from rotting, especially in streets where high buildings are already constructed on both sides; and it [the widening of streets] alleviates the burden of the covers, which the inhabitants are forced to put up on balconies of houses too close to each other."[48]

Article five stipulated that "it is not allowed to build at places of worship, the port area, the coast, in public places, and parks. Similarly it is not permitted to transform these places in any way into private property except if the municipal departments saw it necessary to replace the old constructed locations." Yet, any renovation or restoration had to be made in the 'original, customary form.' Part two of the construction law specified the procedures for street alignment. Before construction work was to begin, a profile map and a bird's eye map were to be drawn of the street in question. The file with the maps was then kept at the municipality's public information bureau ('ilm wa khabr) for fifteen days for general access. The governor had to approve the plans before the municipality could put them into practice. The following parts of the law were concerned with fire regulations and prevention, unifying the facades of houses facing the street, the norms for raising buildings, permissions, fees, and prohibitions of restoration, registration fees, and penal codes.[49] Throughout the text the

sustenance of the public and private domains was a recurrent theme.

On the basis of these rules the Ottoman government set about to regularize Beirut's public and private spaces. When Ismail Kemal Bey arrived as the new *vali* of Beirut in 1892, he declared Beirut "une source d'opulence et un foyer d'instruction" and promised to "hater le progrès de la civilisation et de propager les lumières et les connaissances de cette époque."[50] Despite his short term of office, Kemal Bey became one of the leading Ottoman architectural figures in Beirut during Abdülhamid's reign. The inhabitants of the old city soon realized what model of progress the *vali* had in mind when he ordered the construction of two aligned streets through the old city. One was to connect the port with the bazaars and the other linked Sahat al-Burj to Bab Idriss, effectively piercing through Souk al-Fashkha, Souk al-Tawileh, and Souk al-Jamil.[51] The scheme, put on hold for two years by the premature departure of Kemal Bey, demolished a large number of houses and aroused considerable opposition by the inhabitants. But the plan was approved by Istanbul and the municipality carried out an estimation of the property concerned and raised the necessary sums of compensation money to alleviate the effect on the population. The British consul, reporting this affair to his superior in Istanbul, speculated that "maybe the ill-feelings on the part of some Muslims [affected] caused the removal of the *Vali*."[52] Time and again during this period, the municipality found itself anxiously poised between its task to modernize the city's infrastructure and its role to protect the well-being of its inhabitants. As a local institution it had to play a difficult role in reconciling long-term projects in the imperial and regional context with the more immediate local interests.

Nevertheless, the municipality of Beirut was grateful to the departing *vali*, Kemal Bey. According to his memoirs, "the town of Beyrouth presented me with a souvenir album of photographic views of the place and its monuments bound in massive gold with an emerald in the center."[53] The nature of the gift and its value were expressions of both the acute awareness of the municipality of their city as an artifact and the gratification for the *vali* who helped 'sculpt' it. Some members of the merchant community also benefitted from the development of the old city. A series of advertisements in the press, coinciding with the completion of the alignment project in 1894, announced the opening of two luxury shops near the intersection of the new streets in Souk al-Tawileh, Souk al-Fashkha, and Souk al-Jamil.[54]

With spatial regularization came registration. Since the latter half of the nineteenth century, passports and travel permits caused recurring problems between the Ottoman authorities and the local as well as foreign residents. In the 1890s a new variation of the struggle over registration emerged over the *Tanzifat* – or street cleaning – taxes. In 1891, the municipality imposed a new tax for cleaning the streets on all occupants of houses, shops, and cafés, both foreign and local. To this effect, the houses of Beirut were inspected, registered, and graded according to size and value. Backed by their consuls, the foreign residents refused to pay this tax until the *vali* convoked a meeting with the council of the

consular corps in 1898, in which the consuls finally agreed to the tax on the condition that the tax's application be properly documented. The new income of the municipality, an estimated five to six thousand pounds sterling, was to be reserved for cleaning, repairing, and constructing the streets of Beirut.[55]

The publication of the first Beirut directory in 1888, the year of the creation of the province of Beirut, was a seemingly less political example of registering Beirut's urban space. Nonetheless, the directory effectively facilitated a new way of imagining or 'reading' the city without actually knowing, seeing, or living in it. Indeed, its editor, Amin al-Khouri, introduced his pioneering work as a way to "facilitate the connections of the local, the regional, and the distant which connected our works and our communications with the rest of the empire."[56] The directory was used by local businessmen and notables in Syria and in Egypt. One such notable congratulated al-Khouri: "Your Beirut [*sic*] is on my desk."[57] The directory listed all local politicians, names and owners of schools, hotels, printing presses, factories, etc., and specified their locations in the bazaars or the quarters. In a way, then, the book mapped Beirut's political, economic, and social life for residents and outsiders dealing with the city from, say, Istanbul, Marseilles, Cairo, or Damascus.

Public Health Institutions

Public health was an important issue in Ottoman Beirut. Soon after the creation of the province of Beirut, a health council was established to deal with hygiene under ever increasing cholera risks in the wake of greater human mobility in the region.[58] When in 1889 cholera raged in Tripoli and Lataqiyye, the city authorities imposed a *cordon sanitaire* around Beirut.[59] Consecutive *valis* appealed to the Porte to be allowed to move the *lazaretto*, that is, the quarantine for maritime visitors, to Beirut away from the quarter of Rumail. Finally, in 1899, the construction of a new quarantine area near Nahr Beirut was approved.[60]

Missionary schools and convents excelled at providing medical facilities for their respective communities. At the same time, continuous criticism was directed at the Ottoman authorities for failing to improve public health. The quarantine, for example, was deemed to do more "to spread disease than to prevent it."[61] The dilemma the Ottoman government was facing with regard to hygiene became apparent in a 1910 episode when cholera cases occurred within the quarantined areas. It prompted the *vali* to hold two meetings on the state of hygiene in Beirut. In the first one with his staff, the director of the Ottoman Bank declared that the treasury of the municipality was so depleted that even the most urgent sanitary measures could not be taken. He estimated that the municipality needed at least ten million 'lire' to improve conditions and complained about the difficulty of collecting dues from the foreigners. The next day the *vali* invited the most important medical doctors and notables of Beirut and suggested to them that a new loan was necessary and that the foreigners had to pay their share. A foreign representative intervened brusquely arguing that the two thousand 'Europeans' would not make a difference in a city of '180,000.' The *vali* retorted that new regulations were urgently needed. In any event, the issue was assigned to a newly formed committee, consisting of de Brun, the dean of the French Medical Faculty, Graham, a doctor at the Syrian Protestant College (later the American University of Beirut), Nur al-Din Bey, the director of the Ottoman Bank, and Martindale, the director of the British water company. Reportedly, the *vali* was deeply disappointed with the widespread resistance to any *ad hoc* measures. He had sought to find a way to increase the municipal budget for a long time and had hoped that the threat of the cholera epidemic would release local investment or loans for the municipality.[62]

The Spatial Distribution of Ottoman Urban Management: The Corps de Garde and the New Quarters

The distribution of *corps de garde* posts in Beirut had a profound impact on the location and the operating hours of cinemas, cabarets, casinos, taverns, and liquor stores. Policemen patrolled the streets to ensure that all the taverns and alcohol vending shops which mushroomed in Minet al-Husn, Zaituna, and Sahat al-Burj between 1901 and World War I were closed at sunset.[63] Places which were allowed to remain open until midnight, or where music was played, needed special permission from the police. Permits were only granted after the immediate environment of the proposed establishment had been examined. Such places were forbidden in residential areas, near mosques, and – curiously, given their potential threat to public security – in the vicinity of *corps de garde* posts. In addition, private houses could not accommodate alcohol vending shops. The task of the police was not just to secure public order and collect taxes from these establishments, but also to watch over public morality. They were assisted by municipal agents, *chawushs* in Ottoman Turkish, who made their rounds checking on the correct compliance with regulations on dress, parking, storing, alcohol consumption, and fire precautions.[64]

Underlying the forces of regularization, registration, and hygiene was the centralizing state's drive to make the cities of the empire accessible, 'legible,' and thereby establish public security. The new spatial regularizations were reinforced by police laws and watched over by Ottoman police units – or *corps de garde* – whose posts were strewn strategically across the burgeoning quarters of Beirut. A map of the British water company of 1908 shows twenty-five such *corps de garde* posts and two cavalry barracks – one on the Damascus road near the pine forest and the other on Sahat al-Burj, the point of departure for freeway travelers to Mount Lebanon, Damascus, and beyond. It is striking that in the old city itself there were no *corps de garde* posts, the nearest one being on Sahat al-Sur. One post was situated behind the customs office at the port and one east of Souk al-Tawileh in Santiyye/Zaituna. It is also notable that there were only three *corps de garde* on the coast, in Minat al-Husn at the ancient Port des Français, in 'Ain al-Mreisse near the Druze fishing harbor, and in Saifi/Gemmayzeh at the Bay of St. Andrew. All of these

natural inlets had been alternatives to the port which had become highly estranged from the coastal population with ancestral ties to the sea ever since the port company monopolized sea access for commercial purposes.[65]

As for the *corps de garde* post on Zukak al-Blat (later Maurice Barrés Street), close to the Grand Serail, contemporary physical evidence suggests that it accommodated high-ranking Ottoman officers since the complex, which still survives today, consisted of two two-story houses with an extensive annex for horse stables, arranged in such a way as to frame a rectangular courtyard with a well in its center.[66]

Two more *corps de garde* posts were placed on the main arteries east and west along the tramway lines to Nahr Beirut and the lighthouse, respectively. But the highest density of Ottoman *corps de garde* was found in the southern, inland quarters of Basta, Bashura, Musaitbeh, and Mazra't al-'Arab near the two southern tramway lines. These quarters were well-known trouble spots which necessitated a strong police presence.[67] However, in September 1903, all police presence in these quarters proved unable to quell riots between Greek Orthodox and Sunni groups. The riots spread from Mazra'a to Basta and caused grave tensions between Rashid Bey, the *vali* of Beirut, who was rumored to have close ties to the Sunni 'mob,' and Muzaffer Pasha, the *Mutasarrif* of Mount Lebanon, who was accused of harboring Christian outlaws. In any event, an estimated 15,000 Beiruti Christians fled to the mountains in fear of Muslim reprisals and, as a consequence, Rashid Bey was removed from office by the Porte.[68] Ultimately the crisis was resolved by cross-party negotiations by Sunni and Orthodox notables.

An article in the Beiruti newspaper *al-Iqbal* revealed the serious difficulties the Ottoman police faced in maintaining public order in Basta. Although a *corps de garde* post was placed next to the tramway stop al-Nawiry, passengers successfully resisted to pay the fare and demolished some carriages.[69] Given the powerlessness of the Ottoman police, the tramway company had to close down the line for several days. To prevent widespread attacks in the area against its carriages, the company had to employ local strongmen as guards. In a sense the company here functioned as a 'corporate *za'im*' for the guards and, in order to become more efficient, it was absorbed into the local rhythm of society and the local system of clientelism.[70]

In terms of maintaining public order and security, the *corps de garde* system was often strained. Sometimes only manned with one guard, the posts tended to be ineffectual in quelling large-scale unrest. Occasional prison riots took days to subdue, even if they occurred inside the domineering Grand Serail.[71] When 1,400 Ottoman soldiers returning from a military campaign in Yemen passed through Beirut and were kept in the Grand Serail for a medical check up, they staged a mutiny for arrears in their pay in front of the Grand Serail. Unable to disperse them, the *vali* was forced to give in to their financial demands. This decision earned him the contempt of the French consul. According to him, this was not how a modern administration dealt with uprisings, as it would erode the government's authority and set a case of precedence.[72]

Yet, overall, the period between 1876 and 1908 was one of relative calm and social cohesion, despite the great riots of September 1903 and contrary to diplomatic scaremongering. After occasional small-scale eruptions of violence in the *suq*s, order was quickly restored by the speedy arrival of patrols. On September 6, 1909, a consular dispatch reported on the first public execution in Beirut for twenty-five years.[73] The dispatch considered the absence of state violence a sign of inefficiency and corruption on the part of the Ottoman government in Beirut, but one could, in fact, also read the infrequent use of capital punishment as an indication of an effective, if informal, system of social control, since the lobbying of Beiruti notables, who supported their convicted clients, is a clear demonstration of existing patron-client relationships.

Public Construction and the Ritual of Commemoration

In the latter half of the nineteenth century, the construction of public buildings – whether administrative or educational, in public places, infrastructural, or recreational – was the result of the discourses on regularization and registration of space and time, on policing and public health. Together, these practices merged to produce a specifically Ottoman "system of coherent relations between [Beirut's] society and the space in which it expanded."[74] In Beirut, the development of the urban fabric was a conscious joint effort of the Ottoman government and the local population which was played out between the different *vali*s and the municipality. Within this dual process, the border between the Ottoman state and the local society was not a topographical dichotomy, but rather involved discursively produced spaces.[75] The construction of public buildings and places signified the presence of Ottoman central authority in Beirut. Yet, at the same time, this presence made the authority more tangible, accessible, and accountable. Moreover, the buildings acquired a highly local meaning through the choice of local architects and building materials, and through the fact that the buildings were largely financed locally, that is, with municipal funds.

The ritualistic opening ceremonies of such public buildings and places in honor of Sultan Abdülhamid were intended to bring across the distinctly personal and homogeneous idiom of Ottoman space and time. As pro-Ottoman demonstrations and celebrations took place simultaneously across the Ottoman Empire on September 1, there were front page stories in most Ottoman newspapers often making cross-references to the commemorative rituals in other cities. What Beirut's clock tower did in a routine, daily manner, exhibiting public, distinctly 'Ottoman' time, these simultaneous celebrations conjured on a larger scale: on September 1, 1900, the twenty-fifth anniversary of Abdülhamid II's reign, all Ottoman citizens performed – or were supposed to perform – the same collective ritual wherever they were in the empire. Simultaneity of action would thus bring about the imagining of a common community on a common geography in a common time frame. As Anderson put it: "The idea of a social organism moving calendrically through homogenous, empty time is a precise analogue of the idea of the nation, which is also conceived as a solid community moving steadily down (or up) history."[76]

1. *The Ottoman Clock Tower*

At the turn of the century, a new imperial symbol feeding the Ottoman 'public image' was imported from Istanbul: the clock tower. The first Ottoman clock tower under Abdülhamid II was built in Tophane, Istanbul, in 1888, while the one built in Beirut ten years later was the first of its kind in the Arab provinces. Others soon followed suit in Tripoli, Aleppo, and Jaffa. There had been a few towers with clocks and bells before in Beirut, for example the church tower of the Anglican parish on Kantari Hill. In contrast to the religious structures, these Ottoman "towers were considered 'civic art' as they expressed the dissociation of time and religion," while the omnivisible chronometer signaled a new regularity, discipline, and order in the city.[77]

In 1898, the twenty-five-meter high clock tower became the highest building in Beirut (fig. 4). According to Louis Sheikho's eulogizing description in his journal *al-Mashriq* in 1899, "the viewer on the roof can have a panoramic view of the whole city. Nothing would escape his eyes. His view stretches to the outskirts, as far as the coastal plains and to the border with Lebanon."[78] It was erected in 1897–98 in the center of the Ottoman skyline to the west of the old city between the military hospital and the Grand Serail. To quote Sheikho again: "The public laying of the first stone of the clock tower took place on January 9, 1897 – the birthday of the Sultan. The celebration was carried out in the presence of the high

Fig. 4. View of Beirut with the Grand Serail, the clock tower, and the military hospital in the background

officials of the province, military rank and file, and members of the municipality. A military orchestra played a most delightful melody, and later a speech was delivered in Arabic and Ottoman calling upon the Sultan's resplendent and eternal nature, and the assembled crowd believed in these emotional exclamations. After the celebrations the *vali* symbolically laid the first two stones with a silver hammer. At the end of the party, several photographs were taken." The inauguration took place eighteen months later on September 1, with a similar ceremony to mark the anniversary of Abdülhamid's coronation.

The tower was built from a variety of local wood and marble, Jounieh limestone, Beiruti sandstone, Damascene basalt, and red stone from Dair al-Qamar. The obligatory Hamidian *tughra* was installed above the entrance. Inside its four-by-four-meter square shaft, 125 steps lead up to the top. The steps were pioneering in that they are made entirely of iron. On the third floor a 300-kilogram bell with a diameter of eighty-five centimeters was suspended. This floor boasts four miniature, neo-orientalist balconies to which *mashrabiyya*-style doors lead. Above the bell, four large clock faces imported from Paris by the Ottoman embassy, two with Arabic and two with Latin numerals, soberly herald the exact time. All in all, the building cost the municipality 126,000 gold piasters, about one thousand pounds sterling at the time.

Despite its arabesque style, its rectangular shape and the rooftop battlements reminded the European traveler to Beirut of a freestanding version of the Florence or

Bruges belfries. To the Ottoman eye, however, the tower would trigger connotations from Anatolian, Balkan, and Arab provinces of the Ottoman Empire, where such clock towers became common landmarks. It was a striking feature of the Hamidian clock towers that they represented on the one hand the uniformity of the empire through their recurring theme and location in all cities. However, the building material and the outer shell tended to be specifically local. This symbiosis of the imperial and the local was also reflected in the planning procedures of Beirut's clock tower. In fact, they probably exemplified those of other Ottoman public works. First, the *Vali* Rashid Bey had "put together a construction cadre and asked for the permission from the authorities in Istanbul for the municipal agency to build, out of its own financial allocations, a grand tower in oriental style, and to install a huge clock and a bell to announce the time in Arabic." Once the *irade*, or imperial decree, was read out in Beirut amidst great public celebration, a planning committee of ten was established consisting of two municipal engineers, two members of the municipal council, the president of the municipality, Abd al-Qabani, the provincial chief engineer, and four Ottoman military officers. Together, they decided the location and charged Yusif Aftemos, a local architect who had worked for the Ottoman emporium at the World Exposition in Chicago and for the Egyptian pavilion at Antwerp, with designing the building. The marble masonry was carried out by Dionysos Sawan, a Greek Orthodox from Mousaitbeh, and the *muqarnas* was carved by the Damascene artisan Yusif al-'Anid.[79]

2. *The Orosdi Bek Department Store*

The Orosdi Bek building accommodated the first large-scale department store in Beirut. It was part of an Egyptian commercial chain that opened branches in many cities throughout Egypt and in *bilad al-sham*, of which the one in Beirut was the first and the largest. It was opened to the public on September 1, 1900, as part of the city-wide celebrations in honor of Sultan Abdülhamid II. Situated on the quays next to the customs warehouses at the port, it lay at the intersection between maritime trade, that is, the import of luxury goods from Europe, and the inland trade, the export of regionally produced goods. The opening of a railway station on the port premises, which coincided with that of the department store, further enhanced the central location of the building. Thus its customers constituted not only residents of Beirut, but also regional and international visitors, especially since the port-railway compound became a transit stop for Muslim pilgrims to Mecca.

The international character of its merchandise and customers was clearly reflected in the building's architectural style. On the ground floor of the two seaside facades that faced onto a wide plaza, large shop windows offered an easy and attractive view of the merchandise presented inside. The upper floors impressed visitors through their rich variety of structuring and ornamenting elements, such as pilasters, windows of various shapes and sizes, statues, shells, garlands, and small towers, purposefully rendering an eye-catching effect from afar. Inside, an elevator facilitated consumers' access to the assorted commodities. The back of the building, however, was left unadorned. On the whole the building was strongly ostentatious, even exhibitionistic. As such the Orosdi Bek building held every feature of an *en vogue* contemporary European consumers' temple. The *magazins des nouveautés* or shopping galleries in Paris were, in fact, originally based on the perception of an oriental bazaar that tended the world expositions.[80] The only trace of Ottoman influence on the building itself were the token small stars atop the pilasters. Yet, through the simultaneous inauguration ceremonies of the Orosdi Bek Department Store and the fountain on Sahat al-Sur, the building became part of the stage setting, perhaps even an actor, for the self-projection of the modern Ottoman state.

3. *The Petit Serail*

The Petit Serail was built by the municipal president, Fakhri Bey, between 1882 and 1884 (fig. 5). Designed to accommodate municipal and *Mutasarrifiyya* offices such as the city's legal court, the *Mahkama al-Shari'a*, the civil and the military officers, it became the seat of government of the *vali* after 1888. A correspondence in 1885 between the *vali* of the old province of Syria, Hamdi Pasha, and the Porte in Istanbul reveals considerable difficulties in financing the construction. Hamdi Pasha was forced to take out a loan from an Ottoman bank to mortgage public buildings, and finally to impose new taxes on the population to buy furniture for the Serail.[81]

The building was given a historicist, or rather eclectic, outer appearance. It consisted of two floors above a semi-basement, erected on a rectangular ground plan with a central courtyard. The two floors were lined with tall windows set off by Neo-Baroque marble frames producing a marked contrast to the dark Beiruti sandstone facade. The monumental white marble portal opening onto Sahat al-Burj stretched over the basement and the first floor, recalling an entrance to an Italian Renaissance palazzo. Over the entrance a flowing gable with ornate volutes decorated the roof. The corners of the protruding rectangular corner towers and the central part of each facade were topped and accentuated by miniature octagonal towers which, in harmony with the miniature battlements lining the roof, evoked a medieval European castle.

The reinvention of medieval and Gothic architecture was in fact a common symbol of independent municipal authority in European cities.[82] However, the Petit Serail's features also reflected contemporaneous architectural trends in Istanbul. The second half of the nineteenth century witnessed an Ottoman architectural revivalism that was highly eclectic in character. It was initiated by the Neo-Baroque and Neoclassical interpretations of Ottoman architecture by European or European-trained architects, such as the Fossati and the Baylan brothers, who went to Istanbul and were commissioned by the sultans to design new palaces and public buildings.[83] It is this context that determined the Petit Serail's mixture of playful ornamentation and solid geometric structure. While the image of the Petit Serail stood in contrast to that of its counterpart on the other side of the old city, the Grand Serail, it did absorb the leisurely concept of Sahat al-Burj, in a way appropriating the square as an extension of its own structure. This impression was strengthened when, at the turn of the century, the square's park was embellished with an octagonal kiosk and a sumptuous fountain, both popular architectural features in Ottoman urban design.

4. *Comparing Two Public Squares: Sahat al-Sur and Sahat al-Burj*

In the late nineteenth century, Sahat al-Sur (later, Riadh al-Solh) and Sahat al-Burj (Sahat al-Hamidiyye, Place des Canons, or later, Martyrs' Square) were subjected to a

became disconnected from its immediate spatial and social environment.

In many ways Sahat al-Sur (Wall Square) became the main local traffic junction in late nineteenth-century Beirut. Situated on the southwestern side of the old city, it "was a natural outlet for the district of Zukak al-Blat and for the more working-class area of Bashura and its prolongation, Basta."[84] A new Ottoman telegraph office was installed

Fig. 5. The Petit Serail on Burj Square

series of major physical and functional transformations. The reshaping of both squares ostensibly represented Beirut's modern character through the agency of Ottomanization. Yet, comparing the development of both squares, sharp contrasts between their levels of integration emerge. While Sahat al-Sur maintained its local organization and function, Sahat al-Burj became a place of regional integration and imperial ostentation. In the process of serving these larger functions and by way of succumbing to the external rhythms of life, the square

at the northern side of the square next to the public bath, or *hammam*, Zahrat Suriyya. By the end of the century the square had become a popular spot for coffee houses, generating a new kind of market, one of local gossip and regional, even global information, given the proximity of the Ottoman telegraph office. The construction of the tramway between 1907 and 1909 connected Sahat al-Sur with the quarters of Mazra't al-'Arab and Ras al-Naba' in the south, Khan Antun Bey at the port, and Nahr Beirut in the east.

However, despite the profound effect of expanding the radius of the site, the 'square' resisted the regulatory forces of the municipality and "a gardé cette curieuse forme triangulaire qui semble avoir toujours agacé les urbanistes."[85] There were designs to turn Sahat al-Sur into a public park dating from 1869, when the newly formed municipality bought the stores that were erected on the square and tore them down. Lack of funding aborted all further development until 1892, when the *vali* decided to construct a public building on the square and create a public park around it. With the dismissal of the *vali* the incomplete building was torn down again and the idea of a public park was dropped due to pressure from some of the local inhabitants.[86]

The celebrations commemorating Abdül-hamid II's jubilee on September 1, 1900, brought Sahat al-Sur into the limelight of imperial, regional, and municipal affairs. To the sound of military music and under flying imperial banners, an eight-meter-tall white marble fountain was unveiled in the square's center. The *vali* turned on the water and drank the first cup from the fountain's pipes. As with the clock tower, Yusif Aftemos was the chief architect and Yusif al-'Anid the sculptor. The golden Arabic and Ottoman calligraphy, engraved by the local artist Shaykh Muhammad 'Umr al-Barbir on commemorative plates in honor of the Sultan, clearly reflected the larger phenomenon of employing architecture to promote the Hamidian personality cult. In a sense, such commemorative plates on monuments were a constant reminder of the noble patron (although most public constructions were paid for out of municipal funds). As a way to express the city's gratitude, a delegation of Beiruti notables which included Iskander Tuéni, Amin Mustafa Arslan, and As'ad Lahud paid a personal visit to the Sultan Jubilant in Istanbul carrying valuable presents.[87]

The square continued to function as a kind of people's place, as the meeting point for public processions, and the venue for popular festivities when "swings and merry-go-rounds [were] installed around the square's famous cafes."[88] The square's spatial boundaries remained intrinsic and irregular. West of the square, past the Anglican cemetery, the most direct route to the Grand Serail led up a set of steep stairs, physically linking – and in a sense mitigating – the conflicting social and spatial rhythms of the imperial observer and the observed local. While the transition of the square into Amir Bashir Street in the east was smooth, the general absence of encircling pavements around the square accounted for its intimate character. In a way, the privacy of the houses lining Sahat al-Sur to the north and south disseminated into the public square while, inversely, the boundaries of the public square incorporated these houses.

Amir Beshir Street formed the axis between the two squares. From Sahat al-Sur wide pavements lined with trees led the way to the 'other' square, Sahat al-Burj. On this "three hundred by one hundred and fifty meter square," Poujoulat, writing in 1861 as a member of the French military mission, relished the sight of different color "omnibuses" which took the leisurely to the pine forest at fifteen-minute intervals. More so, he enjoyed the dominance "des restaurants, des cafés, des magazins ou des boutiques *tenues par des Français*" who had arrived in numbers in the wake of the Crimean War.[89] Significantly, following this description of the 'Frenchness' of Sahat al-Burj, he appealed strongly for a French military intervention in Lebanon.

Such colonial designs having been thwarted by Fuad Pasha, the square gradually became a model of Ottomanized Beirut, the "jewel in the crown of the Padishah," the Ottoman Empire, as the German Emperor William II called the city during his visit in 1898.[90] But compared to the organic development of Sahat al-Sur, the effectual regularization of Sahat al-Burj gave the square something external, severed from its natural local environment. This impression was expressed in a polemic article in the biweekly *Lisan al-Hal* comparing the two squares' histories: in the 1880s, the few scattered *azdarahit* plants, the last reminders of the 'old' Sahat al-Burj, had been fenced in to constitute a picturesque oval garden. The article complained that entry to this garden was forbidden, subject to an entrance fee, and that it had been turned into a commercial area: "The municipality had built some small huts on the edge of its fences and today [1913] large shops made of stone and lime are built for revenue, in the knowledge that in Beirut there are a number of very rich people who hope to buy them for no less than 150,000 lira. But if the municipality sells this garden, it is like somebody selling his eyes to buy glasses. It is easy for every Beiruti to witness the beautification of this square in how it is surrounded by stores and shops. What is the need for a garden if it is inside a wall? It is upon us to remove

these constructions [around the gardens] and open its gates to everyone who wishes to enter them. For the park which represents for us the fabric of the previous century is not worthy of an enclosed area."[91]

Far from being merely of aesthetic value, the square had become a political space and was used as a venue for pro-Ottoman demonstrations. For example, when Austria annexed Bosnia-Herzegovina on October 5, 1908, the Beiruti notables organized an anti-Austrian demonstration on Sahat al-Burj – or the "jardin de la liberté" as it was then called – five days later.[92] The newspaper *al-Ahwal* reported that "numerous Beirutis gathered last Saturday in the 'jardin de la Liberté' and formulated an address against Austria's violation of the Berlin Treaty. Amongst them were Beiruti intellectuals like Hassan Beyhum, Chibli Mallat, Ahmad Tabbara, 'Arif Ramadan, Felix Farés, Mustapha Gailani, and Selim Ya'qubi."[93] Large public squares or parks such as the ones in Beirut were purposefully targeted by the Ottoman authorities for these rituals, because they provided political order despite a high degree of popular, urban mobilization.

The barracks of the imperial light infantry on the square's western side clearly signaled the maintenance of this political order, as it was conveniently situated at the intersection between the square and the newly aligned street that led west through the old city. Next to the barracks, a large office accommodated the Hijaz Railway Company, the epitome of Hamidian development of the Arab provinces. On the rooftop of its three-floor office building, a square peak displayed the local time to the leisurely flaneurs and to those newly arrived from the mountain as the Beirut-Damascus road led directly onto the square.

In sum, the comparison between the two main squares of Beirut has shown that analyzing specific places reveals their differentiated historical trajectories in the context of Ottomanization. In the late nineteenth century, Sahat al-Burj never really represented the specifically local character in the way that Sahat al-Sur maintained it. While the latter successfully resisted the imposition of larger, external rhythms, the former became an agent of external change, whether as the French-dominated Place des Canons Poujoulat described, or as Abdülhamid's Sahat al-Hamidiyye. Indeed, by the turn of the century, Sahat al-Burj had become the showpiece of Ottomanized Beirut, just as it was to become a symbol of French rule during the Mandate period.

Summary

This essay has attempted to overcome problems inherent in projecting Beirut as a modern city by viewing an important but neglected and misrepresented period of its history from the vantage point of the people who were subjected to the urban transformations under Abdülhamid II. While the economic forces of change have not been covered in this essay, they are by no means intended to be portrayed as insignificant. However, the above elaborations complement them to render a more complete picture of the production of meaning within the urban expansion and transformation that Beirut underwent at the time. As Weber suggested in his article "The Nature of the City," the economic life of a city also depends on non-economic conditions peculiar only to urban areas.[94]

What emerged, then, was a period of profound urban change, both in terms of physical manifestation and social imagining which brought Beirut closer than ever before into the orbit of the Ottoman state and in terms of local opposition to certain elements of change. This process of Ottomanization involved the interplay of the imperial, the regional, and the local levels. The conscious will to develop Beirut as a safe, orderly, and hygienic modern city represented a common denominator for Ottoman and Beiruti officials alike. As such, the conceptualization of Beirut's evolving modernization in the late nineteenth century took its shape through Ottoman agency.

Notes

1. A. Raymond, "Islamic City, Arab City: Orientalist Myths and Recent Views," *British Journal of Middle Eastern Studies* 21, 1, 1994, p. 4.

2. M. Ghorayeb, "L'Urbanisme de la Ville de Beyrouth sous le Mandat Français," *Révue des Études du Monde Muselman* 73–74, 3–4, 1994, pp. 297–309. The volume is dedicated to manifestations of Orientalism in architecture.

3. I. Yazbeq, ed., "Sabil Sahat al-Sur sara athar ba'da la 'ayn," *Awraq al-Lubnaniyya* 3, 1957, p. 132.

4. See for example, "al-Saray al-kabira: bada' i'mar al-tabqa," *An-Nahar*, 9/13/96.

5. Raymond, "Islamic City, Arab City: Orientalist Myths and Recent Views," p. 17.

6. S. Rosenthal, *The Politics of Dependency: Urban Reform in Istanbul* (Westport, Conn: 1980).

7. Archives du Ministère des Affaires Etrangères (M.A.E.), Nantes, Beyrouth Consulat, carton 332, 5/2/1868.

8. Ibid.

9. S. Kern, *The Culture of Time and Space, 1880–1918* (Cambridge, Mass.: Harvard University Press, 1983), p. 34.

10. S. Deringil, "The Invention of Tradition as Public Image in the Late Ottoman Empire, 1808–1908," *Comparative Studies in Society and History* 35, 1993, p. 5.

11. Paradoxically, the genre of military march music had originally arrived in Europe via Istanbul around the seventeenth century.

12. As part of the inauguration ceremonial of the creation of the *Vilayet* of Beirut, Abdülhamid II gave medals for service to the Ottoman Empire to Selim Takla (*Lisan al-Hal*, 12/17/87), Nicola Naccache, George Sursok (*Lisan al-Hal*, 3/22/88), Selim Malhame, the director general of the Dette Publique in Syria (*Lisan al-Hal*, 5/26/88), Abdallah Ghazawi, Iskender al-Haddad, and Muhamed Pasha Jazairy (*Lisan al-Hal*, 7/30/88, 9/24/88, 10/88, 10/1/88).

13. Deringil, "The Invention of Tradition as Public Image," p. 6.

14. Much has been written on the effect of European trade on Beirut, Mount Lebanon, the Syrian geographical entity at large, and the reaction of the local populations. See for example, R. Owen, *The Middle East in the World Economy, 1800–1914* (London, New York: Methuen, 1981), and B. Labaki, *Introduction à l'Histoire Éconimique du Liban* (Beirut: Librairie Orientale, 1984).

15. L. Fawaz, *An Occasion for War: Civil Conflict in Lebanon and Damascus in 1860* (London, New York: Centre for Lebanese Studies and I. B. Tauris, 1994), pp. 101–31.

16. E. Akarli, *The Long Peace: Ottoman Lebanon, 1860–1920* (London, New York: Centre for Lebanese Studies and I. B. Tauris, 1993).

17. L. Fawaz, *Merchants and Migrants in Nineteenth Century Beirut* (Cambridge, Mass.: Harvard University Press, 1983) and M. Davie, *Beyrouth et ses Faubourgs (1840–1940): Une integration inachevée* (Beirut: Les Cahiers de CERMOC, 1996).

18. Bashbakanlik Arshivi (B.A.), Istanbul, *Yildiz-Esas Evraki (YEE): Idare 'Umumi Vilayetler* 37/302/47/112.

19. B.A., Istanbul, *Dahiliye Iradeleri 37280*, 4/29/1865. For an in-depth analysis of the Beiruti petitions to the sultan, see B. Abu-Manneh, "The Establishment and Dismantling of the Province of Syria, 1865–1888," in *Problems of the Middle East in Historical Perspective: Essays in Honour of Albert Hourani*, edited by J. Spagnolo (Oxford: Oxford University Press, 1992), pp. 9–26.

20. Public Record Office (P.R.O.), London, Foreign Office *195/1613*, Beirut, 3/14/1888.

21. L. Fawaz, "The City and the Mountain: Beirut's Political Radius in the Nineteenth Century as Revealed in the Crisis of 1860," *IJMES* 16, 1984, pp. 489–95.

22. A.M. Rafiq Bahgat, *Wilaya Bayrut*, 2 vols. (Beirut: Matba'a al-Iqbal, 1333/1916).

23. Abd al-Aziz M. Awad, *al-Idara al-'uthmaniyya fi Wilaya Suriyya, 1864–1914* (Cairo: Dar al-Ma'arif, 1969), p. 107.

24. *Salname: Beirut Vilayet*-i.n.p., 1326, 1908, pp. 217–19. See also S.J. and E.K. Shaw, *History of the Ottoman Empire and Modern Turkey*, 2 vols. (Cambridge: Cambridge University Press, 1977); *Reform, Revolution and Republic: The Rise of Modern Turkey 1808–1975*, vol. 2, p. 230.

25. Politisches Archiv d. Auswärt. Amts, *Acta Betreffend den Libanon, Türkei*, no. 177, 1–2, leaf 6383–23/7. See also E. Akarli, *The Long Peace*, p. 197.

26. R. Tresse, "Histoire de la Route de Beyrouth à Damas," *La Géographie* 56, 1936, p. 248.

27. M.A.E., Paris, *CCC Beyrouth, 1868–1888*, 7/10/1868.

28. E. Vasif, *Son Altesse Midhat Pacha* (Istanbul, 1908), p. 180.

29. P.R.O., London, *FO, 195/1648*, Beirut, 5/28/89.

30. M. Davie, "Trois cartes inédités de Beyrouth," *Annales de Géographie de l'Université Saint Joseph* 5, 1984, pp. 37–82.

31. T. al-Wali, *Bayrut fi-l-tarikh wa-l-hadhara wa-l-'umran* (Beirut: Dar al-'ilm lil-malayyin, 1993), pp. 167–80.

32. Writing his autobiography at the beginning of the twentieth century, Jirgi Zaydan would refer to these townspeople as the "crooks of 'Asur square – and spread to Burj Square – whose only occupation was pimping, stealing, and provoking the passers-by; they would run around almost naked" and he speculated whether "perhaps they were the rest of the 'Ayyarun of the Islamic empires." T. Philipp, trans. and ed., "The Autobiography of Jirgi Zaydan," *Beiruter Texte und Studien* 1 (Wiesbaden: Steiner, 1979), p. 143.

33. M. Davie, *Beyrouth et ses Faubourgs*, p. 20.

34. G. Goodwin, *A History of Ottoman Architecture* (London: Thames and Hudson, 1971), p. 420.

35. *Hadikat al-Akhbar*, 3/29/1888. To mark the occasion of the inception of its service, a huge fireworks display took place in the 'municipal garden' in front of the Petit Serail where the notables and officials were assembled.

36. At the time coal, petrol, and dry gas were used to generate electricity. M.A.E., Paris, *Nouvelle Serie, Turquié, Syrie-Liban 109, 1903–1905*, 9/11/05.

37. M.A.E., Nantes, *Consulat de Beyrouth 253, 1905–14*.

38. Wali, *Bayrut*, p. 187.

39. M.A.E., Paris, *Nouvelle Serie, Turquié, Syrie-Liban 111, 112*, 1908, 1909, 10/8/08, 9/30/1909. On 9/17/09 the workers posed an ultimatum, "demanding a reduction of their daily work to 8 hours, an increase of salary by 30 percent, regular holidays, and in case of illness, payment of half the salary for 6 months."

40. Wali, *Bayrut*, p. 188.

41. H. Lefebvre, "Rythmanalysis of Mediterranean Cities" in *Writings on Cities, Henri Lefebvre*, eds. E. Kofman and E. Lebas (Oxford: Blackwell, 1996), pp. 228–40.

42. Wali, *Bayrut*, p. 187.

43. F. Braudel, *Afterthoughts on Material Civilisation* (Baltimore: Johns Hopkins University Press, 1977), p. 78.

44. E.Y. Özveren, *The Making and Unmaking of an Ottoman Port-City: Beirut in the Nineteenth Century* (Ph.D. diss., Binghamton, 1990), p. 170.

45. M.A.E., Nantes, *Correspondances des Echelles, Beyrouth, 1894–1911*, 1/7/07. On the ambiguity of the borders between the two entities, see J.P. Hanssen, *The Effect of Ottoman Rule on Beirut: The Wilaya of Beirut, 1888–1900* (Oxford University, M.Phil. thesis, 1995).

46. A. Abd al-Nur, *Tarjim wa sharah qanun al-abna' wa qarar al-istimlak* (Beirut: al-matba'a al-adabiyya, 1896), p. 7.

47. Ibid., p. 5.

48. Ibid., p. 8.

49. The text of this legal document conformed very much to the spatial regulations in those European cities Charles Mulford Robinson surveyed in 1901: "In 1887 municipal regulations in Rome established explicit standards that fixed a height limit in proportion to the width of the street. In Vienna there were new rules to regulate sanitation, the height of buildings, and the location of balconies, and to establish a 'general harmony of appearance.' " See C.M. Robinson, *The Improvement of Towns and Cities* (New York, 1901), pp. 63–79 quoted in S. Kern, *The Culture of Time and Space*, p. 188.

50. M.A.E., Paris, *CPC Turquié, Beyrouth 37*, p. 26, 1/1892.

51. *Lisan al-Hal*, 12/9/1894. By extension, the newly aligned streets also mapped out the office of the Commercial Council, which was established on June 23, 1887, in Tawile Street near Khan Antun Bey. P.R.O., London, *Details and History of the Chamber of Commerce. FO, 226/209, 1887*.

52. P.R.O., London, *FO, 195/1761, Beirut, Aleppo*, 8/2/1892.

53. S. Story, *The Memoirs of Kemal Ismail Bey* (London: Constable and Company, 1920), p. 206.

54. *Lisan al-Hal*, September to December, 1894.

55. P.R.O., London, *FO,195/2024, Beirut*, 7/6/1898. The first annual revenue could well have financed the ambitious construction plans in Beirut around that time. (See below on Public Construction.)

56. A. and K. al-Khouri, *al-Jami'a au dalil Bayrut* (Beirut: al-maktaba al-jami'a, 1889), p. 7.

57. Ibid.

58. *Lisan al-Hal*, 10/15/1888.

59. M.A.E., Nantes, *Correspondance des Echelles, Beyrouth, 1890–1891*, 11/18/1890.

60. P.R.O., London, *FO, 195/2056, Beirut*, 6/24/1899.

61. Fawaz, *Merchants and Migrants*, p. 34.
62. M.A.E., Paris, *Nouvelles Series – Supplement, Turquié, Syrie-Liban 428*, 1908–14, Beirut, 11/19/10.
63. M.A.E., Nantes, *Consulat de Beyrouth 340, 363*, 1887–1914.
64. G. Young, *Corps de Droit Ottomane* 5 (Oxford: Clarendon Press, 1906–07), p. 156.
65. In 1899, Abdülhamid II issued an *irade* enforcing existing regulations and decreeing that all fishing boats, foreign or native, required a license of ten piastres to fish in 'Ottoman waters' (*sic*). P.R.O., London, *FO, 195/2049*, 6/13/1899.
66. A. Mollenhauer and R. Bodenstein, *A Quarter Study of Zukak al-Blat* (unfinished Master's thesis, University of Frankfurt, 1997).
67. M. Johnson, *Class and Client in Beirut: The Sunni Community and the Lebanese State, 1840–1985* (London: Ithaca Press, 1986), pp. 18–22.
68. M.A.E., Nantes, *Correspondance avec les Echelles, Beyrouth, 1912*, 9/11/03 and 9/28/03. The feud seems to date at least to early 1888, when public security was threatened by a series of stabbings and heavy-handed responses by the Ottoman police. The consuls in Beirut were "convinced that it has to do with the Porte's decision to separate the Provinces of Damascus and Beirut" while no new government in Beirut had actually been set up. P.R.O., London, *FO, 195/1613*, Beirut, 1/20/1888.
69. Wali, *Bayrut*, p. 188.
70. Johnson, *Class and Client in Beirut*.
71. M.A.E., Paris, *Nouvelle Serie, Turquié (104–105), 9/28/01*.
72. M.A.E., Nantes, *Correspondence avec les Echelles, 1912, 1/12/04*.
73. M.A.E., Paris, *Nouvelles Series – Supplement, Turquié, Syrie-Liban 428*, 1908–14, 9/6/09. For the stabilizing role of urban patronage, see G. Denoeux, "Informal Networks and Political Stability: Old and New Perspectives," in his *Urban Unrest in the Middle East: A Comparative Study of Informal Networks in Egypt, Iran and Lebanon* (New York: State University of New York, 1993), pp. 13–19.
74. Raymond, "Islamic City, Arab City: Orientalist Myths and Recent Views," p. 17.
75. T. Mitchell, "The Limits of the State: Beyond Statist Approaches and their Critics," *American Political Science Review* 85, 1991, transcript.
76. Anderson, *Imagined Communities*, p. 26.
77. Z. Celik, *The Remaking of Istanbul: Portrait of an Ottoman City in the Nineteenth Century* (Los Angeles: University of California Press, 1986), p. 130.
78. L. Sheikho, "Al-sa'a al-'arabiyya fi Bayrut," *al-Mashreq* 2, 1899, pp. 769–74. It is not clear from the Sheikho text whether 'Arabic time' referred to a different way of counting the hours of the day or whether he merely referred to the Arabic numerals on the clock face.
79. Sheikho, "Al-sa'a al-'arabiyya fi Bayrut," p. 771.
80. M. Girouard, *Cities and Societies* (New Haven, London: Yale University Press, 1985), p. 293.
81. B.A., Istanbul, *Yildiz Tasnifi Sadaret Hususi Maruzat Evraki, 180/77*, p. 13. Rabi' al-awal, 1302, 12/19/1884.
82. One can speculate whether, if the Serail had been built after the creation of the *vilayet*, its facade would have had a more commanding appearance to represent imperial rather than municipal authority.
83. Goodwin, *A History of Ottoman Architecture*, pp. 421–27.
84. F. Debbas, *Beirut, Our Memory* (Beirut: Naufal Group, 1986), p. 90.
85. J. Tabet, "Trois plans pour une ville," *Méditerranées* 5, 1993, p. 131.
86. *Lisan al-Hal*, 11/6/13.
87. Yazbeq, ed., "Sabil Sahat al-Sur," p. 132.
88. Debbas, *Beirut, Our Memory*, p. 90.
89. B. Poujoulat, *La Vérité sur la Syrie et l'Expédition Française, 1861* (Beirut: Dar al-Khater, 1986), p. 229 (emphasis added).
90. P.R.O., London, *FO, 195/2024*, 10/10/1898.
91. *Lisan al-Hal*, 11/6/13.
92. M.A.E., Paris, *Nouvelle Série, Turquié, Syrie-Liban 111*, 10/17/08.
93. *Al-Ahwal*, 10/12/08.
94. M. Weber, "The Nature of the City" in *Classic Essays on the Culture of Cities*, ed. R. Sennett (New York: Meredith Corp., 1969), pp. 23–46.

On Solidere's Motto, "Beirut: Ancient City of the Future"

by
Farès el-Dahdah

"Beirut: Ancient City of the Future" is a commonly used motto in the promotional literature of the Beirut Central District (BCD) project. Aside from its declarative urban program, this seemingly simple phrase encapsulates a classic debate found in modernity's varying conceptions of the post-industrial city relative to its pre-industrial form. Turning the words 'ancient' and 'future' into values and then attempting to resolve oppositions between them – with linguistic swiftness, in this case – is, in essence, a central theme in the far lengthier treatises of such foundational thinkers as John Ruskin, Camillo Sitte, or even Viollet-le-Duc, among others. The debate stems from a nineteenth-century realization that the city, rather than its collection of monuments, is indeed an object of study that ought to be considered as such, in order either to be preserved or replaced. Modernity itself was, in fact, built on this myth of 'ancientness' versus 'newness,' contemporary versions of which are being played out in the patrimonial politics that surround Beirut's reconstruction efforts. To this old myth we must add a number of late twentieth-century, 'postmodern' variations that include cultural tourism, real estate development, and the ever-changing norms of post-colonial national identity.

With respect to current excavation and reconstruction efforts in Beirut, it is important to make a distinction between ruins and archaeology, for it is to the former that the above mentioned motto is actually referring. In the words *ancient city*, one is to imagine the ruins of Beirut, caused either by time or war (fig. 1). Rather than addressing urban archaeology as a practice on its own terms, ruins are here to be regarded as a general

Fig. 1. Beirut's "ancient" urban fabric

rubric under which the totality of Beirut's urban fabric is implicated, be it above or below ground, be it the result of natural or artificial disasters. One must also discern in the motto a conceptual model that perceives the city in two ways: as an object that ought to be remembered and thus protected, or as an object that must be historicized and thus transformed in an endless temporal continuum.

The conceptual opposition between *ancient* and *future* in large urban projects is not exactly recent and certainly not restricted to Beirut. Origins of this ancient-future dyad in urban planning may indeed be debatable. In her book, *L'Allegorie du Patrimoine*, Françoise Choay traces the history of such a conceptual opposition to two rather clear instances in the work of Ruskin and Sitte.[1] For Choay, current patrimonial politics and other claims to defend a cultural heritage against the so-called onslaught of urbanization would be very much in line with a rather famous precedent: the critiques that Baron Haussmann suffered from Victor Hugo's pen. The difference, however, between current critiques of city planning and their mid nineteenth-century antecedents is that Hugo was lobbying against aspects of the emperor's project that were going to threaten famous monuments, not urban fabrics. Parisian districts were only considered in terms of their insalubrious standing, and were cleared either in favor of traffic or in order to reveal the beauty of French monuments. It is only when in the process certain monuments deemed of lesser importance were threatened that Hugo and others intervened. Hugo was concerned with the ruins of historic monuments, not those of historic districts.

The reasons for this belated distinction are complex and deserve lengthier attention. Choay points out, however, that the city and its districts became mnemonic or historic objects of knowledge most probably after the development of cadastral and other cartographic documents that may have at first served military purposes and were later used for real estate development. Other factors that contributed to this novel (and proto-modern) conception of the city are the major transformations of the built environment after the industrial revolution, which introduced a new system of difference at the level of scale against which the ancient city could suddenly be seen and thus examined by contrast. Colonial expansion is also a factor in the conceptualization of this new problem of what to do with old city centers, either in North Africa or India for instance, in contrast with the imported projects of French and English architects.

As to the example of nineteenth-century Paris, it merely serves to illustrate that for Haussmann the city did not exist as an autonomous patrimonial object, when the motto's words *ancient city* are in fact referring to an old way of life, an urban morphology, streets, souks, etc., that are supposedly to be projected in the future (fig. 2). Haussmann aside, it was basically not until ancient forms of the city became an obstacle for real estate development that urbanism as a discipline was invented and that the 'old city' acquired its conceptual identity.

Choay credits Ildefonso Cerdà for actually having coined the term *urbanism*, and thereby understanding the city as an object

Fig. 2. Souks area during archaeological excavations

would otherwise belong to an intelligible past, the end of which exists in the future, not the present. By wishing to preserve the modest aspects of a city (neighborhoods, street corners, etc.), Ruskin actually fixes quaint urban fabrics into their past and dis-

Fig. 3. Excavation in progress in souks area

of study, and as such, that which cannot be reduced to the sum of its monuments. This is to be distinguished from the conception of an ancient city in need of preservation, which, as a notion, is most probably owed not to Hugo, but to the English poet of stones, John Ruskin. For it was around the time of the great Parisian urban works that Ruskin began alerting public opinion against that which threatens the very fabric of ancient cities, be they Venice, Florence, or Oxford, in his case. A city's original "texture" is in his words to be protected at all costs. His conceptual discovery consists of qualifying the whole city as an unintentionally historic monument: as a kind of mnemonic guarantee of national, temporal, and spatial identity. Ruskin's vision of what makes a city ancient, however, is paradoxically void of historicity, wherein history

engages them from historical vicissitudes to which they would otherwise be subject.

Such a mnemonic approach with regard to what is considered ancient can be discerned in both contemporary patrimonial politics and current archaeological practices whereby the "old Beirut," for instance, is recognized as a value that ought to be preserved as is, just as a Roman edifice, for instance, is dismantled stone by stone, reduced to a mnemonic instance, in the hopes of reconstructing it in some future archaeological park (fig. 3).

The flipside of the same model consists of conceptualizing a city's ancient form as having expired and in need of updating. This view, which is in the camp of history rather than memory, is illustrated by Choay in Camillo Sitte's *The Art of Building Cities*, written a century ago. Sitte, we are told, is not concerned with the loss of an ancient city's preindustrial form, which by then had lost its meaning, but rather is keen on finding the urban grammar upon which older cities were built. Unlike Ruskin, Sitte does not suffer from a severe case of nostalgia and simply considers the so-called ancient city in terms of its architectural consistency at the service of a city of the present which is in turn pregnant with its future. For Sitte, ancient urban configurations such as the paradigm of the public square, to which he consistently refers, need not be reproduced yet must serve as a design lesson for a postindustrial metropolis that has, in his opinion, grown beyond measure. His reflection on history is not at all dogmatic, Choay insists, and is simply a form of questioning meant to insist on aesthetics in postindustrial urban design. Just as Viollet-le-Duc had done two decades before in the field of architecture, Sitte simply operates a form of historical rationalism that renders evident the succession of urban morphological systems, the principles of which can be put to good design use.

In essence, Ruskin believes in the endurance of certain urban "fabrics," while Sitte advocates the persistence of certain design principles. Inherent, therefore, in the memory-history model are two distinct utopian projects, one being a utopia of form located somewhere at the end of history, looking back, while the other is a utopia of principles, which looks ahead.

There are, of course, other high modern conceptions of the city in which the past plays an altogether different role. One need not go further than Le Corbusier to illustrate an 'ahistorical' approach to urban design whereby history is of no utility, and absolute beginnings are a must. As far as one can tell, this conception is not at all being considered in Beirut, and clearly does not belong to the connotations of the motto in question.

In fact, this motto, in its own terms, fits Sitte's historical approach to urban planning rather than Ruskin's, for one would hope that somewhere in Beirut's reconstruction efforts there is a utopia of ancient principles, not forms. Phoenician, Greek, or Roman settlements are, after all, not about to be used as a model of urban design for the year 2000. Yet inevitable and more serious questions remain unanswered: if we are indeed not projecting ancient forms into the future, what are those principles from which Beirut was once built and which we are now going to keep? What constitutes "ancient Beirut" and what is so great about its ancientness that must be projected into its future?

The answers to these questions are difficult, and without a familiarity with conservation policies concerning what in Beirut is going to be kept, used, abused, or destroyed, one cannot set parameters of value on the basis of which one could conceive an urban preservation project. It is also clear that the motto has more to do with public relations than with the history of city planning, and that it does not exactly correspond to what is actually being undertaken in either archaeology or urban design. The

Fig. 4. Radio City Center, Joseph Philippe Karam, architect

topic of cultural heritage has, in recent years, indeed become a hot one, full of ideological traps and political intrigue. The problems that face urban archaeology today are many, not the least of which are those that link archaeology and architecture to the construction of national identity.

In order to address, however, the problem of what ruins must be kept in postwar reconstruction, one might need to take advantage of a late twentieth-century twist on this history traceable to Ruskin and Sitte. As a notion, cultural heritage keeps growing younger and seeks to include just about

Fig. 5. The International and Permanent Fair in Tripoli during construction, Oscar Niemeyer, architect, 1962

Fig. 6. The International and Permanent Fair in Tripoli during construction, Oscar Niemeyer, architect, 1962

everything, which is not exactly the case in Lebanon, where urban artifacts that do not fit the rubric of 'ancient' remain unprotected. Lebanese law on this matter is quite clear: "antiquities are those human products that belong to whatever civilization prior to the year 1700. To this law can be submitted real estate objects dating back to the 18th [century] and later, should their conservation be of any public interest from the point of view of history or art."[2]

In order to address the problem of cultural heritage in terms of urban design, an altogether younger ruin may be used as an example that departs from both Beirut and its hopeful motto. The ruin in question is that of what was once projected to be a new district in Lebanon's second largest city, namely Tripoli. It belongs to an architecture that current reconstruction efforts tend to regard as unworthy of critical attention. Re-

cent developments in the BCD project have eliminated exemplary modern buildings, which are not likely to be regarded as architectural heritage when Lebanon's registry of historic sites and monuments does not include a single building not made of stone. Contemporary trends are aimed toward preserving the region's colonial legacies and do not value the architecture of the '50s and '60s (fig. 4). Just about any masonry building with a red tile roof thus becomes a candidate for preservation, while modern architecture – which helped construct an identity for a young republic's post-colonial freedom – remains 'unseen' and ultimately demolished or disfigured at will.

A project likely to suffer from a kind of patrimonial myopia is Oscar Niemeyer's partially built compound that was designed in 1962 for Tripoli's International and Permanent Fair (fig. 5). The fact that this

Fig. 7. Aerial view of the International and Permanent Fair in Tripoli during construction, Oscar Niemeyer, architect, 1962

rather extensive project was never completed – compounded by seventeen years of civil war – is probably the reason why such an example of modern architecture in the Middle East has escaped much of modern architectural historiography.

Niemeyer described this project as providing the city of Tripoli with all the advantages of "a modern quarter" punctuated, amid vast gardens, by housing units, schools, shops, clubs, churches, mosques, and cinemas, all unified across a heightened horizon line. Unlike other fairs, Niemeyer writes, Tripoli's would abide by the "fundamental principles of unity and harmony demanded by any comprehensive architectural project."[3] Niemeyer's statement is aimed at a contradiction that occurs between a fair's architectural value at a small scale and its seemingly chaotic whole, for which it

is usually forgiven when any other project of that size would not be. The fair's unit, the pavilion (figs. 6 and 8), would consequently be "reduced to a mere roof, and not plastered with the sugary characteristics of a palace."[4] Niemeyer proposed a unifying colossal roof structure, 750 meters in length, under which all pavilions were to be located using as many bays as each country required (fig. 7). Besides democratizing the world under a single roof, this strategy had also the advantage of being economically recoverable through rent or sale of space, speedily built, and, of course, architecturally spectacular. Having never been completed, the Fair has acquired the ambiguous position of being a double ruin caused by both abandonment and the ravages of war. It is not difficult to imagine, however, what it could have looked like since its structure is essentially complete and, as with most of Niemeyer's architecture, little remains to be done once the concrete has been cast. One enters the Fair from an elevated ramp, which offers a sweeping view of the entire compound as it intersects a giant portico. The

of Housing, a small *unité d'habitation,* and a model private residence (figs. 9 and 10).

Niemeyer's project is one of many commissions the Lebanese government sponsored at a time when it sought to construct an identity for its newly acquired indepen-

Fig. 8. The International and Permanent Fair in Tripoli during construction, Oscar Niemeyer, architect, 1994

sequence that ensues is a long walk marked on one side by the arch of the pavilion roof structure and by a string of functions on the other. A pool would have provided a reflective podium for all these functions, thus linking together such programs as the Museum of Lebanon, the Space Museum, the Experimental Theater, and the Open-Air Theater. An elevated helicopter landing pad stands guard next to a low bridge that crosses the pool and links the string of functions with the long roof structure. The walk ends at the Housing Section, which includes the Museum

dence. Until recently, the Fair still served as a military base for the Syrian army and its future remains uncertain. A year or so ago, it was intended to be leased out to a consortium which would restore it, add a hotel, rename it, and presumably develop it for Tripoli in the same way the BCD project is intended to transform Beirut.

The future of Niemeyer's project is uncertain, and the architect himself has yet to be consulted about his unfinished work. Should the recent reconstruction of the presidential palace be any measure, the only

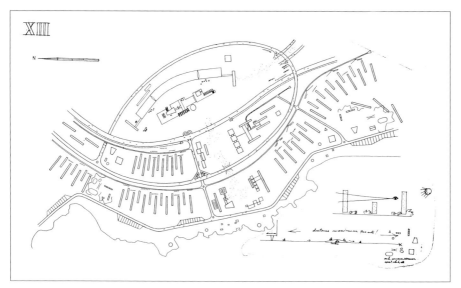

Fig. 9. General plan of the International and Permanent Fair in Tripoli during construction,
Oscar Niemeyer, architect, 1962

possible certainty is that the project might easily be disfigured and replaced with something more 'contextual' or 'regional' and even made of 'local' stone. The presidential palace, which was once a pure glass and concrete cantilever structure, has been turned into some kind of visual gag of so-called Lebanese architecture.

Any plans for rehabilitating the Fair will undoubtedly be ideologically tainted by 'contextually sensitive' design approaches that end up promoting idealized visions of colo-

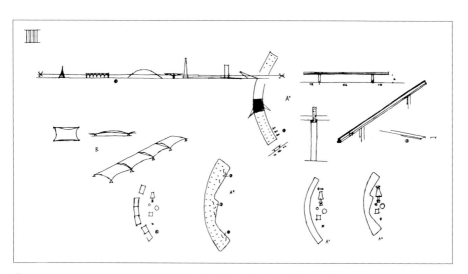

Fig. 10. International and Permanent Fair in Tripoli, sketches of main exhibition hall,
Oscar Niemeyer, architect, 1962

nial Lebanon. This is usually done with an incomprehensible bias against what a young republic chose as its architectural image in contradistinction to what it had inherited from the Ottoman Empire or France. Granted, one cannot expect a country frozen by seventeen years of civil war to have its conservation laws updated when many countries in 1975 lacked any provisions for the preservation of modern architecture. The late '60s and early '70s saw the destruction of many buildings that today would be under strict protection, namely, Victor Horta's Maison du Peuple in Brussels (destroyed in 1968), F.L. Wright's Imperial Hotel in Tokyo (also destroyed in 1968), among many others. One might also expect that in Lebanon, the whole project of conservation is a luxury a Third World country cannot really afford. Yet this fact does not make the potential loss of such an architecture any less regrettable, for it is just as evident that any likely transformation will probably not be free of wastefulness.

At the risk of having to share Ruskin's views on urban patrimony (seeking to preserve things as they once were), one must also recognize that there is a utopia of principles (à la Sitte) to be derived from Niemeyer's architecture. Tripoli's Permanent Fair might, in fact, serve as a model for those urban strategies recently adopted for the reconstruction of Beirut. The BCD project basically consists of liquefying land into assets which are in turn given to shareholders who had once owned or leased any portion of the whole area to be developed. The image of the proposed city, however, does not acknowledge this rather unprecedented condition and insists on emulating a cadastral vision of urban life based on traditional singular ownership of real estate. In other words, urban planning strategies deployed in Beirut do not correspond to proposed designs that seek to represent a preindependence vision of Lebanon's civic life. Niemeyer's architecture, as exemplified in Tripoli's International and Permanent Fair, manifests such a liquid vision of urbanity whereby ownership of property does not correspond to singular rights (framed within allotments), but to a bundle of rights diffused over a larger whole. Such a *tabula rasa* condition punctuated with a variety of mutable programs becomes the public domain owned by all and for whom property rights apply to public infrastructure just as they do to private quarters.

A project such as Niemeyer's is, therefore, in the awkward position of representing notions of uprootedness at a time when returns to ancient origins are in vogue. This position may prove fatal for an architecture that wants to be divested from rooted political notions, which is precisely what a democracy in its youth would want to have abolished (such as political systems based on dynastic or genealogical rights). The difficulty is that what is currently being returned to, namely that ancientness to which our motto refers, predates the very identity of the country itself, born in modern times.

Notes

1. F. Choay, *L'Allegorie du Patrimoine* (Paris: Editions du Seuil, 1993), pp. 135–57.
2. Direction du Service des Antiquités, Arrêté no. 166, LR du 7 Novembre 1933 portant réglement sur les Antiquités (Beyrouth, 1935), pp. 3–4.
3. O. Niemeyer, "Feira Internacional e Permanente do Líbano en Trípoli," *Modulo*, 1962, p. 10.
4. Ibid.

Section Two
The Modern Architecture of Beirut

Modern Beirut

by
K. Michael Hays

The motivation for much of the recent scholarship in the history of modern architecture is the desire to fill a gap in the record or to rehabilitate some previously underestimated period, event, or aspect of an architect's work. Surely such remedial work is crucial to a more adequate understanding of modernism. But too often the hopeful but uncritical assumption that a work deserves to be saved from obscurity ends up simply revalidating the canonical view of modernism by adding new but self-confirming information; or alternatively, it reacts against the canon (as is the case with many 'postmodernist' revisions), but simply by reversing its values, not by challenging its various stylistic definitions and theoretical categories. Here such concepts as 'functionalism,' 'utopianism,' 'abstraction,' etc., or chronological categories such as 'early,' 'middle,' and 'late' immediately come to mind.

Two characteristics in particular have usually been maintained as definitive of modern architecture. The first is functionalism, the intersection of brute facts of utility with objective design methodologies and standardized means of production. Functionalism, of course, is linked with the need for an enormous amount of housing, especially in Germany after World War I, and for a wider distribution of products, including architectural products, to an emergent mass public. The second characteristic is the avant-garde, involving, in one form or another, some notion of a self-critical formal practice as well as the incorporation of advanced technology. The architectural avant-garde sought to invent and deploy new formal techniques, modes of production, and modes of reception against the life habits of the nineteenth-century bourgeoisie and install an altogether new set of habits, preparing its subjects to inhabit the next, more demanding stage in the development of modernity, training them to develop the new modes of perception needed to function in some future, utopian situation. For example, think of the Russian productivist and constructivist attempts to represent collectivity in their design products and establish the subjective conditions for simultaneous collective reception of revolutionary information. Or think of the spaces of Mies van der Rohe or Le Corbusier as radical clearings in the decrepit fabric of the nineteenth-century city, interventions that, infectiously, would continue to spread and eventually transform the city by the sheer power of the 'new.'

The concepts of functionalism and the avant-garde have been supposed to describe fundamental demarcations within modernism, yet neither is very useful for understanding architecture in modern Beirut, either during the Mandate or after. Functionalism attributes to any building an absolute fusion of form and content, the organization of spaces (form) being a direct index of the programmatic intent (content). But even if such a fusion were possible in the case of a well-described program like mass housing, and even if we expand the category of function to include *symbolic* function – which we must, if the assertion of Beirut modernism's search for national identity is to be taken seriously – functionalist doctrine nevertheless assigns as already accomplished what is in fact architecture's necessary but impossible vocation: to strain toward an exactitude of reference or identity that it can in reality never fully achieve. As for the avant-garde, Beirut modernism seems never to have shared either a productivist desire for proletarianization or Western Europe's utopia of the new, receiving as it did a modern 'language' fully formed, as a limiting condition, or at the very least as a legacy on which to elaborate, more than a goal to be won.

What are the new interpretive apparatuses, then, that will have to be invented to expand our conception of modernism so as to include modern Beirut? The dialectic of a globalized modernism and local, 'regional,' or Arabic particularities – along the lines of Kenneth Frampton's 'critical regionalism' – seems to be the only model we have for the moment, and it remains modestly valuable as far as it goes. But critical regionalism was devised as a strategy of resistance to a modernization regarded as one-sided – a call for a tectonically dense 'place-form' intended to supersede the depleted experiential effects of profit-driven building, without entirely abolishing the existing institutions of rationalized finance and production that now make building possible, and to overcome the negative values of private property (like self-interested, utility-maximizing calculations) without necessarily doing away with private ownership. To that extent, critical regionalism is something like a compromise with colonialism itself – a plea for a balance, all the while wishing to tip things the other way. What must be recognized is that this strategy is also driven by Frampton's extreme distaste for today's global techno-scientific and media culture that tendentiously obliterates all local particularities. In the end, Frampton's propositions require us to think that some system other than the market system may be the only way to support the architecture he proposes.

The questions we must ask of critical regionalism, then, are of two different sorts: one regarding its usefulness as a category of historical interpretation, and one regarding its promise for a model of contemporary practice, which is a very different matter. To what extent did Beirut modernism maintain the highly variegated building culture conjoining advanced modern technology and local crafts? Here, Jad Tabet's mention of the hand-built curtain wall is one example. And can that model then be projected into the present? Can the desirable architectural future proposed by critical regionalism ever derive from a dialectical refunctioning of the *actual* present – including the perceptual conventions of popular culture and the technology of metal studs and gypsum board – or is critical regionalism merely an idealized perspective from which present history can be seen only as a fall?

In any case, Beirut modernism as a unique event, an occurrence in that particular geography, during that particular historical moment, and therefore qualitatively different from, say, Italian modernism of the same time, or other 'regional' modernisms in cities such as Tripoli, does not just mean something we know already – not functionalism, avant-gardism, or regionalism. It must be *made* to mean; it must be encoded differently and specifically, in order to then stand as a representative of some generic category of modernism of which it is itself a member.

As a Western historian whose knowledge of Lebanese architecture comprises only what I have learned from the conference which generated this book, I can offer two provisional suggestions for a future historiography of modern Beirut. First, the history of Beirut modernism must be written from Beirut's present – from the knowledge of the physical, cultural, and psychic destruction of a fifteen-year civil war and the current plans for redevelopment. While one wishes to salvage whatever optimism possible, it takes little imagination to foresee an immense commercialization of Beirut, which in some ways is the completion, now by global capital itself, of the process of colonialization begun under the Mandate and before. Under these conditions, it is not merely the regional identity figured by modern buildings, but rather their contradictory endurance and immediate incompatibility relative to the present conditions of production that will constitute the true experience of their historical vocation.

It may seem a paradox that this vocation is nevertheless completely consistent with what Jad Tabet detects in his 'golden age' of modern architecture in Lebanon. For what the buildings of this age accomplished was the registration, in isolated instances, of innovations and desires that could not be accomplished at the general scale of urban planning. The difference now is that, with the replacement of title deeds of ownership by shares in government-created-yet-private development corporations (see the account by Assem Salam), what remains to be found is the architectural solution to the new spatial organizations and programmatic imperatives that will inevitably result from this disappearance of the very distinction between public and private. That liquidation of the very distinction between public and private, and all that it entails for how buildings get built, will tend to obliterate the possibility of distinguished buildings that stand out, heroically and monumentally, from the endless series of built things, each different from the next. And the modern buildings that remain will then spell out not so much what is left to be accomplished as what can no longer be done, or what would be redundant to try to do again. But still – lest this seem like an overly austere minimalism (or even pessimism) structurally inscribed in the new urban economics and therefore inescapable through architecture – we should be reminded that, in the history of modern architecture, such prohibition has mostly felt like a liberation, such limits have mostly been seen as provocation, to which architecture responds with an exhilarated flush of new forms and arrangements, optimistic and rightly full of hope.

From Colonial Style to Regional Revivalism: Modern Architecture in Lebanon and the Problem of Cultural Identity

by
Jad Tabet

Common views about the impact of modern architecture on developing countries often describe it as a violent process whereby imported modern patterns, created in Western industrialized countries, were imposed by force on native cultures, destroying their values and traditions. Local modern architects assimilated to post-colonial elites are also described as being brainwashed by imported Western images, suffering from alienation and schizophrenia, and incapable of producing anything but pale copies of the International Style. Fortunately, modern architecture's impact is being assessed today in more complex terms. The simplified image of locals being passive recipients of concepts and techniques that are foreign to their cultures appears to be too excessive.

Although local architects' approach to Western modernity was admittedly and in most cases superficial, lacking any deep knowledge of the socio-economic processes and cultural background that gave rise to modern forms, some architectural experiences in Third World countries suggest the possibility of successfully domesticating modernism.

In addition to seeking to partake in the global modernization project, local architects had to address their own societies'

concerns, demands, and aspirations. Modernization involved dynamic exchanges between the local and the global, despite the fact that the representation of local architectural traditions was often deformed by Orientalist schemes. Thus, the resulting changes in urban forms, spaces, architecture, physical patterns, and functions were the result of a complex dialectic between center and periphery.

In the present essay, this process will be explored in terms of the development of modern architecture in Lebanon. Lebanese architecture of the eighteenth and nineteenth centuries has been extensively studied during the past decades.[1] Indeed, some research is currently being conducted on the emergence of a transitional style, generally referred to as 'colonial' during the French Mandate period.[2] By contrast, the post-World War II period, during which most of the present urban environment in Lebanon was built, remains mostly unexplored, if not deliberately neglected, and subjected to prejudiced interpretations.[3]

Although a comprehensive approach would require a study of the relation between Western influences and local patterns since the beginning of the nineteenth century, this essay will concentrate on the 'unexplored period' in the history of architecture in Lebanon, i.e., the two decades that followed Lebanese independence. It will try to show that, during this period, attempts were made to find an architectural language which was not simply a degraded version of Western architectural models. On the contrary, despite the widespread use of standard commercial clichés, which have overwhelmed the architectural scene in Lebanon since the late '60s, and despite the present malaise, some of the architectural works produced during the '50s and the '60s represented serious attempts to overcome the dilemma of choosing between 'local traditions' and 'imported modernity.' Moreover, these attempts have more than a mere historical value. They offer interesting alternatives to the problem that seems to prevail today in the architectural debate everywhere in the Arab world, that of local identity versus globalization.

Most of the information on which this essay is based was collected through direct interviews with the architects themselves. Few of these architects have kept real archives or records of their works. However, some information could be found in various issues of *Al-Muhandess* magazine, a journal that was published in the '60s by the Order of Engineers and Architects in Lebanon.

Finally, the discussions with my father, the late Antoine Tabet, have helped me to understand the atmosphere of this period and, above all, to appreciate the spirit of this highly creative age. Architecture never comes about in a vacuum, but expresses emerging tendencies, changing social and technical patterns, and conflicting cultural values.

The Age of Pioneers and the Classical Rationalist Tradition

When Lebanon received its independence in the early '40s, the prevailing style in the architectural scene could be described as being 'colonial.' During the French Mandate period, and following the collapse of the Ottoman Empire after World War II, traditional forms were reinterpreted without introducing drastic changes to the conception of space and without dislodging the hold of previous building typologies. For instance, the typology of new apartment buildings maintained the organization of the nineteenth-century bourgeois house, with its symmetrical layout of rooms around a central '*dar*.'[4] The symmetrical composition of facades was also maintained, and the triple arch motif, a key element of nineteenth-century architectural iconography, was mildly reinterpreted in various forms. Although new materials and techniques were introduced, little attempt was made to find a new architectural vocabulary that would express these materials and techniques. Decorative elements, molded in concrete, tried to copy stone cornices, balustrades, and columns, sometimes tinted with Orientalist accents, other times influenced by classical forms or *Art Nouveau* ornamentation.

In the same period, however, some pioneers tried to formulate new approaches by attempting to find an architectural vocabulary that would better express the emerging social, economic, and technical conditions. Among these pioneers were Farid Trad (1906–1967) and Antoine Tabet (1907–1964). Both were engineers with solid academic training. Farid Trad graduated from the Ecole des Arts et Métiers in France, and Antoine Tabet, after getting a degree in engineering from the Ecole Supérieure d'Ingénieurs in Beirut, joined the atelier of the famous French architect Auguste Perret in the Ecole des Beaux-Arts in Paris.

Reacting against the formalism of colonial style, both Trad and Tabet sought alternatives in the creative potentials and technical constraints of new construction systems, especially reinforced concrete, in the belief that a rational architectural language might be the best solution to the dilemma of modernity versus tradition. This rationalistic, theoretical outlook, coupled with a thorough knowledge of the classical principles of composition and proportion, tried to convey a feeling for the essential qualities of site and usage, rather than a respect for superficial architectural idioms.

In an article written in 1942, entitled "My Profession and Its Impact on the Consolidation of the Nation,"[5] Antoine Tabet transposed the universal properties of classical architecture into a sophisticated hybrid of political doctrine and stylistic explanation. On the one hand, he claimed different styles were not "narrations put together by one nation, which remains itself the same, secure in just one image of its own civic identity through the different periods of development and throughout generations." On the contrary, these styles developed out of the evolution of different polities which, in themselves, were not stable. Tabet thus refuted the notion of a singular origin of any work of art or nation, in favor of a more hybrid understanding of culture and nationhood. By arguing against the essentialism or the inherent characteristics of any one style, Tabet presented a vision of architectural history which was both autonomous and continuous, containing its own internal dynamic and linked to the development of construction techniques and the changing laws of design and production.

Among the seminal experiments that reflect this tendency was the Saint Georges Hotel, designed by Antoine Tabet in 1931 in association with French colleagues from Perret's atelier (fig. 1). A simple cubic

Fig. 1. St. Georges Hotel, Antoine Tabet, architect, 1931

volume, the building stood at the tip of a rocky headland on Beirut Bay, with splendid views of the sea and the mountains. It featured a simple rectangular plan, with guest rooms surrounding a central courtyard. Furthermore, this building, based on the potential of a rectangular concrete-frame construction, was the first to use wide-span concrete beams in Lebanon. As its designer said, it was based on "truth to structure and truth to program." But what made the St. Georges Hotel's architecture superior was not just its progressive construction, but also the way these practical intentions were given a clear tectonic form. The lowest floors, consisting of the hotel lobby and restaurants, were expressed as an individual, separate unit, while the unity of the upper floors was emphasized by continuous overhanging balconies and long, vertical, and regularly-spaced openings (fig. 2). The underlying rectangular frame was clearly legible in the building's elevations, and the presence of non-load-bearing panels were suggested by contrasting colors and textures. At the fourth floor, though, the volume was recessed, hinting to the attic element used in modern buildings a generation later. A raised water tank served as a popular landmark, displaying the hotel's name to the city.

In the Hikmeh School, built in 1937 by the same architect on Ashrafiyyeh Hill overlooking Beirut's Central District, order was brought to the design by the subtle placement of the window panes to give the right sense of depth, and by organizing the pattern of vertical and horizontal structural elements into a simple rhythm of primary and secondary accents (fig. 3). This classical

tradition persisted during the first decades following Lebanese independence after World War II. In the Union Nationale Building, designed by Tabet in 1952, the attention to proportions, composition of facades, details, and articulations gave a sense of sobriety and repose typical of classicism, yet without the overt use of classical orders, i.e., the slightly rectangular window openings punctuating the reconstituted stone panels, the vertical slit windows marking circulation and services, the loggias extending beyond living spaces, the volumetric setback defining the entrance, the upper, abstracted cornice, and the recessed top floor creating roof terraces (fig. 4). The whole is suffused with a discrete elegance that reflects the ideals of the educated bourgeoisie of the period.

This classical rationalist inspiration was sometimes tinted with accents of monumentality, particularly in projects in which the continuity of certain symbolic references was considered important. This was the case in the numerous churches designed by Tabet, which look like softer versions of Perret's prototypes, and in his project for Kaslik Holy Spirit University, where the giant portico stands like a stripped down interpretation of classical colonnades. This was also the case in most of Farid Trad's designs for public buildings. In the UNESCO Palace, built in the late '40s, for instance, Trad adopted a symmetrical axial composition, inherited from *beaux-arts* planning (fig. 5). The balanced equilibrium of masses, the classical proportions of facades, and the details in stone and iron seem inspired by the European tradition of civic monuments of the '30s.

Fig. 2. Aerial view of
St. Georges Hotel
showing the
Zeytouneh area in
the background,
Antoine Tabet,
architect, 1931

Fig. 3. Hikmeh
School, Antoine
Tabet, architect, 1937

Fig. 4. Union
Nationale Building,
Antoine Tabet,
architect, 1952

PAVILLON DE L' U. N. E. S. C. O.
VUE VERS LA FACADE PRINCIPALE

Fig. 5. UNESCO Palace, perspective drawing, Farid Trad, architect, 1946

The Beirut Palace of Justice, designed by the same architect in the late '50s, expresses the same search for monumentality (fig. 6). Here, the ceremonial character of the building is amplified through the massive treatment of the bold rectangular stone volumes that flank the two-story central portico and the horizontal canopy that projects over the steps leading to the forecourt. The monumentality of the composition is further accentuated by the float-ing cornice, emphasizing the dignity of the place.

In later works, this classical rationalist tradition started evolving toward a more abstract aestheticism, closer to Giuseppe Terragni's modern rationalism. Such was the case in the Mobil Office Building in Beirut, designed by Antoine Tabet in the late '50s (fig. 7). Here the details and moldings inspired by the classical tradition disappear, symmetrical composition is abandoned in

Fig. 6. Palace of Justice, Farid Trad, architect, 1959

Fig. 7. Mobil Office
Building, Antoine Tabet,
architect, 1958

مشروع تنظيم وبناء املاك البطريرك
الحازمية

Fig. 8. Housing project in
Hazmieh, Antoine Tabet,
architect, 1959

favor of a purified language, and the simple cubistic volumes are articulated using the archetypal elements of the modern movement, pilotis, brise-soleils, concrete struts, etc. The same applies to the housing scheme designed by Trad in 1959 on the hills of Hazmieh, in the eastern suburbs of Beirut (fig. 8).

The Early '50s and Local Interpretations of Modern Prototypes

The classical rationalist approach that characterized the architectural language of design pioneers attempted to negotiate the transition between the colonial model of architecture, that, in turn, strove to avoid

abrupt formal changes, and the social, economic, and cultural disruptions introduced by modernity. It represented an intermediate solution that tried to reconcile a rather conservative approach toward classical forms and types with a radical attitude toward structure and materials. Challenges to this approach mounted, after World War II, with the spread of modern prototypes and models that introduced new aesthetic values and the search for innovative forms. Among the architects who studied abroad and imported these new ideas, several key figures emerged. They were George Rayes and Théo Kanaan, on one side, and Karl Chayer with Fritz Gothelf on the other. George Rayes was born in Haifa, Palestine, in 1915, and studied architecture at both the Bartlett School of Architecture and the Architectural Association in London. There he met Théo Kanaan, and after founding their practice in Palestine in 1940, the two moved to Lebanon in 1948, following the establishment of the Israeli state. In 1951, they were commissioned to design the Arida Apartment Building in the Sanayeh neighborhood of Beirut, a structure

with a large commercial center on the ground floor (fig. 9). Already in this first building appears Rayes and Kanaan's main concern, the achievement of "an architecture dynamically balanced through the interplay of volumes, solids, and voids, a pure language of lines, shapes, colors, and materials."[6] Abandoning any reference to classical forms and types, this building articulates many of the idioms of the modern vocabulary, consisting of simple geometric forms, sliding volumes, and freestanding planes.

This tendency was further elaborated in the Pan Am Building in Beirut, designed in 1955 by the same architects in association with Assem Salam (fig. 10). Here, a formal language of tensely composed simple forms and shapes recalls essential *de Stijl* principles: controlled asymmetry, rectilinear grids, and intersecting planes. The treatment of the corner at ground-floor level with a free-standing round column, an unexpected architectural comment that produces a marked contrast against the background of the austere facade, brings the typically Corbusian tension between a rational body and its playful elements to fruition. But unlike Le Corbusier, George Rayes seems always to have been obsessed with perfecting details. One of the problems that faced modern architects in the early '50s was the inability of local technology to produce

Fig. 10. Pan American Building, George Rayes and Théo Kanaan, architects, 1955

building components that departed from traditional crafts and skills. Unable to resort to industrial production, architects were forced to design every single component of the building and have the whole put together by craftsmen.[7] The attitude of these architects was similar to that of German Werkbund architects who viewed themselves as mediators between formal invention and standardization, between the dexterity of the contemporary world and reliance on age-old principles.

This attitude was clear in the design of the headquarters for the American University of Beirut Alumni Association in Ras Beirut, conceived by Karl Chayer in association with Fritz Gothelf and Bahij Makdissi in 1953. Chayer was a Polish architect who immigrated to Lebanon during World War II and collaborated with Fritz Gothelf, a German architect educated in the spirit of the Bauhaus, and with Bahij Makdissi, a Lebanese structural engineer. Chayer conceived architecture as the creation of 'type forms' for a new, modern world – be they objects of industrial design, building elements, or pieces of urban structure. The Alumni Club design was a winning scheme in a competition launched by the Alumni Association of the American University of Beirut. The choice of this scheme, strongly influenced by the abstracted rectilinear style of the Bauhaus, reveals that the search for a new architectural vocabulary was a shared concern among the educated elite of the time. In this case it included the tension created by the simple horizontal stretches of window, as well as the location of the glass panes, at times flush with the facade to reinforce the overall volumetric character of a space enclosed by a skin, and at other times recessed to accentuate the hovering white horizontal floor planes.

What is most striking about Chayer's buildings in retrospect is the precision of the formal thinking and the fusion of the major architectural choices with the construction details. This attitude was clear in his design of the first curtain wall in Lebanon, for the Horseshoe Building on Hamra Street, one of the major commercial streets in the modern quarter of Ras Beirut (fig. 11). In this building, designed in 1958, curtain wall details were drawn to full scale and tested on prototypes before being executed. The same applied to the Hamra movie theater designed by Rayes during the same period, for which a complex system was

Fig. 11. Horseshoe Building, Karl Chayer and Wassek Adib, architects, 1958

invented to allow a certain grouping of windows. Chayer and Rayes coordinated the floor heights and the continuity of horizontal lines on the main street elevations of both buildings, but the owners insisted on employing a vertical wall projecting beyond the facade plane to maintain physical separation, a choice which makes it difficult today to appreciate this first effort in Beirut to define a street wall with modern buildings.[8]

In the Zahar Office and Factory Building in Ashrafiyyeh, Beirut, built in the late '50s after the death of Théo Kanaan, George Rayes pursued his search for the means to authenticate the already ratified modern architectural language with new building technology. Setting a precedent in Lebanon, he used prefabricated concrete elements for the facades. Steel window frames were inserted in the molds to avoid any leakage and ensure perfect air- and waterproofing. On the street elevation, a double facade system was used to provide for mechanical services and to ensure good soundproofing.

It hardly needs emphasizing that Chayer and Rayes, each in his own way, was attempting to find a new architectural idiom that would constitute a local adaptation of the ideas developed by the modern movement in Western countries. The Amlieh School in Ras el-Nabeh, Beirut, designed by the Brothers Itani in association with German architects, provides a further example of such an approach. Here, the influence of Eric Mendelsohn and the German Expressionists is obvious, but it is combined with elements borrowed from William Dudock's vocabulary and from the Dutch school.

Another example of Dudock's influence can be found in the Makassed School built in the late '50s by Amin Bizri, in which the play of volumes and shifted planes, long horizontal windows, high, glazed attic, and stripped, white geometries are intended to provide a counter-model to the traditional archetype of school building design (fig. 12). What is striking about all these experiments is their creative potential and their ability to pick up different elements from various strands of modern architecture, and to combine them with local technical conditions and specific uses in order to produce a clearly defined new architectural vocabulary.

The different pursuits of modernism (as contradictory as they were in the West)

In the absence of planning legislation, the only existing reference was a building code, adopted in 1933 and superficially amended in 1954. The economic post-World War II miracle '*à la libanaise*' initiated by the flow of capital and men from Arab countries after the successive political, economic, and

Fig. 12.
Makassed School,
Amin Bizri,
architect, 1958

found equivalents in Beirut, but they also found a different synthesis. Modernism in Beirut was not conceived of as a representation of 'the West,' as opposed to traditionalism representing 'the East.' Rather, the different aspects of modern architecture were reinterpreted and became integral to the local architectural scene. The history of modern architecture in Lebanon was a dialectic of different schools reacting to each other. Moreover, this dialectic was inherent to modernism.

However, and in contrast to this optimistic attitude, architects of that period were struggling against the constraints of obsolete building regulations to expand on the possibilities offered by avant-garde experimentation in form and stylistic vocabulary.

social upheavals of late '40s and early '50s, acted as an alibi for the *laissez-faire* policies of public authorities. A shared belief among the architects in the late '50s was that this situation could not last long, and that something had to be done to initiate a comprehensive planning policy to control the chaotic urban growth. Renewal in architectural form, they claimed, should be extended to the level of urban planning, and they hoped that their claims would be heard by public authorities.[9] Surveying the scene forty years later, one can understand how all these experiments and hopes tended to converge around 1960, and to culminate in what retrospectively could be called the 'golden age' of modern architecture in Lebanon.

The 'Golden Age' of Modern Architecture in Lebanon

The early '60s in Lebanon witnessed the birth of a dream, that of planned and balanced development. On the fringe of an Arab world which, at that time, seemed to be marching toward unity, the Lebanese regime, under the leadership of President Shihab,[10] wanted to develop a modern society, and a financial and economic center to the scale of the whole region. This necessitated the reduction of the disequilibrium between the capital city and its peripheries, and the restructuring of Beirut's agglomeration to cope with mounting new demands and plans. A new policy was thus adopted, characterized by the strengthening of the central state and the belief in the unlimited capacities of planning in solving development problems.

In 1963, the first town planning legislation applicable to all of Lebanon was adopted. According to this legislation, all matters related to town planning were to be concentrated in one single authority: the Directorate-General of Town Planning, assisted by the Higher Council for Town and Country Planning. General master plans, detailed regional plans, specific regulations for the acquisition of land for public use and for the constitution of mixed real estate companies – all these tools were introduced for the first time. At the same time, large-scale projects were launched by the new regime. Constantine Doxiadis, the famous Greek planner, was commissioned to choose the location of a new Governmental City, a huge complex where all ministries would be grouped. Four sites, located at the periphery of Beirut, were identified and one of them was finally chosen in the southern suburbs at Bir Hassan. The French urban planner Michel Ecochard was called back in order to help plan the development of Greater Beirut, a metropolis which would extend from Jounieh in the north to Naameh in the south.

In order to prevent anarchic urban growth and to replace the mononuclear structure of the city, which could not adapt anymore to the conditions of its growth, with a polynuclear structure organized around green spaces, Ecochard developed a further proposal he had already presented in the early '40s. The idea was to create a new town on the sandy dunes of the southern suburbs near the airport in order to absorb the major part of the population increase. The wooded hills around Beirut would be protected by the imposition of low building densities, and new construction would be prohibited on beaches and in forests.[11]

Dozens of other projects were commissioned to a new generation of Lebanese architects, some of whom had studied abroad in the late '40s and early '50s and were already well acquainted with the post-World War II experiences of Europe in urban planning. Among these were Assem Salam, who studied in London and witnessed the birth of the English new-towns movement, Henri Eddeh who, after receiving a degree in civil engineering, worked in France during the reconstruction period, and Pierre el-Khoury, who graduated in 1956 from the Ecole des Beaux-Arts in Paris.

Out of the numerous urban planning projects that were prepared, covering major Lebanese cities (Tripoli, Sidon, Tyre) and

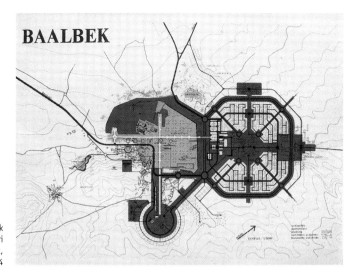

Fig. 13. Baalbeck Master Plan, Henri Eddeh, architect, 1964

other smaller towns, two plans, one for Baalbeck and one for Tyre, seem most representative of the atmosphere of the period. The Baalbeck Master Plan was launched in 1964 through a large competition, and the winning scheme, proposed by Henri Eddeh, was considered by the jury as exemplary in its handling of the problems related to the control of urban growth (fig. 13).[12] Eddeh's scheme was based on the following two assumptions: the Roman city of Baalbeck represented a major archaeological site of international importance; and the modern city of Baalbeck, which comprised at that time 20,000 inhabitants, was covering part of this Roman city, and its growth was unavoidable. To solve this conflict, Eddeh's scheme was all but conventional. It consisted of displacing the modern city in order to "liberate the archaeological remains from the yoke that confines them," and in rebuilding a new octagonal town to the north, established along the main axes of the Roman city. Of the existing city, only one quarter would be preserved, namely the one hosting beautiful samples of nineteenth-century Lebanese architecture.

The Tyre Master Plan was prepared by Pierre el-Khoury in 1964 (fig. 14).[13] Here

Fig. 14. Tyre Master Plan, Pierre el-Khoury, architect, 1964

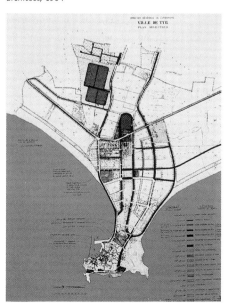

Fig. 15. Defense Ministry, André Wogenscky and Maurice Hindieh, architects, 1965

again, the question to be answered was that of the relation between archaeology and urban growth. Two main axes organized the whole composition: an east-west touristic axis, linking the archaeological zones and dividing the city into two distinct zones, and an administrative north-south axis, which would constitute the main spine of development for the city's future extensions.[14] Although this plan looked less radical than Eddeh's, it shared the same planning strategy of superimposing abstract forms over the built environment. Indeed, a recurrent theme among Lebanese planners of the '60s was that planning could restore a supposed harmony between social order and the physical environment, a harmony that had been lost in cities' anarchic growth. Master plans were therefore conceived of as formal figures, balanced and well organized, com-

bining, in turn, grids, zoning, and a segregation of land uses. The numerous ideal city plans produced in the early '60s suggest that planners were moving in a utopian direction. For them, the political and social project seemed to indicate that it was possible to start afresh, to rebuild the world anew, and to rid Lebanese society once and for all of the detritus of 'dead old forms.'[15]

A similarly enthusiastic visionary attitude prevailed in the architectural scene. Famous international architects were called upon to design public and private buildings. Oscar Niemeyer was commissioned by the Lebanese government to conceive of a Permanent International Fair in the second major Lebanese city of Tripoli. Michel Ecochard, besides his urban planning schemes for Beirut, Tripoli, and Sidon, designed major school projects in different parts of the country, such as the Collège Protestant Français and the Lycée Français de Beyrouth, where Le Corbusier's five points were rigorously applied, but also the Marist Brothers' schools in Baabda and Sidon, and the German Hospital in Hazmieh.

André Wogenscky, Le Corbusier's last senior collaborator, was also called upon, in association with a young Lebanese architect, Maurice Hindieh, to design the new Defense Ministry in Hazmieh (fig. 15) and the Lebanese Public University in Shwayfat. The American architect Edward Stone was commissioned by the Intercontinental Hotel chain to design the Phoenicia Hotel, the largest hotel in Beirut at that time. Even Alvar Aalto, in association with the Swiss architect Alfred Roth, got involved in the architectural boom of that period, designing

Fig. 16. Electricité du Liban headquarters, Pierre Nehmeh, architect, 1966

a major office building and commercial center in Beirut.

Parallel to these ventures, some of which were private, the government launched a series of projects of symbolic value, aimed at embodying the new collective spirit of the time. A Swiss firm, Adord et Julliard, was commissioned to design the Presidential Palace in Yarzeh and the new Central Bank in Beirut. This latter project was conceived of as a prototype, which would be reproduced at a smaller scale in other locations, and acted as a recognizable symbol of the central government's power and regional development policy. Competitions were launched for the design of public primary, secondary, and technical schools, and post office buildings, as well.

A large competition was organized in 1963 for the design of the Governmental City, the location of which was chosen after the Doxiadis study. The winning scheme was that of Pierre Nehmeh, a Lebanese architect educated in France, who proposed to build a series of tall longitudinal slabs, lifted from the ground and linked with vaulted galleries. The architectural vocabulary of this project seems inspired by some of Jose Luis Sert's experiments on building in hot climates.[16]

The same architect was also the winner of a competition organized in 1966 for the design of the Electricité du Liban headquarters, which, the architect claims, was inspired by the Brazilian version of International Style (figs. 16 and 17). Indeed, the Brazilian school seems to have had a major influence on the development of architecture in Lebanon during the '60s. Lebanese architects found a good precedent for responding to special climatic conditions, strong sunlight, and a tradition of outdoors social life in the reinterpretation of modern movement principles by Brazilian architects.[17] Many examples of this influence can be signed by Joseph Philippe Karam, with its direct Corbusian references, its colored panels, and its detached attic floor (fig. 19). Further away, on Verdun Street, the Fabriano Building by the same architect shows an

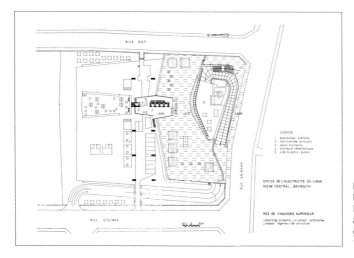

Fig. 17. Electricité du Liban headquarters, Pierre Nehmeh, architect, ground floor plan, 1966

found in the buildings of the early '60s along the Beirut Corniche. Among the most noticeable figures in architecture who produced this interesting 'urban ensemble' stands on the one hand a veteran, Karl Chayer, this time associated with a younger Lebanese architect, Wassek Adib, and on the other hand an engineer, Joseph Philippe Karam who, despite being somewhat despised by his peers at the time for his 'vulgar taste,' appears today as one of the major designers of the '60s.

Among the seminal buildings designed by Chayer and Adib are the Carlton Hotel, with its planted gardens and terraces, the Shell Building (fig. 18), with its airplane-wing roof, and the Ghandour Building, with its terraces carefully composed with prefabricated 'claustra' panels. On this same urban fringe stands an apartment building de-

accentuated treatment of the streets' acute intersection, with a blunt reference to Rietveld's hovering planes (fig. 20).

However diverse their approaches, however varied their personal styles, the architects who came to maturity in the mid '60s had certain features in common. They were all educated according to Western principles of modern architecture but, while respecting the guiding tenets of the modern movement, they did not advocate a slavish orthodoxy. Influenced by the Team X investigations, their position was characterized by the tension between the allegiance to the lessons of the founding fathers and the need for self-expression. By extension, and since the mid '60s, the genuine optimism that characterized architectural production in the preceding period began to be questioned.

Fig. 18. Shell Building, Karl Chayer and Wassek Adib, architects, 1962

Fig. 20. Fabriano Building, Joseph Philippe Karam, architect, 1963

Crises and Critiques in the Late '60s

Indeed, what is striking about the architects' attitude during these 'glorious years' is their general lack of concern for political issues, their ignorance of the real forces that were struggling to strengthen their

Fig. 19. Apartment Building in Raouché, Joseph Philippe Karam, architect, 1962

control over the territories (religious institutions, political feudal lords, landowners, and financial corporations), as well as their amazing lack of knowledge of the powers that resisted the implementation of their plans. Whereas individual commissions for villas, schools, factories, housing projects, and public buildings allowed architects to realize fragments of larger dreams in microcosm, the power to build urban totalities was never granted them nor the planners.

The Ecochard plan for building a new town in the southern suburbs remained on paper, as did Henri Eddeh's octagonal utopia and Pierre el-Khoury's axial composition. The ambitious project for building the Doxiadis Governmental City ended up implanting, in the selected site, an orphan building, the Ministry of Telecommunication. The Lebanese Public University Campus in Shwayfat was never completed.

The failure of the planning policy of the '60s reproduced, on a larger scale, the effect of the previous *laissez-faire* era. The radiocentric structure of Beirut was inflated further by the addition of successive suburbs,

Fig. 21. House in Yarzeh, Pierre el-Khoury, architect, 1958

and the decomposition of the rural traditional world intensified rural migration, exacerbating all the imbalances associated with rapid and uneven urban growth. Disillusion started corroding the simplistic intellectual constructions of early '60s planners. Similarly, in the field of general construction, a banal international corporate style did triumph, with its standard cheap clichés. The resultant dull reductionism looked like a mockery of the pioneers' passionate quest. Lebanese architects of the '60s were confronted with a series of dilemmas which pushed them toward the search for new tracks.

Since his early works in the late '50s, Pierre el-Khoury had been preoccupied with the question of adapting a modern vocabulary to local typologies.[18] In his own house,

designed in 1958, he developed the theme of central space as an interpretation of the traditional Lebanese *dar* (fig. 21). Although following a strict modern orthodoxy in their architectural language, other buildings designed by the same architect in the early and mid '60s, like the Directorate of Public Transportation Building in Shiyyah and the Civil Aviation Safety Center near Beirut airport, developed this exploration of introverted spatial organization (fig. 22). In the late '60s, Pierre el-Khoury also took up a search for monumentality. His Harissa Cathedral (fig. 23), designed in 1970, was strongly influenced by Kenzo Tange's works, developing a lyrical language which, as the architect describes it, was intended to "express the spiritual meaning of the space."[19]

The search for new means of expression also took other forms. Pierre Nehmeh tried to bypass the conventionality of brise-soleil treatments by transforming them into decorative features in his Concord Building, designed in 1970. Another attempt by the same architect came close to mannerism, in his treatment of precast concrete supports emulating traditional arches for the Artisanat Show Room in al-Mryseh, built in 1966. Meanwhile, the influence of Michel Ecochard on the younger generation of architects who started their independent practice in the mid '60s was visibly strong. Grégoire Serof, born in 1930, became Michel Ecochard's primary Lebanese assistant in 1962. Together with Khalil Khoury, born in 1930, and Raoul Verney, a French architect born in Lebanon, they soon formed a new direction. While respecting the principles of their mentor, they reacted against the rigidity of previous

Fig. 22. Civil Aviation Safety Center, Pierre el-Khoury, architect, 1964

The attitudes toward the vernacular, intrinsic in the late works of Le Corbusier, Aalto, and Team X had a strong influence on the new generation of Lebanese architects. Among these, two tendencies emerged in the early '70s. The first tendency evolved toward the adoption of a Brutalist language, influenced by Paul Rudolph's rough expressionism, and mostly by Japanese Metabolists, discovered at that time through the large diffusion of *Japan Architect* magazine.[21] This tendency was best expressed in Khalil Khoury's later works, such as his office building in Spears Street or his Manar beach resort in Maameltayn, where a vocabulary made up of rough concrete volumes, heavy crates of brise-soleil, and rugged overhangs appeared as a reaction against the puritanism of the '50s.

schemes, and tried to develop an architectural language capable of expressing growth and change. Their preoccupations were directed toward bringing together mass production and the sense of place, modern programs and local conditions.[20]

In the late '60s, these three architects met as a team to design the Mont La Salle school complex on the eastern hills overlooking Beirut. On an uneven site, covered with pine forests, they produced a pattern based on small-scale modular elements articulated in different sequences, resulting in a series of spaces that connected loosely with one another. The result was a compact, village-like ensemble that attempted to engender richness and complexity from repetition, similar to some of Candilis, Josic, and Woods' seminal experiments.

Fig. 23. Harissa Cathedral, Pierre el-Khoury, architect, 1970

Fig. 24. Serail of Sidon, Assem Salam, architect, 1965

The second tendency evolved toward a more contextual approach, preoccupied with issues of identity, scale, and meaning, which required a reconsideration of modernist principles in the light of regional traditions. The main representative of this tendency was Jacques Liger-Belair, a Belgian architect practicing in Lebanon, who had been trying, since the mid '60s, to respond to the 'genius of the place' by developing an architectural language that would link architecture to nature.[22]

But the works that best express the search by Lebanese architects of the period for a blend between the principles of modern architecture and local traditions were those of Assem Salam. In an article written in 1966 entitled "Architectural Expression and Handling in the East and the West"[23] Salam develops the idea that architectural expressions in the East and the West spring from different roots: while Western architecture has been the direct product of Renaissance humanist tradition, Near Eastern traditional architecture is "founded on the attitude of a community that is profoundly governed by the religious philosophy of Islam," with little freedom left to individual innovation. "The sociological

Fig. 25. Broummana High School, Assem Salam, architect, 1966

conflicts which caused an aberration of cultural traditions," he argues, "have exposed the contemporary architecture of the Near East to undigested principles, a pseudo-

building, according to Salam,[24] was inspired by Morabites' *ksars* architecture that he discovered at that time in Tunisia and Morocco. Moreover, in the Broummana High

Fig. 26. Pine Forest Mosque, Assem Salam, architect, 1968

sophistication leading in most instances to vulgarity." As a matter of fact, Salam claims, while contemporary Eastern architects "have lost the spontaneous and human nature of their traditional architecture," this architecture offered an "untapped source of architectural inspiration" which the West could exploit and "mold into its own twentieth-century vernacular."

The doubts expressed by Salam were representative of the malaise felt by many Lebanese architects of the period, who were preoccupied with the question of regional identity and local architectural vocabulary. However, while adopting a 'critical regionalist stand,' they considered themselves part of the modern architectural tradition: the dialectic was still internal to modernism. For instance, in the Sidon Serail, built by Salam in 1965, building was organized around an open central courtyard, in accordance with the traditional *serail* typology, and the stone walls were punctuated by concrete arches and small openings, reminiscent of fortress architecture (fig. 24). The language of the

School, built by the same architect in 1966, the reference to regionalist influences, although less obvious, appears in the protruding bay windows similar to the kiosks of Ottoman architecture (fig. 25). Overall, this modern regionalist tendency sometimes appeared iconoclastic, particularly when it dealt with religious buildings. In the mosque designed by Salam near Beirut's pine forest (fig. 26), the traditional cupola is replaced by a floating white concrete shell, and the minaret conceived as a simple square campanile!

Conclusion

Today, such a non-conventional, refreshing attitude towards architecture seems unusual. With the new situation created after the 1967 war, the Arab defeat, the emergence of new regional alliances, the increasing influence of petroleum-producing, traditional societies of the Gulf, and with the outbreak of civil war in Lebanon and the resurgence of fundamentalist identities, the cultural debate has become totally distorted. Architecture could not remain immune for long, and the backlash against modern values, in the name of reclaiming cultural identity, soon condemned all the architectural production of the '50s and the '60s as being emblems of demonic secularism or boring imitations of alien, puristic models. With the vulgarization of so-called architectural postmodernism, and ignoring the toil of preceding generations, young architects were trapped in the dilemma of choosing between slick, cynical technology and dogmatic regional revivalism. In most cases, the desperate search for the expression of a singular identity produced a simplistic combination of the two: gingerbread historical detail pasted onto ill-conceived concrete structural boxes, and sometimes even combined with colored mirror-glass walls. Lebanese architects of the '50s and the '60s were convinced that they were breaking new ground and that their search would lead them to discover new cultural territories. They shared a commitment to social improvement through design, and a feeling for the progressive potential of modern technology. They were united in their belief in a new language appropriate to the spirit of the period, and in the hope that lessons might be learned from the past, without slavish imitation.

Despite a degree of alienation intrinsic to their avant-garde position, despite an elitist tendency, which often restricted the scope of their influence, despite, in some cases, an amazing naiveté in dealing with problems that could not be reduced to the architectural language they were employing, these architects were able to create a climate of outstanding creative intensity during a phase of social and cultural transition. However, the problems that they set out to solve are still very much with us. Unlike what they once believed, architecture cannot change the world. But, as art historian and previous mayor of Rome, Giulio Carlo Argan, used to say,[25] architecture has an iconoclastic task to perform: that of challenging intellectual comfort and the self-satisfaction of mediocrity.

Notes

1. R. Friedrich, *Architecture in Lebanon*, American University of Beirut Publications, 1974.

2. The French Mandate was established in Lebanon after World War I and the collapse of the Ottoman Empire. It lasted till the country achieved independence in 1943. Several studies have been conducted on architecture and planning during this transitional period, particularly: Robert Saliba, *Beirut Baroque*, to be published by the Order of Engineers and Architects, Beirut, December 1997; Marlène Ghorayeb, "De l'art urbain à l'urbanisme progressiste: Desseins pour une ville levantine sous mandat Français" in *Beyrouth, regards croisés, URBAMA, Tours-France*, 1997; and Mona Sharara, "Les maisons ocres de Beyrouth" in *Mediterranean's*, no. 5, Winter 1993, Paris.

3. A few studies should be excepted, mainly Raymond Ghosn, "Beirut Architecture," in *Beirut: Crossroads of Cultures* (Librairie du Liban: Beirut 1970).

4. *Dar*, the central hall around which traditional Lebanese houses were organized.

5. A. Tabet, "My Profession and Its Impact on the Consolidation of the Nation," in *Al Tariq*, October 3, 1942, Beirut.

6. Interview with George Rayes, March 1997.

7. Interview with Assem Salam, August 1994.

8. Interview with George Rayes, March 1997.

9. Interview with Assem Salam, July 1994.

10. Fuad Shibab was elected president in 1958, following a series of riots that lasted several months. His rule, which lasted until 1964, was characterized by political, economic, and social reforms, and the attempt to strengthen the role of the Central State.

11. For futher details on Ecochard's plan, see Marlène Ghorayeb's essay in this publication.

12. For further information on this project and those of Tripoli and Sidon, see *Al-Muhandess, Special Issue: Urban Planning in Lebanon* (Beirut: The Order of Engineers and Architects, 1966).

13. *Al-Muhandess*, ibid.

14. Interview with Pierre el-Khoury, July 1994.

15. Interview with Assem Salam, August 1994.

16. Interview with Pierre Nehmeh, August 1994.

17. Interviews with Assem Salam (August 1994), Khalil Khoury (September 1994), and Grégoire Serof (September 1997).

18. Interview with Pierre el-Khoury, July 1994.

19. Interview with Pierre el-Khoury, August 1994.

20. Interview with Khalil Khoury, September 1994.

21. Interview with Grégoire Serof, September 1997.

22. Interview with Jacques Liger-Belair, April 1995.

23. A. Salam, *Architectural Expression and Handling in the East and the West: Conditions in the Twentieth Century,* International Union of Architects Colloquium Orient-Occident, Beirut, 1966.

24. Interview with Assem Salam, March 1997.

25. G.C. Argan, *Projet et destin: Art, architecture, urbanisme* (Paris: Les Editions de la Passion, 1993), pp. 7–56.

The Work and Influence of Michel Ecochard in Lebanon

by
Marlène Ghorayeb

Understanding the activity of Michel Eco-chard in Lebanon, which lasted for about thirty years, requires, beyond the analysis of the projects themselves, capturing the impact of this architect's intervention in the context of a country that was itself already receptive to the modern movement by mid century. Through his numerous projects in Lebanon, Ecochard became a major propo-nent of CIAM-inspired ideas in the Near East and North Africa. He was commissioned to produce plans for the major cities and towns of Lebanon. Of the numerous Lebanese cities for which he prepared master plans, Beirut was the subject of two, one in 1943 and the other in 1963. He was also responsible for the conception of the coastal highway in Lebanon in the early '30s.

As an architect, Michel Ecochard was known for applying the principles of modern architecture to institutional buildings such as schools and hospitals, and his built archi-tectural projects also include institutional buildings in both Lebanon and the region. In what follows, an attempt will be made, through analysis of some of Ecochard's work in Lebanon, to bring to light some of the primary conceptual themes and strategies of realization – always partial when it came to the planning projects – as well as the pre-vailing methodology.

Professional Formation: Archaeology, Urbanism, Islamic Architecture, and 'Modernity'

Ecochard's initiation and formative years took place in the Levant of the French Mandate. From the beginning, Ecochard worked in diverse fields of operation – early on as a restorer in the Department of Antiquities before becoming the director of the urban planning services in Syria. This position, in turn, led him to produce master plans for the major Syrian cities, and later for Beirut. All the while he continued to realize his first architectural projects. When he arrived in the Levant in 1932, Michel Ecochard – a 1931 graduate of the Ecole des Beaux-Arts in Paris – did not possess any real professional experience. Therefore, his early work for the services of antiquities and his work as a restorer had a long-term influ-ence on his professional career. Restoring Islamic monuments, drawing and redrawing sketches, dismantling and reassembling buildings in order to understand their con-struction logic before restoring them in-evitably led him into the historical dimen-sion of Levantine culture.[1] Archaeology, contradictory as it may appear, helped initiate Michel Ecochard into both architec-ture and urban planning:

"Allow me to tell you how I came to urban planning. Having completed an archaeological survey of a public bath in Damascus, an Orientalist asked me to survey all the baths of the city. I did, and with sixty surveys of buildings from the eleventh to the twentieth century, I formed a general view of the Arab civilization. But I needed to find a link between all these baths, and a geographer advised me to survey all the canals that serviced them. By following these canals, I entered into housing and mosques, which exposed to me the hidden life of the city. This gave me deep satisfaction and decided my future as an urban planner."[2]

As the French Mandate became established in the Levant, the era of travelers ended and was replaced by that of researchers representing or making contact with the avant-garde of mainland France. Michel Ecochard, still a young architect, found himself thrust into this context. At the end of 1932, the Directorate of Antiquities put him in charge of the restoration of certain monuments, such as the door of Palmyra's Bel temple. He studied the evolution of Muslim baths with Claude Le Coeur and Damascus' Ayyoubide monuments with Sauvaget.[3] This work, however, was not restricted to the sole, albeit very noble, task of restoring different monuments from the twelfth and sixteenth centuries. It also included a survey of baths in Damascus dating from the eleventh to the twentieth century, a study spanning nearly a thousand years of the evolution of this type of monument. Possibly the most important aspect of his training was in the evolution of urban forms, which he learned while attempting to reconstruct the Hellenic and Roman plans based on contemporary ones for Mandate Damascus. His discovery that a correlation between forms and numbers and geometric calculations was key to interpreting Muslim architecture established his credentials: "Attempting to turn descriptions into numbers was a wrong approach. Rather, everything else follows from architectural meaning."

A new approach to architecture emerged from his experience with the Directorate of Antiquities, and the training he received there prepared him for the practice of urban planning. The French Institute in Damascus[4] played a formative role for Michel Ecochard (fig. 1). Collaborating with the scholars at the French Institute of Damascus in the 1930s presupposed an allegiance to a school of thought which was bolstering the Institute's reputation. Despite their varied backgrounds, the scholars at the Institute were all 'Arabists' and shared an interest in discovering the culture of an Arab country, whether through history and archaeology, as Sauvaget[5] did, or through ethnology like Seyrig, or geography like J. Weulersse. The deployment of all these disciplines to solve a single problem was a novel approach at the time, and so was the adoption of a single shared methodological approach that relied on evidence produced through fieldwork in the discovery of a civilization.

Another borrowing from archaeology was the methodology that approached 'site' and history simultaneously. In his proposal for the urban planning of Damascus, dated 1968, Ecochard wondered "how to superimpose the major arteries over the Roman ways" still legible in the city. An understanding of the evolutionary aspect of urban history can emerge in the process of searching for traces of the past, seeking to explain them, and becoming one with the history of the city through repeated sketching of its monuments. Ecochard's double training as an archaeologist aware of cultural specificity and as an ethnologist gave him the confidence to approach any culture, particularly an Arab one, and to understand it from

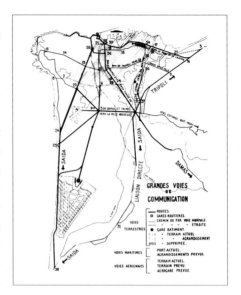

Fig. 2. Master Plan for Beirut: Main Circulation Networks, Michel Ecochard, 1943

within. This would allow him to become the best available spokesperson for CIAM in those countries and elsewhere. Ecochard was convinced of the universal values upheld by the CIAM theories. Rather than importing knowledge and know-how, he sought to open for others access to a modernity expected to transform not just cities, but men as well. Ecochard's undertakings in Morocco cannot be separated from his efforts in the Levant. His experience in North Africa is at the source of the theoretical strength conveyed by the conception of the grid, the perception of Moroccan urban realities, and the necessary courage to apply the precepts of the Athens Charter in an Arab country. The ability later displayed by Ecochard to reconcile the CIAM principles of architecture and urbanism with reality, whether geographical or social, represented a new and personal dimension. This ability can only be explained by the training acquired during his Levantine sojourn. Ecochard's work must be understood at the heart of this apparent antinomy. This may be what later made him the most tenacious 'agent' for the transfer of knowledge and know-how in both architecture and urban planning.

Michel Ecochard's Urban Planning in Lebanon

Enriched by the Syrian experience, Ecochard reaffirmed his guiding principles in the framework of the master plan for the city of Beirut executed in 1943 (fig. 2).[6] This plan was made up of three main components: the major arteries, the new city, and the *'quartiers congestionnaires'* at the center of town. The city as an object was the center of global attention. Before new settlement began, it was necessary to establish a prospective plan to orient the future evolution of urban growth. By then, it was becoming clear that only a specialist could attempt to solve such complex urban problems, and the undirected growth of the city was no longer acceptable. Functionalism and rationalism defined a form of urban zoning in which the segregation of functions became the key concept. At the core of this urbanism were principles that would become the norm for planning after World War II. The road network was seen as the armature of all urban propositions, involving both a hierarchy of roads and a priority for pedestrian networks. Housing was treated separately because of 'its special needs,' particularly with regard to climatic and lighting conditions. The description of the new city, proposed in the master

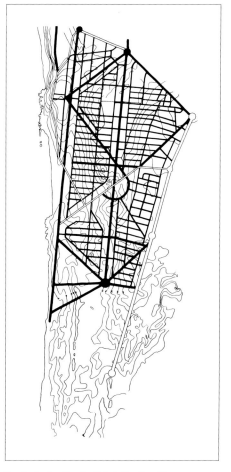

Fig. 3. Master Plan for Beirut: The New City, Michel Ecochard, 1943

plan, clearly showed the choices being made. "We have to completely reject the old principles of construction that view roads as corridors aligned with attached houses. The land allocated to each residence should be large enough to allow not only for setbacks from the streets, but also to allow the residence to be located in the middle of a garden."[7]

Ecochard did not reproduce the models of colonial urbanism, and even less its practices. His task was to think of the city

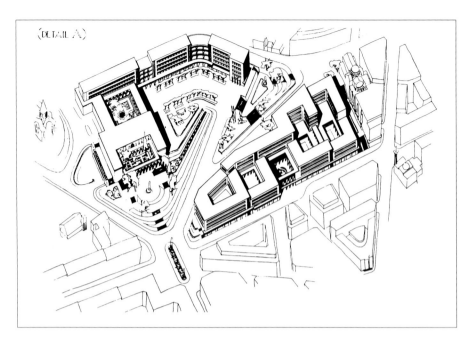

Fig. 4. Proposal for the redevelopment of the Serail Hill in Beirut, Michel Ecochard, architect, 1943

through the 'modern means' of urban planning. The planned extension of the new city (fig. 3) proposed a new way of living associated more with 'the workers,' who were to be offered, in addition to 'modernity,' greater 'equality.' Thus, the modification of existing roads, in order to double their vehicular carrying capacity, constituted a universal principle of this urbanism. Indeed, in the course of his Levantine experience, Ecochard would establish a new approach by introducing the modern principles of urbanism, a strategy that was introduced in part by his predecessors working elsewhere, such as Prost and Danger, both of whom were pillars of the SFU (The French Society of Urban Planners). In so doing, Ecochard presented a new way of intervening in urban planning under the French administration, an approach, however,

which would not prevail until after independence in the 1960s. Had the ideas advanced in this plan for Beirut been realized, the city would have been one of the world's most modern centers. The three main ideas were: 1) to differentiate uses spatially, employing the idea of regrouping public buildings in the same location and creating an administrative center; 2) to separate vehicular and pedestrian circulation using distinct spatial articulations; and 3) to give priority to the main roads.

Ecochard's value judgments on neighborhood aesthetics are also very telling about this form of urbanism. Monumentality was established by detaching a building from its environment in order to emphasize it. Composing in space, by carefully arranging or creating buildings, streets, and gardens, was, effectively, the manifestation of an architectural approach that redefined the target as a set of objects instead of a single object (fig. 4). Ecochard's understanding of the role of the architect and the urban planner, in these regards, is very clearly expressed in the following words delivered to the first class held at the Lebanese Academy of Architecture in Beirut on November 8, 1943[8]:"It is true that our times require excessive specialization, and specialization is necessary at the executive level; but I think that at the superior level of conception, no difference should exist between the architect and the engineer ... in defining the higher attributes of a program and expressing them in a composition that balances volumes, numbers, and colors.... This formation, for which the compositional mind (I insist on the word) would give all its value, is only partially acquired through education. But do not forget that every large composition is but a sequence of smaller compositions. If you only study one group of buildings in the city, or only one building in this group, or even one room in this building, you could, if you wanted to, make a piece of art out of the fragment as much as out of the whole.... These programs allow you to take part in the movement of our times, in the smallest details in the life of a particular family as in the life of the city as a whole. Your creations will be the expressions of your times." Clearly, Ecochard had also not forgotten the deontological aspect of the profession since he concluded by saying that "disinterestedness, honesty, and professional conscience" were indispensable in the practice of the profession.

Contrary to the earlier proponents of modern urban techniques, such as the Danger brothers, Ecochard's urbanism was situated at the heart of the political and the social milieu. In Beirut, and before his struggles during the Moroccan period, Ecochard tried to implement the idea of an urbanism that would remain outside private interests, whatever they might be. His field of intervention would not be limited only to regulating and foreseeing urban growth, but would extend into management and project execution from both the financial and administrative vantage points. Always guided by the utopian ideal of the urban planner as neutral and disinterested, and of urbanism as a defender of the public interest against large private concerns, Ecochard positioned himself against the liberal capitalism introduced by the Mandate. This was accentuated even further by his attempt to allocate decision making to the state and to the municipality[9] – which, at the time, remained more or less independent of the Mandate powers. Barely two months after he presented his scheme, Ecochard wrote a report regarding "a plan for financing urban projects in Beirut"[10] which confirmed his interest in those aspects of the project and gave further instruction on urban planning. But his approach also defined caveats: "By virtue of the added value to the land, any well-conceived urban work cannot but be a profitable operation.... It is the collective and not individuals which should benefit from the improvements achieved through urban planning."[11] On the practical side, he proposed the creation of an autonomous body within the Lebanese government that would have a triple function: the first would be technical, for the study of plans and expansions, as well as for development projects in

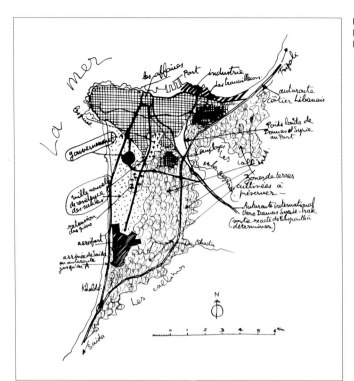

Fig. 5. Master Plan for
Metropolitan Beirut,
Michel Ecochard, 1963

the new town; the second would be administrative – it would take on the study of constraints and the regulation of expropriation; the third would be financial, involving reselling land destined to be built in the new town for private and public clients. It would also finance development projects in the new town and major developments in the existing city.

This urge to organize the administration of all things related to urban planning was not particular to the 1943 plan, but was seen by Ecochard to be inherent in his mission as a planner. In "A Free Point of View on the Management of Urban Affairs in Lebanon,"[12] a memo Ecochard wrote in 1959, he addresses this issue once again by criticizing the association of urban affairs within the Ministry of the Interior. He claimed

that this association based itself upon an outdated notion of urban planning, one that defined its mission as a mere service of municipal assistance for 'alignments.' By then, Ecochard had established a more global vision, that of regional planning. Influenced by the methods he discovered during a trip to the United States, where he met some of the authors of the Charter of Athens, notably Le Corbusier, Ecochard returned to Lebanon with a broadened conception of his field.

What he understood was that urbanism should be at the root of regional planning, especially in a young and developing country. Regional planning gives the broad directives of urban and rural development, after which urban planning can be applied to coordinate these efforts throughout the country.

After that, the administrative and executive services can put the plans into effect.

From this, we can deduce the general approach that was apparently applied in Lebanon. First, the Ministry of Planning had to identify the objectives. The regional planning services had then to decide on the geographic allocation of these objectives and, therefore, on the relative development of each region. Finally, the urban planners had to design the new urban extensions based on these regional plans. At the request of urban planners, the Ministry of the Interior then issued executive decrees and oversaw their implementation through its agencies. It seems a natural development, therefore, to make the regional and urban planning agencies into a single institution under the tutelage of the Ministry of Planning.[13] In effect, what withstood time was not the vehicular beltway – which Ecochard did help finalize, but which would have been realized anyway – but the newly introduced means of urban planning and related institutions, in short, the framework which actually influences the production of urban space and its perception.

The Master Plan for the City of Beirut, 1963

Like Damascus, Beirut would in turn experience a 'new version' of a master plan at the beginning of the 1960s (figs. 5 and 6). Once again, and with the same purpose of absorbing the urban population that had 'grown madly during the period,' the new city that was proposed in the 1943 plan was reintroduced along with another new city to the

Fig. 6. Master Plan for Metropolitan Beirut: The New City, Michel Ecochard, 1963

west. The founding principle of this proposal also remained the same: to build a 'healthy city' next to an 'ailing city.' Similarly, the transportation network constituted the armature of urban development and planning, and, in this regard, the 1963 plan proposed six exchange points, as well as a number of service roads and bypasses to circumvent the city center. Thus, the 'transportation knot' would be located outside municipal Beirut. The regional dimension of the plan was further elaborated by proposing an extra-urban peripheral beltway, a north-south national highway, and by including a study of the interregional road network. For the first time, Beirut, through the instrument of zoning which remained flexible in its definition, was conceived of as a city of varying densities. As a matter of fact, the Building Density Factor varied so widely that the allowed density in bordering mountainous areas was virtually indistinguishable from rural density. The motivation behind this urban strategy was the safeguarding of the site and the beauty of the surrounding landscape. Two new 'centers of attraction' were planned to allow the decongestion of the saturated traditional center (fig. 7). Located at the southeast and the southwest extremities of the urban agglomeration, respectively, they emphasized the suburbs and helped to justify – along with the new city, of course – the low densities imposed beyond these limits. This functionalism would naturally lead to a regrouping of uses by category. These categories included govern-

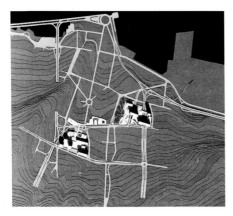

Fig. 7. Proposal for the development of the city center, Michel Ecochard, 1963

mental institutions as well as a City of Ministers, to be built south of Sidon Boulevard.[14]

Throughout, the spirit that would animate the struggle against real estate speculators within the framework of the first development plan for Beirut in 1943, and maintain the interest of concessions and the civil servants of the Mandate, remained intact, and perhaps even gained momentum. As Ecochard noted, "One can make the paradoxical observation that the middle-class residential areas were developed on agricultural land, whereas the sandy areas closer to

the city remained unbuilt in order to allow their owners to make substantial profits later, by the time the abutting land would have been built up.... If one then asks where the poor people would live, one finds them on the land least appropriate for construction, i.e., in the trough of the adjacent hills. But then these houses were stacked in more incoherent groups than the others, and mixed with industry without a discernable boundary between these two different land uses.... I know of nothing more painful for an urban planner than to visit these hills and to see how man has been able to destroy such a beautiful landscape without even benefitting from it for his own well-being."[15]

As in the 1943 project, the new cities, along with the City of Ministers, would never be built. The highway project would barely become established and the recommended policy of protecting natural sites would never be carried out. The sum total of the 'technical' propositions very rapidly became outdated. The plans produced for Damascus and Beirut were criticized by Ecochard's colleagues, especially in Lebanon, from the very beginning. Apart from the debate of the time that opposed opening the market to foreign architects, the proposed plans were attacked for a lack of precision. The 1963 plan, for example, determined a zoning strategy without delineating the perimeter of each zone. This lack of specificity, in this case regarding precise parameters for planners to follow, appears, in fact, to have been a deliberate choice on the part of the author. As he put it, "the Master Plan aims to provide general directives for the development of a city, reserving zones for growth, establishing the principles for constraints, and determining the main axes of circulation."[16]

However, in spite of these planning propositions, the idea of a different building coefficient for each zone would pervade the plan, thus fixing and guiding – until recently – the development of the city (fig. 8). The idea that motivated this proposition was simple in its conception. It departed from the principle that "a capital could not expand to infinity in order to absorb the whole population of the country,"[17] and, in the process, responded to a particularly Beiruti problem. The role of the new city was to absorb the future citizens and to reabsorb the slums, and in this context, the need to 'control' the density of surrounding areas became obvious.

An account of Ecochard's urbanism would not be complete without underlining

Fig. 8. Photomontage of an urban renewal project in the city center, Michel Ecochard, 1963

Fig. 9. Collège Protestant
in Beirut,
Michel Ecochard,
architect, 1956

two distinctly personal aspects of his work, namely, the interest he accorded natural and archaeological sites. This interest in nature and archaeology seemed to him to be compatible with the principles of the Charter of Athens. Ecochard would not accept the *tabula rasa* attitude toward overseas territory that offered the opportunity to achieve these principles. The concern, described earlier, for safeguarding the mountainsides bordering the capital from unsightly settlements would later become amplified with respect to Sidon. There, he paid special attention to the "archaeological monuments of historical or picturesque value." Even if historical quarters of the city center were destroyed, draconian constraints could be applied to zones of archaeological, historical, or picturesque value (to use the Charter's terms).[18] In the hope of long-term protection in Sidon, construction was completely forbidden in these zones. Ecochard wanted even the possibility of future archaeological finds during 'random digs, new constructions, or agricultural work' to be covered by this provision.[19]

An Architectural Sample

Other than public projects, Ecochard received several architectural commissions. He built a school for the Marist Brothers in Sidon, and one for the Antonine Priests in Baabda, the Collège Protestant in Beirut, and the Charity Hospital in Baabda.

An analysis of the Collège Protestant in Beirut sheds some light on its architect, since this building, one of the first built by Ecochard after his Moroccan stay, exemplifies his unquestioning approach (fig. 9). For a long time, Ecochard would boast having built one of the most modern and functional schools anywhere. The Collège Protestant project was executed between 1954 and 1956, parallel to the design of the University of Karachi – the latter in association with Riboulet and Thurnauer, whom he had met in Morocco. From then on, Ecochard would practice his profession free-lance from his architectural studio in Montparnasse, Paris. This change offered him more space for expression, given the broad range of projects and his return to architecture.

The architecture of this educational facility, composed of various buildings, is characterized by a strong, pure line, an elegant rhythm in the facades, a continuity between the exterior spaces and the enclosed spaces, as in the teachers' library, which extends into outdoor areas called the *iwan* by the architect (alluding to a local space-type), and the use of the brise-soleil – the architect's favorite – for some of the buildings. Ecochard did not mask his references when it came to aesthetic matters. The source of his inspiring concepts is clearly exposed, obviously in harmony with his theoretical motivations. As he stated, "the general equilibrium of the building has been achieved through a very careful study of proportions. These proportions have been based on the employment of the golden mean, as codified by the *Modulor*.... The southern facade, in particular, where the height of the rhythmically arranged bays was determined according to this principle – this geometric figure was based on the golden mean.... The gaiety and freshness were sought through a careful study of color, mainly inside the classrooms, each of which is thus made different from the others.... On the facades, only the differences in materials are played out, such as white coating, plain concrete, and bush-hammered concrete. Only the linking elements, such as the bridge leading to the science rooms and some of the circulation platforms, have been vigorously colored."[20]

The originality of the scheme adopted for this building cannot be reduced to the use of fair-faced concrete, the introduction of ramps, or the use of the brise-soleil elements which convincingly express the times. Rather, it comes through in the personal style of the architect who used these elements to handle modernism in architecture. Furthermore, the dialogue with the site appears to be one of the main criteria. Ecochard intelligently used the slope and put emphasis on the landscape and on the climatic conditions. The natural parameters became the structuring and determinant conceptual elements. A southern orientation was chosen for the buildings since it allows optimal use of the sun's warming rays in the winter, and, because the sun's trajectory is higher in the summer, it affords easy protection from sunlight during the hot months. The 'master builder' proudly elaborated the ingenious nature of such solutions. Indeed, the angle of the brise-soleil was calculated in such a way as not to allow direct sunlight into the classrooms except during specific hours of the day, adjusted to the season. Natural light entering the classrooms was similarly researched and controlled via rigorous arrangements of opaque and transparent elements in the facades exposed to the sun. Planting also played a major role in the overall conception. Ecochard even sought to preserve and integrate the existing fig orchard, using the alignment of trees as a screen to shield an intimate outdoor space immediately beyond the complex. The buildings were also oriented in such a way so as to allow an unobstructed view of the sea which, according to the author, was an 'extraordinary thing.'

The architectural conception was also understood from the beginning to be in close conjunction with the engineering. The plan of the Collège Protestant in Beirut reflects a functionalist attitude and a sound understanding of the day-to-day workings of a school. The school for the Antonine Brothers built a few years later would be cited as an example of the "persistence in the convenience of space," a quality it still preserves to the present day.[21] Finally, a consistent will to associate with local *savoir-faire* would lead to professional relationships that would exceed their professional framework to become friendships. In summary, Ecochard adapted the building to the social and natural climate while proposing an avant-garde architecture. Subsequently, Ecochard would refuse to publish this project in *L'Architecture d'Aujourd'hui* due to a conflict with his former partner of early days, Claude Le Coeur. This offer of a public venue by a well-known publication testifies to the importance of the project for the disciples of modernism. In fact, Le Corbusier, who had known the plans since the Paris days, would witness the 'proud allure' of the project firsthand during a stopover on his way to India.[22]

As the author of this project, Ecochard became an authority in the field. The type of architecture exemplified by the Collège Protestant flourished in Beirut, a city then experiencing a construction boom. The building remains a good example of intelligent adaptability. The impact of the proliferation of French influence, starting from the role that Ecochard played, was well appreciated by the representatives of the French government in Lebanon, as clearly expressed in the following letter:

"This embassy, having followed the construction of the school closely, and in view of the State's vested interests in this educational institution built on land belonging to the 'Domaines,' is in a position to recognize the remarkable feat accomplished by Mr. Ecochard in such a short period of time. The success of this project, the exemplary character of this ensemble that has attracted legitimate admiration even from outside the Lebanese frontiers, honors the great talent of this architect. Thus, it appears to me highly desirable that credit for this work be given to its author, who is being nominated by the French government and the United Nations to lead various urban planning and architectural missions in the Orient. I am convinced that you will share my feeling that French prestige is at stake, and that the committee may therefore not remain insensitive to this issue."[23]

To proclaim this project and many others built by Ecochard (or colleagues sharing his sources of inspiration) as architectural successes by no means obviates a critique of the relevance (or lack thereof) of such an architecture in a city freed from the imperial Ottoman context by just a few decades. Some of what follows are cases in point.

The Architect's Impact: Three Decades of Work and Influence

Whether criticized, loved, or defended, Ecochard symbolized for many countries, especially those in the Levant, French know-how and a particularly effective form of urban intervention. As can only be illustrated by the full listing of his achievements in the Levant, Ecochard truly embodied French ingenuity in architecture and urban planning. On the other side of the coin, however, it is also clear that through his interventions, French urban planning – rather, its local forms – would continue to dominate those countries. Rarely had an architect or an urban planner known so much popularity as Ecochard did in Lebanon. Associated with the highway projects and with a new law on urban planning, his name was integral to all local discourse about urban growth. Even citizens minimally interested in urban planning found themselves preoccupied in finding out if the new Ecochard Avenue would absorb their land holdings or, to the contrary, increase its value.

Which city did not aspire to or claim its own modernity in the 1960s? Ecochard has been criticized by his Lebanese colleagues often, but the criticism has been directed to the urban-technical aspects of his proposals without fundamentally questioning the modernity of his urbanism. Whether Ecochard is to be considered an accelerating force behind an ongoing process, or as its initiator, one thing is certain: he symbolized modern ideas and modern skills to the people in whose countries he worked.

With every episode of Ecochard's work, the basic issue to be addressed is the degree to which his plans have been able to influence urban planning and the perception of urban space. What has survived from his projects are the tools of urban intervention that he introduced, the institutional organization, the urban regulations often associated with the projects, and, finally, new modes of perception and new means of producing urban space. The very existence of a plan, tucked away as it may have been in some ministerial filing cabinet, created an irreversible precedent. For example, the 1950 Egli Plan for Beirut refurbished the

main ideas of Ecochard's plan of 1943 under the French Mandate. The same applies to the 1963 plan produced by Ecochard himself which, despite its more sophisticated appearance, reiterates the main points of the 1943 plan, namely, the new city, the clearing of the town center, and the northern and southern highways serving as links to two other major coastal cities.

The legacy of the plan goes beyond the existence of a file for a new study of the city. Its most important aspect is the legacy of concepts conveyed by the plan. These end up shaping the perceptions of the decision makers who determine the fate of urban space, as well as the approaches they might take in solving urban problems. Urban planning, as claimed by Ecochard, implies a strong central authority empowered to make and impose decisions required by a plan. It also implies social consensus about the nature of the general interest that the plan should serve. Beyond the requirements of the plan, this regulation gradually becomes the reference point for urban planning and architecture. The administrative apparatus is assumed to be consonant with the magnitude of these programs. Indeed, this set of requirements may explain why the plans were not easily applicable in their national contexts.

The Ecochard Legacy: A Patrimony to Protect or a Memory to Discard?

The heritage we seek to understand presents itself in a field that surpasses the temporality of the urban plan in order to propose a model toward which the city should aspire.

The sum total of the various urban plans' 'technical' propositions rapidly become outdated, whereas the concepts of modern architecture and urbanism have penetrated and impregnated many minds, thanks to practitioners such as Ecochard.

How can we assess this heritage at the end of the century? The 'export' of his theories has been severely criticized for lack of coherence in different cultural contexts. This modernity has no doubt created some ruptures, but should it not now be assimilated and assessed as patrimonial heritage? Ecochard's plans – whether realized or not – like his architectural products, belong to the history of the cities for which they were produced. They belong equally to the history of contemporary Western architecture and urbanism. This history, and particularly that of the modern movement, would remain incomplete without a chapter on projects realized overseas.[24]

The wealth produced by the intersection of different experiences, together with the feedback and impact in France, combine to create a common legacy, many facets of which remain to be discovered. The work achieved by Ecochard offers a new dimension to the history of urbanism, one that transgresses frontiers, crosses cultures, and sheds light on moments in the history of the city, and on ideas that have been shared at both ends of the Mediterranean. Ecochard's work, which is at the heart of this intersection, should find its place in the history of twentieth-century architecture and urbanism.

Michel Ecochard, whose bible would have been the Charter of Athens, was not the only one in Lebanon to transmit, with so much conviction, the architecture and urbanism of CIAM. Numerous Lebanese and foreign architects have contributed to transforming the Beirut of the '60s into a significant nexus of international architecture. However, Ecochard's influence in Lebanon remains significant for several other reasons. He has left his imprint on the urban landscape through his large-scale institutional buildings, such as schools and hospitals. More significantly, his impact is felt in the dynamic discussions he set in motion and from which further debate has sprung. The collaborators who remained constitute a major part of the Ecochard legacy. It was common practice for him to work jointly with colleagues abroad; these colleagues quickly familiarized themselves with his concepts. As intermediaries, and well after Ecochard stopped serving as its spokesman, they have insured the longevity of this modernity. An analysis of the practices and products of some of these collaborators in the post-Ecochard period would no doubt further reveal the extent of his influence.

Notes

1. Technically, the working method consisted of building reinforcements in masonry, resurfacing, and sometimes even disassembling and reassembling the building. Modern techniques were being utilized, such as the injection of concrete under pressure. However, Ecochard favored the Syrian craftsmen over the French technician. On this topic, see M. Ecochard, "La Restoration des Monuments Historiques en Syrie," 1943.

2. M. Ecochard, "Conférence Inaugurale de l'Enseignement de l'Urbanisme," October 13, 1967, p. 7, private archives of M. Ecochard.

3. M. Ecochard and J. Sauvaget, "Le Tombeau de Safwat-El-Molk," in *Les Monuments Ayyoubides de Damas* (Paris, 1938), pp. 1–13. Ecochard praises Sauvaget repeatedly.

4. For a history of the French Institute of Damascus, see R. Ave, ed., *IFD, L'Institut Français de Damas au Palais Azem (1922–1946)*, 1993.

5. J. Sauvaget, *Esquisse d'une Histoire de la Ville de Damas* (Paris: Librairie Orient, 1935).

6. On January 15, 1942, at the request of General Catroux, High Commissioner of Free France in the Levant, the chief of urban planning services in Syria was put at the service of the Lebanese government.

7. M. Ecochard, "Proposition du 27/7/42," Ministere des Affaires Etrangeres, Fonds de Nantes, inv. 17, carton 2927.

8. Inaugural lecture at the Lebanese Academy of Architecture in Beirut on November 8, 1943, private archives of M. Ecochard.

9. Treating this aspect of the question would in itself constitute a topic of research. I have chosen not to present all the information collected from the different archives, and to use only the material that sheds light on the career of the urban planner.

10. M. Ecochard, "A Plan for Financing Urban Projects in Beirut," a report written on September 16, 1942, Ministry of Foreign Affairs, Fonds de Nantes, inv. 10, carton 1347 (reference n25), Fonds Ecochard.

11. Ibid.

12. M. Ecochard, "A Free Point of View on the Management of Urban Affairs in Lebanon," private archives of M. Ecochard (Agence Montparnasse).

13. Ibid.

14. Different zones are established, and for each zone a building code (COS) based on the following criteria: Zone A: mountainous area with very low density; Zone B: existing mountainous agglomerations; Zone C: cultivated zones, generally with no building allowed; Zone D: to be urbanized first; Zone E: mixed zone; and Zone F: medium density residential.

15. M. Ecochard, "Plan Directeur de la Ville de Beyrouth, 1968," p. 62, Fonds Ecochard, IFA.

16. Ibid.

17. Ibid.

18. M. Ecohard, P. Riboulet, G. Thurnauer, and A. Bizri, "Sidon et sa région, problèmes d'urbanisme," 1957, Institut Français d'Architecture, Centre d'Archives du XXe Siècle, Fonds Ecochard.

19. Ibid., p. 20.

20. M. Ecochard, note concerning the project, without any further details, op.cit.

21. Interview with Antonine Father Elie on August 15, 1992, on the school building built at Baabda by Michel Ecochard in collaboration with Gabriel Tabet in 1960.

22. Letter from Michel Ecochard to Louise Wegmann, Paris, January 29, 1956, Fonds Ecochard, IFA.

23. Letter from the French ambassador in Lebanon to Mr. de Rouville of the "Comite des Œuvres Protestantes" of Syria and Lebanon, Beirut, June 15, 1956, Fonds Ecochard, IFA.

24. This question was first raised in *Architecture Française d'Outre-Mer,* under the directorship of M. Culot and J.M. Thiveau, Collections Villes, IFA, ed. Mardaga, 1992.

The Role of Government in Shaping the Built Environment

by
Assem Salam

A discussion of reconstruction in Lebanon necessitates probing into the role of public administration and the agencies entrusted with the task of promulgating and monitoring legislation dealing with the just and equitable management of the country's territory and ecological resources. In presenting the government's role in shaping the built environment in Lebanon, the urban growth of the capital Beirut is a useful example. The capital and its outskirts represent about 2 percent of Lebanon's land area, and are occupied by half the population, or 1.5 million inhabitants.

The Site and Its History

Urban growth in the city of Beirut has always been dependent on exceptional circumstances of varying intensity. Moreover, the site has offered very definite limitations for natural growth. The double barrier of mountain ranges is a physical handicap to communication with the interior, and other Mediterranean coastal cities like Tripoli, Sidon, Tyre, and Haifa, all have definite geographic advantages. Flat areas for easy expansion are very limited in Beirut, and the mountain slopes reach down to the sea.

Built on a cape protruding from the coastline of Lebanon, the medieval city grew up over the ruins of a prosperous Roman law school which had been destroyed earlier by an earthquake. This city remained of relatively little importance until the latter part of the nineteenth century, when it was designated as a provincial capital of the Ottoman Empire. It was then that extramural expansion began, and army barracks, government buildings, schools, and private residences were built outside the medieval city walls and on the hills surrounding the old Casbah.

Just before the end of World War I, the Turks undertook extensive improvements in the city, demolishing large areas of its medieval fabric. When the French moved in after the war, they found an old city partly demolished, and they immediately developed an ambitious scheme for its improvement. New axial roads were established and named after French and other Western European celebrities such as Foch, Allenby, Gouraud, Monot, Clemenceau, etc., and a renovation of the Place de l'Etoile was planned. Only two pockets of the medieval city survived the onslaught of the Westernizing planners. However, their ambitious schemes became bogged down by the Lebanese mercantile mentality, and efforts to implement them were thwarted by corruption and political manipulation. The Westernization of the city center, nevertheless, continued in a piecemeal and informal fashion under the French Mandate, resulting in an architectural environment more in keeping with the vernacular of southern France than a truly Arab oriental style.

Beirut first grew as a small Phoenician port of little commercial or strategic importance, and obtained its name from the multitude of water wells in the area (*beryte*, the Canaanite word for well, is the original name for Beirut). In the Hellenistic period, it became a medium size town of no great importance, and it wasn't until the fifth century that Beirut became a large Roman city. The reasons behind this sudden significance are not very clear. Excavations in the center of the town reveal aspects of Roman planning that perhaps were destined for military ends, most probably for barracks and a military town. However, the real role of Beirut under the Romans was of a cultural nature. The law school founded there gave the town cultural significance and an area of specialty that was envied by important Mediterranean towns such as Antioch and Alexandria. This strong regional role of Beirut was only lost when the whole town was erased by an earthquake in the sixth century.

For over twelve centuries afterwards, and all through Arab and Ottoman rule, Beirut was a relatively insignificant town. It was only toward the end of the nineteenth century that Beirut became a Turkish *vilayet*, due to the restructuring of the political system in Lebanon.

After World War II, the city continued to play its role as a port for the territories of the French Mandate, and maintained a slow and unspectacular growth until 1948.

Independence brought with it prosperity from the oil boom, and building in the International Style began where tenure and existing property outlines permitted. The urban memory of Beirut thus came to be associated with the extensive layers of the Arab Casbah, French vernacular, and, finally, the International style.

The spectacular circumstances that have fed urban growth in the last fifty years can be traced to many factors, among which the following appear to be of prime importance. They are:

a. the neutralization of the main competing port, Haifa, to the south in Israel;

b. the availability of a human capacity to improve the technical facilities necessary for the development of the port and airport;

c. the conversion of a limited industry that grew during World War II into a more productive industrial base to meet the needs of neighboring Arab countries;

d. the adoption of an economic system of free enterprise that has attracted foreign investment and offered almost unlimited horizons for imaginative Lebanese entrepreneurs; and

e. the adoption of a political system that has given better guarantees of stability in a rather troubled region.

The pressure of urban growth in the last fifty years has given Beirut the image we see today. It consists primarily of high-density urban sprawl built upon a medieval fabric and supported by a badly equipped infrastructure and a lack of adequate programmatic implementation. Spectacular as the urban volume may be, it is not difficult to see that the result is not a happy one.

In attempting to outline the government's involvement in Beirut's urban planning, it is worth mentioning that such efforts began under the French Mandate. Five stages in the urban planning efforts can be identified, both including that period and since then. They are:

a. the French Mandate, 1922–1946;
b. the early years of independence, 1946–1958;
c. the Shihabist and post-Shihabist period, 1958–1975;
d. the Civil War, 1975–1990; and
e. the postwar reconstruction, 1990 to the present.

Each is described in the following text, especially with regard to government activities.

Stage One – The French Mandate, 1922–1946

Under the French Mandate, serious efforts were initiated to prepare master plans for Beirut, the city that became the capital of the newly created Lebanese Republic. The earliest city plan drawn up for Beirut was prepared in 1932 by Danger. It was the first attempt at a comprehensive study of the capital taking geographic, climatic, geological, and human factors into consideration. In particular, it determined the major axes of circulation, such as those from Beirut to Tripoli, Beirut to Sidon, and Beirut to Damascus. It also determined the zoning coefficients, densities of occupation and property holdings, and created dwelling quarters planned in the spirit of garden cities. In addition, it recommended and located all the necessary utilities (parks, transportation, sewers, and garbage disposal) and recommended, for the first time, that the outskirts of Beirut, as we know them now, be considered as independent villages. However, the Danger Plan was never approved and, therefore, never put into effect.

Commissioned in 1942, the Ecochard Plan took two years to be developed and was finally submitted for consideration in 1944. It should not be confused with the present plan of Beirut, commonly referred to as the Ecochard Plan, which will be discussed later in detail. The first Ecochard Plan was extremely detailed and precise. The following are its major features:

a. It considered that the planning of Beirut should go beyond administrative boundaries, and as such the area covered by the plan stretched from Nahr al- Mawt in the north to Ouzai in the south.
b. It provided the main transportation arteries, and proposed a commercial ring around the center.
c. It provided for the link between Ras Beirut and Ashrafiyyeh.
d. It indicated the location of the present airport.
e. It offered an intensive survey of existing open spaces and gardens. In these regards, the plan and accompanying report contained a list of all the trees that should be maintained in Beirut.
f. It went into detail about zoning, industrial location, housing for workers,

popular housing, civic centers, and all the other categories of dwellings, from those for middle-income groups to those in the luxury class.

g. It proposed twelve land-use zones in Beirut (commercial, industrial, and residential) of varying densities, and it proposed a complete study for the protection of natural sites.

The Ecochard Plan was never approved, though many of its basic concepts were preserved and introduced in later plans.

The Egli Plan was submitted in 1950. In fact, it was more of a limited consultation than a comprehensive plan. Essentially, it recommended the adoption of the Ecochard Plan and reduced the number of zones involved to five. However, like the Danger Plan, it was never approved.

Stage Two – The Early Years of Independence, 1946–1958

This stage covers the period between initial independence from the colonial powers and the year 1958. By this time, Lebanon had inherited some semblance of an administrative hierarchy, namely that established by the French Mandate and based mainly on allegiance and loyalty to the mandatory power, largely without any framework or structure that set out guidelines or powers of control and inspection. These institutions were maintained during the first two presidential regimes (the Khoury and Chamoun periods) and displayed serious defects when confronted with the dynamism of the private sector, which was enjoying an interlude of exuberant, unguided growth and economic prosperity. During the two regimes, these institutions were mostly used as instruments in the hands of the ruling bodies, answering their own desires rather than acting as a strong and reliable governmental framework accountable and devoted to the service of the public, and as guardians of the interests of the state. During this period, Beirut continued to grow rapidly to meet its rising political and economic aspirations without a master plan. Development was guided only by the building code.

In 1954, under the pressure of an intense building boom, the municipal administration appointed a commission of experts to establish a plan. This was submitted and approved, but the plan was nothing but a network of roads, derived essentially from the earlier Ecochard proposal, too narrow to cope with the volume of traffic and neglectful of the elementary principles of traffic circulation. It provided no zoning, i.e., definition of density, occupation, and function in various areas. It never touched on any of the factors that could affect future trends and developments, such as ports, airports, industry, tourism, and major roadway developments. It made no study of or attempt to preserve the natural sites and historic monuments of the city. Above all, it never looked at Beirut in its regional context nor, for that matter, at the role the city was to play in the area during the coming years. Indeed, it is this plan of 1952–1954 that is in effect even now within the administrative boundaries of Beirut, and has been responsible for its development as we see it today.

Among the primary features of the plan were intersecting grids of roads that created traffic congestion everywhere. A lack of zoning resulted in commercial centers invading residential areas. Most commonly, offices have located themselves in apartment buildings and on ground floors, and shops have been built in what should have remained gardens. Unfortunately, the streets planned for residential circulation are unable to cope with commercial traffic, such as along Hamra Street in Ras Beirut and along Ashrafiyyeh. Extremely high densification factors, established in an arbitrary manner, have led to the continuous erosion of the urban tissue, and the lack of planning for open spaces and gardens, coupled with the uncontrolled land costs, have made it impossible to provide for adequate green areas. Moreover, the lack of protection for the natural sites and monuments has resulted in a barbaric destruction of the national heritage. Nevertheless, the most serious flaw of this plan was that high densification factors were set, standards commonly known as the "Coefficient of Exploitation." In fact, this factor which was established in 1954 without any serious study, and is still in force today, has resulted in high levels of congestion, degradation, and environmental dilapidation.

Stage Three – The Shihabist and Post-Shihabist Period, 1958–1975

This stage covers the period from 1958 until 1975, when the foundation of the modern state was established in Lebanon, which is also commonly known as the period of Shihabist reforms. It effectively established rules of appointments, hierarchy, terms of reference, and accountability for civil servants. In fact, this was the first serious administrative reform attempted in Lebanon and constitutes, to a large degree, the foundation of the present administrative system.

The reforms also established governmental agencies and institutions such as the Council of Public Administration, the Central Inspection Agency, the Public Audit Agency, the Institute of Public Administration, the Central Bank, and Social Security. With regard to urbanization and the development sector, the reforms introduced, for the first time, legislation governing urban planning. Both the Higher Council of Planning and the General Directorate for Town Planning were established, and the first extensive survey of the country's resources and development needs was carried out (the IRFED Mission), resulting in the establishment of five-year sectorial plans to accomplish major public works, including those involving highways, ports, water, electricity, schools, and public housing. The state also reclaimed most of its ailing or malfunctioning concessions, leased previously to the private sector, and embarked upon the task of building up its basic infrastructure. For the first time Lebanon was equipped with the necessary tools to acquire an efficient and powerful administration capable of meeting the challenges of development and the resource base needed to sustain growth. In no time, however, these novel institutional structures and agencies began to reveal shortcomings. These were not inherent to the weaknesses of their conceptual framework, but were rather an expression of the fact that the Shihabist reforms touched only the administrative structures. They were not able to introduce the reforms needed to sufficiently

Fig. 1. Aerial photograph of Martyrs' Square, ca. 1963

overhaul the political system. Soon the administration became politicized and reflected the same weaknesses which beleaguered the political system in the past. In particular, confessionalism and favoritism reduced the administration's efficiency and credibility.

In urban terms this period is marked by two major landmarks. First, there was the preparation and approval of an urban plan taking all Beirut, both the capital and the outskirts, into consideration. Second, there

was the drawing up of the legislation necessary for urban planning. For the preparation of the plan for Beirut and the outskirts, a commission was appointed and assisted by Ecochard. In 1964, the plan was submitted and was approved after modifications. It is this particular plan that is commonly referred to as the Ecochard Plan and which is in application now in Greater Beirut, from Nahr al-Kalb to Khaldeh.

More specifically, the plan deals with Beirut's city proper only insofar as it identifies the main arteries leading to the center. As for the rest, the 1954 plan remained unchanged, since Beirut itself was too deeply committed to it to accommodate any major changes or basic reconsiderations. By contrast, attention was concentrated more on the outskirts, and here the plan sets the densities and regulations for all the areas, as well as designating an area for the heavy industries, protecting the coast and the beaches, preserving the woods and natural sites, and establishing two governmental precincts.

Manipulation of the proposed plan led to basic changes. The restrictions of the plan were not severe, but the densities it approved gave Greater Beirut a capacity to accommodate many millions of inhabitants, in itself much too high a density. Ecochard has publicly dissociated himself from the officially published plan. Naturally, the greatest opposition, in spite of its moderate restrictions, came from developers. They wanted fewer restrictions and more room for exploitation. The disastrous effects of this plan can be seen now, thirty years later, in the sad conditions that plague Beirut.

The new town planning regulations also delegated all matters related to town planning to one single authority: the Directorate General of Town Planning under the aegis of the Ministry of Public Works. Administratively, the Directorate was also coupled with the Higher Council for Town and Country Planning, a totally independent body comprising representatives of the concerned ministries and independent professionals, representing planning, tourism, antiquities, public works, and the municipalities. Furthermore, the regulations gave the

town planning authorities the right to decide which areas needed planning. These authorities had to follow the priorities established by the government development planning policy. They also made it mandatory that the planning of urban areas be done in two stages: the first being the master plan, and the second the details.

The master plan, as originally conceived, is basically the conceptual framework which defines the main options that have been chosen, such as major roads, natural sites, green belts, general densities, industries, public buildings, infrastructural equipment, etc. It is only a broad guideline which defines urban orientation and controls overall development. Above all, it does not go into details, and thus it maintains flexibility. Within this framework, the detailed plans are established according to approved priorities. It is a lengthy process and a continuous one that is left to the administration to work out at the project execution stage.

By contrast to earlier approaches, the new law tightens the control of the administration over construction permits, architectural aesthetics, and parcellation. One of the major contributions of the new legislation has been the capacity for acquisition of land for public use (parks and green spaces) and the possibility of creating urban development on a large scale. The only way to achieve this under the old regulation was to expropriate the necessary areas for public facilities. However, the land cost was so high that it was impossible to think of expropriation except for roads, ports, and public utilities. Faced with this difficulty, the new law stipulated the constitution of mixed public-private real estate companies in which the government would become a shareholder in proportion to the amount instigated by the expropriation laws, i.e., 25 percent of the property value, with the private owners holding the remaining 75 percent. The mixed company would then undertake the planning of an entire zone, allowing for all facilities (open areas, parks, schools, public spaces, etc.), and would proceed to sell or develop properties in accordance with the master plan prepared for the zone. Such a system seemed to ensure that no one would be penalized by expropriation for the benefit of others. The evaluation resulting from urbanization would be shared by every owner on a *pro rata* basis. This law, though in existence since 1963, has been paralyzed by the interference of the large property owners in districts where mixed companies were declared. So much so that in 1991 a new strategy was drawn up for reconstruction of the Beirut Central District.

Stage Four – The Civil War, 1975–1990

The beginning of the Civil War found an administration too enfeebled to address the tasks of reconstruction. At the end of the first two years of war, when Lebanon was believed to be on the road to recovery, the Elias Sarkis regime created the Council for Development and Reconstruction (CDR). This agency was empowered with the necessary tools to bypass all routine and normal regulations encumbering other governmental institutions. Released from conventional bureaucratic constraints, the CDR was expected to perform its reconstruction tasks with the speed and efficiency characteristic of the private sector. Indeed, the CDR was conceived of as an instrument to assist public institutions, whenever possible, in carrying out their tasks in a more expeditious manner.

During the first six years of its life, the CDR was careful not to become a state within a state. It laid down the general development plan, secured the necessary financing for major projects, but refrained from getting embroiled in the execution of reconstruction projects, except when other government agencies were either too inept or too sluggish. Its primary task was to act as a reinforcement to the ailing administration, not to replace it.

The ruinous devastation caused by protracted hostilities further debilitated state institutions. The CDR, like other governmental agencies, became too fragmented to be effective, much like the country. For almost five years, Lebanon was run by two parallel administrations receiving instructions from two political heads. Nevertheless, during this most gruesome period in Lebanon's history, and in spite of continuous recurrence of violence and destruction, two major efforts were made toward urban planning in Beirut and its outskirts. They were the Beirut Central District Plan of 1977–1986, and the Urban Master Plan for Beirut and its outskirts, or the IAURIF Plan.

1. *The Beirut Central District Plan of 1977–1986*

During a lull in the fighting, based on false hopes for a political settlement, the government nominated a special committee to draw up a master plan for the damaged Central District (BCD) and oversee its implementation. Assisted by the APUR (Atelier Parisien d'Urbanisme) a plan was established (fig. 2), and approval obtained. It also went partially into effect.

The conceptual framework of this plan was drawn up with the following guidelines in mind: the first was to maintain the urban tissue in its original condition whenever possible, and to maintain original property

2. *The Urban Master Plan for Beirut and the Outskirts*

The continuing Civil War led to a radical change in the demographic fabric of Beirut's overall urban structure. The resulting population shifts and migration due to conflict changed the distribution of the population in and around the city radically. New subcenters grew around the capital to meet

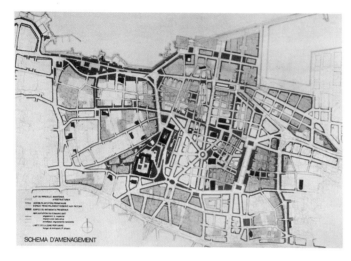

Fig. 2. APUR Plan for Beirut, 1977

tenure. The second was to encourage the legal owners and occupants of the BCD to return to their previous activities. The third was to accelerate the return of the BCD to its traditional role as a unifying ground for Lebanon's multiconfessional communal structure. The fourth was to introduce infrastructural improvements to the BCD, and finally, the fifth was to revitalize areas that had been badly damaged through the creation of real estate companies and other methods of intervention stipulated in town planning laws. As stated earlier, the plan went partially into effect, but was thwarted by renewed military conflicts and, finally, stalled in 1986.

the ever-increasing demands caused by the population shifts, and the authorities' waning ability to exercise control led to an unprecedented increase in illegal construction and unregulated growth. Against this backdrop, the IAURIF Plan was initiated in the hope that it would provide new directions for Greater Beirut. This was a bold and courageous move by those in government, considering the climate of war that existed at the time. To their credit, this plan is still the cornerstone for generally evaluating and guiding prevailing conditions in Greater Beirut, although no official approval of the plan has yet been fully granted.

Stage Five – The Postwar Reconstruction, 1990 to the Present

The Taif Accord and the political reforms agreed upon therein led to the re-establishment of a centralized political authority. Nevertheless, the residue of sixteen years of war and communal strife left the government with an extremely weak administration, almost nonexistent in certain sectors, and rife with all the deficiencies of Lebanon's various communities. At its outset, the colossal task of reconstruction after the hostilities had ended was centralized mainly in the capital. Efforts toward resettlement of the refugees and the reconstruction of destroyed villages, vital as they are for the political stability of the country, have been limited to financial remuneration to displaced populations. Efforts toward the physical reconstruction of destroyed villages are nonexistent, and where efforts for the return of the refugees have been made, the built environment has been neglected and is being replaced by totally chaotic urban growth, often threatening the natural beauty of the countryside. Efforts in the capital have been concentrated on three major schemes. They are the reconstruction of the BCD by Solidere, the reconstruction of the southern region by Elisar, and the rehabilitation of the northern coastline by Linord.

If the destruction of Beirut Central District during fifteen years of civil war has been an agonizing experience for Lebanese citizens, the plan for its reconstruction has exposed them to an intolerable vision of their capital's future. With the battered municipal administration in a state of almost total bankruptcy, it is not hard to see how the plan, which reflects no pressing need, but is a high priority for symbolic reasons, has fallen into the hands of developers with barely disguised commercial interests and political ambitions. A law passed in December 1991 gave the municipal administration the authority to create real estate companies in war-damaged areas, and to entrust them with the implementation of the urban plan and the promotion, marketing, and sale of properties to individual or corporate developers. The role of the state is limited to the formation of the company, the delimitation of the physical boundaries for its activities, and the compensation of companies for the cost of infrastructure. This entails the total and uncontrolled privatization of the reconstruction operations. The Société Foncière, or Real Estate Company henceforth referred to as the REC, has been formed by the compulsory association of property owners and occupants with property investors, the former offering their rights as equity and the latter the equivalent, after evaluation, in cash. Thus shares will, in effect, replace title deeds of ownership.

It is not possible to address here the constitutional aspects of this operation, nor its financial, economic, and legal implications. These have been the source of growing discontent, resulting in loud protests from large sectors of the community and proving a major source of embarrassment to the present government which, as it happens, is headed by the architect of the December 1991 legislation and a major share holder in the REC. However, two aspects of the operation, which have a direct bearing on the preparation of the urban plan, must be explained: first, the compulsory participation of owners and occupants in the REC and the conversion of their deeds and leases into shares will automatically deprive them of the right of occupation, or the right to return to their premises. Moreover, those who still legally reside in the center will be obliged to vacate their dwellings. Second, this compulsory association dissolves the physical boundaries between property lots and merges them into a single unit to be divided into parcels and sold off to developers. It is not hard to imagine the consequences of this on the formulation of the urban plan. The eviction of the existing population will quite simply eliminate the social fabric, while the dissolution of the medieval patterns of property within the city will decimate the physical fabric. The two main obstacles to the destruction of the heritage and the memory of the old city have thus been removed, and the town center has become a dead city, an empty field open to the speculative ambitions of developers. For instance, the plan proposes to demolish 80 percent of the town center and to increase its density fourfold. Effectively, a fatal blow has been dealt to the memory of this very ancient city, only to be replaced by a 'mirage' of a new city, one better suited to the oil-rich Arab countries, with a wealth of new buildings, perhaps, but a dearth of architectural traditions. In a city such as Beirut, which has more than two thousand years of history, the idea of memory must not be belittled. To pretend to protect this memory by preserving a few monuments while obliterating the context onto which they were inscribed can only

diminish their real nature. They will be like desecrated tombs, witnesses to the death of the city. Moreover, if we respect the memory of the city, we should also recall its unconscious memory: the great archaeological heritage that lies underground. The plan ignores this, taking no account of a possible need to record, let alone preserve, the relics of the ancient city which will be revealed in the creation of a new one, for such recording could only diminish or delay the investors' profits.

The southern outskirts of the capital are the city's most degraded urban fabric. Settled by squatters since 1958 and immensely inflated with refugees during the sixteen years of civil war, this area needs special attention. Attempts to handle its renovation in a similar manner to the BCD were met by the diehard opposition of the indigenous populations, together with a similar opposition to the idea of privatization. The legal framework for Elisar springs from the legislation established in 1991 for the Beirut Central District, which allows temporary expropriation for urban renewal, and stipulates the return of the owners and occupants to areas adjacent to their previous habitat. The task is to be carried out by an association between the state and the residents, without the involvement of a third party. Work in Elisar has been going on for almost two years now, and the scheme is showing slow progress, primarily due to factional and intercommunal struggles.

Linord is a project for the rehabilitation of the coastline area north of the capital degraded by a large refuse dump in the sea, covering an area of around two million square meters of land reclamation. The mechanism for implementation is similar to the Real Estate Company of Solidere, although the work is still in its infancy.

Conclusion

In this presentation, the role of the public institutions in Lebanon that control the built environment has been outlined. As mentioned, Beirut and its outskirts accommodate half of the population of Lebanon in an area that represents just over 2 percent of the country's total area. It is platitudinous to mention that without an effective and well-equipped administration, there is little hope to meet the challenges of the future. Emigration has already seriously damaged the functioning of many major institutions in Lebanon, and the intercommunal struggles have paralyzed its efficiency still further. Clearly, privatization should never be a choice when the administration is weak and its institutions are ailing. Instead, priorities should be directed at the reinforcement of those state institutions capable of playing their role in formulating development policies, exercising control, and supervising successful implementations. It is only when this is achieved that the private sector should be invited to contribute and invest in the reconstruction effort. Ideally, the Taif Accord and its envisioned political reforms should take us from a state of factional and lethargic administration to a state of dynamic institutions capable of holding a constructive dialogue with the private sector.

Section Three
The Socio-Economic Framework
for the Reconstruction of Beirut

Spatial Aspects and Socio-Economic Processes

by
Peter G. Rowe

Most discussions of city building either assume or confirm a certain reciprocity between the spatial aspect and outcome of urban development and the influence of underlying socio-economic processes. After all, down through the ages, cities have been primary sites of economically viable production and transaction, as well as the prime quarters of institutions concerned with various forms of social organization. Fundamentally, urban plans and projects are made with particular socio-economic factors and trends in mind. Modern real estate developers, for instance, usually assess the risk of their building decisions and their economic returns according to this kind of logic. Similarly, government planning officials might canvas various user groups in order to determine what to build and how much to build. Likewise, what is ultimately constructed dictates, in turn, many socio-economic outcomes, such as how the environment is actually used both now and in the future, as well as how it shapes the lives of those who occupy it and how it comes to express or symbolize their existence. It is comforting to see, for instance, how the de-

sign of a park or public place in a humane yet formal manner can somehow put people using it on their best behavior, instead of encouraging the loitering and anti-social behavior that abandoned and neglected spaces might within the same urban area.

In postwar Beirut, an important social phenomenon that has become dramatized in the process of reconstruction is the question of identity. Indeed, one might argue that the physical reconstruction of the city has a special responsibility in this regard, precisely because of the very physical way identity was defined during the war, through safe and contested territories, as well as by both the destruction and construction of symbols of faith and confessional membership. Clearly places at least partially take on and express the character of those who occupy and shape them. One way to recover a sense of identity, rather than to accept what is left in the torn urban remnants of war, is by rebuilding. However, where to reconstruct and in what way immediately become very important questions. So too does the expression of the event that precipitated the rebuilding in the first place, unless one wishes to partake of some form of collective amnesia and face its consequences. How to commemorate the ugly events of the war, therefore, and turn them into redemptive as well as didactic experiences, is an issue which must be confronted squarely in the urban-architectural conformation of the city.

In what follows, the Beiruti sense of identity, according to Samir Khalaf, has been dramatized by several circumstances and conditions, even though the issue may also be strongly present elsewhere. The first is the loosening of certain cultural and collective meanings through the ordeal of civil war and the process of what he refers to as 're-tribalization.' Any collective sense the downtown of Beirut might have had, for instance, that associated with well-known places such as the Place de l'Etoile or Martyrs' Square, was not only physically obliterated but rendered inoperable by the inevitable retreat into confessionally and tribally defined precincts. What remains intact are those places – at least some – of clan significance rather than of cross-confessional, city-wide, or even national significance. Surely this is one of the high prices of civil war. The second threat to a healthy and robust sense of identity, according to Khalaf, is that many places constructed during the postwar boom have become simply places of consumption, thus leveling the local differences and positive distinctions which might have otherwise emerged during the reconstruction process. Thus Beirut today finds itself on the horns of a dilemma in which parochial, local expressions of identity are likely to be well taken care of, and yet much beyond that seems likely to be overrun by consumer self-interest.

No doubt this dilemma also exists elsewhere. Many in academia, as well as in political circles, have decried the modern loss of civic enterprise in recent years and the surrendering of the public realm to those with less than high-minded interests. Nevertheless, in Beirut this situation has been exaggerated still further, according to Freddie Baz's analysis, by the present requirements for rapid economic redevelopment sustaining precisely the kind of boom that Khalaf sees as potentially encouraging indiscriminate consumerism. By Baz's account, the Civil War resulted in huge losses, both economic and otherwise. The human toll was appalling, both in terms of lives squandered and the potential for leadership lost, and there was significant damage to the infrastructure. Direct loss alone probably amounts to U.S. $19 billion, not to mention a foregone opportunity cost on the order of $60 billion. The general economic trajectory at the end of hostilities showed inflation running at 92 percent per annum, depreciation at 82 percent per annum, and production down by at least 50 percent of normal peacetime levels. What Lebanon needs, according to Baz, is to get the economic fundamentals correct, requiring huge investments in modern infrastructure, along with the acquisition of significant levels of foreign capital, an emphasis on private enterprise, and the encouragement of liberal trade practices. The key to success, however, is timing. Moreover, the sooner and quicker the better – in short, what is needed is a real and sustained economic boom.

The third essay in this section brings the dilemma of broader collective identity and economic progress home to roost, so to speak, in the southern suburbs of Beirut. Here, Mona Harb el-Kak rather poignantly presents a case study of stark contrasts among the densely populated Shi'ite populations and official efforts from on high to make way for more prosperous redevelopment and, with it, a more visually acceptable entryway to the city from the airport located in the south. On the one hand, the Elisar Project is seen as the means by which valuable property adjacent to the southern seashore of Beirut can realize its full developmental potential. On the other, it is seen as a form of 'coastal cleansing' involving forcible demolition of illegal settlements to make way for different uses and social groups. Without a broader common ground, the processes of retribalization, occasioned by the war and described by Khalaf, only seems likely to continue, along with the equally destructive singular penchant for pecuniary self-interest.

By now, much of this might sound familiar. In effect it is a phenomenon taking place in many places around the world where heterogeneous communities have gathered and where urban economic development is occurring. Moreover, this is not a new phenomenon, albeit peculiarly exaggerated in the case of Beirut. It has happened before in the past and, in this regard, one has only to recall the urban renewal eras in various places to find ample cases in point. Unfortunately, exactly what to do better is not developed explicitly in any of the three essays, certainly not from an urban design perspective. Khalaf and Baz present overviews and analyses of current circumstances, while Harb el-Kak presents a case study and a condemnation of modernism as such. Never-

theless, useful hints can be discerned in all three contributions.

Taking up Khalaf's suggestion, one approach would be to make the postwar period more reflective of its social circumstances, countering tendencies toward collective amnesia and the perpetual mardi-gras syndrome of the boom period. In urban design terms, this might translate into a policy of remixing urban uses and activities at the finest grain possible, especially in areas where economic groups and merchant classes ought to be encouraged to work together, and where the blandness of contemporary merchandizing agglomeration in search of economic scale ought to be discouraged. The old area of the souks in downtown Beirut is a fairly clear example. Another approach might be to program place-making activities and urban-design solutions which call attention to recent events, but from a broader vantage point than the circumstances surrounding the specific events might otherwise allow. Here the manner in which the rich Beiruti urban history is revealed and yet simultaneously made a part of daily life seems like a promising design strategy. There is ample opportunity to 'commemorate,' again using Khalaf's terminology, but to place spatially and symbolically such commemoration into a much larger and, therefore, more salutary perspective.

Counterproductive though it might initially seem, yet another strategy might well be to design very explicitly and well for particular groups, exaggerating in particular the nuances of a specific locale. This would certainly counteract any tendency toward the bland commercialism that Khalaf fears and, if handled appropriately, the tendency to create lasting tribal enclaves as well. The commonplace yet locally-specific built environments of cities do, afterall, change hands and even uses over time. Various economic situations, for instance, make some areas more or less favorable than others, and the spaces of one class or social group give way, temporally, to another. Usually the most long-lasting, robust, and successful urban districts in this respect are those which are constructed generously and well in the first place, together with a sense of their being permanent. Marginal or cheap settlement and real estate investment has no place in such a strategy. By architecturally asserting specific aspects of postwar confessionalism, especially those in dwelling and settlement which are held in common, environments both of quality and distinction can be obtained, regardless of future occupation.

As Baz stipulates, infrastructure investment is undoubtedly a key to Beirut's continued recovery. Moreover, in urban areas this usually results in a common property resource both enabling and guiding subsequent property investment and building. In some places it is one of the few means to effectively provide this important controlling and managerial function. As a common property resource it is also a site for expressing and symbolizing the hopes and aspirations of a collective, regardless of any internal differences. For this public aspect to flower usually requires a strong presence of both the state and civil society, together with a strong creative tension between them.[1] Unfortunately, at this stage in Beirut's reconstruction, the missing ingredient appears to be the strong presence of civil society, although the recent emergence of various grass-roots organizations, suggested by Harb el-Kak, is an encouraging sign. Typically, such community groups emerge around specific issues and controversies and, in the long-run interests of the reconstruction process, should be encouraged. Unless large-scale master plans have the benefit of review, comment, and negotiation with empowered interest groups on the side of civil society, they are likely to be much worse off and far less well-tuned to local circumstances and the possibilities for heterogeneous expression. Moreover, in the planning and design of public improvements, both the state and representative elements of civil society must not only aim highly, but also reach out toward disenfranchised groups as well. In this very important regard, needed social and institutional reform must precede design, otherwise nothing more fitting seems likely to occur than improvements which satisfy the preferences and tastes of some elite or monoculture.

Similarly, as Harb el-Kak points out, property rights must also be treated with considerable care and respect. Especially in conditions such as postwar Beirut's, hard-earned territory is likely to be very difficult to give up unless questions of equity and the future opportunity for very real development are addressed adequately. More often than not, these questions hinge on at least two crucial aspects. First, there is the matter of the locational advantage of the tract to be given up and, second, there is the matter of the real quality of the environment being substituted in return. Further, the latter is often difficult either to convey convincingly in contentious circumstances, or to guarantee in any efficient and plausible manner.

This usually leaves at least one reasonable choice, and that is to direct additional infrastructure investments in such a manner that an acceptable equivalence is struck based upon the locational advantage of some other site.

In the final analysis, progress and civic improvement need to be made without the loss of local identity. At this stage in Beirut's reconstruction, this may require a fairly radical shift in thinking, away from ideas about mixed use and mixed social groups on the same or nearby sites. Instead, it may mean a heterogeneous mosaic of separate precincts or territories, where each piece is relatively socially homogeneous in its specific spatial identity.[2] Clearly the edges of the mosaic and the boundaries between precincts would then become the negotiated terrain, the common ground, and the cross-cultural meeting places. In certain senses this is what usually happens in cities anyway, when particular groups move into the territory of other groups. The difference here in Beirut is that these territories have already largely been defined. What is needed now is to fill in the gaps, so to speak, with civility and mutual respect.

Notes

1. See P.G. Rowe, *Civic Realism* (Cambridge, Mass.: The MIT Press, 1997).
2. See S. Khalaf, *Beirut Reclaimed* (Beirut: Dar An-Nahar, 1993).

Contested Space and the Forging of New Cultural Identities

by
Samir Khalaf

Lebanon today is at a fateful crossroads in its political and socio-cultural history. At the risk of some oversimplification, the country continues to be imperiled by a set of overwhelming predicaments and unsettling transformations. At least three stand out by virtue of the ominous implications they have for the massive reconstruction underway and the prospects for forging a viable political culture of tolerance and peaceful coexistence.

First, Lebanon is in the throes of postwar reconstruction and rehabilitation. Given the magnitude and scale of devastation, the country will most certainly require massive efforts in virtually all dimensions of society to spearhead its swift recovery and sustained development. Processes of postwar reconstruction, even under normal circumstances, are usually cumbersome. In Lebanon, they are bound to be more problematic because of the distinctive character of some of the residues of collective terror and strife with which the country was besieged and which set it apart from other instances of postwar reconstruction. Among such disheartening consequences, two are particularly poignant and of relevance to the concerns of this essay. First, the salient symptoms of 'retribalization' apparent in reawakened communal identities and the urge to seek shelter in cloistered spatial communities. Second, a pervasive mode of lethargy, indifference, weariness which borders, at times, on 'collective amnesia.' Both are understandable reactions which enable traumatized groups to survive the cruelties of protracted strife. Both, however, could be disabling, as the Lebanese are now considering less belligerent strategies for peaceful coexistence.

Lebanon is not only grappling with all the short-term imperatives of reconstruction and long-term need for sustainable development and security, but it has had to do so in a turbulent region with a multitude of unresolved conflicts. Impotent as the country might seem at the moment to neutralize or ward off such external pressures, there are measures and programs, already proved effective elsewhere, which can be experimented with to fortify Lebanon's immunity against the disruptive consequences of such destabilizing forces. Such efforts can do much to reduce the country's chronic vulnerability to these pressures. As will be argued, urban planning and design, architecture, landscaping, among other overlooked forms of public intervention, can offer effective strategies for healing symptoms of fear and paranoia and transcending parochialism.

Finally, Lebanon as of late is also embroiled, willingly or otherwise, in all the unsettling forces of postmodernity and globalism: a magnified importance of mass media, popular arts, and entertainment in the framing of everyday life, an intensification of consumerism, the demise of political participation and collective consciousness for public issues, and their replacement by local and parochial concerns for nostalgia and heritage.

Unfortunately, many of the public manifestations of nostalgia so rampant today in Lebanon have scant, if any, concern with what Christopher Lasch has called a 'conversational relationship with the past.'[1] Instead, they assume either the construction and embellishment of grandiose and monumental national symbols, or the search for roots, the longing to preserve or invent often contrived and apocryphal forms of local and communal identities. More disheartening, this valorization of or escape into the past, particularly at the popular cultural level, has taken on some of the garish symptoms of commodification of heritage into kitsch and the vulgarization of traditional folklore and indigenous artifacts.

Within this context, issues of collective memory, contested space, and efforts to forge new cultural identities begin to assume critical dimensions. How much and what of the past needs to be retained or restored? By whom and for whom? Commonplace as these questions might seem, they have invited little agreement among scholars. Indeed, the views and perspectives of those who have recently addressed them vary markedly.

To Ernest Gellner, collective forgetfulness, anonymity, and shared amnesia are dreaded conditions resisted in all social orders.[2] Perhaps conditions of anonymity, he argues, are inevitable in times of turmoil and upheaval. But once the unrest subsides, internal cleavages and segmental loyalties resurface.

D. MacCannell goes further to assert that the ultimate triumph of modernity over other socio-cultural arrangements is epitomized not by the disappearance of premodern elements, but by their reconstruction and artificial preservation in modern society.[3]

Similarly, Jedlowski also maintains that a sense of personal identity can only be achieved on the basis of personal memory.[4]

Benjamin Barber however, argues that successful civic nations always entail a certain amount of "studied historical absentmindedness. Injuries too well remembered," he tells us, "cannot heal."[5] What Barber is implying here, of course, is that if the memories of the war and its atrocities are kept alive, they will continue to reawaken fear and paranoia, particularly among those embittered by it. Without an opportunity to forget, there can never be a chance for harmony and genuine coexistence.

Both manifestations – the longing to obliterate, mystify, and distance oneself from the fearsome recollections of an ugly and unfinished war, or efforts to preserve or commemorate them – coexist today in Lebanon. Retribalization and the reassertion of communal and territorial identities, as perhaps the most prevalent and defining elements in postwar Lebanon, in fact incorporate both these features. The convergence of spatial and communal identities serves, in other words, both the need to search for roots and the desire to rediscover, or invent, a state of bliss that has been lost; it also serves as a means of escape from the trials and tribulations of war.

Expressed more concretely, this reflex or impulse for seeking refuge in cloistered spatial communities is sustained by two seemingly opposed forms of self-preservation: to remember and to forget. The former is increasingly sought in efforts to anchor oneself in one's community or in reviving and reinventing its communal solidarities and threatened heritage. The latter is more likely to assume escapist and nostalgic predispositions to return to a past imbued with questionable authenticity.

Either way, concerted efforts need to be made to reinvigorate or generate meaningful public spaces in order to diminish fear and transcend parochialism and the compulsion to withdraw into the compact enclosures of family and community. If this essay has a plea, it is a call to go beyond what Nan Ellin terms 'defensive urbanism' and to generate conditions germane to the articulation of a more 'offensive urbanism.'[6]

More than in any other time in recent history, architects and urban planners in Lebanon now have a rare opportunity to step in and assert and validate the reconstructive and radical visions of their profession. With all the disheartening manifestations of the war, we catch Lebanon at a critical and propitious threshold in its urban history. The massive reconstruction underway, particularly the historic core of Beirut's Central Business District, has provoked a rare mood of nascent and growing public awareness of spatial and environmental issues. Perhaps for the first time growing segments of the Lebanese are becoming increasingly conscious and verbal about what is being done to the spaces around them.[7]

If there are visible symptoms of a 'culture of disappearance' evident in the growing encroachment of global capital and state authority into the private realm and heedless reconstruction schemes, elements which are destroying or defacing the country's distinctive architectural, landscape, and urban heritage, there is also a burgeoning 'culture of resistance.' It is this which is contesting and repelling such encroachment and dreaded annihilation, or the fear of being engulfed by the overwhelming forces of globalization.[8]

Within this setting, urbanists have considerable latitude for advancing strategies to awaken and mobilize silenced, lethargic, and disengaged segments of the society to become more vigilant and actively engaged in pacifying some of the forces ravaging their habitat and living space. It is my view that in this ameliorative interlude of postwar reconstruction, such involvement can do much in healing and transcending sources of fear and division in society. Also through such involvement, an aroused public can begin to assist in transforming 'spaces' into 'places.' After all, the way spaces are used is a reflection of people's identities and commitments to them. The more we live in a particular place – as we become part of it, so to speak – the more inclined we are to care for it. It is in this sense that 'spaces' are converted to 'places.'

As concerned citizens, it is of vital interest to us to be involved in safeguarding, repairing, and enriching our experience of space. Indeed, these are basic human rights, almost universal needs. If they are abused, we all are diminished. Consider what happens when a country's most precious heritage either is maligned or becomes beyond the reach of its citizens. This is precisely what has been happening to many Lebanese. Their country's scenic geography, its pluralistic and open institutions, which were once sources of national pride and inspiration, things around which they wove dreams that made them a bit different from others, have either become inaccessible to them, or worse, are being redefined as worthless. At best, they have been reduced to mere 'spaces' for commercial speculation.

To better understand the nature and character of this ongoing interplay between collective memory or obsession with 'heritage,' the reassertion of space, and the forging of new cultural identities, this essay addresses three related dimensions. First, it will highlight briefly a few of the most striking spatial transformations associated with the war, particularly those that have some bearing on the dialectics between space, memory, and collective identity. All three are in flux and are being contested today. How they will be resolved will prefigure much of the emerging contours and future image of Beirut. Second, an attempt will be made to identify and account for a few of the responses communities are having in resisting or accommodating some of the global forces presumed to undermine their local heritage and identities.

Finally, the question will be raised as to what role urban planning and design can play in recovering or reclaiming Beirut. Who is to reclaim what and how much of the old heritage should be restored and rehabilitated?

The Spaces of War

For almost two decades, Lebanon was besieged and beleaguered by every possible form of brutality and collective terror known to human history: from the cruelties of factional and religious bigotry to the massive devastations wrought by private militias and state-sponsored armies. They have all generated an endless carnage of innocent victims and immeasurable toll in human suffering. Even by the most moderate of estimates, the magnitude of such damage to human life and property is staggering. About 170,000 people have perished, twice as many were wounded or disabled; close to two thirds of the population experienced some form of dislocation or uprootedness from their homes and communities. By the fall of 1982, UN experts estimated that the country had sustained U.S. $12 to 15 billion in damages, i.e., $2 billion per year. Today, more than one third of the population is considered to be below the poverty line as a result of war and displacement.

For a small, dense, closely-knit society of about 3.5 million, such devastations are, understandably, very menacing. More damaging, perhaps, are some of the socio-psychological and moral concomitants of protracted hostility. The scars and scares of war have left a heavy psychic toll which displays itself in pervasive post-stress symptoms and nagging feelings of despair and hopelessness. In a culture generally averse to psychoanalytic counseling and therapy, these and other psychic disorders and fears are more debilitating. They are bound to remain masked and unrecognized and, hence, unattended to.

The demoralizing consequences of the war are also visible in symptoms of vulgarization and impoverishment of public life and erosion of civility. The routinization of violence, chaos, and fear only compounded the frayed fabrics of the social order. It drew groups into the vortex of bellicose conflict and sowed a legacy of hate and bitterness. It is in this fundamental sense that Lebanon's pluralism, radicalization of its communities, and consequent collective violence have become pathological and uncivil. Rather than being a source of enrichment, variety, and cultural diversity, the modicum of pluralism the country once enjoyed is now generating large residues of paranoia, hostility, and differential bonding.

The first striking and, perhaps, unsettling feature is the way the Lebanese have been, since the outbreak of the war in 1975, caught up in an unrelenting process of redefining their territorial identities. Indeed, as the fighting blanketed virtually all regions in the country, few have been spared the anguish of uprootedness from their spatial moorings. The magnitude of such displacement is greater than commonly recognized. Recent estimates suggest that more than half, possibly two thirds, of the population has been subjected to some transient or permanent form of uprootedness from their homes and communities.

Throughout the war, in other words, the majority of the Lebanese was entrapped in a curious predicament: that painful task of *negotiating*, *constructing*, and *reconfirming* a fluid and unsettled pattern of spatial identities. No sooner had they suffered the travails of dislocation by taking refuge in one community, than they were again uprooted and compelled to negotiate yet another spatial identity or face the added humiliation of re-entry into their profoundly transformed communities. They became homeless, so to speak, in their own homes, or furtive fugitives and outcasts in their own communities.

The socio-psychological consequences of being dislodged from one's familiar and reliable landmarks, those of home and neighborhood, can be quite shattering. Like other displaced groups, the Lebanese became disoriented and distressed because the terrain had changed and because there was no longer a neighborhood for them to live in and rely upon. "When the landscape goes," says Erikson "it destroys the past for those who are left: people have no sense of belonging anywhere."[9] They lose the sense of control over their lives, their freedom and independence, their moorings to place and locality and, more damaging, a sense of who they are.

Bereft of place, they become homeless in at least three existential senses. First, they suffer the angst of being dislodged from their most enduring attachments and familiar places. Second, they also suffer banishment and the stigma of being outcasts in their neighborhoods and homes. Finally, much like the truly exiled, they are impelled by an urge to reassemble a damaged identity and a broken history. Imagining the old places, with all their nostalgic longings, serves as their only reprieve from the uncertainties and anxieties of the present.

Equally devastating has been the gradual destruction of Beirut's and, to a large extent, the country's common spaces. The first to go was Beirut's Central Business District which had served historically as the

Fig. 1. 1960s aerial view of the city center looking over the Burj toward the port and the Gemmayzeh area

undisputed focal meeting place. Beirut without its 'Burj,' as the city center is popularly labeled, was unimaginable (figs. 1 and 2). Virtually all the vital public functions were centralized there: the parliament, municipal headquarters, financial and banking institutions, religious edifices, transportation terminals, traditional souks, shopping malls, entertainment, etc., kept the pre-war 'Burj' in a sustained state of day and nighttime animation. There, people of every walk of life and social standing came together.

Fig. 2. Clearing of the Burj

With decentralization, other urban districts and regions in the country served as supplementary meeting grounds for common activities. They, too, drew together, albeit on seasonal and interim bases, groups from a wide cross-section of society, thereby nur-

turing outlets germane for coexistence and plural lifestyles. Altogether, there were very few exclusive spaces beyond the reach of others. The social tissue, like all seemingly localized spaces, was fluid and permeable.

Alas, the war destroyed virtually all such common and porous spaces, just as it dismantled many of the intermediary and peripheral heterogeneous neighborhoods which had mushroomed with increasing urbanization in cities like Tripoli, Sidon, and Zahleh. The war did not only destroy common spaces. It also encouraged the formation of separate, exclusive, and self-sufficient spaces. Hence, the Christians of East Beirut need not now frequent West Beirut for its cultural and popular entertainment. Likewise, one can understand the reluctance of Muslims and other residents of West Beirut to visit resorts and similarly alluring spots of the Christian suburbs. With internecine conflict, quarters within urban districts, just like towns and villages, were often splintered into smaller and more compact enclosures. Spaces within which people circulated and interacted shrunk still further. The socio-psychological predispositions underlying this urge to huddle in insulated spaces is not too difficult to trace or account for.

Massive population shifts, particularly since they are accompanied by the reintegration of displaced groups into more homogeneous, self-contained, and exclusive spaces, have also reinforced communal solidarity. Consequently, territorial and confessional identities, more so perhaps than at any other time, are beginning to converge. For example, 44 percent of all villages and towns before the outbreak of hostilities included inhabitants of more than one sect. The sharp sectarian redistribution, as Salim Nasr has shown, has reshuffled this mixed composition. While the proportion of Christians living in the southern regions of Mount Lebanon (i.e., Shouf, Aley, Upper Metn) was 55 percent in 1975, it shrunk to about 5 percent by the late 1980s.[10] The same is true of West Beirut and its suburbs. Likewise, the proportion of Muslims living in the eastern suburbs of Beirut has also been reduced from 40 percent to about 5 percent over the same period.[11]

The war has also transformed the perception and use of space in a more compelling sense. When a 'playground' (as prewar Lebanon was legitimately labeled) turns into a 'battleground,' inevitably this is accompanied by a dramatic turnover in land use. Hashim Sarkis has demonstrated how, during episodes of civil strife, space develops its own logic and propels its own inhabitation.[12] He claims that "it precedes, resists, yields to, and survives those who assume it to be a neutral site for their control." He also advances the view that "inhabitants are more elusive in their relationships with places they inhabit. They move across given boundaries, negotiate, and renegotiate their spatial identities." Much can be added to substantiate both of these seemingly antithetical viewpoints.

The most graphic, of course, is the way spaces of war have asserted their ferocious logic on virtually every nook and cranny of public and private space. Equally telling is the ingenuity of its besieged hostages in accommodating this menacing turnover in their spatial surroundings.

Public thoroughfares, crossroads, hilltops, bridges, and other strategic intersections which served as links between communities were the first to be converted. They became 'Green Lines,' treacherous barriers denying any crossing. Incidentally, the infamous 'Green Line' acquired its notorious label when shrubs and bushes sprouted from its tarmac after years of neglect. It is ironic that this great divide which rips the city in two was none other than the major thruway (i.e., the old Damascus Road) connecting Beirut to its hinterland and beyond. Likewise, major squares, traffic terminals, and pedestrian shopping arcades, once the hub of gregarious activity and dense interaction, became a desolate 'no-man's-land': *al-Mahawir al-taqlidiya* (traditional lines of confrontation) or *khutut al-tamas* (lines of confrontation).

While prominent public spaces lost their identity, other rather ordinary crossings, junctures, hilltops, even shops, became dreaded landmarks. The war produced its own lexicon and iconography of places.[13] By virtue of their contingent locations these, and other such inconsequential places and spaces, became fearsome points of reference and demarcating lines, part of the deadly logistics of contested space.

Private space was not spared these tempestuous turnovers in land use. Indeed, the distinctions between private and public space were blurred and lost much of their conventional usages. Just as basements, rooftops, and strategic openings in private homes became part of the logistics of combat, roadways were also 'domesticated' as family possessions, discarded furniture, and bulky items spilled into the public domain to improvise barricades. Balconies, verandahs, walk-ups, doorways, and all the other open, airy, and buoyant places the Lebanese craved and exploited with such ingenuity became dreaded spaces to be bolted and shielded. Conversely, dingy basements, tightly sealed corridors, attics, and other normally neglected spaces became more coveted simply because they were out of the trajectory of snipers and shellfire. They became places of refuge.

Of course, the symbolic meanings and uses of a 'house,' 'home,' or 'dwelling' space, as Maha Yahya has demonstrated, were also overhauled.[14] The most compelling, of course, is the way the family unit and its private spaces have been broadened to accommodate other functions, as disengaged and unemployed household members converted or relocated their business premises to their homes. The thriving informal war economy reinforced such efforts and rendered them more effective.

Altogether, and perhaps most unsettling, is the way the tempo of war has imposed its own perilous time frames, dictating traffic flows, and spaces to be used or avoided. Time, space, movement, and interaction all became enveloped with contingency and uncertainty. Nothing was taken for granted anymore. People lived situationally, so to speak. Short-term expediency replaced long-term planning. Everything had to be negotiated on the spur of the moment. The day-to-day routines, which once structured the use of space and time, played havoc with their lives. Deficient communication and irregular and congested traffic rendered all forms of social interaction fortuitous and unpredictable. One was expected to accomplish much of his daily activities at unexpected hours depending on the merciless whims of fighters or the capricious cycles of violence. Beirutis became, as a result, astonishingly adept at making instant adaptations to such jarring modulations and precipitous shifts in the use of time and space.

Finally, it must be noted that the post-war mood in Lebanon has generated its own pathologies and disheartening manifestations. Postwar interludes normally generate public moods of moderation and restraint. People are more inclined to curb their conventional impulses and become more self-controlled in the interest of reappraising and redirecting their future options. Rather than freeing them from their prewar excesses, the war has paradoxically induced the opposite reaction. It has unleashed appetites and inflamed people with insatiable desires for acquisitiveness and unearned privileges.

Mercantilism and its concomitant bourgeois values were always given a free reign in Lebanon. The outcome of such excessive commercialization was already painfully obvious in the prewar years. With staggering increases in land values, commercial traffic in real estate became one of the most lucrative sources of private wealth. Hence, that ruthless plundering of the country's scenic natural habitat and the dehumanization of its living space became starkly visible. With the absence of government authority, such excesses became rampant. What had not been ravaged by war was eaten up by greedy developers and impetuous consumers. Hardly anything was spared. The once pristine coastline is littered with tawdry tourist attractions, kitschy resorts, and private marinas as much as by the proliferation of slums and other unlawful, shoddy, makeshift tenements. The same ravenous defoliation has blighted the already shrinking greenbelts, public parks, and terraced orchards. Even sidewalks and private backyards are stripped and defiled.

Rampant commercialism, greed, and enfeebled state authority could not, on their own, have produced as much damage. These are exacerbated by the pathos of a ravenous

postwar mentality. Victims, wracked for so long by the atrocities of human suffering, become insensitive to these seemingly benign and inconsequential concerns or transgressions. It is understandable how the moral and aesthetic restraints which normally control the growth of cities become dispensable virtues. They all seem much too remote when pitted against the profligate postwar mood overwhelming large portions of society. Victims of collective suffering normally have other rudimentary issues on their mind. They rage with bitterness and long to make up for lost time and opportunity. The environment becomes an accessible surrogate target on which to vent their wrath. In a culture infused with a residue of unappeased hostility and mercantilism, violating the habitat is also very lucrative. Both greed and hostility find an expedient proxy victim.

In such a free-for-all context, any concern for the aesthetic, human, or cultural dimensions of living space is bound to be dismissed as superfluous or guileless. As a result, it is of little interest whether cities are ugly, whether they debase their inhabitants, whether they are aesthetically, spiritually, or physically tolerable, or whether they provide people with opportunities for authentic individuality, privacy, and edifying human encounters. What counts is that the unconditional access to land must satisfy two overriding claims: the insatiable appetite for profit among the bourgeoisie, and the vengeful feeling of entitlement to unearned privileges among the disenfranchised.

By the time authorities step in to restrain or recover such violations, as happened repeatedly in the prewar years, the efforts were always too little, too late. By then, officials could only confirm the infringements and incorporate them into the legitimate zoning ordinances.

The Cultures of Disappearance and Resistance

All wars, civil or otherwise, are atrocious. Lebanon's encounters with civil strife, it must be suggested, are particularly galling because their horrors were not anchored in any recognizable or coherent set of causes. Nor did they resolve the issues which had sparked the initial hostilities. It is in this poignant sense that the war was altogether a wasteful and futile encounter with collective violence.

The muted anguish and unresolved hostilities of the war are now being compounded by all the ambivalences and uncertainties of postwar reconstruction and the encroachment of conglomerate global capital as it contests the efforts of indigenous and local groups in reclaiming and reinventing their threatened spatial identities. What we are witnessing, in fact at the moment, is a multilayered negotiation or competition for the representation and ultimate control of Beirut's spatial and collective identity. Much of Beirut's future image will be largely an outcome of such discrepant claims and representations. The contesting groups (i.e., funding and state agencies, planners, property owners and shareholders, advocacy groups, voluntary associations, and the concerned public), by virtue of their distinct composition and objectives,

vary markedly in their proposed visions and strategies.

The ongoing competition and the public debate it has incited has also served to accentuate the fears of the public, particularly since the struggle is now intimately aligned with the intrusions of global capital, mass culture, and consumerism. Hence the fears of disappearance, erasure, marginalization, and displacement are assuming acute manifestations. The overriding reactions have much in common, in fact, with the three neurophysiological responses to fear and anxiety, namely: 'freeze,' 'flight,' and 'fight.' While the first two normally involve efforts to disengage and distance oneself from the sources of fear, the third is more combative since it involves a measure of direct involvement, negotiation, and/or resisting the threats of erasure.[15] All three, in varying proportions, are visible today in Lebanon.

The first, and perhaps the most common, is a relic of the war. To survive all its cruelties, the Lebanese became deadened and numbed. Like other victims of collective suffering, they became desensitized and overwhelmed by muted anguish and pain. During the war, such callousness (often masquerading as resilience) served them well. It allowed them to survive but also to inflict and rationalize cruelties on the 'other.' By distancing themselves, or cutting themselves off, from the 'other,' the brutality of embattled communities was routinized. Violence became morally indifferent. People could engage in guilt-free violence and kill with impunity precisely because they had restricted contact with their defiled victims. To a large extent, it is 'the group boundaries,' as Randall Collins tells us, "that determine the extent of human sympathy; within these boundaries, humanity prevails; outside them, torture is inflicted without qualm."[16]

There is a painful irony in this mode of response. That which enabled embattled groups and communities to survive the atrocities of strife is clearly disabling them now as they are considering options for re-arranging and sharing common spaces and forging unified national identities. Here again, Collins is quick to remind us that "the point is not to learn to live with the demons, but to take away their powers."[17] The issue, here as well, converges on who is to mobilize or speak on behalf of those who have been rendered 'frozen;' namely, disengaged, inactive and bereft of speech.

There is, after all, something in the character of intense pain, Elaine Scarry tells us, which is "language destroying." "As the content of one's world disintegrates, so the content of one's language disintegrates ... world, self, and voice are lost, or nearly lost, through the intense pain."[18] This is also a reflection of the fact that people in pain are ordinarily bereft of the resources of speech. It is not surprising that the language for pain should in such instances often be evoked by those who are not themselves in pain, but by those who speak on behalf of those who are. Richard Rorty expresses the same thought. He, too, tells us that "victims of cruelty, people who are suffering, do not have much in the way of language. That is why there is no such thing as the 'voice of the oppressed' or the 'language of the victims.' The language the victims once used is not working anymore, and they are suffering too much to put

new words together. So the job of putting their situation into language is going to have to be done for them by somebody else."[19]

A second more interesting and complex response is not purely one of 'flight,' but an effort to distance oneself from the atrocious residues of protracted strife and the disenchanting barbarism of postwar times. This nostalgic retreat is a search for 're-enchantment' evident in the revival of heritage or the imagined nirvana of an idyllic past. Three manifestations of such escapist venues are becoming increasingly visible in various dimensions of daily life and popular culture: 1) the reassertion of communal solidarities, 2) nostalgic longings, and 3) the proliferation of kitsch.

As mentioned earlier, it is understandable why traumatized and threatened groups should seek shelter in their communal solidarities and cloistered spaces. Confessional sentiments and their supportive loyalties, even in times of relative peace and stability, have always been effective sources of social support and political mobilization. But these are not, as Lebanon's fractious history amply demonstrates, unmixed blessings. While they cushion individuals and groups against anomie and the alienation of public life, they also heighten the density of communal hostility and enmity. Hence, more and more Lebanese are today brandishing their confessionalism, if we may invoke a dual metaphor, as both emblem and armor. Emblem, because confessional identity has become the most viable medium for asserting presence and securing vital needs and benefits. Without it groups are literally rootless, nameless, and voiceless. One is not heard or recognized unless confessional allegiance is first disclosed. It is only when an individual is placed within a confessional context that his ideas and assertions are rendered meaningful or worthwhile. Confessionalism is also being used as armor, because it has become a shield against real or imagined threats. The more vulnerable the emblem, the thicker the armor. Conversely, the thicker the armor, the more vulnerable and paranoid other communities become. It is precisely this dialectic between threatened communities and the urge to seek shelter in cloistered worlds which has plagued Lebanon for so long.

There is a curious irony here. Despite the many differences which divide the Lebanese, they are all in a sense homogenized by fear, grief, and bafflement. Fear, as it were, is the tie that binds and holds them together. But it is also fear which keeps them apart. This 'geography of fear' is not sustained by walls or artificial barriers, as one observes in other comparable instances of ghettoization of minorities and ethnic groups. Rather, it is sustained by the psychology of dread, hostile bonding, and ideologies of enmity.

The implications of such heightened forms of spatial and communal solidarities for urban planning are clear. Expressed in more concrete terms, if urbanization normally stands for variety, diversity, mix, and openness, then what has been happening in Lebanon, at least in a majority of areas, is ghettoization. In this sense, the Lebanese are inverting what might be assumed to be the most typical course of evolution in social systems. How, where, and when can such fairly 'closed' spaces become more 'open'? At the least, how can public spaces be made more malleable and accessible to divergent groups which continue to harbor residues of indifference or latent hostility toward each other? Clearly, any premature or imposed schemes which attempt to open up spaces for groups reluctant to mix and interact with others might be counterproductive.

Escape into a reenchanted past has obviously a nostalgic tinge to it. This tinge, however, need not be seen as a pathological retreat into a delusionary past. It could well serve, as Bryan Turner has argued, as a redemptive form of heightened sensitivity, sympathetic awareness of human problems and, hence, it could be 'ethically uplifting.'[20] In this sense it is less of a 'flight' and more of a catharsis for human suffering.

There is much in the vulgarization of traditional forms of cultural expression and the commodification of kitsch and sleazy consumerism, so rampant in postwar Lebanon, which needs to be curtailed and challenged. This nostalgic longing, among a growing segment of disenchanted intellectuals, is at least a form of resistance or refusal to partake in the process of debasement of aesthetic standards or the erosion of *bona fide* and veritable items of cultural heritage. Impotent as such efforts may seem, they express a profound disgust with the trivialization of culture so visible in the emptiness of consumerism and the nihilism of the popular cultural industry. They are also an outcry against the loss of personal autonomy and authenticity. Even the little commonplace, mundane things and routines of daily life – street smells and sounds and other familiar icons and landmarks of place – let alone historic sites and architectural edifices, are allowed to atrophy or be effaced.

Here again this nostalgic impulse is beginning to assume some redemptive and engaging expressions. A variety of grass-roots movements, citizen and advocacy groups, and voluntary associations have been established recently to address problems related to the preservation and protection of the built environment (fig. 3). Earlier special interest groups have had to redefine their objectives and mandates to legitimize and formalize their new interests. A succes-

At the popular cultural level, this resistance to the threat of disappearance is seen in the revival of folk arts, music, and lore, flea markets, artisan shops, and other such exhibits and galleries. Personal memories, autobiographies, nostalgic recollections of one's early childhood and life in gregarious and convivial quarters and neighborhoods of old Beirut are now popular narrative genres.

Fig. 3. A Mandate era building on Damascus Road that has been saved from destruction by public campaign

sion of workshops, seminars, and international conferences have been hosted to draw on the experience of other comparable instances of postwar reconstruction. Periodicals and special issues of noted journals, most prominently perhaps the feature page on 'heritage' by the Beirut daily *An-Nahar*, are devoting increasing coverage to matters related to space, environment, and architectural legacy.

So are pictorial glossy anthologies of Beirut's urban history, old postcards, maps, and other such collectibles. They are all a thriving business. Even the media and advertising industry is exploiting such imagery and nostalgic longing to market their products.

Finally, another mode of retreat or escape from the ugly memories of the war and the drabness or anxieties of the postwar era is the proliferation of kitsch. While kitsch, as an expression of the appeal of popular arts and entertainment whose objective is to "astonish, scintillate, arouse and stir the passions," is not normally perceived as a mode of escape, its rampant allures in Lebanon are symptomatic of the need to forget and, hence, it feeds on collective amnesia and the pervasive desire for popular distractions.[21] It is clearly not as benign or frivolous as it may appear. At the least it should not be dismissed lightly, for it has implications for the readiness of the public to be drawn in and become actively and creatively engaged in the processes of reconstruction and safeguarding the edifying beauty of their natural habitat and built environment.

It is not difficult to account for the allure of kitsch in postwar Lebanon: the need to forget and escape the atrocities and futility of a senseless war; the mindless hedonism and narcissism associated with an urge to make up for lost time; the dullness and trivialization of everyday life; the cultural predispositions of the Lebanese for gregariousness, conviviality, and fun-loving amusement; all of these have contributed to its appeal. So has the ready access to the vectors of high technology and 'infotainment.' Lebanon is not spared the scintillations of such postmodern and global incursions. Indeed, bourgeois decadence, mediocrity, and conspicuous consumption have compounded the public seductions of kitsch.

Its fundamental allures, then, are inherent in the ability of kitsch to offer effortless and easy access to the distractions of global entertainment. It is compatible with the public mood of lethargy, disengagement,

and disinterest. It is also in this sense that kitsch becomes a form of 'false consciousness' and ideological diversion; a novel opiate for aroused and unanchored masses. To the rest, particularly the large segments who have been uprooted from their familiar moorings, kitsch feeds on their hunger for nostalgia. Altogether, it is a form of collective deception since it is sustained by the demand for spurious replicas or the reproduction of objects and art forms whose original aesthetic meanings have been compromised. As Calinescu puts it, kitsch becomes "the aesthetics of deception; for it centers around such questions as imitation, forgery, counterfeit. It is basically a form of lying. Beauty turns out to be easy to fabricate."[22]

In Lebanon, the pathologies of kitsch display more ominous by-products. They do not only debase the aesthetic quality of high culture; folk arts and vernacular architecture are also vulgarized. National symbols, historic, and other cherished monuments become expendable trophies or vacuous media images. This frenzy for the prostitution of cherished cultural artifacts and the consumption of pseudo-art cannot be attributed merely to the impulse for status seeking and conspicuous consumption, potent as these predispositions are in Lebanon today. What constitutes the essence of kitsch, as Adorno among others reminds us, is its promise of 'easy catharsis.'[23] The object of kitsch, after all, is not to please, charm, or refine our tastes and sensibilities. Rather, it promises easy and effortless access to cheap entertainment and scintillating distractions.

Here again the implications for urbanists and architects are vital. How much can they accomplish in restraining or redirecting the distracting allures of kitsch into more redemptive and creative venues? This is not an easy task. Above all, it involves the incorporation or reconciliation of two seemingly opposing options: to tame and restrain the excessive manifestations of kitsch, while acting as sentinels who arouse the disengaged and disinterested by infusing their world with some rejuvenated concern for edifying and embellishing the aesthetic quality of their built environment.

Providing outlets for the release of such creative energies should not be belittled or trivialized. As Nietzsche was keen on reminding us, an aesthetic solution through artistic creation could well serve as a powerful expression for releasing individuals from the constraints of nihilism and resentment. "It is in art that we appear to realize fully our abilities and potential to break through the limitations of our own circumstances."[24]

By far the most promising are the strategies to which various communities have been recently resorting in order to resist threats to their local heritage and identity. Here responses to fear and uncertainty – whether generated by internal displacement, global capital, or mass culture and consumerism – have reawakened and mobilized local groups to reclaim their contested spaces and eroded cultural identities. The emergent spaces reveal more than just residues or pockets of resistance. There are encouraging signs of so-called 'third spaces' or in-between cultures of hybridity, mixture, and tolerance.

This is, after all, what Bennett implied by 'cultures of resistance,' i.e., how a "local spatial system retains many of its traditional institutions and utilizes these to manipulate and control the extreme forces."[25] Hence,

many of the public spaces, more the work of spontaneity than design, are in fact spaces of bargaining and negotiation for national memory and indigenous reemergence. More so than in other such instances of 'globalization,' what we are witnessing in Lebanon today are manifestations of local groups becoming increasingly globalized and, conversely, global incursions being increasingly localized. In other words, we see symptoms of 'inward shifts' where loyalties are redirected toward renewed localism and subnational groups and institutions. We also see 'outward shifts,' where loyalties and interests are being extended to transnational entities.[26]

This is, incidentally, a far cry from the portraits one can extract from recent writings on the spatial and cultural implications of this global/local dialectics. For example, in his polemical but engaging work on the interplay between 'jihad' and 'McWorld,' Benjamin Barber pits McWorld, as the universe of manufactured needs, mass consumption, and mass infotainment against jihad, the Arabic word meaning holy war, as a shorthand for the belligerent politics of religious, tribal, and other forms of bigotry.[27] The former is driven by the cash nexus of greedy capitalists and the bland preferences of mass consumers. The latter is propelled by fierce tribal loyalties, rooted in exclusionary and parochial hatreds. McWorld, with all its promises of a world homogenized by global consumerism, is rapidly dissolving local cultural identities. Jihad, by recreating parochial loyalties, is fragmenting the world into tighter and smaller enclosures. Both are a threat to civil liberties, tolerance, and genuine coexistence. "Jihad pursues a bloody politics of identity, McWorld a bloodless economics of profit. Belonging by default to McWorld, everyone is a consumer; seeking a repository for identity, everyone belongs to some tribe. But no one is a citizen."[28]

We see little of such sharp dichotomies and diametrical representations in postwar Lebanon. While many of the emergent spatial enclaves are cognizant and jealous of their indigenous identities, they are not averse to experiment with more global and ephemeral encounters and cultural products. Likewise, global expectations are being reshaped and rearranged to accommodate local needs and preferences. Expressed in the language of globalization and postmodernity, the so-called 'world without borders,' 'of spatial boundaries,' is not a prerequisite for global encounters. At least this is not what has been transpiring in Lebanon. Indeed, as Martin Albrow argues, one of the key effects of globalization on locality is that people "can reside in one place and have their meaningful social relations almost entirely outside it and across the globe." This, Albrow goes on to say, "means that people use the locality as site and resource for social activities in widely different ways according to the extension of their sociosphere."[29]

Recent case studies of three distinct sites in Beirut (Ain al-Mryseh, Gemmayzeh, and the 'Elisar' project in Beirut's southern suburb) provide instructive and vivid support of how local groups and communities have been able to resist, avert, and rearrange the powers of global agendas. Indeed, in all three instances, globalization has contributed to the strengthening and consolidation of local ties and, thereby, has reinforced the claims of Persky and Weiwel regarding the 'growing localness of the global city' and the globalization of urban structures.

Ayn al-Mryseh, arguably one of the oldest neighborhoods of Beirut, huddles on a picturesque cove on the waterfront of the western flank of the city center. It adjoins the hotel district devastated during the war. In the prewar period, Ayn al-Mryseh, like the rest of Ras Beirut, was a mixed neighborhood with fairly open and liberal lifestyles. Indigenous groups, mostly Sunni, Druze, Shi'a, Greek Orthodox, along with Armenians and Kurds, lived side by side. The location of the American Embassy and the American University of Beirut also drew a rather large portion of foreign residents – diplomats, free-lance intellectuals, journalists, artists, and other itinerant groups. The neighborhood's politics were progressive; its culture cosmopolitan and pluralistic. By virtue of its proximity to the city center and seaport, its inhabitants were mostly merchants, retailers, and clerks in the burgeoning tourist sector of hotels, nightclubs, bars, and sidewalk cafés. The bulk of its indigenous population worked at the port or were fishermen, serving as the mainstay of the neighborhood and its defining character.

The war, more so than in other neighborhoods of Beirut, profoundly changed its character. Because of heavy internecine fighting, Christians and Sunnis were compelled to leave, along with, of course, most of the foreign residents. These were replaced by displaced Shi'a, mostly from the south and Beirut's suburbs.

The massive reconstruction of Beirut's center and adjoining hotel and resort district has enhanced the economic prospects of the neighborhood. Real estate and land values have increased sharply. Traditional property holders and homeowners could not resist the tempting offers of conglomerate capital in collusion with local entrepreneurs. Hence, many of the edifying suburban villas and red-tiled roofs which once graced the shoreline have given way to high-rise office buildings and smart, exclusive resorts.

The inroads of foreign capital is not only transforming its skyline. It is also undermining its moral character and public image. The social fabric is becoming more fractious; its culture more raucous, strident, and kitschy. Shi'ite squatters, awaiting gentrification and other speculative projects, resist eviction from the premises they unlawfully occupy. Hence, fashionable hotels and global resorts stand next to dilapidated homes and squalid backyards. The most jarring event, perhaps, was the invasion of the Hard Rock Cafe, less than fifty yards away from two of the neighborhood's most imposing landmarks: the mosque and Gamal Abdul-Nasser's monument.

Armed with a city zoning law which outlaws the location of entertainment functions too close to religious establishments, the neighborhood association organized to resist such intrusion failed in its efforts to relocate the 'offensive' café. Now, the muezzin's righteous calls to prayer are competing with the impertinent din of loud music just one block away.

The fishermen did not fare any better in their opposition to the construction of Ahlam, a towering forty-floor high-rise comprising an upscale residential complex with a direct underground passage to the Mediterranean and private landings for yachts and speedboats. Ahlam's site is none other than the traditional cove, a miniature harbor, that the fishermen of Ayn al-Mryseh have used for centuries to tend to their time-honored trade and only source of livelihood.

The Mosque Association and that of the Revival of Heritage of Ayn al-Mryseh came to the assistance of the fishermen by lobbying the authorities and mobilizing the support of local politicians to thwart the project. The outcome, after nearly three years of embittered negotiation, was naturally in favor of Ahlam. As compensation, the fishermen have been offered an alternative site as a fishing harbor (three miles further south) which they refuse to recognize or use.

As this local-global tug-of-war has continued, two rather interesting groups or strategies for coping with global intrusions have recently emerged within the neighborhood. Both seem likely to prefigure or presage the direction Ayn al-Mryseh is bound to take in the future. First, a growing number of young fishermen, enticed by the new and appealing jobs the global-resort sector is generating, no longer seem as virulent in their opposition. Indeed, quite a few, to the chagrin of the older generation, are beginning to break away and accept new jobs. A second group, largely members of the Association for the Revival of Heritage, have opted for a more nostalgic and retreatist response. Recognizing that they can do little to contain or tame the forces of global capital, they have taken shelter in preserving and rediscovering the threatened legacy of their history and culture. This is evident in a couple of makeshift 'museums' and galleries established to collect and display items emblematic of its colorful past. [30]

Gemmayzeh, at least spatially, is Ayn al-Mryseh's counterpart on the eastern flank of Beirut's city center. It also adjoins the port with its outlying resort attractions, warehouses, and traffic terminals. Much like Ayn al-Mryseh, the neighborhood emerged as the city's population started to spill beyond the confines of its medieval walls during the second half of the nineteenth century. Both also harbor strong communal loyalties and pride in their unique history and collective identity.

But this is where all similarities end. While Ayn al-Mryseh was confessionally mixed and socially heterogeneous, Gemmayzeh was predominantly an enclave of the Greek Orthodox and Maronite communities. It also remained as such: fairly prosperous Greek Orthodox propertied families were 'invaded' by successive inflows of more modest Maronite craftsmen, retail, and small-scale merchants. This symbiotic association between the two rather distinct socio-economic strata has been one of the defining elements of the neighborhood.

Although located on the demarcating lines separating East and West Beirut, Gemmayzeh was spared the devastations other comparable communities witnessed. Nor was it beleaguered by any dislocations or permanent displacements of its indigenous inhabitants. Except for two moderate high-rise apartments at its remote eastern limits, its skyline has remained largely intact.

As the city center is being virtually reconstructed from scratch, Gemmayzeh is simply remaking and embellishing its original identity. Through APSAD (Association for the Protection of Sites and Ancient Dwellings) and other voluntary associations, efforts are being made to preserve the architectural character of the neighborhood. Plans are being finalized for a joint project with the European Commission to paint and beautify the facades of all buildings originally earmarked for restoration.

The neighborhood is experiencing more than just a cosmetic facelift. Voluntary associations, youth clubs, and local businessmen are collaborating in efforts to revitalize its image and cultural identity as the 'Montmartre' of Beirut. This is in fact how some of the young generation speak of Gemmayzeh. A seasonal festival, *Daraj al-Fann* (Stairway of the Arts), now attracts a devoted following. So do the rehabilitated craft shops, sidewalk cafés, and upscale boutiques.

The neighborhood, finally, does not seem reticent or furtive about announcing its Christian character. Festive decorations during Christmas, a graffiti of crosses and other religious emblems, adorn walls and windows. During the pope's historic visit, his posters were decked with white and yellow ribbons. His only competitor was the equally imposing portrait of the late Bashir Gemayel, the neighborhood's deceased leader.

Altogether, postwar Gemmayzeh does not feel any threat to its identity or future prospects. In fact, the destruction and long-term reconstruction of the city center is largely viewed with indifference and disregard, mixed with some derision and sarcasm. Indeed, Beirut's center is often contemptuously dismissed as 'Solidere.' [31]

While Ayn al-Mryseh and Gemmayzeh are neighborhoods rich in history and uncontested collective memory, the Elisar Project is an attempt to forge an identity for a suburban slum with no history to speak of other than the besmirched and defiled image of a squalid space. It is, to borrow Benjamin's apt label, Beirut's "site of dereliction," an eyesore defamed with every slur possible. Indeed, the neutral expression, *dahiya al janubiyya* (literally, the southern suburb) has been debased to become a synonym for degradation, squalor, anarchy, squatters, illegality, and aberrant behavior.

Late in the 1960s, as successive waves of displaced Shi'ite refugees were fleeing the chronically embattled villages in southern Lebanon, the *dahiya* quickly acquired the label of Lebanon's 'Misery Belt': a ghetto seething with feelings of neglect and abandonment and, hence, accessible to political dissent, mobilization, and violence. This constructed global image, spawned and reinforced by the international media, belies, of course, much of the reality of the suburb. It is not so monolithic in its composition or misery. Nor is it a hotbed of dissidents and marginalized groups eager to wreak vengeance on a neglectful government and an indifferent public. As an open, coveted space, though, it has always managed to attract a much larger share of the dispossessed than other marginal and impoverished suburbs. During the war, its demographic and sectarian composition was sharply altered as other displaced groups – predominantly from the Beqa' and the south – sought it for shelter. Initially, for example, the Shi'ite-Maronite balance was slightly tilted in favor of the latter. Today, approximately 80 percent of the southern suburbs' inhabitants are Shi'ites, as described in Harb el-Kak's chapter in this volume.

The political mobilization of the *dahiya* began before the war. First, the relatively moderate Amal Movement, inspired by the late Imam Musa al-Sadr, gained considerable popularity. Early in the 1970s it was joined by Hizbullah and other more radical 'Islamic' factions. Hizbullah, by virtue of its aggressive outreach programs of social, educational, and medical welfare, has been able to gain great inroads and consolidate its virtual hegemony over the area. It is, however, still rivaled by other, lesser political factions in the production and management of urban services. Today, this plethora of political actors has to reckon with the growing efforts of the government to regain its legitimate presence.

It was largely part of such efforts, and to convey Rafik Hariri's public image as someone obsessively and exclusively interested in the rehabilitation of downtown Beirut, that the Elisar Project was launched in 1992.[32] Conceived as an infrastructure rehabilitation works, it evolved by 1994 into a real estate company legitimized by the same law which established Solidere. Amal and Hizbullah immediately challenged and contested its formation as a private company. The ensuing power struggle resulted in some significant modification whereby the company was transformed into a public establishment with the state becoming in effect the major actor in the reorganization of the project. More important, perhaps, Amal and Hizbullah gained their own representatives on Elisar's board.

Despite the sharp antagonisms between the three major rivals (Hariri, Amal, and Hizbullah), the project was uniformly conceived and perceived as a scheme for development and modernization. The vision and underlying ideology of the overall design comply with other such urban 'utopias' intended to introduce a hygienic element of 'cleansing' and relocation through social housing and supportive public rehabilitative strategies.

Prospects for Urbanists

Paul Rabinow, in his analysis of the socio-cultural history of France between 1830 and 1930, delineates a constellation of thought, action, and passions underlying what he terms the "social technologies of pacification" or tools for reforming and controlling the inherent antagonisms between space and society, the forms and norms France was experiencing during that eventful century.[33] Rabinow identifies a set of actors – ranging from aristocratic dandies, governors, philanthropists, to architects, intellectuals, and urban reformers – who were all infused with this passion to 'pacify the pathos' and, consequently, articulated a set of pragmatic solutions to public problems in times of crisis such as wars, epidemics, strikes, etc. Despite their divergent backgrounds, they shared two common perspectives: bitterness about the institutional and cultural crisis of their society, and an unshaken faith in positive science or the consolidation of power and knowledge in the production and regulation of a peaceful and productive social order.

Hard-nosed positivism might have fallen onto hard times. One can, however, still glean several persuasive examples of such successful consolidation from Rabinow's analysis. The recent experience of the Lebanese themselves has also been reassuring in this regard. It is at least proof that as intricate as the problems are, pacifying Lebanon's pathos is not insurmountable. Much can and has already been done to prepare for this blissful eventuality.

In my view, urban designers, architects, intellectuals, humanists of all shades and persuasions, along with other outraged but muted groups, are particularly qualified to play this role. Until recently, they had been shunted aside and trivialized. They now have to shed their timidity and reclaim the redemptive promises of their professions. By mobilizing aesthetic sensibilities, other artistic energies, and popular cultural expressions in everyday life, they can do much to arouse the public to redeem its maligned heritage. More importantly, they can prod the Lebanese to turn outward and transcend their parochial identities and to connect with others. City life is, after all, an ideal environment for acting out and working out personal and social conflicts.

Three more reasons can be advanced by way of justifying why today such groups are ideally suited to articulate this new language and vision on behalf of their besieged compatriots. First, a disproportionate number of such groups has been, for much of the duration of the war, in diaspora. Every culture has its own diaspora. Lebanon's trials with exile and dispersal have been quite acute. They were, however, also enabling. Mavericks, as histories of itinerant populations tell us, rarely stay at home. Just as the traditional Lebanese *mkari* (peddler) always wandered beyond the narrow confines of his bounded village and came back with tales, goods, and tidbits of the world beyond, we have today the makings of a growing generation of global multiculturalists. Both established and young cohorts of gifted professionals and entrepreneurs have been expanding their skills and experiences abroad. Many are rightfully disillusioned, perhaps bitter, but nonetheless have not been 'frozen stiff' by the harrowing events. They only experienced the war vicariously, from a distance. Hence, they have not become as numbed or cynical as others. Nor do they harbor deep-seated hostility toward other groups. Second, though exiled, they have not severed their ties to nor lost their nostalgia for their native culture. They bring in comparative visions, not the alien constructs of 'foreign experts' imposed on unfamiliar and unreceptive milieus. Finally, by virtue of such multicultural and global sympathies, they are less likely to perceive their projects as efforts for privileging or empowering one group or community over another. Hence, they are predisposed to transcend their parochialism as an antidote for doing away with the geography of fear and its demarcating lines and enclosures.

The first and most vital task confronting architects and planners is to arouse among the Lebanese a few cardinal but overlooked realities about the interplay between space and well-being. Self-evident as it may be, they must be made to realize that the quality of the environment has an impact on their lives, in the sense of who they are and their attitudes toward others. Indeed, repeated research findings in fields such as photobiology, color therapy, and other fairly novel areas of exploration all substantiate the extent to which physical and emotional well-

being, even creativity, are intimately associated with the aesthetic and enriching attributes of environment.[34] Put simply, the places where we spend our time affect the people we are and can become. Hence, as the places around us change – whether fortuitously or by design, carelessly or in good faith – we too are bound to change. As such, despoiling our natural habitat does not only damage our cities and living spaces, it can also damage the quality of our lives.

Second, the Lebanese must be reassured that their territorial commitments, aberrant as they seem at the moment, are understandable and legitimate. But so is their need to break away. Being spatially anchored reinforces their need for shelter, security, and solidarity. Like other territorialized groups, they become obsessed with boundary delineation and safeguarding their community against trespassers and interlopers. The needs for wonder, exhilaration, exposure to new sensations, world views, the elevation of our appreciative sympathies – which are all enhanced through connectedness with strangers – are also equally vital for our sustenance. Witness the euphoria of children in an urban playground who, as they play, cut themselves off from the ties of family and home; observe the excitement of visitors in a bustling city street. Look how accomplished, gifted, and daring Lebanese students have become in foreign capitals and universities, once they have broken their ties with their familiar surroundings.

The village *mkari*, in an admittedly much different time and place, played much the same role. He, too, broke away, crossed barriers and was a 'cultural broker' of sorts precisely because he availed himself of new sensations and contacts. He had no aversion to strangers. He wandered away but always managed to return home. We need to revive and extend the ethos of the *mkari* as the prototype of an idyllic national character. With all his folk eccentricities, he epitomizes some of the enabling virtues of a 'traveler' and a 'potentate.'

Edward Said employs this imagery to construct two archetypes for elucidating the interplay between identity, authority, and freedom in an academic environment. In the ideal academy, Said tells us, "we should regard knowledge as something for which to risk identity, and we should think of academic freedom as an invitation to give up on identity in the hope of understanding and perhaps even assuming more than one. We must always view the academy as a place to voyage in, owning none of it but at home everywhere in it."[35] Are these not also the attributes we should seek in equipping our cities or the places and institutions within them to render them more permeable for this kind of journey? Insightfully, Said goes on to tell us that "the image of the traveler depends not on power, but on motion, on a willingness to go into different worlds, use different idioms, and understand a variety of disguises, masks, and rhetoric. Travelers must suspend the claim of customary routine in order to live in new rhythms and rituals. Most of all, and most unlike the potentate who must guard only one place and defend its frontiers, the traveler crosses over, traverses territory, and abandons fixed positions, all the time."[36]

Ideally, this could well serve as a leitmotif of urbanists and town planners, i.e., to create the conditions germane for this transformation of Lebanese 'potentates' into 'travelers.' In other words, we have to find some way of making 'ghettos' and all other cloistered spaces more open to facilitate voyaging, traversing, and crossing over. They should be like all other envisioned public spaces, redesigned in such a way that people can move on when the need for communal support and shelter is no longer essential. We must all bear in mind that any form of confinement, in the long run, becomes a deprivation. Conversely, open urban spaces can also be rendered more genial to cushion groups against the vicissitudes of city life.

The image of the Lebanese as a spatially anchored people, compulsively huddling in and defending its domains (i.e., the compact enclosures of family and neighborhood) against potential trespassers, needs to be modified. The same goes for the phobic and nostalgic drive for heritage and the longing to reclaim seemingly unique communal legacies, something that today borders on becoming a national pastime. The Lebanese once longed for the outdoors, at least until the war terrorized their public spaces. Here again, urban design can do much to restore the conviviality of such open spaces. Street life, after all, is emblematic of urban provocation and arousal precisely because one lets go, so to speak, and drops one's conventional reserve toward 'others.'

This impulse to venture beyond familiar enclaves is always driven by mixed emotions. There is the exuberance of strange places, the pleasure and excitement of being drawn out of one's secure routines to encounter the novel and surprising. This induces an element of anxiety and fearfulness. But we also take pleasure in being open to and interested in people we experience as 'different.' Both these impulses, the need for intimacy and the need for distance; the urge to break away and the equally trenchant urge to reconnect with one's original moorings, are essential for human sustenance. They also account for much of the vitality of open and permeable spaces. To borrow a trite but apt metaphor, we need at different interludes in our lives, both "roots" and "wings." Roots nourish our need for security, solidarity, commitment, and heritage. Wings express our longing for movement, breaking away, and taking occasional flights of fancy. It behooves us to heed and incorporate both impulses in strategies for spatial re-arrangement.

The urbanist, in other words, has to design weak borders rather than strong walls. This means spaces constructed malleably enough to permit constant alterations and shifts. There is still much to commend in Robert Frost's adage that "good fences make good neighbors." Fences are not, after all, impregnable barriers. They merely delineate borders, often through hedges, shrubs, and other demarcating but scaleable objects. Indeed, fences are borders and not boundaries. Borders are usually more porous and malleable; hence they are less likely to serve as partitions between one area and another. Boundaries, on the other hand, conjure up images of confinement and exclusion.

Finally, urbanists must not shy away from another redemptive role not conventionally linked to their constructive or reconstructive ventures. Whatever strategies they propose, they must bear in mind that the mere involvement of the Lebanese in such common and shared interests (i.e., recovering their country's maligned heritage) could bring them closer together and help in transcending their parochial identities. By doing so, they are also creating opportunities for disengaged groups to reclaim their right to be engaged in redefining their collective memory and stewardship over the spaces they inhabit and bequeath to future generations.

Notes

1. See C. Lasch, "The Communitarian Critique of Liberalism," in C.E. Reynolds and R.V. Norman, eds., *Community in America: The Challenge of Habits of the Heart* (Berkeley: University of California Press, 1988), p. 178.
2. E. Gellner, *Culture, Identity and Polities* (Cambridge: Cambridge University Press, 1988).
3. D. MacCannell, *The Tourist: A New Theory of the Leisure Class* (New York: Schoken, 1989).
4. P. Jedlowski, "Simmel on Memory," in M. Kaern, B.S. Philips, and R.S. Cohen, eds., *George Simmel and Contemporary Sociology* (Dordrecht: Kluwer, 1990).
5. B. Barber, *Jihad vs McWorld* (New York: Ballantine Books, 1996), p. 167.
6. N. Ehm, *Architecture of Fear* (New York: Princeton Architectural Press, 1997).
7. A critical care of established architects and urbanists, particularly those who had taken part in prewar construction (Assem Salam, Henri Eddeh, Pierre el-Khoury, Jad Tabet) have been very active in launching campaigns to disclose the foibles and shortcomings of Solidere and associated projects and schemes. These critical mentors have been recently joined by a growing number of a fairly young, mostly Western-trained architects and urbanists. On their own or through APSAD (Association for the Protection of Sites and Ancient Dwellings) and the revived Order of Engineers and Architects, they too have added their dissenting voices and proposed more viable alternatives. Hashim Sarkis, Habib Debs, Joe Nasr, Maha Yahya, Joumana Ghandour Atallah, Oussama Kabbani come to mind.
8. Chadwick Alger (1996) has employed these terms adapted from Barri Anne Brown's initial usage for elucidating some of the local responses to global intrusions.
9. K. Erikson, *Everything in its Path: Destruction of the Communily in the Buffalo Creek Flood* (New York: Simon and Schuster, 1976).
10. S. Nasr, "New Social Realities and Postwar Lebnaon," in S. Khalaf and P. Khoury, eds., *Recovering Beirut: Prospects for Urban Reconstruction* (Leiden: E.J. Brill, 1993).
11. Ibid.
12. H. Sarkis, "Territorial Claims: Post-War Attitudes Towards the Built Environment," in S. Khalaf and P. Khoury, eds., *Recovering Beirut: Prospects for Urban Reconstruction* (Leiden: E.J. Brill, 1993).
13. In an evocative, often searing memoir of her encounters with civil strife in Beirut, Jean Said Makdisi (1990) provides an amusing but instructive "Glossary of Terms Used in Times of Crisis."
14. M. Yahya, "Reconstituting Space: The Aberration of the Urban in Beirut," in S. Khalaf and P. Khoury, eds., *Recovering Beirut: Prospects for Urban Reconstruction* (Leiden: E.J. Brill, 1993).
15. A recent edited volume by Nan Ellin (1997) contains meaningful theoretical and empirical evidence and instructive case studies substantiating the interplay between architecture, urban design, and fear.
16. R. Collins, "The Three Faces of Cruelty: Towards a Comparative Study of Violence," in *Theory and Society*, vol. 1, 1974, p. 417.
17. Ibid., p. 416.
18. E. Scarry, *The Body in Pain: The Making and Unmaking of the World* (New York: Oxford University Press, 1985), p. 35.
19. R. Rorty, *Contingency, Irony, and Solidarity* (Cambridge: Cambridge University Press, 1989).
20. B. Turner, "A Note on Nostalgia," in *Theory, Culture and Society*, vol. 4 (1), 1987, p. 149.
21. M. Calinescu, *Five Faces of Modernity* (Durham: Duke University Press, 1987), p. 238.
22. Ibid., p. 228.
23. T. Adorno, *Philosophy of Modern Music* (New York: Seabury Press, 1973).
24. G. Stauth and B.S. Turner, "Nostalgia, Postmodernism and the Critique of Mass Culture," in *Theory, Culture and Society*, vol. 5, 1988, p. 517.
25. Bennett as cited in Z. Mlinar, ed., *Globalization and Territorial Identities* (England: Avebury, 1996), p. 80.
26. R.B.A. DiMuccio and J. Rosenau, "Turbulence and Sovereignty in the World Politics: Explaining the Relocation of Legitimacy in the 1990s and Beyond" in Z. Mlinar, ed., *Globalization and Territorial Identities* (England: Avebury, 1996), p. 62.
27. Barber, *Jihad vs McWorld*.
28. Ibid., p. 8.
29. M. Albrow, "Traveling Beyond Local Cultures," in J. Eade, ed., *Living in the Global City* (London and New York: Routledge, 1977), p. 53.
30. For further details see A. Swalha, "Gloc-

alization: Community Responses to Global Initiative in Ayn al-Mryseh," unpublished paper, 1997.

31. For further elaboration see D. Genberg, "The Mutagenic Maquette of Beirut: A real-estate company's claim to a city," unpublished paper, CBR, American University of Beirut, 1997.

32. Incidentally, Elisar derives its name from an ancient legend of a Phoenician queen who escaped Tyre to establish the city of Carthage. Prime Minister Hariri, a Sunni from Saida, suggested the name to commemorate this prehistoric myth. Nabih Berci, leaders of Hizbullah, and other Shi'ite notables were of course delighted to adopt the name to reassert, thereby, Shi'ite control over the southern suburb.

33. P. Rabinow, *French Modern* (Cambridge, Mass.: MIT Press, 1989).

34. T. Hiss, *The Experience of Space* (New York: Vintage Books, 1990), p. 23.

35. E. Said, "Identity, Authority, and Freedom: The Potentate and the Traveler," in *Transition*, 54, 1991, p. 18.

36. Ibid., p. 8.

The Macroeconomic Basis of Reconstruction

by
Freddie C. Baz

From a macroeconomic perspective, the reconstruction of Beirut cannot be conceived of successfully and independently from that of the nation. The present plans for reconstruction not only cover the rehabilitation of what has been physically damaged by two decades of war, but also aim to reposition Lebanon as a focal point of business in the Middle East. Moreover, such a repositioning will be necessary if high standards of living and individual welfare are to be secured for the generations to come.

The following presentation will begin with a review of the war damages which largely determine the challenges for reconstruction and the fundamental aspects of economic recovery which must lie at the foundations of the reconstruction plan. This will be followed by a basic outline of the plan and its relevant components. Commentary will then be made on the likely future investment environment in Lebanon, together with some concluding remarks on overall economic prospects in the relatively near future.

The Consequences of War and Economic Recovery

Seventeen years of war in Lebanon led to heavy human, material, and, consequently, economic losses. Around 170,000 persons died, 800,000 were displaced, and 900,000, or 27 percent of the Lebanese population, emigrated. The result was a massive brain drain.[1] The major components of the basic infrastructure were destroyed. Less than half of the 450,000 existing phone lines were functioning, only 35 percent of the 1,350-megawatt capacity of power plants was available, 80 percent of water reserves were polluted, and all filtering stations of the water-waste treatment facilities were out of service. In addition, the road infrastructure required total rehabilitation and only half the public schools were operational.

At the private sector level, the production capacity of industry was reduced to 25 percent of its potential. About 300,000 dwellings were damaged and 40,000 cars were burned. The hospital capacity dropped to 30 percent and that of hotels to 50 percent. Material damages were estimated to be U.S. $12 billion, while opportunity costs rose to a minimum of $60 billion. Needless to say, these developments completely disrupted the equilibrium of public finance, as well as the functioning of markets. This, in turn, resulted in a drastic fall in the level of income and the standard of living and welfare of most Lebanese. Between 1982 and 1990, real Gross Domestic Product (GDP) decreased by 50 percent in volume. Inflation was reported to be 92 percent per annum on average, and the Lebanese pound depreciated, again on average, by 82 percent per annum.

After such dramatic developments, the present challenge of economic recovery is to raise per capita income quickly to its prewar level and, within an acceptable time limit, to a higher, steady-state position. The challenges ahead are numerous (fig. 1) and involve ensuring, over the period between say 1995 to 2007, a cumulative volume of investment of about $60 billion in order to generate the requisite average GDP growth of 6 to 8 percent per annum needed to raise per capita income in 2007 to its real 1974 level. Only later on, in the 2030s, can a steady-state income level be achieved under such conditions. Throughout, reconstruction is required, since private investment, the major drive of economic growth, will not materialize without a fully rehabilitated infrastructure, despite an otherwise favorable business climate prevailing in Lebanon.

The Fundamentals of Lebanon's Recovery Plan

The fundamentals of Lebanon's recovery are threefold (fig. 2). First, a macroeconomic adjustment policy must be instituted in order to reduce the fundamental imbalances and to stabilize the domestic currency. These measures aim to improve conditions for public finance, contain inflation, align interest rates, improve output growth rates, and, in short, firmly establish the fundamentals of future sustainable growth. Second, a reconstruction plan for the economic, physical, and social infrastructure must also be instituted, extending over at least thirteen

years and aimed at improving the efficiency of the private sector, and at reestablishing Beirut as a focal point for business in the Middle East (fig. 3). Third, a comprehensive administrative reform must be undertaken to improve the efficiency of the public sector and to increase the effectiveness of private investment.

As alluded to earlier, the reconstruction plan – titled Horizon 2000 – is currently under execution and extends over the next thirteen years. It primarily consists of securing the basic infrastructure necessary to stimulate the development of productive sectors, ensuring a balanced regional distribution of public investment and actively sustaining private initiatives. A total of $18 billion worth of investment has been targeted, of which 32 percent will be allocated to physical infrastructure, 22 percent to social infrastructure, 15 percent to public services, 14 percent to productive sectors, and 17 percent to various investment expenditures.

The rehabilitation of the basic infrastructure primarily covers increasing power plant capacity to 2000 megawatts, extending the phone network to 1 million electronic lines and 250,000 cellular lines, and enlarging the road network to 8,000 kilometers, as well as integrating it into the existing regional network (fig. 4). These projects; with a global cost of $5.7 billion, have a double strategic importance for Lebanon that is both local and regional. At the domestic level, the improvement of the local communication and distribution network will generate productivity gains, probably on the order of 10 percent of GDP per annum. At the regional level, the investment will allow a better integration of Lebanon into the emerging Middle

Fig. 1. The challenges of Lebanon's economic recovery

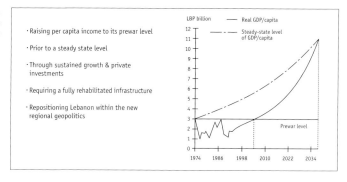

· Raising per capita income to its prewar level

· Prior to a steady state level

· Through sustained growth & private investments

· Requiring a fully rehabilitated infrastructure

· Repositioning Lebanon within the new regional geopolitics

Fig. 2. The fundamentals of Lebanon's recovery plan

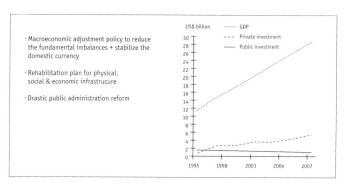

· Macroeconomic adjustment policy to reduce the fundamental imbalances + stabilize the domestic currency

· Rehabilitation plan for physical, social & economic infrastrucure

· Drastic public administration reform

Fig. 3. Horizon 2000: Sectoral components

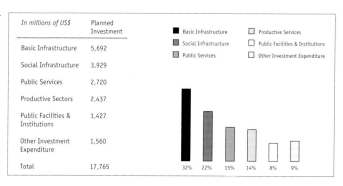

In millions of US$	Planned Investment
Basic Infrastructure	5,692
Social Infrastructure	3,929
Public Services	2,720
Productive Sectors	2,437
Public Facilities & Institutions	1,427
Other Investment Expenditure	1,560
Total	17,765

Basic Infrastructure
Social Infrastructure
Public Services
Productive Services
Public Facilities & Institutions
Other Investment Expenditure

32% 22% 15% 14% 8% 9%

Fig. 4. Horizon 2000: Basic infrastructure

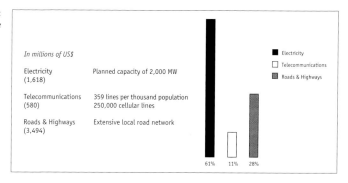

In millions of US$	
Electricity (1,618)	Planned capacity of 2,000 MW
Telecommunications (580)	359 lines per thousand population 250,000 cellular lines
Roads & Highways (3,494)	Extensive local road network

Electricity
Telecommunications
Roads & Highways

61% 11% 28%

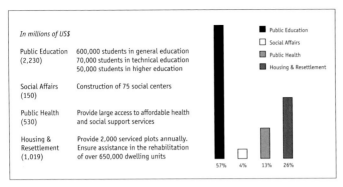

Fig. 5. Horizon 2000: Social infrastructure

In millions of US$

Public Education (2,230) — 600,000 students in general education / 70,000 students in technical education / 50,000 students in higher education

Social Affairs (150) — Construction of 75 social centers

Public Health (530) — Provide large access to affordable health and social support services

Housing & Resettlement (1,019) — Provide 2,000 serviced plots annually. Ensure assistance in the rehabilitation of over 650,000 dwelling units

Legend: Public Education, Social Affairs, Public Health, Housing & Resettlement

57% 4% 13% 26%

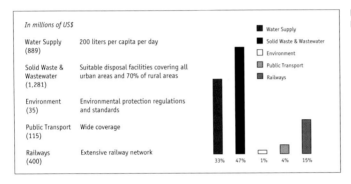

Fig. 6. Horizon 2000: Public services

In millions of US$

Water Supply (889) — 200 liters per capita per day

Solid Waste & Wastewater (1,281) — Suitable disposal facilities covering all urban areas and 70% of rural areas

Environment (35) — Environmental protection regulations and standards

Public Transport (115) — Wide coverage

Railways (400) — Extensive railway network

Legend: Water Supply, Solid Waste & Wastewater, Environment, Public Transport, Railways

33% 47% 1% 4% 15%

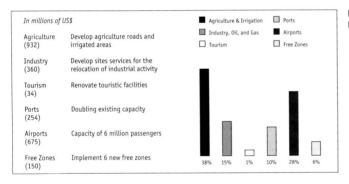

Fig. 7. Horizon 2000: Productive services

In millions of US$

Agriculture (932) — Develop agriculture roads and irrigated areas

Industry (360) — Develop sites services for the relocation of industrial activity

Tourism (34) — Renovate touristic facilities

Ports (254) — Doubling existing capacity

Airports (675) — Capacity of 6 million passengers

Free Zones (150) — Implement 6 new free zones

Legend: Agriculture & Irrigation, Ports, Industry, Oil, and Gas, Airports, Tourism, Free Zones

38% 15% 1% 10% 28% 6%

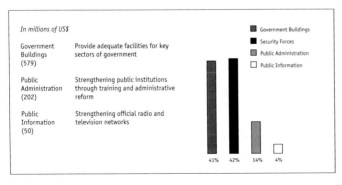

Fig. 8. Horizon 2000: Public facilities and institutions

In millions of US$

Government Buildings (579) — Provide adequate facilities for key sectors of government

Public Administration (202) — Strengthening public institutions through training and administrative reform

Public Information (50) — Strengthening official radio and television networks

Legend: Government Buildings, Security Forces, Public Administration, Public Information

41% 42% 14% 4%

Fig. 9. Horizon 2000: Regional facilities

	Total amount millions of US$	US$ per capita	Index per capita
Beirut	897	1,554	100
Beirut suburbs	1,513	2,444	158
Other regions of Mount Lebanon	1,992	3,138	203
North Lebanon	1,855	2,688	174
Biqa	1,250	3,048	197
South Lebanon	1,221	3,392	220
Nabatiyeh	693	3,499	227
Non distributed expenditures	8,343		

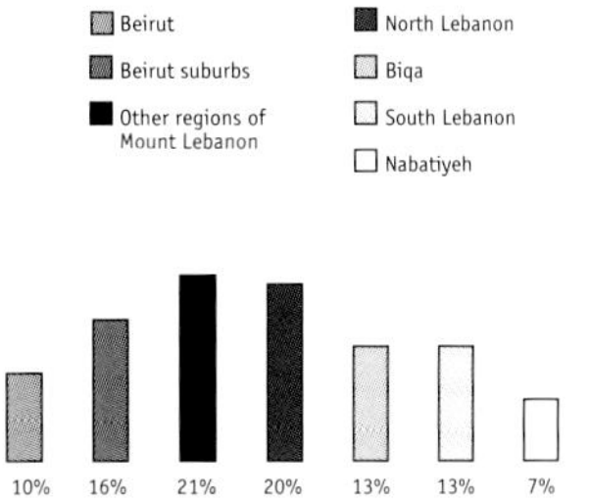

Legend: Beirut · North Lebanon · Beirut suburbs · Biqa · Other regions of Mount Lebanon · South Lebanon · Nabatiyeh

Bar chart values: 10% 16% 21% 20% 13% 13% 7%

East, as well as safeguarding its significant role and position and avoiding the risk of economic marginalization.

The rehabilitation of the social infrastructure primarily consists in securing 2,000 serviced residential plots annually, and in assisting in the restoration of damaged dwelling units (fig. 5). It also aims at increasing public-sector school enrollment to 600,000 students in general education, 70,000 students in technical education, and 50,000 students in higher education. The plan also provides for broad access to affordable health and social support services. These projects, with a global cost of $3.9 billion, will certainly improve the social circumstances of Lebanon, which, according to UN statistics, are already historically above the average of neighboring countries.

The improvement in public services will include developing an extensive public transport network, ensuring 160 liters per capita of drinking water per day, and the installation of a comprehensive waste-water and solid waste treatment system (fig. 6). In addition, the protection of the environment, a strategic issue for Lebanon, is at the heart of the plan, which allocates $2.7 billion for achieving these objectives.

Support of productive industrial sectors within the plan entails, for agriculture, the extension of irrigated areas, the safeguarding of agricultural lands, and extensive reforestation (fig. 7). For manufacturing industry, the plan provides for adequate infrastructure and for the relocation of industrial activity to more productive sites, including improvement of oil warehousing and refining facilities. Finally, for tourism, specific facilities and other related premises will be fully developed and renovated. The plan also provides for doubling Beirut's port capacity through the creation of a fifth basin, and for raising the airport capacity to 6 million passengers. The execution of all these projects will cost around $2.4 billion.

A major objective of the reconstruction plan is to secure a balanced regional distribution of projects. The government is aware of the prevailing discrepancies in the distribution of access to public facilities and services, and of the uneven regional impact of direct war damage (fig. 8). This concern is best denoted in terms of per capita investment by region, which reveals higher concentrations in the rural areas when compared to Beirut and its suburbs (fig. 9).

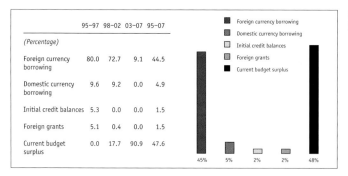

	95–97	98–02	03–07	95–07
(Percentage)				
Foreign currency borrowing	80.0	72.7	9.1	44.5
Domestic currency borrowing	9.6	9.2	0.0	4.9
Initial credit balances	5.3	0.0	0.0	1.5
Foreign grants	5.1	0.4	0.0	1.5
Current budget surplus	0.0	17.7	90.9	47.6

Foreign currency borrowing
Domestic currency borrowing
Initial credit balances
Foreign grants
Current budget surplus

45% 5% 2% 2% 48%

Fig. 10. Horizon 2000: Financing issues

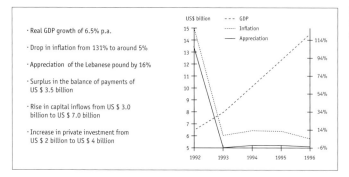

· Real GDP growth of 6.5% p.a.

· Drop in inflation from 131% to around 5%

· Appreciation of the Lebanese pound by 16%

· Surplus in the balance of payments of US $ 3.5 billion

· Rise in capital inflows from US $ 3.0 billion to US $ 7.0 billion

· Increase in private investment from US $ 2 billion to US $ 4 billion

US$ billion   - - - GDP
.... Inflation
——— Appreciation

Fig. 11. Investment environment: macroeconomic stability 1992–1996

At this stage, it is worth commenting on how $18 billion can be secured to finance all these projects (fig. 10). No doubt, sources of funding will vary substantially as the program proceeds. Nevertheless, in order of priority, the sources seem likely to be: foreign currency borrowing, domestic currency borrowing, initial credit balances, foreign grants, and current budget surpluses. To date, available and promised foreign financing amounts to around $3 billion, consisting of soft loans and grants, of which approximately 80 percent have been allocated, with the agreement of donors, to specific projects or sectors. Still, domestic financing issues are pressing and are tied to the materialization of the basic macroeconomic assumptions of the plan, mainly the achievement of an average real GDP growth of 6 to 8 percent per annum, an average interest rate of 10 percent on the Lebanese pound, and a resource mobilization ratio of 24 percent. So far, available indicators show that these assumptions are achievable, provided a political consensus is secured among decision makers. Within this perspective, the rehabilitated infrastructure, coupled with a favorable business environment, will certainly contribute to securing foreign capital and to channeling it toward productive investment and improvement of the Lebanese level of income and the standard of living.

The Investment Environment

At this stage it is important to focus on the comparative advantages of the emerging business environment, without which it is difficult to assess the full dimensions and scope of the reconstruction plan (fig. 11). Essentially, reconstruction takes place within the context of a positive macroeconomic outlook, aimed at luring investment incentives and extensive investment guarantees. First, at the level of macroeconomic stability which is a prerequisite for any investment decision, major goals have already been reached. Four years after its implementation, the macroeconomic adjustment policy is showing very positive results over the period from 1991 to 1996. For instance, real GDP grew by an average of 6.5 percent per annum, inflation fell from 131 percent to around 6 percent, and the exchange rate appreciated by 16 percent.

Consequently, capital inflows increased from $3 billion to $7 billion, and private investment rose from $2 billion to approximately $4 billion today. In addition, these investments were realized within a very favorable business environment, characterized by a renovated infrastructure, skilled human resources with a literacy rate of 81 percent, flexible business laws allowing ten different types of companies, and very extensive private, commercial, and investment banking services.

Second, what has made Lebanon attractive to foreign direct investment has been its long tradition of liberal trade and investment policies. Government intervention has historically been minimal, and the private sector contribution to the economy has always been around 80 percent. There are no restrictions on entry, exit, or access, for instance, to foreign exchange in Lebanon. Foreign investors can import and export capital freely in any form they wish. Taxation is very lenient with a flat 10 percent corporate tax rate and 5 percent withholding tax. In addition, there is essentially free access for foreign investors.

Lebanon has certainly gone through some difficult times, but today, with the return of peace and stability, its favorable economic conditions are increasingly confirming its potential as a significant emerging market in the region. With an economy currently operating at 70 percent of full capacity, where companies are in the process of replenishing their capital assets, Lebanon does seem likely to attain the annual growth rates of 6 to 8 percent. Furthermore, international financial sources anticipate a $7 billion capitalization for the Beirut Stock Exchange in the year 2000. Moreover, at the beginning of 1997, Lebanon was awarded its first international credit ratings, paving the way for additional foreign involvement in the reconstruction process and putting Lebanon under careful scrutiny from the international investment community.

A third and further incentive for private investment is the extensive guarantees that have been made available. In fact, Lebanon is included in the export credit guarantee schemes of COFACE, ECGD, and HERMES, which can provide for a mixture of political and economic risks. In addition, the EXIM Bank of the United States decided in November 1994 to resume its financing programs in Lebanon after twenty years of absence. Furthermore, Lebanon joined the American Overseas Private Investments Corporation, the Multilateral Investment Guarantee Agency, and the Arab Investments Guarantee Organism. Domestically, the National Investment Guarantee Corporation offers a ten-year insurance policy which covers fixed assets against non-economic risks, such as wars, riots, revolutions, and nationalization.

Conclusion

As stated earlier, the efficiency of the Lebanese reconstruction plan cannot be assessed independently of the macroeconomic and business environments, which together underlie the increased competitiveness of the Lebanese economy and the generation of supplementary value added ultimately required to boost the standard of living and welfare. Today there is a rising debate in Lebanon as to the plan's dimension and priorities, especially with regard to infrastructure. Nevertheless, many believe that this debate is somewhat misplaced if consideration is given to the major efforts, mentioned earlier, required to reach even one measure of success, such as the steady-state level of per capita income. Whatever the plan's gaps, and they definitely do exist, their costs do not outweigh the costs of waiting and delay, which would almost certainly result in economic marginalization in a rapidly evolving Middle Eastern economic environment.

In all cases, it is difficult to determine precisely the actual standard of infrastructure and services required to reach the plan's goals, but the available measures suggest that present service is poor. The waiting time to obtain a telephone connection, for example, and the percentage of unsuccessful calls

are high by all standards. Road maintenance is poor, with less than 50 percent of paved roads in good condition. Electrical losses range between 12 and 16 percent of total production.

Clearly the need for more advanced infrastructure services is high. Comparing the current supply of basic infrastructure services to what is available today in countries within the $2,000 to $4,000 annual income range gives us some indication of the actual need for upgrades. On this basis, power generation should be increased six times. Telephone lines per capita should be multiplied 1.7 times. The access to safe drinking water should rise by 5 percent, and paved roads per capita should be doubled.

In the years of recovery that lie ahead, Lebanon is still confronted with two major challenges. The first is to undertake structural institutional reforms, and the second is to restore confidence in its productive capacities. One must remain confident in the final outcome of the national reconciliation process and economic recovery since the pragmatism of the Lebanese has always offset their worries. Regardless of specific political outlook, Lebanon and Beirut will undeniably maintain their privileged position as a focal point of business in the Middle East.

Note

1. All data was provided by the Economic Analysis Unit of the Banque Audi Sal, Beirut, Lebanon, 1997.

Transforming the Site of Dereliction into the Urban Culture of Modernity: Beirut's Southern Suburb and Elisar Project

by
Mona Harb el-Kak

The southern suburb is a space that several players want to control, each working more or less autonomously from the public sphere, and each having their own strategy, ideology, and manner of representing themselves. They manage their territories through a network of organizations acting on different levels in the fields of education, culture, social services, and sanitation. Their relationships vary between alliances or conflicts according to time and space. They gather around issues common to their territories which intersect, overlap, and are redefined according to the evolution of their power relations. Negotiations over common issues reflect the tensions and coalitions inherent to their relations, and the making of the Elisar Project is an illustration of these dynamics.[1]

This chapter starts by presenting the general social, political, and urban characteristics of Beirut's southern suburb, followed by an overview of Elisar's urban conception and a description of the project's actual conditions. The chapter ends with a reflection upon the implied social and spatial consequences of the project, especially in the light of the proposed urban culture of modernity.

Before beginning, however, it is important to point out some terminological issues.

The phrase southern suburb is the common translation of *dahiya janubiyya,* which has been the Arabic designation of this space since the early 1980s. *Dahiya* conveys emotionally charged referents that can be found in the press where discourse about this part of the city is either produced or reported by journalists. The discussions, produced in this manner, describe the southern suburb as a 'misery belt' distinguished by its 'illegal urbanization,' its 'squatters,' and its 'underdevelopment.' It is also referred to as 'Hizbullah's suburb' which is 'Islamist' and where 'poor Shi'ites' live. Generally, such reports are those of political leaders, who discuss the 'Shi'ite ghetto,'[2] the 'anarchical space'[3] which is inhabited by people living in a 'tragic' situation.[4]

Together, both kinds of discussions refer to the southern suburb as an illegal, anarchical space inhabited by poor Shi'ites led and/or manipulated by the Hizbullah (Party of God) which is an Islamist Iranian party aiming to establish an Islamic republic in Lebanon.[5] These representations are only partially correct, however, and citing some of the facts that contradict them will show their inaccuracy. On the one hand, the southern suburb is not a homogeneous space. It is divided into several territories managed by different players. Hizbullah is hence not its sole constituency or authority. A good number of residents are neither close to Hizbullah nor to the Amal movement, the other major political party active in the area. Hizbullah's territorial markings, with an iconography praising Iran's religious leaders or local 'martyrs' of the Islamic resistance in southern Lebanon, coexists with shops that bear Western names offering the 'latest fashion from Paris' and with schools bearing Christian saints' names.[6] Also, the services and the equipment proposed by the Hizbullah, such as the free distribution of potable water, financial aid, schools, dispensaries, supermarkets, etc., are distinguished by the efficiency of their organization as well as by their professional and bureaucratic 'modern' character.[7] We thus see that the Islamism and the underdevelopment of the southern suburb must be reconsidered.

On the other hand, the southern suburb is not a totally poor, under-equipped, and illegal space. Several neighborhoods are inhabited by well-to-do people and closely resemble other parts of the city. We can find there, for instance, the same general external signs of wealth, such as marble and stone facades, expensive cars, etc. The presence or absence of equipment is related to the socio-economic situation of the neighborhood. As for the illegality, which, incidentally, is not always related to real estate, it varies widely from one place to another, and it frequently concerns the laws of construction. Consequently, it is similar to illegalities found in other Beiruti suburbs such as Aramoun, Bshamoun, Mkales, Mansuriyyeh, Zalka, etc.

When considered together, these facts show that the social and political realities of the southern suburb are much more complex than the widespread representations that are propagated by the press. The southern suburb is not a space of misery that one should bypass or an area of urban anarchy to be reorganized. It is quite simply one of the multiple components of Beirut's urban agglomeration. Consequently, we need to think of other designations for this space,[8] requiring a more thorough study. Nevertheless, in the present article we will content ourselves with the common term of 'southern suburb.'

Multiple Players in a Coveted Space

The southern suburb is inhabited by one third of the population of Greater Beirut, almost 500,000 people, and occupies an area similar to that of municipal Beirut (respectively 16 and 17.6 square kilometers). For this study, as shown in the accompanying map, the perimeter was limited by the Mediterranean sea to the west, the airport to the south, the old Beirut-Saida road to the east, and the southern limit of municipal Beirut to the north. The southern suburb can be morphologically and socially differentiated into two zones divided by the north-south axis of the airport road. The eastern zone combines dense old villages (Burj al-Barajneh, Mrayjeh, Harit Hrayk, Ghobeyri, Shiyyah) and peripheral illegal sectors (Amrussyeh, Hay al-Sillom), while the western zone groups major illegal sectors (Jnah, Uzai), legal low-density urbanization (Bir Hassan, Ramlit al-Baydah), together with relatively large non-urbanized areas.

Beirut's southern suburb was for a long time, and prior to the Lebanese war, abandoned by the public urban authorities whose interests there were both partial and intermittent.[9] During the war, the demographic structure of the southern suburb was greatly altered by the multiplication of waves of internal displacement and by intersectarian conflicts. The Shi'ite-Maronite balance that first favored the Maronites changed gradually toward a Shi'ite hegemony strengthened by the population displacements from the northeastern suburbs of Beirut, from the Biqaa and from South Lebanon. Today, the displaced Shi'ites of the southern suburb form 70 to 80 percent of the total population.[10]

Already mobilized since the beginning of the 1970s by Imam Musa al-Sadr, the Shi'ite community was structured a few years later around two major political forces. They were

Fig. 1. The southern suburb and the Elisar Project

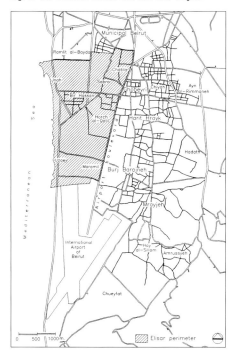

the Amal movement in the mid 1970s and Hizbullah in the early 1980s. Amal slowly lost the military and political monopoly to Hizbullah, which, during the past ten years, skillfully structured its operations in the southern suburb. With a state that was long absent from the social, educational, and medical fields, Hizbullah's activities in those sectors were accepted without many hesitations by large parts of the population.[11]

Hizbullah is rivaled by other players, also active in the management and the provision of urban services. Some of those players are their political and/or religious allies, such as al-Mabarrat, an organization led by Sayyid Fadlallah, close to Hizbullah but very independent, as well as associations, administratively autonomous, that are directly sponsored by the Islamic Republic of Iran. The private sector of real estate agents has non-declared relations with the 'Party of God' that allow it to flourish. Two players can be distinguished from this *hala islamiyya* (Islamic situation) by their structures, their affiliations, and their strategies: the Supreme Shi'ite Council, whose role is more consultative than political, and the Amal movement, led by Nabih Berri, who is also the parliamentary speaker of the house. Today, these different local players also have to deal with the intervention of a state that wants to regain the confidence of the inhabitants, especially after the government, presided over by Rafik Hariri, was formed in 1992. This intervention was achieved mainly through infrastructure rehabilitation – law 246/93 for the southeastern suburb – and the Elisar Project[12] for the southwestern suburb: two faces of an operation conducted by the 'private bureau' of Rafik Hariri (fig. 1).[13]

Elisar or the Urban Culture of Modernity

Elisar is a public establishment that aims at the reorganization and the restructuring of the western part of the southern suburb, thus allowing for the spatial expansion of Beirut toward the south and for a more 'decent' urban linkage between the airport and the city center (fig. 2). The total project area is 560 hectares, from which 230 legal constructions and religious as well as social buildings are exempted from demolition. The remaining 330 hectares were placed under study, including the illegal sectors of Jnah, Uzai, Horsh al-Qatil, Sabra, and Chatila. These areas, in turn, are distinguished by their high density and their irregularity, from Bir Hassan, Ramlit al-Baydan, and the adjacent area next to the airport road, and will likely be destroyed and reconstructed according to regulations set in the general plan. Not coincidentally, the seashore occupied by these illegal sectors will be freed and thus could be developed as a tourist zone with high potential. The displaced residents will be relocated in 7,500 housing units to be built along the airport road. The shops and small industries that are an integral part of the illegal sectors will also be relocated in industrial zones situated near the residential areas.

The Elisar Project was first revealed to the public in early 1994, when the press announced the creation of a real estate company in the southwestern suburb based on law 117/91 – the same law which created downtown's Solidere. This immediately provoked vehement reactions from both Amal and Hizbullah. Indeed, the power relations that underlie the making of the project can be recounted by the following anecdote. Prime Minister Rafik Hariri wanted to use the name 'Elisar' borrowed from the story of the Phoenician Queen Elisar who escaped Tyre to found the city of Carthage. However, during a discussion of the project amongst Shi'ite leaders (Hizbullah's and other Shi'ite notables), Nabih Berri said that, "Elisar is from Tyre not from Sidon," alluding to the fact he is originally from Tyre while Rafik Hariri is from Sidon, and asserting Shi'ite control over the southern suburb. Bearing this in mind, one can better understand how the project is continually elaborated and reshaped as a negotiation between the major players involved, namely Rafik Hariri, Amal, and Hizbullah.

The latter two political groups were able to achieve three significant changes in the original formulation of the project. First, the idea of a real estate company was abandoned in favor of a public entity. Since the state and municipalities own large plots of land within Elisar, the structure of a public entity is legally more adequate and more financially sound. A public entity also makes the state a major participant in the reorganization of the area and it is represented by a board of administration in charge of the urban operations. Further, the public entity is supposed to carry out temporary expropriation of relevant areas, to acquire 25 percent for public use, and to reparcel and redistribute plots to the owners. Hence property rights are fully retained.

The second modification instigated by Hizbullah and Amal was their ability to make Elisar consider, theoretically at least, the inhabitants of the illegal sectors as having

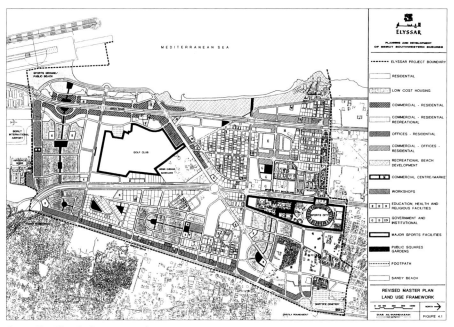

Fig. 2. The Elisar Project, master plan

property rights and to deal with them accordingly. This was consolidated by the state's decision to deny the allocation of financial compensation to the inhabitants who would be, in the majority, relocated. The third achievement was having Amal and Hizbullah representatives on Elisar's administrative board, a body which was formed in July 1994.

Thus Elisar is the result of an equation that brings together real estate and economic and urban parameters. The project's zone is formed mainly by large plots of land that are not parceled out and of 'muchaa,'[14] belonging mainly to the public domain and to the municipalities. By being situated along the coast, those plots can produce an important real estate surplus, which is today totally paralyzed by illegal urbanization. Through expropriation, regrouping, and par-

celing procedures, Elisar wants to reclaim these plots and to recover the surplus. The benefits will be large enough to finance the construction of social housing, allowing for the relocation of almost two thirds of the illegal inhabitants.[15] Elisar's board will study the case of each family and will then offer them apartments of their own.[16]

If Elisar seems to succeed as a restructuring operation in the real estate and economic fields, how successful is it on the urban level? Here, the project's guidelines can be summed up by two ideas: the regularization of space and its organization into homogeneous zones. The first stage concerns the Maramil neighborhood where 1,800 dwelling units will be constructed below the future highway linking the Sports City to Cocody. One hundred housing units of six to eight stories are organized into fifteen

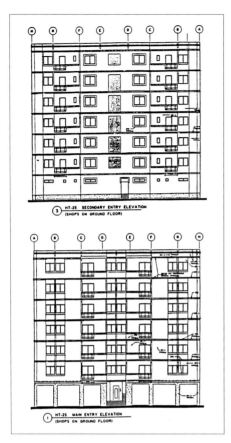

Fig. 3. Elevations of housing units in Maramil, Dar al-Handasah, 1996

blocks, each grouping five basic units, as shown in the accompanying plans and elevations (figs. 3 and 4). The buildings are separated by twenty-five meters to allow for light and ventilation. The roads, which are set twelve meters apart, are planned for easy traffic movement and for opening views toward the sea. The introduction of garden apartments will allow those who already have a garden to recover their *qarawi* (village-like) lifestyle.[17] Public spaces will be managed by the residents and municipal authorities, and parking areas will serve as playgrounds during off-peak hours. Finally,

functional specialization of space is a strict rule. Industrial zones are isolated from residential areas, and social services are grouped together in the center of the plots.

For the past two and a half years, the project has been developed in ways not always similar to the declared directions and guidelines. This can be seen in a number of instances. Compensation, for instance, is being paid to families who live in the path of the planned highways and roads, although this contradicts the initial intentions of the plan. The expropriations being made are permanent and not temporary, as the rules of the public establishment state.

The Maramil Project, which is the first stage of Elisar, has not yet started due to delays in the release of funds from the government, although all architectural plans and construction drawings have been finalized by the designers – Dar al-Handasah – Shair and Partners. Current rumor has it that Elisar is not going to proceed. Hizbullah and Amal representatives claim that they will counter the project if land continues to be expropriated, and that compensation is owed to the people affected. Moreover, they are only accepting the plan temporarily because it concerns the construction of roads that are crucial as much for Beirut as for the southern suburb.

Urban Conceptions Praising Modernity over Society

Although Elisar is a project led by three antagonistic actors (Rafik Hariri, Amal, and Hizbullah), their conflicts seem to fade away when it comes to its urban conception.

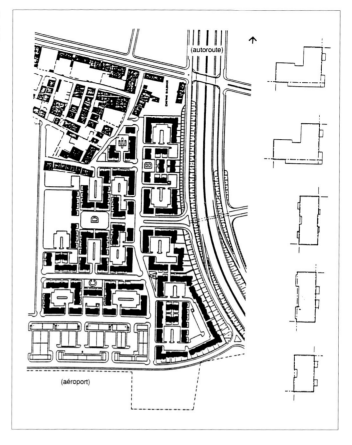

Fig. 4. Mass plan of the housing units in Maramil, Dar al-Handasah, 1996

(autoroute)

(aéroport)

Essentially, their friction concerns only the economic and real estate issues, and in the cases of Amal and Hizbullah, the control of the social groups that legitimize their power. For its part, Amal thinks the urban projects proposed by Elisar are adequate in the way of development and modernization (*tamaddun*).[18] Hizbullah's delegate praises the quality of Elisar's urban concepts,[19] and even Rafik Hariri's collaborative asserts the urban planners' visions as unquestionable. "Only the urbanists know what is adequate; even myself, a civil engineer, cannot think in terms of spatial planning; what would be then the cases of Amal or Hizbullah?"[20]

The underlying concepts of Elisar can easily be retraced to those that shaped the ideology of modern urbanism in the beginning of the century and were epitomized in Europe after World War II.[21] Along these lines, urbanism is presented as a science that wants to remedy the problems of the city,[22] and is thus a means toward social and political modernization. The basic urban guideline of modern urbanism was zoning which, in turn, was seen as the rational, hygienic planning of space where functions were segregated to create homogeneous sectors, thus excluding all social dimensions.

It is not necessary here to sum up the findings of numerous analyses of the ideology behind modern urbanism and its leading concept of zoning. It suffices to cite only two of the major principles that can also be found in Elisar's general approach to urban planning. The first claims that urbanism is capable of social reform and the second asserts that form creates use. This approach to space and society has given way to some successes and many failures. Consequently, several years ago, many authors denounced the idea of such an urban *utopia* and the illusions upon which it was based.[23] The principle of 'ordering' urban space by zoning can be detected in Elisar. It is seen through the division of space in dissociated zones that do not integrate the existing mixture of functions. It continues with the modeling of the public spaces that are conceived of as leftover voids. And it appears in the suppression of the streets that act today as places favoring rapid circulation. Ordering is also expressed through the 'hygienic' approach that aims at 'cleansing' space by razing it.[24] Relocating Elisar's inhabitants to social housing units is an illustration of this logic. First, these people will no longer be differentiated by their housing.[25] Therefore, they will no longer represent a social menace, since they will have access to a higher standard of living, and, furthermore, they can finally be integrated more fully into society. It is the logic of "interventionism that aims at transforming the city and the society in one motion."[26]

Conclusion

It is true that the illegal residents of Elisar are not living in ideal urban conditions. It is also true that the real estate potential of this space is substantial and cannot be immobilized permanently. Nevertheless, there are serious threats in the fact that only economic considerations are determining the choices adopted by the project and that no debate is being initiated about its urban or social dimensions. The urban model proposed by Elisar was widely tested in several Arab cities in Egypt, Algeria, Tunisia, and Morocco, and proved to be both economically constraining and socially poorly adapted.[27] Despite the fact that, under the pressure of international agencies, those states have been engaged for several years now in the problematic logistics of recognizing and regularizing illegal urban spaces, repression and coercion unfortunately remain the dominant methods of spatial regulation in Lebanon.[28]

However, this does not seem to worry any of the planners involved in the project, nor the concerned political powers who are reusing the modern discourse to back up Elisar with the reluctant inhabitants, nor even the 'intellectuals' concerned with the reconstruction of the city. Is it because they all agree with those modern concepts of urbanism for social reform? Or is it because Elisar deals with a space that lacks all historical dimensions and thus, in their opinion, lacks a potential cultural value? Or, is it that Elisar concerns an area inhabited by the Shi'ite community which has been considered throughout Beirut's recent history as rural and poor and hence having no 'right to the city'? The lack of debate around Elisar is largely contributing to the social and spatial segregation that has begun to characterize the urban structure of Beirut.

Notes

1. Revealed by the formation of Elisar's board of administration, necessitating long negotiations. The board was announced on 7/14/95. President: **J. Helu**, an engineer close to Rafik Hariri. Six members: two represent Amal and Hizbullah, respectively: the lawyer and South Lebanon deputy **A. al-Khalil** and the engineer **N. Krayyim**; the other four are considered collaborators of Rafik Hariri: the deputy **A. Andraos**; the political scientist **W. Saab**; the engineer and businessman **E. Sehnawi**; and the General Director of Urbanism **S. Khaled**.
2. Interview with A. al-Khalil, 5/17/96.
3. The term 'anarchical' was used by a leading figure in the Consultative Center for Studies and Documentation (CCSD), a structure close to the Hizbullah and in those of Bassim Sabeh, South Metn deputy, in a TV interview, on 8/22/96.
4. Ibid.
5. The slogan of Hizbullah is "the Islamic revolution in Lebanon." However, the 'Islamic' ambitions of the Party of God have been more and more belittled by its leaders and press articles that discuss the 'Lebanonization' of Hizbullah.
6. Those observations are derived from our numerous visits in the southern suburb.
7. M. Harb el-Kak, *Politiques urbaines dans la banlieue-sud de Beyrouth* (Beirut: CERMOC, 1996), pp. 51–59.
8. Bassim Sabeh, south Meten deputy, one of the 'old' notables' representatives and close to Rafik Hariri, uses the term "coast of south Meten" or *sahel janubi* (southern coast).
9. W. Charafeddine, *La Banlieue-sud de Beyrouth: structure urbaine et économique, thèse d'aménagement*, ss. la dir. de X. de Planhol (Paris: Université de Paris 4, 1987), pp. 1–17.
10. *Al-markaz al-istichari lil buhuth wal tawthiq*, CCSD, 1991, report.
11. Harb el-Kak, *Politiques urbaines dans la banlieue-sud de Beyrouth* (Beirut: CERMOC, 1996), pp. 39–44.
12. *Projet de développement des banlieues et de construction d'autoroutes (loi n 246); plan de développement pour améliorer les services dans les banlieues de Beyrouth, le niveau de vie de ses habitants et les accès à la capitale*, Beirut, 8/12/94.
13. The dividing line between the two projects is the airport road.
14. The '*muchaa*' groups "territories which parceling is of community origin"; J. Weulersse, *Paysans de Syrie et du Proche-Orient* (Paris: Gallimard, 1946), pp. 98–101.
15. The 7,500 housing units that are going to be constructed cannot house all the residents in the existing 13,000 units. Almost 5,000 families – including over 2,600 tenants – will receive compensation either from Elisar, the Ministry of the Displaced, or the Ministry of Housing. (Interview with J. Helu, 5/29/96; interview with N. Krayyim, 12/17/96.)
16. Theoretically, an apartment is given for free in exchange of the destroyed unit. In practice, things are more complicated; i.e., the resident of a two-room apartment who will be given a three-room dwelling will pay for difference; the owner of both a building and a house will have an apartment and a piece of property equivalent to his assets. (Interview with N. Krayyim, 12/17/96.)
17. Interview with J. Helu, 5/29/96.
18. Interview with A. al-Khalil, 5/17/96.
19. Interview with N. Krayyim, 12/17/96.
20. Interview with J. Helu, 5/29/96.
21. J.P. Gaudin, *Les Nouvelles politiques urbaines* (Paris: PUF, 1993), p. 14.
22. F. Choay, *L'Urbanisme: Utopies et réalités* (Paris: Seuil, 1965), pp. 8–9, 33.
23. Ibid., pp. 74–83; G. Dupuy, *L'Urbanisme des réseaux, théories et méthodes* (Paris: A. Colin, 1991), p. 10–11, 72–80.
24. Interview with J. Helu, 5/29/96. He uses the Arabic word *tandif*.
25. Interview with J. Helu, 5/29/96. However, we find his statement debatable: a population housed in 7,500 identical housing units seems strongly differentiated by its urban structure; on another level, Elisar's proposed spatial organization does not exist in Beirut.
26. Gaudin, *Les Nouvelles politiques urbaines*, p. 14.
27. F. Tebbal, "Habitat insalubre: Thématique et rôle des différents acteurs," in *Habitat insalubre et stratégies d'intervention*, Meknès, ANHI, USAID, 1994, p. 7.
28. The 'bulldozing' of Khaldeh, Damur, and other squatter areas during July 1996 is an illustration of this logic.

Section Four
The Postwar Planning of Beirut

The Postwar Project

by
Rodolphe el-Khoury

*Great monuments are erected like dikes, op-
posing the logic and majesty of authority
against disturbing elements.... The taking of
the Bastille is symbolic of this state of things:
it is hard to explain this mass movement other
than by the animosity of the people against
the monuments that are their real masters.*

Georges Bataille

*... If thinking is to be true – if it is to be true
today, in any case – it must also be a thinking
against itself. If thought is not measured
against the extremity that eludes the concept,
it is from the outset in the nature of the
accompaniment with which the SS liked to
drown out the screams of its victims.*

Theodor Adorno

The reconstruction of Beirut has generated
considerable interest. Although architecture
and urban planning hardly qualify for prime
time news, local and foreign media have
been unusually attentive: they regularly
feature Beirut's building efforts in more or
less sensational stories. Typically, the scenario of reconstruction provides a 'happy
ending' to the Civil War's undramatic and
inconclusive close. The event of reconstruction naturalizes, as it were, the fiction
of a peaceful and potentially prosperous
Lebanon, although the ideological and
material investments that have sustained fifteen years of civil war – which may prove to
be entirely consistent with Beirut's history of
conspicuous consumption – have yet to yield
the expected returns.

If the intensity of building activity were
commensurate with peace and stability, the
Civil War would have had to have been a
prosperous and peaceful time. Indeed, the
volume of new construction broke all records
during the war years and exceeded, by far,
the relatively limited extent of destruction
by artillery. Far more devastating was the
developer's assault on open-hence-buildable
space. The coastline was the first casualty
of this wartime building campaign: the
zoning laws which barely managed to protect
it from entrepreneurial zeal before the war
were swiftly swept aside with the collapse
of governmental authority. How different,
we must then ask, is the so-called 'reconstruction' from the mass of wartime con-

struction when governmental intervention remains minimal and the grounds of operation barely legal, still? Can we confidently speak of "postwar reconstruction" or should we refer to this latest stage in the building boom as "war construction?"

A more provocative question comes to mind: has the Civil War ended or is the feverish building activity the persevering manifestation of its polymorphous process?

'Reconstruction' is a term that ongoing media campaigns reserve for the building project in the Beirut Central District, the long deserted target of daily wartime artillery. Construction and reconstruction currently involve several sectors of the city at different scales of intervention. But media attention has focused, almost exclusively, on the BCD. Other sites and projects may be essential to the daily life of today's Beirut, but none can compete with the material and symbolic investments in the BCD's past and future. In mass media representations as much as in the collective imagination, the BCD represents the city; its fate implicates, metonymically, the entire country.

The fate of Lebanon may now be in the hands of a private real estate company: The Lebanese Company for the Development and Reconstruction of the Beirut Central District, better known as Solidere. The vicissitudes of Solidere, in its various incarnations and negotiations with the government, has been the subject of many adequate studies. Suffice it here to restate the essential facts: the Lebanese government expropriated the land of the BCD (under the law of December 7, 1991) and delegated, for a twenty-five-year mandate, the legal and managerial responsibilities of its reconstruction to Solidere, whose capital is constituted by the shares that were granted to property owners/tenants and sold to investors. Solidere tasks include, within a comprehensive master plan, the rehabilitation and extension of infrastructure, the restoration of select buildings, and the development and management of the real estate.

The premature presentations of the master plan were understandably met with unanimous skepticism. Many revisions later, and thanks to the assistance of several eminent experts, Solidere's plan has earned some respect but still cannot escape the perpetual disapproval of a small but vigilant opposition. When the criticism persists against ostensibly 'well-behaved' proposals which do not readily inspire contempt, one can only suspect deeper sources for the underlying hostility.

Angus Gavin has been closely involved in Solidere's design efforts. In "Heart of Beirut: Making the Master Plan for the Renewal of the Central District," he reports on "the most important undertaking in urban rejuvenation taking place in the world today," with all the enthusiasm expected of an architect presented with "one of those rare opportunities in city-making and renewal." He speaks eloquently of the many assets of Solidere's plan, noting its sensitivity to topography, its judicious mixture of residential, commercial, and institutional amenities, and its contextual architectural language.

If the professed virtues of the architecture fail to seduce, it is because of a lingering uneasiness with the project's economic infrastructure: highly fluid and volatile real estate conditions set in motion in extraordinary legal and political circumstances and unlikely to be harnessed but for the benefit of the privileged few. There is, in fact, little to worry about in the latest incarnation of Solidere's project. The trouble is with its latent plasticity: given the lack of legal and physical resistance in the deterritorialized BCD, the plan has the alarming capacity freely and unexpectedly to mutate with the shifting pressures of the market. Chances are that it will inevitably yield to such pressures.

The sheer materiality of the surviving urban fabric could perhaps have dampened the brutal opportunism of capital, but thorough demolition left no ground for such resistance. Indeed, despite Solidere's advocacy of "Anglo-Saxon contextualism," the fact remains that its 'reconstruction project' has been more efficient than fifteen years of warfare in 'building' a *tabula rasa* in place of what used to be the old downtown. This district had suffered substantial damage from systematic bombing during the Civil War, but was still ready for restoration until Solidere's explosives delivered the coup de grace in 1992. One could consequently ask if critics are necessarily paranoid when they note the troubling convergence of military and planning maneuvers in the BCD.

Joumana Ghandour Atallah's tone is fittingly belligerent in the discussion of the recent proposals for the Northern Sector of the Beirut Metropolitan Region. The plans call for a stretch of landfill along the coastline and a variety of strategies for its development. Ghandour Atallah traces the transformation of various features of the plan from their original conception by Bofill to subsequent iterations in Dar al-Handasah's proposal. Her analysis demonstrates how the financial interest of the development agencies has consistently precipitated the degradation of these features. The compromising symptoms are familiar: shrinking public space, encroaching privatization, boundaries designed for the isolation of privileged enclaves, etc.

For Ghandour Atallah, the challenge that urban design and planning face in the aftermath of the Civil War is largely political: "the citizens have yet to regain their city and the power to reshape it." Her reading implicitly recognizes in the ongoing planning and building activity the recurring patterns of the struggle which have violently reshaped the city since 1975, and which continue to compromise public interests and marginalize the disenfranchised segment of the population.

The disenfranchised Lebanese, who constitute the overwhelming majority of the population, have depleted their material wealth and suffered countless casualties to support an indifferent war machine in its territorial maneuvers. These maneuvers may now be proceeding, unhindered and uninterrupted, in postwar planning and building. Indeed little has changed in the strategic map: the constellation of vectors and forces which guided the war continues to exercise its influence in the abrupt if not violent reconfiguration of the territory. The means may now be different, but the objectives are the same and no less fulfilled: bulldozers and office buildings are nothing short of grenades and barricades when it comes to clearing the ground, demarcating the field, and enforcing exclusions.

After seventeen years of violent warfare, the citizens of Lebanon naturally welcome the reconstruction efforts as the healthy, vital signs of the "recovering peace economy." But when the deployment of streets, fences, and buildings is alarmingly consistent with recent territorial struggles, the naturalized distinction between 'war' and 'peace' may have to be questioned. I would not risk trivializing the pain and suffering of war by denouncing seemingly benign but no less insidious processes in peace, and, yet, we may have to recognize a covert warfare in the project of architecture.

Dances with Margaret Mead: Planning Beirut since 1958

by
Hashim Sarkis

The title of this essay, concerning the political and social challenges of planning Beirut, is inspired by a photograph of the Greek planner and architect, Constantinos Doxiadis, dancing with American anthropologist Margaret Mead (fig. 1).[1] The photograph was taken on Delos in 1969 where Doxiadis, who boasted one of the largest practices in the world at the time, and who

Fig. 1. Constantinos Doxiadis dancing with Margaret Mead on Delos, 1969

had produced a master plan for Lebanon in 1958, sponsored a yearly symposium.[2] Around the topic of *ekistics*, the science of human settlements, some thirty-five highbrow scholars from different disciplines would gather on Delos, and, together, they would cruise the Aegean aboard Doxiadis' yacht, the *Semiramis,* talking about cities and dancing across disciplines in order to come away with a shared vision of an improved urban life. The photograph captures the sanguine mood of such cross-disciplinary collaboration in the '60s, and figures like historian Arnold Toynbee, economist Barbara Ward, and inventor Buckminster Fuller were all working together even when they displayed their disciplines' highly particularized fetishes (Doxiadis in Mediterranean white and Mead in Samoan prints).

Imagine the intensity and impact of interdisciplinary discussions aboard the *Semiramis*. This is the '60s, and most of these scholars were also highly influential public intellectuals who served as government consultants on several critical issues, especially on inner cities and their social problems. Yet imagine the possibility of confusion that could be caused by discussions across disciplinary boundaries. The terms of communication would have to be extremely lucid (which even today, after several failures and successes, they are not). Consider, for example, the concept 'community,' which will recur in this essay. To a planner, 'community' is always a place, a locality of a certain scale and number of inhabitants. For instance, Doxiadis used the *ekistic* unit of 10,000 people to define a neighborhood. To an anthropologist, community is a shared bundle of habits and customs, to a politician it is a represented constituency, and to an economist it is an exchange network frequently used by the same agents. Now while these different definitions do overlap, and while the Aegean cruisers could no doubt discern such definitional discrepancies, the differences between their terms were very far-reaching.

The greater confusion, which even today haunts the discipline of planning, is the degree of instrumentality that other disciplines such as sociology and anthropology accord to planning, in view of its pretense to shape the total physical environment. During the '50s and '60s, the interaction between planners and social and political scientists increased exponentially toward total collaboration, so much so that even when the sociologists were not there, the planners, as the case of Beirut will show, took it upon themselves to project such responsibilities as social reconciliation onto physical planning. Social scientists became increasingly aware of the role of the physical environment in shaping human behavior, and planners may have played a very important part in soliciting the attention of the sociologists and anthropologists to such difficult problems as the inner city and suburban growth during that time. But excessive collaboration has ultimately overburdened the planners with unattainable tasks at the expense of the quality of their plans.[3]

Nevertheless, despite the fact that some disciplines danced better with each other (see Barbara Ward's graceful *sirtaki* with Doxiadis) they were all having a good time (fig. 2). Such comprehensive visions were still desirable. They were even deemed possible. Furthermore, the disappointments of the late '60s had not been given the scale that disenchanted both architecture and planning from the hopes of such collaboration. Significantly, the planner in this story acted as the host, and a cordial one at that, rather than the vehicle through which the ambitions of these other disciplines, along with their disappointments, would be projected. In that respect, there is one other aspect of this photograph that is relevant to the planning of Beirut.

In the 1920s, Margaret Mead embarked on a study of the sexual habits of primitive societies, interviewing Samoan women and discovering through very personal exchanges that they led promiscuous lives. The resultant book, *Coming of Age in Samoa*, created an uproar in the United States when it was published in 1928, but was eventually accepted in the West as the authoritative view on Samoans.[4] In a revisit to Mead's island, however, some anthropologists subsequently discovered that, given the embarrassing nature of her questions, the local interviewees resorted to inventing stories

Fig. 2. Constantinos Doxiadis dancing with Barbara Ward on Delos, 1963

that would quench Mead's polemicist spirit.[5] Here, then, we have it, a culture deliberately misrepresenting itself in order to avoid the embarrassments of normality. In Beirut, the sociologists and the anthropologists would continue to look for the exaggerated, discerning qualities of the city's communitarian composition, and, as will be seen below, the planners would slip in and out of this game of cross-cultural perception, occasionally falling for its extravagance.

Apart from describing and comparing two rarely mentioned plans for Beirut, the aim of this essay is to show how these social burdens have distracted planners from their tasks. The essay will also look through the plans toward the prospects of a more feasible approach for planning in Lebanon. The choice of two plans, namely the 1958 Ekistics Program for Lebanon by Doxiadis Associates and the 1986 Schéma Directeur de la Région Métropolitaine de Beyrouth by the Institut d'Aménagement et d'Urbanisme de la Région Ile de France (IAURIF), is partly due to the fact that they were both prepared during periods of heightened civil strife, at a time when community identities would challenge national and civic associations, and, thus, at a time when the social challenges to planning were further heightened.

The Ekistics Program for Lebanon by Doxiadis Associates, 1958

On May 20, 1957, Doxiadis Associates signed a contract with the United States Operations Mission and the Government of Lebanon to prepare a "long-term Ekistics Program for Lebanon." The plan was due one year after the signing of the contract, along with a National Housing Program and the designs and drawings for about 1,500 housing units on sites to be selected by the Lebanese government.[6] The signing of the contract came soon after an increase in United States development aid to Lebanon. This, in turn, followed the Eisenhower Doctrine for intervention in the Middle East against the threat of Soviet expansionism and the mounting unrest in the region and in Lebanon.[7] The choice of Doxiadis was no doubt due to his previous extensive collaboration with United States agencies on postwar reconstruction in Europe. Being a Greek third party, Doxiadis perhaps also helped make the planning process appear more neutral than the political alliances that willed it.

In the months to follow, the months preceding the civil strife of May-October 1958, Doxiadis established an office in Beirut on 382 Rue Madame Curie and began the *ekistics* study by conducting a highly comprehensive survey of Lebanon. He relied on photography in order to document the urban environment of Beirut, and also its architectural character, the life of its streets, souks, inner residential areas, and the faces of its citizens (figs. 3, 4, and 5). He also took personal notes and tape recorded on-site impressions. The survey which was collected in more than twenty volumes also extended to the regions and to the rural areas, adding views of the natural and architectural heritage of all the *cazas*, or administrative regions, of Lebanon. Analyses of the building types and of construction quality were also included in the report. Occasionally, Doxiadis would also include photographs of agricultural fields, factories, and modern

Fig. 3. View of Beirut looking southeast, photograph by Doxiadis Associates, 1957

Fig. 4. The Avenue des Français, photograph by Doxiadis Associates, 1957

Fig. 5. Weygand Street, photograph by Doxiadis Associates, 1958

buildings. This extensive but fleeting tour of the country captured a general condition that was about to change irreversibly. Doxiadis' eye could not miss out on the Mediterranean countenance of the city and the landscape: the fine grain, dense, and highly mixed urban fabric with strong modern influences that did not (yet) endanger its Ottoman heritage, set against a rural but equally fragile hinterland. During this period, Doxiadis also mingled (and probably danced) with the Lebanese intelligentsia, many of whose members were invited aboard the *Semiramis* to listen to his big ideas about modern town planning.[8]

The analytic side of the Ekistics Program was as comprehensive as the visual survey but, in retrospect, less enlightening (fig. 6). With a typical bent on drawing the big picture first, the report started with the study

Fig. 6. Ekistics map of Lebanon (population distribution), from the Ekistics Plan of Lebanon, by Doxiadis Associates, 1958

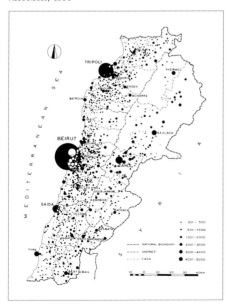

of the location of the Lebanese diaspora in the world and then its distribution within Lebanon, proposing a more even demographic redistribution in the regions. It then went on to identify housing locations, job locations, and possible sites for the new housing based on recommendations for new job locations (fig. 7). And despite its redistributive ambitions, the program did not ignore the physical quality of the existing housing stock, such as the nature of exterior wall construction. Occasionally, the report zoomed in on existing squatter settlements and deteriorating housing stock in order to select stucco colors for exterior walls and the details of cinder block construction for garden fences.

From the map of the world to paint samples: this was Doxiadis' scope of inquiry. And yet, the final proposal involved actual design projects. The practical task came down to the selection of project sites with the Lebanese government. These consisted mainly of: 1) a Beirut New Community Project in Mkalles, 2) a Beirut New Community in Hadeth, 3) a Beirut Amelioration Project, 4) a Beirut Slum Clearance Project, 5) a Tripoli Housing Project, 6) a Sidon Housing Project, and 7) a Beirut First Experimental Housing Scheme. In effect, the Ekistics Program turned out to be a master plan for Lebanon with an emphasis on housing in and around Beirut.

The focus on housing was obviously due to the fact that the *ekistics* approach viewed the built environment as units of inhabitation starting with the individual dwelling and progressing to the neighborhood, to the city, and to larger conglomerations of cities. But the provision of housing was also a

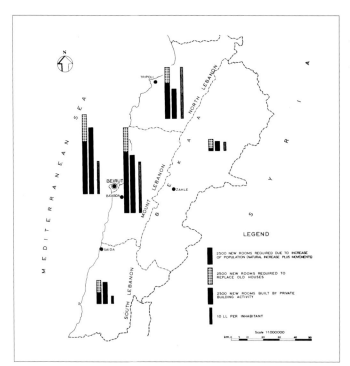

Fig. 7. Annually recurring housing requirements from the Ekistics Plan of Lebanon, by Doxiadis Associates, 1958

Fig. 8. Squatter settlement in the Burj Hammoud area, photograph by Doxiadis Associates, 1957

response to numerous problems stirring around Beirut. Their prioritization contained a degree of political as well as humane urgency. A strong earthquake hit Lebanon in 1956, causing significant damage to some of the low-income neighborhoods, particularly in Tyre and Sidon. During the '50s, Beirut had grown to become the primary regional port on the Eastern Mediterranean, mainly

ect here, a new community for new rural immigrants there, a housing project to re- place the earthquake destroyed areas in the south, and a new experimental housing scheme for testing new developmental approaches.

Yet despite the overwhelmingly political bent of these projects, which would be heightened by the civil unrest in May 1958,

Fig. 9. New Community of Mkalles, the square of a neighborhood unit, by Doxiadis Associates, 1958

due to the loss of competition with the port of Haifa. Continuing a trend that had started in the 1860s, rural populations attracted by the cosmopolitan capital and its modern services settled in a ring of existing villages around the city creating what sociologists immediately called the misery belt.[9] The misery belt of Beirut also overlapped with the refugee camps of the Palestinians and with the by-then deteriorating Armenian camps in Burj Hammoud (fig. 8). The belt was also feared as one of the potential sources of civil unrest in Lebanon agitated, according to the Lebanese government, by the pro-Nasserite sentiments of the time.[10] Thus, the choice of projects and sites with the Lebanese government was a sampling of such social problems: a slum clearance proj-

Doxiadis Associates would go back to the drawing table on Rue Madame Curie and design actual buildings. Despite the highly particular conditions of each of these prob- lem areas, they would produce housing schemes derived directly from such success- ful modernist models as the Roq et Rob Housing Project by Le Corbusier. For exam- ple, the most elaborately worked out hous- ing scheme was for the area of Mkalles, southeast of Beirut's center, in which he pro- posed a set of two-story apartment build- ings, terraced with the terrain, and aggre- gated around a neighborhood center which resembled in many ways the nondescript centers of residential Beirut (fig. 9).

In retrospect, such projects, and the modernist urban planning that inspired them, were adopted partly in order to erase the highly politicized differences among selected projects and among income groups within projects; and yet they remained inexplicably underdeveloped in terms of their formal ambitions, particularly in terms of their relation to the terrain and the internal distinctions between residential and public areas.

The Ekistics Program would be completed in Lebanon by May 1958 as planned, but the work of the office in Lebanon would be interrupted for about six months by the subsequent uprising and Doxiadis would not return to Lebanon until 1959 when the new president, Fuad Shihab, had been elected, the tensions had subsided, and a new, expanded government had been formed.[11] During this year, and following meetings with the new Lebanese president and council of ministers, Doxiadis would be assigned the task of selecting a site for the new Government City (fig. 10), a project that he had initially been reluctant to consider during the first phase of his work, preferring to deal with the more urgent needs of housing supply and improvement. He would soon undertake it following a renewed interest in strengthening the presence and image of centralized government in Beirut and the need to move the government facilities out of the dense commercial center of the city toward the hinterland.[12]

Again, and relying on his *ekistics* model, Doxiadis would study four possible sites selected by the Lebanese government around Beirut, and would push for one of them based on a straightforward locational analysis. Seen on the national map, the proposed new government center is situated at the intersection of two major roads, the east-west road to Damascus and the north-south coastal highway. This location would never be adopted, and instead, the government would build its public institutions in a more distributed fashion.

Doxiadis would soon be solicited by the Ford Foundation to assist in a private program on educational facilities and to develop the designs for three community schools in Lebanon, only one of which was ever implemented. The extensive economic and social survey he had recommended in his Ekistics Program would soon be undertaken by the IRFED commission in 1959, and a more elaborate master plan for Beirut would be undertaken by Michel Ecochard in 1963, who had previously worked on planning Beirut in 1943 and 1956. The Doxiadis Associates office in Beirut would continue to operate as a regional satellite serving Syria and the Middle East.

What is most impressive about the Doxiadis plan is its insistence on viewing Lebanon as a physical entity, a possibility that would escape everybody who came after him. This possibility and the associated potentials of regional planning to cover a country this small would even elude Doxiadis, who stopped short of following up on its potentials. It would also become the major shortcoming of the plans to follow, whether that of Michel Ecochard, the 1973 Livre Blanc, or that of the Schéma Directeur described below.

Despite the burden of these sampled social problems, the planner's primary task remained to provide projects for improving the housing conditions in the city irrespective of the class and ethnic differences of

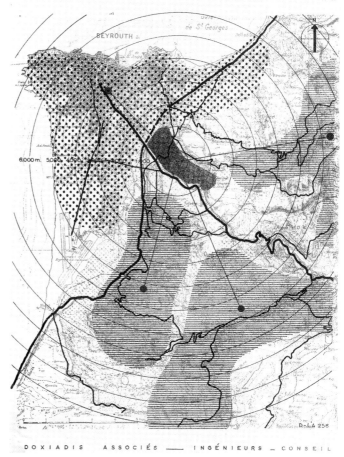

Fig. 10. Proposed location for the new Government City, by Doxiadis Associates, 1959

DOXIADIS ASSOCIÉS ——— INGÉNIEURS — CONSEIL

communities. Doxiadis also turned away from adopting a direction for the national economy or from proposing a comprehensive decentralizing strategy. The planner danced through these commitments and tried not to be burdened by them or to be held responsible for their solution. The unfortunate aspect of the work is that the more detailed, specific projects also failed in their commitments to producing rigorous designs, remaining schematic in their proposal and outlooks. Still, the Doxiadis experience in Beirut demonstrates the possibility of planning to operate both independently of the political regimes that willed it, and between different regimes.

The Schéma Directeur de la Région Métropolitaine de Beyrouth by the Mission Franco-Libanaise d'Etude et d'Aménagement, 1986

In 1983, a series of extensive demographic, housing, and infrastructure surveys were commissioned by the Lebanese government through the Council for Development and Reconstruction and the Directorate of Urban Planning, in order to assess the general conditions of Greater Beirut. The project was supported by an agreement between the Lebanese and French governments signed on April 29, 1983, in order to eventually produce a master plan for metropolitan Beirut. These surveys were being conducted following the Israeli withdrawal from Beirut and the renewed hope that the intermittent civil wars that had started in 1975 were coming to an irreversible end.[13]

By 1983, the city's population had been radically redistributed over the metropolitan region during the war while having remained fixed in size at about 1,200,000. These demographic movements had also created a major shortage in housing supply in the city's suburbs, and the inner city housing stock was suffering from serious, war-inflicted damage. The shift in job locations from the city center to regional centers had also increased the pressure on the infrastructure and transportation networks of the city, both heavily damaged by the war.

The optimism that willed these surveys would soon be proven wrong, and yet despite the resumption of new wars on new fronts in and around Beirut by the summer of 1983, the surveys would be completed. Furthermore, and based on these surveys, the new planning report for metropolitan Beirut was then prepared by the Institut d'Aménagement et d'Urbanisme de la Région Ile de France in collaboration with a group of local architects and planners under the umbrella of the Mission Franco-Libanaise d'Etude et d'Aménagement de la Région Métropolitaine

de Beyrouth. The final report, the Schéma Directeur de la Région Métropolitaine de Beyrouth, providing a vision for the year 2010, was released in June 1986 with the country still at war (fig. 11).

The initial challenge of both the data gatherers and the planners was to define the extent of the Beirut metropolitan region. The conventional criterion of continuous urbanization was cast off under political pressure in search of a boundary definition that would achieve a demographic balance between the Christians and the Muslims in the metropolitan region.[14] The northern and southern boundaries, the Kalb and Damour Rivers, respectively, as delineated by Michel Ecochard in his 1964 metropolitan plan, were readopted here, even though by 1986 the continuous urbanization had crossed over the Kalb River to link Beirut with Jounieh. This problem of amputating regional sprawl from secondary magnet cities would be confronted more acutely in the drawing of the eastern boundary of the metropolitan region. There, and working back and forth between contours and municipal boundaries, the surveyors and planners chose the slightly altered 400-meter-altitude contour to delineate the eastern boundary of the metropolis and achieve the sensitive balance. This line would cut off distant villages from their regional centers, such as the towns of Aley, Broummana, and Bikfaya, and would turn them into a second belt of suburbs around the city. Thus, while it would have made more sense to consider metropolitan Beirut as a conurbation between the central city and the different regional poles, the self-imposed pressure to achieve a half-and-half formula would lead to a suburban

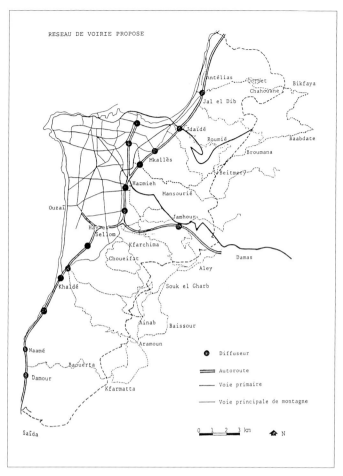

RESEAU DE VOIRIE PROPOSE

Antélias
Qornet Bikfaya
Chahouane
Jal el Dib
Jdaïdé
Roumié Baabdate
Broumana
Mkallès
Beitmery
Hacmieh
Mansourié
Ouzaï
Jamhour
Haret
Sellom
Kfarchima
Choueifat Damas
Aley
Khaldé Souk el Gharb
Aïnab Baissour
Naamé Aramoun
Baouerta
Damour
Kfarmatta
Saïda

● Diffuseur
══ Autoroute
── Voie primaire
── Voie principale de montagne

0 1 2 3 km ⬆ N

Fig. 11. Master Plan of the Metropolitan Region of Beirut for 2010, 1986, IAURIF

conception of the regional areas and to a fundamental definitional mistake in the Schéma Directeur.[15]

Beyond, this initial structural problem, the Schéma Directeur remains, for the most part, clear and rigorous in building its recommendations on four principles which, though sometimes contradictory, offer an adequate framework for several proposals and projects in and around the metropolitan region. For the most part, these were prepared before the Schéma Directeur.

The primary principle of the plan is to reallocate to the city center a role of centrality whether within the city, in relation to the hinterland, or within a larger international setting. This recentering is confirmed by bringing back to the downtown area, both physically and symbolically, the government and its vital institutions. Accordingly, the Schéma Directeur adopted the recommendations of the 1983 and 1977 master plans for the reconstruction of the city center area and for the enlargement of this area: to provide a landfill that included an urban park, and to enforce the road and public transportation networks that emanated from this reclaimed center.

Yet this recentering was coupled with a second principle, a strong decentralization policy. To counterbalance this center, but to help structure the existing dispersed and chaotic growth of the city, the Schéma Directeur proposed the creation of four regional centers, namely, Nahr al-Mawt, Hazmieh, Laylakeh, and Khaldeh (each serving a population of about 300,000) and of several sectoral subcenters, each serving a population of about 70,000.

According to criticisms of this second principle, the number of regional centers corresponded to the confessional/military factions which were controlling the metro-

politan region at the time. Studied carefully in relation to the areas that they were meant to serve, however, these centers do turn out to serve regions that straddle military lines, particularly in the southern and southeastern regions of the metropolitan area (fig. 12). While the experiences of postwar development and growth in Europe and the United States do suggest that both a strengthened center and directed suburban growth could occur simultaneously, a strong center remains incompatible with the creation and enhancement of secondary regional centers as proposed by the Schéma Directeur. Had the planners not succumbed to equating the population on both sides of the demarcation line in the city, the possibility of enhancing the existing regional centers instead of creating new ones would have responded much better to the specific nature of the Beiruti conglomerate and given shape to a particular model that builds the regional plan on the regional geography. Ironically, such a plan remains closer to the social and political organization of the city and its surroundings.

The subsequent selection of subcenters relates more to the intersection of primary roads than to the actual distribution of growth in the city. Under its third principle, the Schéma Directeur assigned a major role in defining the location and character of the regional centers and subcenters to the transportation network. Here, the major road projects proposed were mostly brought together from previous plans and other public authorities: the Arab Highway to Damascus; the peripheral beltway as a link among the four centers; the adoption of the port expansion and the airport expansion projects; and the revitalization of the railroad networks as a system of public transportation.

All these were projects proposed separately under respective authorities and justified together in the transportation framework provided by the Schéma Directeur. Here, more than in any other aspect, the Schéma Directeur's recommendations are closest to what is taking place in the reconstruction process today, even if they lack the coherence provided by the plan.

If in the third principle and the transportation proposal the Schéma Directeur authors come closest to the needs and implementation strategies of postwar reconstruction, their recommendations for the preservation of natural sites, the fourth principle, remain aloof and incoherent both in terms of the selection of sites and in terms of the means of implementation. Geographically, the two major parks are surrounded by large industrial areas and removed from the regional centers. Most of the local parks consist of steep gorges that could not be used for recreation anyway, and yet, the Schéma Directeur did not propose ways in which such large expanses of land could be appropriated for ecological or recreational purposes.

Overall, the exaggerated social and political challenges to the Schéma Directeur enter at such an early level of its conception, at the level of defining the boundaries, that the careful translation of its principles into a physical plan remains misconstrued. Over and above that, the planners of the Schéma Directeur probably provided the last case of planning as a disinterested public agency working with implementable legislation and unlimited resources as its assumed tools. Yet the most difficult aspect of this plan remains the way it solidifies ethnic communities by asserting their territorial presence through the regional centers.

Even at the worst moments of the war, major population displacements and fluid urban networks managed to transcend such simple locational interpretations of community. Overwhelmed by their symbolic tasks, the planners were not able to see beyond the assertion of communal identities through space. Proponents of pluralism, in Lebanon and elsewhere, should not be satisfied with such simplistic interpretations of communal differences.

Comprehensive Thinking
and Local Implementation

In spite of the sketchiness of the Doxiadis scheme and the crude rendering of Beiruti society by the Schéma Directeur, these two plans remain, along with their analytic sections, indispensable surveys of the urban environment at two very important moments in Beirut's history. Both capture the state of the city at a time of rapid and radical change. As such, these two plans provide remarkable historical documents for the study of the city's urban environment against the background of its political history. It is difficult not to succumb to reading historical events through the plans, and yet the strength of these two documents lies precisely in how they reveal patterns in urban history that do not fully correspond to the political narrative.

What is equally distinct about these two plans is that they tend to favor physical means of implementation, despite the large scale of the area being studied (Ekistics Program), and to rely heavily on economic and demographic assumptions (Schéma Directeur). Stressing the physical against legislative or economic means could be justified by the extent of physical destruction, but it could also be viewed as a response to problems that cannot be solved in social or political terms, but that find surrogate, more immediate solutions in the building process. In either case, architects and planners should be encouraged by this, "If you build it, they will come!" tradition, and the way it asserts their role in the reconstruction process. Yet this assertion may result in placing an exaggerated responsibility in the hands

of planners, as it did during the '50s and '60s. It is a responsibility that they should reject so as not to follow in Doxiadis' uncommitted steps, and yet so as not to be crippled by the symbolism of the Schéma Directeur. This does not mean giving up on all the social and political content of planning. Between these two positions, there is a whole spectrum of possible responses that should be tried out but that do not fall victim to the comprehensive visions of politicians.

Even before Doxiadis, there was an unabashedly modern project in Beirut of thinking up better futures through the physical environment. Despite the failures of these proposals, such a project is still indispensable. The comprehensive direction provided by the Ekistics model and the failure of the Schéma Directeur's boundary designation show that it is necessary, given the specific condition of Beirut in relation to the hinterland, to think of comprehensive physical planning strategies. In parallel, such strategies need not depend, as they did with the Schéma Directeur, on national instruments of implementation, but could depart, as were some of the suggestions of Doxiadis, from local amelioration. And yet, lest planning and the seductive terrain it defines fall victim to comprehensive political visions, it is time to adopt a carefully anti-modern idea of robbing the political center of the decision making power about every aspect of human life, and delegating different aspects to different professions and disciplines. Each of these professions, through the means available to it and through the cultural debates it contains about what is good and what is not, would polarize certain debates and positions within the discipline based upon their political content. As such, planners need not abide by existing social visions or political projects, but could expose and direct the social and political content of their profession. At best, their visions should be coordinated rather than collaborated with other disciplines, and in the differences within each discipline and among disciplines and professions, the possible alternatives available to us would be expanded. Amidst the proliferation of excessive forms of pluralism that seek to be asserted in every domain of life, the built environment included, this form of pluralism promises a more effective assertion of diversity.

Notes

1. This particular image is taken from a special issue of Doxiadis' journal *Ekistics* in 1976 to commemorate Constantinos Doxiadis, following his death in 1975.
2. Doxiadis also published a magazine called *Ekistics* which helped disseminate the research conducted by him and his disciples on modern urban planning principles.
3. The late '60s and early '70s witnessed the emergence of alternative approaches in planning to the physical methods of the '50s and '60s. These ranged from transactive planning to policy oriented approaches that avoided dealing with the physical environment directly.
4. M. Mead, *Coming of Age in Samoa: A Psychological Study of Primitive Youth for Western Civilization* (New York: W. Morrow and Company, 1928).
5. See, for example, D. Freeman, *Margaret Mead and Samoa: The Making and Unmaking of an Anthropological Myth* (Cambridge, Mass.: Harvard University Press, 1983).
6. All the material on Doxiadis' work in Lebanon has been provided by the Constantinos Doxiadis Archives in Athens. I am grateful to Lillian Kuri for helping to uncover this material in Athens and to the Doxiadis family for allowing me to survey this material despite the fact that it is still being archived.
7. For an extensive account of U.S. policy in the Middle East and Lebanon during the Eisenhower era and the subsequent military intervention in Lebanon in 1958, see I.L. Gendzier, *Notes from the Minefield: United States Intervention in Lebanon and the Middle East* (New York: Columbia University Press, 1997).
8. From a personal account of Ghassan Tuéni who was a guest aboard the *Semiramis*, April 12, 1997.
9. For a good social history of these suburbs, see F.I. Khuri, *From Village to Suburb: Order and Change in Greater Beirut* (Chicago: University of Chicago Press, 1975).
10. Gendzier, pp. 181–96.
11. The government included Pierre Gemayel as Minister of Public Works, who inherited the support of the United States ambassador from Camille Chamoun, Shehab's predecessor. See Gendzier, pp. 348–56.
12. Doxiadis Archives, vol. 16 (6/30/1959).
13. See Mission Franco-Libanaise d'Etude et d'Aménagement, *Le Schéma Directeur de la Région Métropolitaine de Beyrouth* (Beirut: Conseil du Développement et de la Reconstruction et Direction Générale de l'Urbanisme, June 1986), p. a4.
14. Ibid., fig. 1.
15. Ibid., pp. 2–25.

The Northern Sector:
Projects and Plans at Sea

by

Joumana Ghandour Atallah

Extending four kilometers from the Beirut to the Nahr al-Kalb River, the Northern Sector of the Beirut metropolitan region covers the Dora industrial area, and the commercial areas of Nahr al-Mawt and Jal al-Dib. Commercial and office developments line the eastern side of the north-south highway, and the character of the sector varies from dense commercial and residential areas around the city of Beirut (the Armenian district of Burj Hammoud) and along the north-south highway, to more suburban residential areas as the mountain rises. Traces of an agricultural landscape are also spread along the seashore and in the northernmost part of the sector. In addition, uncontrolled growth, resulting from years of civil war and the decentralization of Beirut, has led to unprecedented urbanization, traffic congestion, and a general abuse of the area's natural environment.

In order to provide more land for development, the 1986 Schéma Directeur (d'Aménagement et d'Urbanisme de la Région Métropolitaine de Beyrouth) proposed a 400-meter-deep land reclamation project stretching over the Northern Sector's coastline. It also proposed an increase in the perpendicular road network leading to the sea in order to relieve the linear urban density along the highway. The first section of the reclamation proposal (from the Beirut River to Antelias, a two-kilometer stretch) is included in the project called Linord, which was initiated in November 1995 and is now a government project under the management of the Council for Development and Reconstruction (CDR).[1] The second section (from Nahr Antelias to Dbayyeh, 1.8 kilometers), commonly known as the Dbayyeh project, is under the management of the Société Nationale d'Entreprises (a privately owned construction company headed by Joseph Khoury) which was established in 1983.[2]

The New Coastline

Reclamation projects unfortunately preclude excessive alteration of the landscape, and planning efforts seem obsessed with the construction of structures that radically compromise the geography of the coastline.[3] The Schéma Directeur determines the layout of public services and the general infrastructure of urban zones without any consideration for the environment and without formulating social and urban concepts for the new areas. Development is seemingly equated with a victory over nature and the ambitious task of gaining land from the sea.

These landfills (Solidere and Linord) began as either a garbage dump or a small fishing harbor, the latter becoming completely landfilled, much like the situation at Ras Beirut. Nevertheless, garbage dumps have grown as remnants of the chaos of the war. Together, both garbage dumps and small fishing harbors seem to herald a pattern of development and to justify planning policies that are, in fact, strictly dictated by the desire to maximize the political and economic gains of a successful 'tourist' industry. In some cases, the surface area of the dump constitutes a significant part of the total surface area to be reclaimed.[4]

Linord

Linord was supposedly created to deal with an environmental problem in the absence of government resources. The project called for the rehabilitation of the Burj Hammoud garbage dump into a municipal park.[5] It also called for the creation of the primary and secondary stations of a sewage treatment plant and for the provision of three sewage pipelines to serve the surrounding areas. Oil and gas storage areas were to be regulated and relocated east of the park, and 2 million square meters of surface area was to be reclaimed and the necessary infrastructure provided.

The master plan developed for Linord divides the project into three zones: an infrastructure zone (sewage treatment plant, oil and gas tanks), a leisure area, and a residential area. A business park will surround the commercial developments of the marina (at the heart of the leisure area) and act as a buffer between the industrial area and the traffic generated by the north-south highway. Conceptually, the business park extends along the highway and provides the 'city facade' of the project.

The notion of safeguarding the residential neighborhoods from the effects of heavy traffic guides the layout of streets and the land use assigned to specific blocks. A seaside promenade is proposed along the coast, and the 'Mediterranean' facade of the project is to be created by means of architectural alternation: every other block will host low-rise apartment buildings with red-tiled, pitched roofs, and in between will stand medium-rise, modern-looking buildings. Within the scheme, ownership of the sewage treatment plants and the park will be returned to the government, along with all public road networks. The remaining holdings would be divided between the developer and the government.

Bofill's Cité de la Mer

The first project drawn for the Northern Sector reclamation area, and by far the most interesting one to date, was commissioned in 1988. A preliminary master plan was outlined by Ricardo Bofill for the zone, extending from Antelias to Nahr al-Kalb,[6] in which he set out to re-create an ideal Mediterranean city, a city open to the sea, with large public spaces set against the dramatic scenery of steeply sloping mountains. He called his project Cité de la Mer (fig. 1).

A uniform grid was laid out, establishing a series of 400-square-meter parcels parallel to the sea and to the present north-south highway. Organizing the overall layout are three main axes: a buffer zone to the east, a central spine, and the 'Corniche' by the sea (figs. 2 and 3).

The relief road runs along the length of the development and distributes local traffic into the project. Bordered by commercial enterprises, the central spine runs through the project and is punctuated by a series of

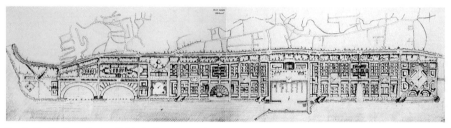

Fig. 1. The Northern Sector, Cité de la Mer, master plan

Fig. 2. The Northern Sector, Cité de la Mer, master plan, detail

Fig. 3. The Northern Sector, master plan, detail view of marina

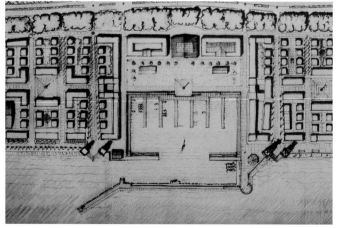

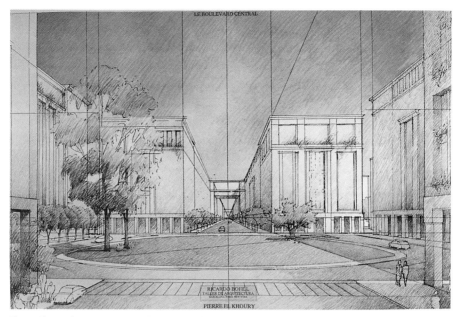

Fig. 4. The Northern Sector, Cité de la Mer, view of central boulevard

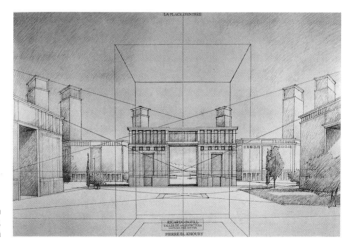

Fig. 5. The Northern
Sector, Cité de la Mer,
view of entrance piazza

public open spaces (fig. 4). The third axis is a twelve-meter-wide seaside 'Corniche' that opens up to large public piazzas established near the water. Intersecting the three main avenues (service road, central spine, and Corniche), are perpendicular roads set at intervals of 100 meters and allowing for views of the sea. The perspective is exagger- ated at the roads intersecting the existing expressway and is framed by two housing towers each eighty meters high, and each set by the water's edge. Three major squares (400 meters by 400 meters in size, with underground public parking) also help define the city: the 'harbor,' the 'entrance piazza,' and the 'beach piazza,' respectively (fig. 5). Essentially, these squares act as focal points for everyday public life of the city: the 'civic,' the 'leisure,' and the 'commercial.'

With a marina for 600 yachts and an arcade of commercial facilities surrounding the quays, the harbor area is at the center of the project. A hotel, a business center, and a city hall surround the upper level of the central plaza. The 'entrance piazza,' located a little further to the south, adopts a layout that addresses both downtown Beirut and the sea. It is planned to accommodate housing projects and a town hall serving the neighboring community. The 'entrance piazza' is accessible, on axis, from the project's southern extension and, therefore, produces a linear interpretation in the plan, with a hierarchy of programmatic functions starting from housing at the southern tip to recreation toward the north.

Symmetrically located about the central harbor, the 'beach piazza' constitutes the edge between the city and its recreation zones. This is a sunken piazza bordered again by a hotel development, office buildings, and a third town hall serving the adjacent community. Between these main squares, two residential neighborhoods appear. Two further squares mark these neighborhoods, the first drawn as an irregular quadrangle in the manner of Piazza San Marco in Venice, and the second featuring an open-air theater. Souks planned for the area behind adopt a tighter street pattern allowing for small commercial enterprises to develop. Districts within the project are mainly residential in character, with about 6,500 dwelling units projected. The remaining 20 percent of the project is commercial and institutional, including offices, two schools, three town halls, a sports club, a marine museum, and a heliport.

Dar al-Handasah's 'Littoral Nord Master Plan'

With the renewal of heavy fighting, Bofill's design was never further developed. The project was placed on hold for several years until the early '90s when the Civil War was over and the CDR, under the Hariri government, reworked the Northern Sector reclamation project. At that time, the land areas were redistributed by the government and the section of the project that extends from Dbayyeh to Nahr al-Kalb was discarded.[7] Dar al-Handasah, the largest engineering consulting firm in Lebanon, was commissioned to produce a master plan for the zone, extending from Antelias to Dbayyeh. The master plan covers approximately 1 million square meters of reclaimed land of which about 61 percent will be built upon. A floor-area ratio of 2 brings the total buildable area to 1.2 million square meters. The main land use of the project will be residential, eventually accommodating 22,000 inhabitants.[8]

The current master plan, issued in May 1996, retains few traces of Ricardo Bofill's urban ideal while using plan-making gimmicks to sell an urbanism shaped by financial gain. The grid proposed in the Dar al-Handasah plan is significantly less rigid, allowing for a transformation and dilution of Bofill's formal organizing layout. The relief road is now connected to the existing road network at only three intersections (Antelias, Naccash, and Dbayyeh) (fig. 6). Mixed commercial and residential developments are created along this relief road to provide a western edge to the existing highway and to protect the residential community, located at the innermost parts of the project, from the nuisance of heavy traffic.

mixed-use, nine-story high-rise buildings, is reduced to a secondary road, distributing traffic within the neighborhoods. To prevent 'through traffic,' the road is regularly interrupted by planted parks and commercial developments.

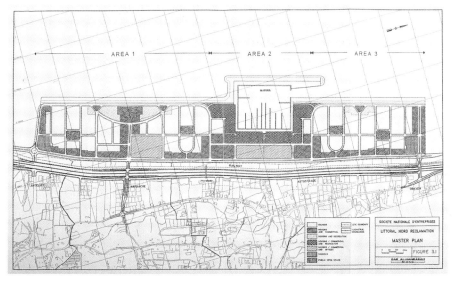

Fig. 6. Dbayyeh reclamation area, master plan, Dar al-Handasah, the Northern Sector

At the two extremities of the relief road, and at major vehicular intersections, two sites have been allocated for primary schools. These two schools are meant to be accessible to the surrounding communities and the area is seen as a buffer zone protecting the development from other 'intrusive activities.'[9] Two predominantly residential areas distributed on either side of the yacht marina divide the project into three distinct areas. Located on the interior of the project and organized around open landscaped spaces, these strictly residential neighborhoods are intended to be "suburban in character."[10] Bofill's central spine, with its

In addition, Bofill's large open piazzas by the sea – the quadrangular piazza, theater, and 'beach piazza' – are now mere roundabouts located to facilitate traffic flow at intersecting roads. The only public open space on the Corniche is a small piazza, and the Corniche is now divided into two separate parts on either side of the marina (fig. 7). A dense belt of mixed housing and commercial developments surrounds the marina. Also, vehicular access to the marina is restricted, thus, making it more exclusive.

Open views are maintained across a series of roads that connect the relief road

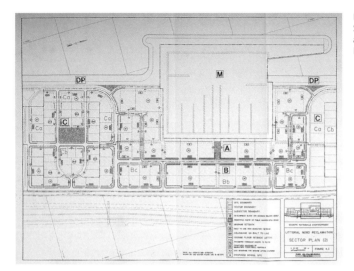

perpendicularly to the waterfront. A T-shaped roadway terminates one of the few perpendicular axes cutting through the project and connecting with the inland developments. This connecting road is mainly commercial, with a large mall scheduled to be located at the northwestern intersection with the relief road. Other axes at right angles are planned as tertiary roads, with building setbacks increasing with proximity to the sea, a reinterpretation of Bofill's forced perspectives. With continuous setbacks, as far as nine meters behind the parcel boundary, Dar al-Handasah's scheme attempts to enlarge the pedestrian green or public domain, provided, of course, that these spaces remain open and are not fenced in. A twenty-meter-wide open space cutting through the center of the marina development is maintained to provide pedestrian

Fig. 8. The Northern Sector, Linord

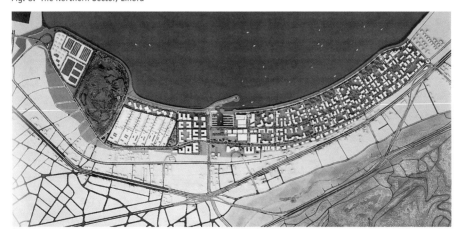

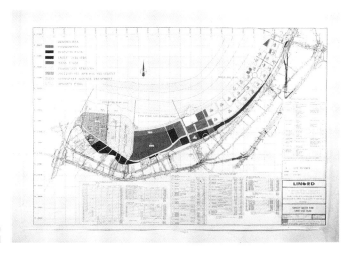

Fig. 9. The Northern
Sector, Linord

access to the commercial developments surrounding the quays, and the commercial core features a double-height colonnade, ideal for commercial "exploitation of the sidewalk."

A Limited Notion of Urban Planning

Bofill's original plan for the Dbayyeh reclamation project seems to have been washed out to sea. Its reinterpretation in the current Dar al-Handasah master plan can be qualified as an aberration of the original, which should be noted for the city-making issues it addresses and the contrast it creates with current planning policy. In the current Dar al-Handasah project, it is difficult to recognize any notion of city-making beyond its immediate commercialization (colonnades are for commercial exploitation of the sidewalk, gardens are roundabouts, schools are buffers to nuisances, etc.). It is difficult to read the urban vision or grasp the social agenda that would underlie any new city proposal. The idea of a

project as an urban design scheme addressing social and formal issues is most ambiguous in the Linord proposal (figs. 8 and 9). The project is looking more and more like the mere framework for a financial transaction. Even the invitation to bid suggests that the present "conceptual plan" can be altered at will by the developer or construction company. The brief calls for the provision of a number of infrastructure projects, whilst urban design issues (open spaces, road layout, building requirements, etc.) are apparently interchangeable.[11]

Reclaimed land, which is fundamentally public property is, in many ways, sold in the development transaction. Treatment of the waste dumps, or the costs of reclamation operations, are paid for in land with planning regulations shaped by the developer. Master plans are altered at the will and seemingly for the benefit of the investors. According to the state, the economic benefits of profitable 'touristic' projects such as Linord and Dbayyeh counter the loss of the public beachfront (fig. 10). Planning guidelines are reduced to specific percentage figures imposed for utilities, such as roads and open spaces, to be returned to the government.

maximize land exploitation, the large piazzas are reduced to small vehicular roundabouts. In the present project, what is called an 'open space' is merely the void opened up by a setback (a colonnade, a small place), or the buffer zone (such as the schoolyard)

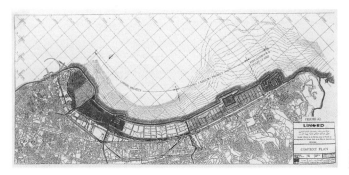

Fig. 10. The Northern Sector, Linord/Dbayyeh

Contempt for Public Open Space

It is quite telling that included in the 30 percent accounting of the public network are all open spaces not specifically dedicated to traffic. Moreover, given both the predilections of engineers in public office to create more roads with a wider right of way, the surface allotted to green spaces is likely to be very small. Unfortunately, this is often the case when promises of public open space are transformed to suit shortsighted commercial interests. An early draft of the plan, developed by Linord, diverted vehicular traffic behind every other residential block on the Corniche, giving the developer added land value for buildings directly adjacent to the water. Now, however, the Corniche is no longer a continuous seaside drive (fig. 11).[12]

The metamorphosis of Bofill's urban spaces into the current plan proposed by Dar al-Handasah illustrates the developer's notion of public open spaces. In an attempt to

designed to protect the development from 'nuisances.' Where a garden is in fact provided, it seems to be for the sole benefit of the surrounding residents. The four squares, which include children's playgrounds, appear scheduled to remain inaccessible to the public at large and, therefore, more attractive to the adjacent property buyers. The provision of a public open space is never a serious part of the design brief or the urban concept behind the plan. Parks seem to be logical conclusions to non-buildable sites. The quality of a so-called public open space, sandwiched between a sewage treatment plant and a tank farm, must be questioned. The Burj Hammoud Park, for instance, is a park by default.

The Grand Avenue for Social Interaction

The Corniche seems to be the only model of a public space approved and emulated by

Fig. 11. The Northern Sector, Linord, view of the Corniche

planning agencies. It symbolizes an urbanization of the coastline, replacing sandy beaches and natural rock formations with a paved seaside promenade. The Corniche is primarily a traffic artery. In a country where public gatherings are considered a security threat, the Corniche seems to be the ideal form of open space. It remains a place of passage.

With the loss of the traditional souks and Martyrs' Square, open spaces of social interaction and public activity have been significantly reduced in Beirut. The Corniche represents the most successful open space left in the city today and captures the positive public spirit. When plans to build an expressway along the Sidon shorefront were met with much criticism, for example, the outcry was tempered with proposals to render the artery more 'Corniche-like,' with slower traffic, pedestrian intersections, and palm trees.

For the municipality, the Corniche remains an 'avenue.'[13] In addition to the Corniche, Bofill locates a grand avenue at the heart of his Cité de la Mer project. The most commercial and the most public street in the plan is the central spine organizing the overall scheme. In an attempt to create a continuous street wall and a strong sense of public spaces, buildings lining the main avenues (the Corniche and the central spine) are given bigger footprints and no setbacks are required. The avenue begins and ends with monuments: symbolic markers in time and space. The design of the central spine is approached from an architectural as well as from a functional perspective, adding urban significance to its infrastructural role. The central spine is made all the more theatrical and all the more public with its monumental buildings. Thus, Bofill refers to memorable moments of successful boulevards.[14]

By contrast, Dar al-Handasah's idea of a grand avenue can be read clearly at the level of the Naccash connector, where a primary road extends toward a public garden by the sea. Palm trees as a border to the street are used to reinforce its formality and to signify 'avenue.' The success of the avenue, as a grand space framed by a line of continuous buildings with carefully controlled frontage, is jeopardized, however, by the large lot located at its southeastern entrance. Perhaps the site of a future mall, this parcel is free of the building regulations that have been imposed upon other parcels along the street. With the obliteration of Bofill's central spine, the 'avenue' and the public life that goes with it are no longer a strong urban gesture.

The Vanishing Public Square

Nowhere is the contrast in the design approach so clear as around the issue of urban squares. Where one project seems to run away from the civic public place, the other seems to reinstate it at every opportunity ('entrance piazza,' 'Piazza San Marco,' 'central piazza,' 'the theater piazza,' 'beach piazza'). Dar al-Handasah's four green squares and Linord's single circular garden are seen as amenities to the surrounding residential developments, while civic and institutional buildings surround Bofill's largest squares, the largest and most perfect of which is the marina with its esplanade and sundial. Symbolically, it represents the center of public life. Unfortunately, Dar al-Handasah's ensuing proposal replaces the esplanade with residential buildings and

limits public access to the marina. Clearly, the European piazza is adopted by Bofill as a model to be imported and emulated as a platform for public life in the city.[15] However, his desire to re-create the Italian piazza, whether centralized or open to the sea, came into conflict with the realities of the Lebanese residential market. A distinct piazza is usually carved out, as it were, from a tight urban fabric. The developer, however, insisted on supplying the market with detached apartment buildings that are the residential norm in Beirut.

Within the revisions of the Dar al-Handasah master plan, the single urban space left to design is the marina. In fact, Bofill has been hired back, together with architect Nabil Gholam, by Mr. Joseph Khoury, to design the urban spaces included in his portion of the Dbayyeh project, namely the marina and its surrounding area. Together, Bofill and Gholam try and imagine the basin as the large paved piazza in the original project. To define the perimeter of the marina, a colonnade wraps around the basin and is echoed by a double row of trees. The sharp five-meter drop in level between the esplanade and the promenade is mediated by an inclined 'green' plane. From there the landscaped 'talus' provides a green backdrop to the horizon of columns. In the willful articulation of the perimeter can be read Bofill's attempt to recover the central square. Thus the open center becomes the 'public interior' of the city. Unfortunately, however, the public piazza is also a sunken piazza, located below the ground level datum. It is therefore public only inasmuch as pedestrians will be allowed into it in order to shop at the adjacent arcade. Otherwise, it is planned as a water basin for yachts and it is surrounded by private development with limited access. Such planning totally diverges from Bofill's Cité de la Mer, which provided straight vehicular connections on either side of the marina, all the way from the expressway to the sea.

Order and Transparency in City Planning

As opposed to the plans developed by Dar al-Handasah and Linord, which are conditioned to a large extent by real estate marketing techniques, the Cité de la Mer plan illustrates an architect's vision of the new city. Bofill's plan represents an attempt to introduce a social dimension to the planning effort. It places faith in the capacity of public space to counterbalance urban elements. It proposes a stage for interaction and dialogue within large urban spaces. The selection of programmatic elements, such as public buildings, museums, sports facilities, and beaches, is an attempt to open up cloistered communities identified by religious confession, thus pushing forth the importance of civic and institutional uses in the planning of a mixed, open community. Furthermore, elements drawn from historic cities are used to recall distinct experiences of urban harmony. The campaniles of Venice which have inspired the Cité de la Mer's housing towers, the Piazza of San Marco, Roman Byblos, etc., raise parallels with memorable cities by the sea and illustrate a nostalgia for a recognizable urban structure. Whether the renderings of Bofill are meant to preach a European classical language or

not, one thing is certain. The idea is to embrace a certain historicism and formal contextualism. The stylistic language applied to the perspective images is a metaphor for notions of order and harmony that have guided the plan making process.

Order and clarity in city planning can also be read in its structural geometry. It can be read in the street grid, in the string of squares, and in the monumentality of public buildings. In addition, the use of urban types becomes essential in a project such as Bofill's first, which relies heavily on regular urban and architectural patterns. Strict alignments are used for organizing spaces, for defining views, and as a framework for building. Bofill seems so obsessed with establishing a continuous urban form, that the necessary disruptions to that order are totally omitted from the scheme.

Interstitial Spaces

The notions of an open city and a clear plan accessible to the public at large are shunned by the developer's desire to create a safe and pleasant environment. Both the Linord and the Dar al-Handasah projects engage community life at local centers and green squares set within tightly built neighborhoods. One can only imagine that these would be fenced off and restricted to the public. The result is a community protected from the surrounding context by careful selection of land uses and the provision of empty buffer zones. The space between the project and the highway is also left as a gap by this brand of urbanism. In this regard, the Dar al-Handasah project ignores the strip as a 'no-man's-land,' where Bofill's original plan suggested a linear park. The fifty-meter buffer zone set between the development and the highway was to include a wall of eucalyptus trees. Extensions of the park into the project (at the level of the northern town hall) were proposed and local squares were to be created across the relief road. Furthermore, the relief road, treated as a commercial strip on the western side of the buffer zone in the Dar al-Handasah scheme, fails to engage the other side, which remains too distant and too disconnected. On its eastern side, the strip is characterized by a series of developments devoid of urban identity. These have sprung up as a result of the extension of the north-south artery, hindering its vehicular capacity. The need to connect different urban settlements should be addressed by those traffic arteries and 'local distributors' which are now thought of as mere circulation corridors. In order for these new developments to succeed in any way, interstitial spaces need to become a focus of the urban design, and should not be treated as zones of separation or forgotten parts of the city.[16]

Locating the schools at the edges of the project is in the end a gesture made (together with the commercial mall) toward engaging the neighboring communities. If one thinks of these projects (created on reclaimed land at the boundary of an existing traffic artery) as appendages to the city, margins of sorts, then one may understand the absence of any attempt to integrate the new community within the surrounding fabric. None of these projects seems concerned with fitting into the context. The projects are often conceived of as independent islands designed to give a new face to the city. Indeed, Bofill was asked, in typical 'developer speak,' to plan an independent city, an island that would distinguish itself from its surrounding context. The management at Linord was quite proud of the fact that the project was a separate entity and should, by virtue of this distinction, be superior to any other project in the city. Clearly, the idea of exclusivity, a marketing tool, guided the urban planning decisions. Quality was equated with difference, and the exclusivity of the project unfortunately reinforced existing isolated and segregated structures.

The Idea of the Mediterranean City

The idea of contextual design is difficult to apply in the creation of completely new urban blocks, such as those on reclaimed land. The design can hardly derive from a collective experience since the land does not exist. It cannot derive from an inherited road system, nor from an existing topography. Only general geography, the Mediterranean, seems to provide a viable physical basis for the planning exercise.

Features of the traditional Mediterranean city inform some of the design decisions in the present projects. The flexibility of the boundary between public and private is manifested in the shared courtyards and open setbacks of all three schemes. Rendered perspective images of the Linord seafront illustrate the Mediterranean facade as a patchwork alternating selected images of the inherited cityscape with more contemporary flat-roofed buildings.[17] Generally, red-tiled roofs are used to re-create the image of the 'Mediterranean city.'

The new face added to the city can in many ways be seen as recovering the city's sense of access to the coast. In the case of Linord, it replaces the industrial installations and the garbage dump with a seaside promenade and a municipal garden. It reclaims access to the coast by overrunning the barrier of the existing highway in the Dbayyeh project. Increasing setback requirements in the Cité de la Mer and the Dar al-Handasah plans, as you proceed toward the sea, are used to reinforce the perspective and large vistas.[18] Nevertheless, the view is actually the other way around. With a fore-shortening of building heights as you move backwards, together with the narrowing of the street framed by 'campaniles,' Bofill has set the stage for the spectacle of the Mediterranean city against the cyclorama of the Lebanese mountainscape. Using scenic effects that make reference to cities of the past, the Cité de la Mer alludes to a Renaissance idea of the city as a stage, an ideal setting. Bofill literally creates *'théâtralise la ville'* to act out a utopia, a planner's utopia. Moreover, the relevance of the Cité de la Mer's unattainable utopia is poignant in the postwar city which has lost all notion of the 'public' as the unifying element of urban life. By contrast, major construction projects on public lands are relegated to private enterprise, and all government regulatory policies are withdrawn to facilitate the rapid construction of the new amorphous zones with undefined 'suburban' spaces. It is imperative that the dead space at the edge of the new zones is addressed and that public open spaces be articulated if the city is to be reconstructed as the center of urban life and not as a collection of enclosed communities. It is only then that the design of those new large-scale projects can be called urban, and that the design would respond to the complexity of the act of 'constructing' the city. In this regard, if every city constructs itself with an image of an ideal, Beirut has yet to formulate a clear idea of what that ideal is.

Notes

1. Now the title of a CDR government project, Linord was originally the name of the private real estate company, "The Lebanese Company for the Development of the Northern Coast of Beirut" given the mandate to reclaim and develop 2 million square meters of land.
2. The initial project extended all the way to Nahr al-Kalb.
3. Such is the case with plans developed for the Ras Beirut Convention Center and the Sidon highway.
4. In the case of Linord, the surface area of the garbage dump is approx. 266,000 square meters as opposed to a total project area of 2,394,000 square meters.
5. The Burj Hammoud dump, which was closed in July 1997, grew over the last two years to include household garbage from Greater Beirut after the Normandy dump was closed for the Solidere works.
6. Bofill was then associated with Pierre el-Khoury, a local architect who was at the time Minister for Public Works and the Lebanese partner on the project.
7. Reclamation operations are at present restricted to the area between Antelias and Dbayyeh. Filling has commenced and is near completion. The outer sea defense wall has been partly completed up to and including the marina basin. Road levels are being filled in around urban blocks.
8. Dar al-Handasah, "Littoral Nord Master Plan Report," May 1996, pp. 30, 33.
9. As stated in the Dar al-Handasah "Littoral Nord Master Plan Report," p. 33.
10. The "Littoral Nord Master Plan Report" cites a medium density projection with a plot coverage of 35 percent, p. 31.
11. Linord's invitation to bid entitled, "See through the cost. This is your coast to coast opportunity," calls for financing the building of the coastal sewage collector, for the provision of land to incorporate a future secondary sewage treatment plant, for land to be sold to oil/gas storage companies, for the rehabilitation of the waste dump, the execution of a primary sewage treatment plant, the construction of a military coast guard harbor, and a fishing harbor.
12. The plan has since been amended and the Corniche is currently a continuous drive.
13. The Ras Beirut Corniche is officially named 'Avenue de Paris.' The term is used loosely to designate a major artery.
14. Hanna Gomez provides an extensive discussion of the avenue in "Center, Park, Avenida," *Lotus* 56, pp. 33–61.
15. It could be argued that this import is yet another manifestation of cultural colonialism reminiscent of the planning techniques of the Mandate period.
16. See Richard Sennett's discussion of interstitial spaces in "The Power of the Eye" in *Urban Revisions*, pp. 59–69.
17. These attempts are reminiscent of the planning guidelines developed for the Beirut Central District (included in the Solidere project) whereby a wedge of medium-rise buildings is assigned limited building heights and red-tiled roofs symbolize the Mediterranean roofscape. The sector's main design concern is in fact to maintain a 'view corridor' to and from the prime minister's headquarters, reinscribing within the perspective of the city (an idealized city) the original viewpoint, the seat of power.
18. Originally, and in keeping with his idea of a Mediterranean city open to the water, Bofill had proposed lower building heights by the seafront. The developer insisted on maximizing revenue on the seafront building sites and on locating the highest buildings at the water's edge (twelve floors), with nine floors for buildings along the central boulevard and seven floors for buildings on the street.

Heart of Beirut: Making the Master Plan for the Renewal of the Central District

by
Angus Gavin

The city of Beirut has since Phoenician times claimed a main role as a trading crossroads and cultural watershed between Europe and the East. Such a role was fulfilled in characteristically flamboyant style by modern Beirut during the oil boom years, up to the outbreak of Lebanon's Civil War in 1975. In spite of a persisting lack of resolution in the regional peace process, the city is now quickly recovering from the scars of the Lebanese war, and the reconstruction of the Beirut Central District (BCD) – the geographic and historic heart of the city (fig. 1) – forms the spearhead of an extensive national recovery program that is rekindling the capital's ambitious regional aspirations. The project represents one of those rare opportunities in city-making and renewal. Unlike much urbanization in the Middle East it has so far managed to avoid the "rush to modernize and impress," and is recognized as perhaps the most important undertaking in urban regeneration in the world today.[1]

Fig. 1. The geographic and historic heart of the city

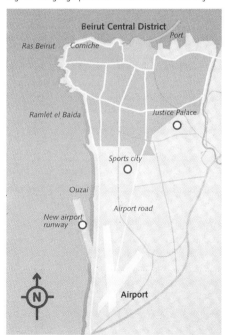

Legacy of the War

Beirut came out of the war in 1990 a city divided, devoid of center and robbed of its regional role as the former financial, trading, educational, cultural, and tourism focus of the Middle East. Today the city remains psychologically split along the scar of the wartime 'Green Line' from Martyrs' Square at the core and out along the axis of Damascus Road. Other dividing lines are evident. As reconstruction of the center proceeds, there is a risk that unresolved relationships may develop between an advantaged core and its immediate periphery. The city needs to reconnect.

Beyond these evident polarizations, Beirut has been affected by other legacies of the war. Among these there is a widespread and permissive atmosphere of unplanned and uncontrolled development, caused not only by the squatter settlements housing refugees from the occupied south, now largely confined to the city's southern approaches, but also by the wartime exodus of urban communities to the relative safety of the suburban fringe, up onto the surrounding mountainsides, and in commercial strip development along the coastal highway to the north.

Contrasts between relative wealth to the north and the poverty of the southern suburbs are marked, and the decentralization has worsened Beirut's transportation problems, already aggravated during the war by the destruction of the city's public transport infrastructure. Furthermore, the pattern of migration away from Beirut's war-torn center has reinforced the city's emerging polynucleated structure. In this there are parallels to the structural changes that have affected many cities in the developed world: but in Beirut the stimulus was not the complex interplay of economic and social forces – it was war.

In beginning to address, five years ago, the task of planning for urban regeneration, of reactivating the city core and redefining its role, these macro-scale issues compounded the more obvious problems in the BCD itself: destruction beyond salvage of almost two thirds of the urban fabric and the city's public spaces; a squatter population in excess of 30,000 occupying largely unsafe structures throughout the city core; virtually total dysfunction of the infrastructure;

extreme fragmentation of existing property ownership; and a shoreline polluted and irrevocably changed by years of uncontrolled dumping of the city's domestic waste, the rubble of destroyed buildings, and the detritus of war.

Master planning for the BCD's revival had made a false start shortly after the end of the war,[2] with a grandiose scheme that combined beaux-arts 'grand planning' and a 1960s infatuation with the car, and the heavy road infrastructure that this love affair engenders. Despite the need for widespread demolition and restructuring in the war-damaged city center, the master plan that replaced it[3] and is now being implemented by the private sector development corporation Solidere shows a much greater sensitivity to the surviving and preexisting urban fabric and a welcome reduction in the impact of the highway on the city. Numerous buildings were preserved for restoration. The process brought with it a focusing of international experience and an application of recent trends in urban regeneration and waterfront development from around the world.

Through the process of evolving the new master plan,[4] a cross-cultural debate continued, essentially between Anglo-Saxon contextualism that sought to restore and rebuild the city from the 'bottom up,' and a 'top-down,' tabula rasa approach that favored the grand gesture, imposing new patterns of order on the city in the continental European tradition. The city center had witnessed a superimposed restructuring of this type during its last great renewal in the 1920s and 1930s under the French Mandate. The dense medieval fabric had been cleared, to be replaced by the star-shaped, beaux-arts grid, focused on the Place de l'Etoile as the symbolic setting for the parliament building, radiating its political primacy over the recently extended borders of Greater Lebanon.

In the Beirut of the early 1990s, the master plan team held strong convictions that, despite the scale of wartime destruction and the need to provide the framework and vision to help stimulate the city's re-emerging role in the region, the plan should deliver a message of cultural continuity and pluralism – not the imposition of a foreign order. The war had not obliterated the past. Where the fabric had been destroyed, the site's topography and historic views to the sea and mountains revealed a preexisting order, other patterns and remembered places that had survived in the collective memory, and the wealth of the city's archaeological heritage that lay beneath the soil awaiting the influence that it might exert, once exposed, in shaping and enriching the city of the future.

The Role of the Center

In 1950 about 80 percent of the city's main commercial establishments were located in the center. This proportion had declined to 42 percent by 1975 as Beirut sustained rapid growth, its population increasing by two thirds over the preceding decade. As the center reached the limits of available space, secondary centers began to emerge in Greater Beirut. The Central District nevertheless maintained a clear centrality and dominance over the metropolitan area as the government, retail, and regional banking center, the microcosm of the country's reli-

gious affiliations, and the focus of the hotel sector and city nightlife.

Beirut's metropolitan strategic plan,[5] completed during the war in 1986, recognized the city's emerging pattern of peripheral centers, much strengthened by the exodus from the destroyed core. The renewed BCD will increasingly be in competition with these secondary centers and must recognize their presence. It will also have to compete with the commercial strip of uncontrolled development that has infilled northward along the coastal corridor. The contrast between the comprehensive planning of the Central District and the desecration of the landscape along Lebanon's coastal fringe and elsewhere points to another type of 'role' that the BCD has adopted, with its relatively sophisticated developmental control procedures and new fire safety, seismic, disabled access, and other standards – that of a 'model project' for Lebanon.

There are superficial similarities between Beirut's wartime dispersal from the core, its expanding suburban fringe, the occupation of the center by squatters, and the patterns of inner city decay that have affected many cities in the developed world since the 1950s. Most marked in North America, the process of central area decline is the result of complex economic and social forces. In the 1960s fashionable urban theories attempted to rationalize the process: in the new 'non-place urban realm,' developments in communications technologies meant that face-to-face contact was no longer necessary and the traditional city center, the preferred location and meeting point of many different activities, was claimed to be a feature of the past.[6]

In the cities of the New World, development pressures continue strongest in the urban fringe, fueled by peripheral highway construction, car-based mobility, and the availability of cheap land. The center, the inner city, the old dockside areas – once the engines of the urban economy – are, nevertheless, beginning to fight back. Boston and Baltimore provide good examples of waterfront city centers reestablishing their role after a pattern of central area decline and explosive peripheral growth had set in, in the 1960s. Achievements like these have both contributed to and benefited from a growing body of experience in urban regeneration[7] from around the world over the past quarter century, demonstrating a considerable advance over the early, simplistic interventions of 1950s urban renewal. They have provided lessons for Beirut, not in building form and architectural expression, but as models of viable central-area and waterfront renewal,[8] place-making, mixed-use development, and as centers of complex urban interaction.

Along with a rapidly improving track record in inner city revitalization, there is also a perceptible shift in public opinion that recognizes a need for the center. The 'New Urbanists' reflect this trend.[9] Just as cyberspace and the freeway offer the ultimate freedoms, we rediscover the need for the central place: a social arena, a meeting point, and a place of exchange for business, culture, and ideas – the city's point of origin.

In many ways this sounds like the historic cities of the Old World. These, too, hold lessons for Beirut. In many historic European cities, centers have succeeded in retaining a role as 'meeting point,' in spite of the ubiquitous pattern of strong peripheral growth. Recent trends toward successful urban regeneration have accompanied a strong revival in urban values and a rediscovery of the commercial, cultural, and residential benefits of the inner city and the hidden assets of rejuvenated waterfronts. No longer are the spread out, auto-age cities of North America fashionable to urban theorists: the relatively dense, historic European city is back in vogue.

Stemming, therefore, from an inquiry into both the Beirut context and international trends in urban regeneration, key master-plan objectives were identified for the BCD. The city center should be much more than a conventional central business district: it must emphasize mixed use and be active round the clock. It should recover its role as an important residential location. Heritage and archaeology are assets that can distinguish Beirut: historic fabric set in a high-quality, pedestrian-friendly public domain are among the features that enable many European city centers to retain their role as 'meeting points.' The city core should strengthen its role as a seat of government, delivering the message of public commitment and attracting other service functions. It should follow the example of successful regional centers in providing the location for headquarters-type office functions and international institutions. Finally, as a multiuse focus and potential visitor destination, it should reestablish its role as seat of tourism, recreation, and cultural uses, and as an important center for retail and leisure activities.

Compared with other current large-scale regeneration projects, central Beirut enjoys the benefit of special features that will help it come back strongly. Firstly, the BCD forms the geographic and historic heart of the city, as shown in the accompanying illustrations. Unlike other major inner city projects – London's Docklands, Paris' La Défense – it does not have to promote a new, off-center location. Largely as a result of wartime land-fill, the BCD also enjoys the benefit of adjacent land that may be used for expansion. Secondly, the BCD represents the one unaffiliated zone in Beirut – it has always been multi-religious and multi-ethnic. Once reactivated, it can be the place where the city reconnects. By creating a mixed-use destination at the heart of Beirut, with extensive areas of public open space, it can rediscover its role as the city's meeting point and 'social arena.'[10] It can also provide a natural and pluralist focus for Lebanon's emerging service economy: if you want to do business with all Lebanese communities, you need a presence in the city center. Lastly, behind the project lies the political will and imperative for it to spearhead Lebanon's national recovery program and lead the way toward a new international role for Beirut within the region.

Grandeur and Context

The making of the plan synthesized an exchange between two sets of ideas – almost between two cultural positions. The first is steeped in the continental European tradition of top-down 'grand planning' – much like the Haussmannian philosophy that gave Beirut its Etoile during the last reconstruction of the city center in the '20s and '30s –

and a new, more Anglo-Saxon search for context and cultural continuity that seemed more appropriate to postwar revival at the close of the twentieth century.

Nothing, however, is very new in the making of cities. To formalism and order there has always been an opposing trend toward the natural and the organic. In the cities of classical antiquity the Greeks made subtle and contextual responses to the landscape, as if interpreting a 'genius loci' – early Ephesus provides an example (fig. 2). The Romans were 'top-downers.' Disregarding the vagaries of nature, they built axial diagrams of imperial power, as at Timgad in Algeria. At Miletus, however, Hippodamus created a masterpiece of balance that seemed to unite the two extremes, fusing the dynamics of the Greek plan with the discipline of the grid.[11]

Comparable opposing responses have been observed in differing approaches to postwar reconstruction in European cities after World War II. In central Warsaw, the salvaging of a national identity in the aftermath of occupation became associated with the faithful reconstruction of devastated historic fabric. Opposing this *patrimonial* stance are the temptations of the *tabula rasa,* represented in Le Corbusier's 'Brave New World' images of the 1920s, in which the old, inefficient structures and narrow streets were to be swept away and replaced by a new order of great boulevards, open spaces, and glass and concrete towers. Such images had a strong influence, but are now widely recognized as having done much damage to many European cities in the 1950s. Both positions, however, had their protagonists in Beirut of the 1990s.

Fig. 2. Lessons from antiquity:
Timgad, Miletus, and Ephesus

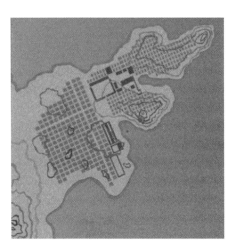

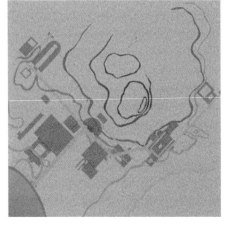

During the process, the grand planning, *tabula rasa* manner of the early master plans gave way to a more contextual approach which valued preexisting visual, townscape, and topographic features of the city, substantially increased the number of salvaged buildings, and placed greater emphasis on the archaeological heritage of central Beirut, locus of the ancient settlement and a site continuously inhabited for more than 5,000 years.

An extensive survey was carried out, covering some 800 buildings in varying states of damage. Of these, a total of 291 were eventually retained, increasing the number of buildings salvaged for restoration by more than 50 percent over those identified in the previously approved master plan. Concentrated in the designated Conservation Area and two traditional residential quarters of the city center, these retained buildings occupying 38 percent of the developable land of the prewar city core, exerting a significant impact as place-makers and a reference context for the city of the future. Much of the new development in the traditional city center will, therefore, have the character of infill development in a historic context, and the master plan contains design guidelines to encourage such a 'contextual' approach (fig. 3).

Historical or 'city' memory has become a fundamental concept of the master plan.[12] Beirut is an ancient, 'layered' city, containing the surviving features of some twelve distinct civilizations, with the earliest substantial remains dating from the Bronze Age. The city is not an instantaneous 'collage,'[13] but has been built up over thousands of years and has many historical layers, layers of 'city memory' (fig. 4). Fragments of each influential era and successive patterns survive to the present day. We need to respect and preserve this continuum and allow such a pattern of layering to survive and evolve into the future. After all, it is the combination and interfacing of these layers that encapsulates, in a real and physical sense, the cul-

east toward Mount Sannine across St. Georges Bay. This view, from city to mountain, has always been the hallmark of Beirut, favored by the Orientalist painters of the last century, but was in danger of being lost through overbuilding and encroachment of the landfill. These realities of modern Beirut also threatened another traditional feature – the avenue that descends to the sea. A common theme of Mediterranean cities, such streets provide not only a relieving view but also allow sea breezes to penetrate the fabric of the city. In addition to those

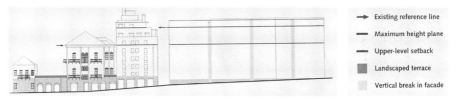

Fig. 3. Street facade guidelines: the Saifi urban village

ture and identity of Beirut and of the Lebanese people themselves.

An appreciation of neighborhood structure, natural landform, historic street patterns, views, and visual references were other features of a more contextualist approach. The past and future city center is not a single district, but desegregates into quarters, each with a different focus and character. Their natural edges became the administrative boundaries of the planning sectors – each with distinctive planning regulations designed to encourage differentiation and identity. The Serail ridge – the most visible natural feature and acropolis of the ancient city – bisects the site into two tracts of land, one facing northwest toward the summer sunset horizon, the other north-

existing streets that provided links to the water's edge, Beirut had dreamed for almost a century of opening Martyrs' Square to the sea.

A form of layering and 'city memory' is present in surviving street grids: existing street alignments and frontages were retained wherever possible. They are important, as is the recognition of hidden relationships and continuities with the new. A rationalized grid was formed on the landfill by extending 'avenues to the sea' – the two existing streets of Allenby and Foch – and transposing this grid to the west of the Serail ridge, focusing on the central axis of the hilltop Ottoman Serail, now restored and once again the capital's seat of government. The new grid terminates in a sweeping waterside

Fig. 4. Layers of 'city memory'

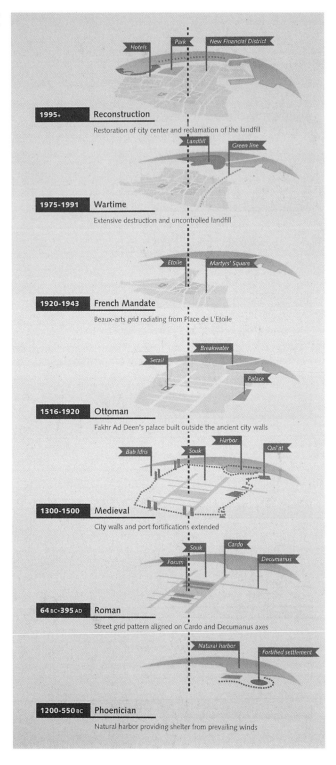

Hotels · Park · New Financial District

1995+ Reconstruction

Restoration of city center and reclamation of the landfill

Landfill · Green line

1975-1991 Wartime

Extensive destruction and uncontrolled landfill

Etoile · Martyrs' Square

1920-1943 French Mandate

Beaux-arts grid radiating from Place de L'Etoile

Breakwater · Serail · Palace

1516-1920 Ottoman

Fakhr Ad Deen's palace built outside the ancient city walls

Bab Idris · Souk · Harbor · Qal'at

1300-1500 Medieval

City walls and port fortifications extended

Souk · Cardo · Forum · Decumanus

64 BC-395 AD Roman

Street grid pattern aligned on Cardo and Decumanus axes

Natural harbor · Fortified settlement

1200-550 BC Phoenician

Natural harbor providing shelter from prevailing winds

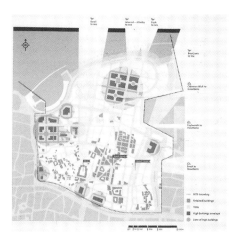

Fig. 5. View corridors and high building zones

drive, extending from the city's existing corniche system into the heart of Beirut.

Several of these themes came together in a combined strategy that defined view corridors and the disposition and placement of high buildings (fig. 5). Important views of the sea and mountains were protected from development. High buildings were restricted to carefully selected zones outside these corridors and to where they could create positive townscape value: as landmark and gateway towers, as infill to the existing high density Hotel District, and forming a man-made continuation of the natural Serail ridge and a bold statement of contemporary urban scale on the reclaimed land.

The reclamation and protection of the landfill, now under way, is a major environmental and marine engineering project in its own right. At the close of the war the uncontrolled landfill extended to some twenty-five hectares in area and represented a major pollution hazard to the Eastern Mediterranean. In its final form, including the two marinas, waterside parks, corniche promenades, and sea defenses, the reclaimed land will extend to almost sixty hectares (fig. 6). The 100-year storm design criteria would normally have called for a

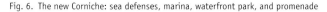

Fig. 6. The new Corniche: sea defenses, marina, waterfront park, and promenade

Fig. 7. Evolution in highway design: first and second master plans

twelve-meter-high sea protection berm, blocking views to the sea and preventing access to the shore. Open sea views and promenade access to the water's edge were the required criteria that led to a pioneering engineering design. Large-scale landfill decontamination works are now under way and the western marina and corniche sea defenses are under construction. However, other aspects, including the disposition of the eastern marina and the ultimate built

form of development on the reclaimed area, remain flexible and subject to future detailed study under broad principles established in the master plan.

The grand scale of the corniche drive, new landscaped boulevards, intersections, and tunnels on the loop road belie the considerable efforts made in the planning stage to reduce highway impact, establish rational central area car parking standards, and encourage appropriate public transport strategies for the Beirut of the future. A ring road configuration around the Central District was a feature of previous master plans and had been made virtually inevitable as a result of urban highway construction since the 1960s (fig. 7). In many cities of the Western world, however, inner ring roads of this type have created divisive barriers and other negative effects, and for these reasons some have subsequently been dismantled or substantially altered.[14] In Beirut, careful planning and engineering design effectively eliminated a northern leg to the ring, turned the western leg into a surface boulevard with through-traffic tunneled out of sight, improved the surface connections to neighboring areas, and considerably reduced the impact of the overall network.

Within the city center itself, the emphasis has been on preserving existing street alignments wherever possible, eliminating grade separation, tightening the road geometry, and devising a set of urban design and building envelope controls to encourage the development of a traditional street form. A family of 'streetwall controls' was derived initially from an analysis of key streets in the historic core (fig. 8), where virtually all buildings constructed since the French

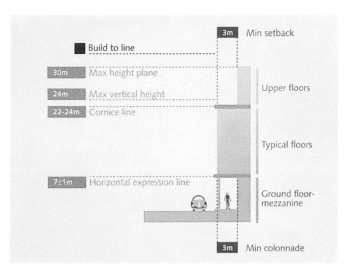

Fig. 8. One of a family of streetwall controls

Build to line

3m Min setback

30m Max height plane

24m Max vertical height

22-24m Cornice line

Upper floors

Typical floors

7±1m Horizontal expression line

Ground floor-mezzanine

3m Min colonnade

Mandate conform to street block and frontage controls applied in the 1920s, creating a streetscape of the highest quality. Such controls will promote continuity between the traditional streets of the historic core and the surrounding new development, with more flexibility permitted in the main residential areas. They prohibit arbitrary setbacks, force developers to build to back-of-pavement lines, and follow a set of coordinating guidelines, thereby contributing to a continuous street form and scale. The process reverts, in some ways, to earlier models of city making – Haussmann's Paris or the cities of Regency England – in which the street as a whole took precedence over individual plot development.

The Unfolding Plan

The master plan and urban regulations as a whole are components of a relatively unconventional planning framework, containing neither land use nor preconceived subdivision plans, other than the allocation of defined sites for utilities and public and cultural facilities. The plan concentrates instead on the definition of a generous and high-quality public domain and on three-dimensional urban design intentions (figs. 9 and 10), leaving parcellation and the choice

Fig. 9. Master plan

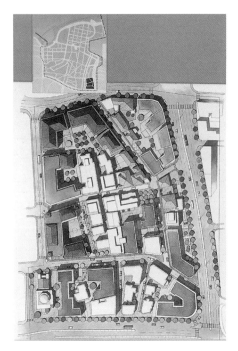

Fig. 10. Detailed plan for Saifi Village

of land use relatively flexible and subject to market demand. An overall mixed-use policy is stipulated in the urban regulations, with residential development projected as the largest single land user, particularly encouraged in 'Special Residential Policy Areas.' Elsewhere, subject to strategic monitoring to coordinate street level uses and avoid overbuilding in, for example, office or hotel sectors, the developer is relatively free to make his own market choices. To date, the approach is seen as helping generate a mixed patina of land uses, responding to the specific location of individual sites, with inspired and unforeseen choices being made by the developer in some cases.

Contrasting with these areas of deliberate flexibility, the massing and volumetrics of development are strictly defined. The plot

Fig. 11. Building massing within a defined envelope

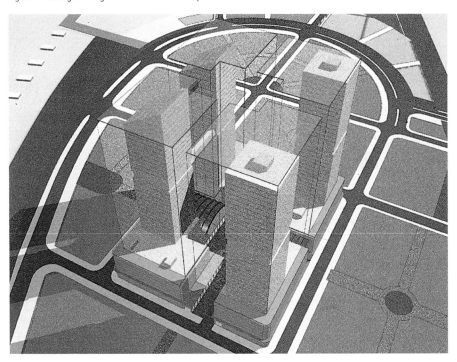

Fig. 12. Sector plans for
the Martyrs' Square
District and the Saifi
urban village

or floor area ratios that feature in Lebanese regulations as difficult to control do not apply in the BCD. They are replaced by maximum building heights and other envelope controls determined on urban design grounds and prescribed for every block and parcel in the Central District (fig. 11). In terms of floor-area ratio, these values would vary from 1:2 in the souks to as much as 1:15 in the high-density blocks of the New Financial District. Together with the streetwall and other frontage and site-coverage controls, these height limits determine the maximum envelopes to which any building design must conform.

The regulations contain subdivision controls that enable parcellation to be carried out in keeping with market demand and as development proceeds. Block massing studies are undertaken as an essential aspect of subdivision planning. Once parcellation has been defined, floorspace limits can be calculated and individual development briefs prepared, giving detailed planning, massing and urban design objectives, infrastructure, survey, and other information for every parcel. Although relatively sophisticated, such development briefs contain criteria and constraints that are easy to understand and apply.

The master plan, as a regulatory document, is split into ten sector plans, defining the cohesive areas or neighborhoods that make up the BCD. The plans indicate the level and range of controls operable on building heights, frontages, setbacks, and other features. These include, for example, the identification of 'key sites' at visually strategic locations, for which a special architectural response is encouraged. Illustrated here are the combined plans for Sector H, Martyrs' Square and its extended axis down to the waterfront, and Sector I, the Saifi residential neighborhood (fig. 12).

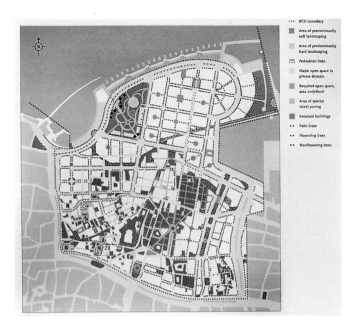

Fig. 13. The landscape framework

The public domain is given precise definition in the sector plans, while the broad design intentions are illustrated in the landscape framework. These are now being fleshed out in the city's streetscape and as individual landscape projects for squares and public gardens, with some of the trees and plant material supplied from a tree nursery established within the BCD. The great majority of streets are planted with trees, providing shaded walkways which, together with a web of prescribed off-road links, create a fine-grain pedestrian network throughout the city center. The precise extent and location of public spaces and connecting links remain undefined and diagrammatic in later phases of development. They are, however, identified on the plan and await future parcellation.

The theme of 'city memory' has been extended into the landscape design. Patterns of avenue planting shown in the framework plan identify street trees as flowering or non-flowering varieties and palms (fig. 13). A landscape tradition is being revived through the reintroduction of tree and plant species historically associated with Beirut. The line of the ancient city wall is to be marked with ficus trees, with the seven city gates identified in paving patterns. Within the historic core, bounded in this way, high-

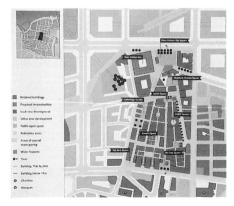

Fig. 14. Detailed plan for the souks district

Fig. 15. Heritage trails

quality traditional paving, lighting, and street furniture based on designs drawn from the 1930s will create a very special environment in this pedestrian-priority area.

The framework plan shows more than thirty parks and public spaces forming a hierarchy, from local squares in residential areas to Martyrs' Square, its associated Archaeology Park, and the extensive waterfront parks and promenades that will have a city-wide appeal. Of the two most important public spaces in the renewed city center, one is quite new – Khan Antoun Bey Square – and the other dates back at least to medieval times – Martyrs' Square.

Virtually obliterated during the war, Martyrs' Square has a wealth of history and association, originating as the medieval *maidan* beyond the city walls.[15] It will be revived as the commemorative space and public arena for the nation, intended to be the subject of an international urban design competition that will address not only its design and built form, but also the character and mix of surrounding land uses. In the master plan, the extended axis of the square

down to the port quayside is turned slightly eastward, reflecting an alignment first proposed in the Danger Plan of 1932, and preserving the spatial integrity of the square itself. But the freeing of this zone from building constraints led to archaeological discoveries of international significance – the Phoenician city walls, Canaanite origins of Beirut, and other important Hellenistic and Crusader remains. The implications of these discoveries for Beirut and for their public display within the Archaeology Park, while also accommodating the essential infrastructure of a modern city, are issues still under study by urban designers and archaeologists. It is clear, however, that the outcome will give a significant added dimension to Martyrs' Square as an important international cultural and visitor destination.

Khan Antoun Bey Square lies at the northern tip of the new Beirut souks and takes its name from the great Ottoman *khan* (bakery) that once overlooked the harbor. Destroyed during the war, it will be reconstructed to house the project's department

Fig. 16. Site model: viewpoint centered on Park Avenue and the Serail axis

store. The square provides the northern focus of the souks (fig. 14), which are planned around a reconstructed network of ancient streets to incorporate archaeological features from the Persian, Byzantine, and Mamluk periods. The main north-south routes converge on Khan Square, making it an important link between the historic core and the new city quarter on reclaimed land.

The new Khan Square will also be the point of convergence of a series of heritage trails that will carry the message of 'city memory' through different 'layers' of the city's past (fig. 15). The 'Old Shoreline Walk' is a linear park that traces the line of the prewar waterfront and Promenade des Français – the origin of the Beirut Corniche that has been erased by the reclamation. The 'Ottoman Wall Walk' cuts diagonally through the orthogonal blocks of the New Financial District, across the surface of the great stone breakwater also buried in the landfill, revealing views of harbor, sea, and mountains beyond. Finally, the 'Archaeology Trail' pro-

vides a circuit through the city that links an entire series of heritage events – landmarks, integrated archaeological features, historic buildings, archaeological parks, and their site museums – offering the visitor displayed and narrated evidence of 5,000 years of history, integrated within the fabric of the modern city.[16]

The main objective for the master plan's first phase is to provide critical mass in and around the historic core in both restoration and new development, thereby reactivating a city center that has been abandoned for a generation. A series of 'poles of attraction' is being developed (fig. 16). These include the core Conservation Area, the souks, new and refurbished hotels, modern office complexes such as the Beirut Trade Center and United Nations regional headquarters, and the Saifi urban village, where new infill development revives a vernacular tradition. These projects are underway, already bringing life back to the BCD. In spite of the faltering regional peace process, Beirut and its Central District are now among the top ten most active areas of development and construction in the world today. Beyond the turn of the century, as the BCD enters its second phase, the focus will shift toward a resurgence of Beirut's international aspirations – nothing less than reclaiming the city's historic role as gateway to the region and world city of the Middle East.

Notes

1. J. Parry, "Out of the Ashes," *Arts & The Islamic World* 30, Spring 1997, p. 24f.
2. Dar al-Handasah (Shair & Partners), *Beyrouth Centre-Ville: Schéma Directeur* (Beirut: Dar al-Handasah, 1991).
3. Dar al-Handasah (Shair & Partners), *Beirut Central District Detailed Plan Report,* vol. 1, *Planning and Urban Design* (Beirut: Dar al-Handasah, 1994).
4. For a detailed account of the making of the master plan, see A. Gavin and R. Maluf, *Beirut Reborn: The Restoration and Development of the Central District* (London: Academy Editions, 1996).
5. IAURIF, *Schéma Directeur de la Région Métropolitaine de Beyrouth* (Paris: IAURIF, 1986).
6. M. Weber, "Order in Diversity, Community without Propinquity," in W. Jones, ed., *Cities and Space: The Future Use of Urban Land* (Baltimore: Johns Hopkins University Press, 1963).
7. I. Colquhoun, *Urban Regeneration: An International Perspective* (London: Batsford, 1995).
8. A. Breen and R. Rigby, *Waterfronts: Cities Reclaim Their Edge* (New York: McGraw Hill, 1994).
9. P. Katz, *The New Urbanism: Toward an Architecture of Community* (New York: McGraw Hill, 1994).
10. For a more detailed discussion of the phasing strategy and theme of the 'social arena,' see A. Gavin, "Beirut Reborn," *Arts & The Islamic World* 30, Spring 1997, p. 18f.
11. Gavin and Maluf, *Beirut Reborn*, p. 96.
12. Ibid., pp. 62–64.
13. C. Rowe and F. Koetter, *Collage City* (Cambridge, Mass.: MIT Press, 1978).
14. Boston Redevelopment Authority, *Boston 2000 – A Plan for the Central Artery* (Boston: BRA, 1990).
15. I. Guerin, *La Place des Martyrs à Beyrouth: Recherche Historique Préliminaire* (Beirut: Solidere, 1995).
16. For a review of archaeological strategy in the BCD, see A. Gavin, "Integration of Past Layers: The Place of City Memory in the Renewal of Central Beirut" (paper presented at the Institute of Field Archaeologists conference, Manchester, Sept. 1997).

Section Five
Recent Projects in Beirut

Beirut and the Facts of Myth

by

Jorge Silvetti

In the foreground there are orange groves, oleanders, and cacti bordering the roads which run downhill. Farmers are working in the fields, and the point where the roads converge appears to be the same as where the frigates and fishing boats are headed. From a high point in the hills, the eye follows the reciprocal sweeping curves of the shore and the mountains cupping the city fabric at their feet. Towers, turrets, cupolas, bastions, gates, and the massive volumes of a few imposing buildings, together with palm trees, all emerge from the uniform grain of the urban fabric – a carpet of masonry and tiles. A breakwater stretches into the sea – the most visible human undertaking – putting a finishing touch to the protective ring of natural and man-made features that make this human settlement so viable. The sky is blue, very blue, with the mountains beyond...

Haven't all we urban lovers seen this image of a city in print, and its vestiges many times more as we moored along the Mediterranean coast? Palermo, Naples, Genoa, and the harbors of the Grand Tour gave Western culture a visual cliché that was the key to the understanding and promotion of an ideal of the Mediterranean city – an early nineteenth-century *guache vedute* exuding the colorful and predictable pace of harbor life, the charming balance of nature and urbanity, as well as the wonder of a sublime and surprising event like the erupting Vesuvius, an ancient ruin, an unusual rock, or a white mountain. Altogether, these form model images for our reading and interpretation of waterfront cities.

However, as we observe these views, I wonder if it is possible to think of the 'other' Mediterranean city of the second part of the same century as the same city? Is this city as characteristic and well defined as the one in the vedute, but deploying an entirely new collection of urban pieces such as *ensanches*, grand boulevards, railroad yards, terminals, and monuments? Probably not, yet this 'other' Naples, Barcelona, Genoa, Alexandria, or Palermo, which in itself was transformed radically by departing in image, dimension, and role from the neoclassical city, managed to reinstitute its 'mediterraneity' anew; its paradigmatic attributes will now be more clearly expressed not by the pictorial illusionism of the veduta, which is too limited to capture with a single pair of eyes the 'image' of a larger city, but by the planner's light pink and green colored map of the city: incorporating a grid made up of rectangular doughnut blocks and regularly distributed green plazas surrounding the medieval center with a grand avenue cutting through its thick and intricate core tissue at right angles to the harbor; stars and *rond-points* setting the locus of monuments and public institutions; the peripheral fans of railroads, opening up as they encircle the center and stop at the city's new architectural showpieces, the train stations themselves; and perhaps the public parks, the *giardini publici* with bandstands and organized botanical displays. These are new protagonists of this new version of the old, eternal Mediterranean city. The new image of an ever reborn myth.

Between these two images, there is the painful process of the emergence of two new systems of order in the new city at the turn of the century, that replace or, more often than not, include and transform the corresponding two previous images. One is physical, an order of new urban morphologies and architectural typologies that is obvious to the eye, and the other is ideological, the order of a new urban mythology entirely transparent and unconscious. Not surprisingly, to this new double order corresponds a new system of representational conventions.

As we are considering the numerous dilemmas and paradoxes that characterize the discussions of the reconstruction of Beirut and the expressed desire to intervene with an eye to the future and another eye to the past, it is helpful to focus on these historical and well-documented urban changes that require a fundamental redefinition of the idea of the Mediterranean city, stemming from a profound reconfiguration of space, in order to maintain an ideological and mythical continuity with history. The ancient city of the future, the emblematic motto chosen to define the drive to reconstruct Beirut, that el-Dahdah has well analyzed earlier in this volume seeks a compromise that I, like many others, also doubt can be reached.

As the bickering between the 'preservationist' and the 'modernist,' so prevalent today all over the world, continues in Beirut and seems to settle on such slogans, it may be illuminating to remember the persistent double lesson arising from such processes of transformation of all great Mediterranean cities during the nineteenth century. On the one hand, all such cities changed by replacing the old city with an entirely new one that created, in its turn, a renewed original image. On the other, while the interventions were radical, the process of physical change responded to the historical and geographic logic of the city itself. Therefore, to find another term that avoids an inevitably failing attempt to reconcile the opposites, it seems that rather than seeking the 'proper' style for a new architecture, one that 'combines' the old and the new, the traditional with changing society, antiquity with modernity, we may be a bit more 'matter of fact' and look at how such cities have actually changed successfully. This task is warranted, if nothing else, because there is so much these cities have had in common since their origins — and so much of this has persisted, in spite of the inevitable emphasis on the particulars that its new makers need to use in their arguments — such as the physical traces left by Greco-Roman urbanism, the maritime networks, the markets and souks, the Crusades, the expansion of Islam, and the protecting geographic features of Mediterranean harbors. Such a focus seems to be not only what Beirut needs, but what all other Mediterranean cities on the verge of change need to consider. Further, although there is no protocol miraculously available to describe precisely such a process, we can at least attempt to enumerate those characteristics necessary to understand it, and to articulate the possible vehicles necessary to implement such a vision.

First, it is not only necessary to accept the idea that the city will change – something everybody sooner or later realizes as being inevitable – but that change is the subject of the exercise. This is not just a semantic or rhetorical ploy, but a necessary stand from which to think of the reconstruction of Beirut. Moreover, by not accepting such a subject for the exercise seems to lead, at best, to disguising change with the clothes of continuity, a strategy of the late twentieth century that has proven to be flawed, not only formally as it belies authenticity, but more importantly ideologically, as it is incapable of accommodating that historical necessity in its true ideological mutation. Thus historical research needs to focus not on the moments when the image of Beirut was at its most paradigmatic, but on the moments when such images were about to change inevitably and forever, and, in doing so, bring to the fore the instruments, mechanisms, and knowledge through which the city has understood itself and implemented change. More importantly, focusing on the moments of

change (events usually not dominated by visual characteristics) and not on the static vedute or plans of the past, will make palpable the new, unimagined elements that are necessary to effect the change and yet also to maintain an idea. It pays to forget, at strategic moments, the particulars of Beirut and its history, and instead to look broadly at the generic 'Mediterranean city.'

Second, if the recommended focus is accepted, we must consider that, historically, the most efficient engines of physical urban change have been the new infrastructural systems. Focusing exclusively on the urban fabric probably leads to the aspect of urban form where innovation is least likely to occur. In particular, those systems intended to accommodate the movement of people, goods, and information, and those concerned with establishing the networks of important new institutions, are the 'infrastructure' that will give new scale and personality to the new, larger city. Points and lines that are the armature of all new strata that comprise the 'geology' of any old city, are the real 'new' elements and become, paradoxically but necessarily, the focus where continuity with any image of the past can be tried and tested. When considered in this light, these infrastructural elements are ideal subjects for the high quality of design that usually requires innovation, if for no other reason than the programmatic needs for new services cannot rely entirely on precedents. But this will happen only if such infrastructure is considered the subject of architecture by those in power who promote the changes. Moreover, this could happen, if and only if the city makers are not shy in considering these infrastructural systems as the most likely locus of a new urban monumentality.

Third, all of this, particularly infrastructural interventions of large scale, should be achieved with serious and considered regard for the natural setting, i.e., topography, views, and natural land resources. As a matter of common sense, this seemingly platitudinous statement would not be put forth here if it were not for the neglect of the engineers of the contemporary city, the consequences of which have been the understandable yearning for the impossible return to the city of old. Nevertheless, just in case we forget, let's review these 'obvious' considerations. In our 'Mediterranean' case, it is important to remember that in waterfront cities the 'draw' toward the shore (views, recreation, and relief from the urban density) is an irresistible force that must be articulated and used as a major planning tool. Consequently, as the city grows and proximity to the sea is diminished by density and distance, the instruments of infrastructure and monuments become crucial mediators between the city and the sea. Luckily, there is a simple and dominant fact that no intervention can change and that is the sea itself. Its dimensions are always larger than the city and it will always be there. Any change must measure itself against this permanence. Quite simply, the further inland the city moves, the more the need for efficient access to the waterfront. The more the city extends along the shore, the more permeable the frontal parallel development needs to be. In addition, a key consequence, due to the adjacency to the sea, and one which should loom large in planners' minds, is that people will always have to abandon whatever means of transportation they are on as they arrive at the boundary between land and sea. The sea, in its multiple manifestations (beach, shore, corniche, cliff, etc.), will always give such cities, if acknowledged in their design, an invincible feature that will assure historical continuity with any chosen 'previous' city. The beauty and allure of Mediterranean cities will always be assured if the presence of the Mare Nostrum remains unequivocal and ever present in the daily life of its inhabitants.

Fourth, great cities persist by adjusting the equilibrium between the myths that give them their ineffable personality and the ever-changing realities of their history. Paradoxically, and now contrary to common sense, myths change in order to be the same. In a perverse way, any attempt to 'reproduce' a mythical structure, usually by means of image and form, is bound to end precisely in its contrary by exposing, and hence destroying, the myth itself. For the traveler, one of the beauties of Mediterranean cities is the expectation of the discovery of vestiges of the old myths, kept physically in the layers of strata that each moment of change tries to cover up or incorporate in the new crust. For its inhabitants, such beauty comes from the fact that the city 'is the same' as one of their ancestors, no matter what physical changes have occurred.

Finally, a word must be said about the process of imagination. New realities and reconfigured myths require new techniques of representation. No specific recommendation can be made here as I believe that the creative process itself will guide the search and possible invention of techniques. Nevertheless, the advice to planners, designers, and promoters is to be open to experimentation in the techniques of finding the appropriate image for 'reconstruction.' In short, the challenge to Beirut, on the eve of 'reconstructing' itself as the 'ancient city of the future,' is simply to reconstruct itself as a new city by proposing and representing its new form as a reconfigured myth of origin. This can be achieved with common sense by studying its real history and geography. The change must be conceptualized as neither erasing nor continuing the old city, but as a new stratum that solidifies the ever thickening crust of Mediterranean cities.

Public Space as Infrastructure:
The Case of the Postwar Reconstruction of Beirut

by

Oussama R. Kabbani

In the aftermath of any war, a ruined city and its devastated society are faced with the challenge of picking their way through the shambles and fixing what took ages to build in the first place. Though the physical damage and human suffering of wars might have many similarities in different places and times, the means and objectives of reconstruction are usually different. Furthermore, the socio-political and economic specificity of each situation inevitably mandates a different approach.

Such is the case of Beirut, a unique postwar reconstruction model that has been in the making since 1992, after some twenty years of continuous civil war, so much so that it is currently the world's largest laboratory for postwar reconstruction. Of prime importance, here as elsewhere, is the question of public space. More specifically, where and what kind of space is needed to bring a war-torn society back together?

To begin with, some observations about the logic of war and its impact on how one

Fig. 1. "Shortly after the end of the war: the British soldier, having thrown off his uniform, starts work on the rebuilding of London," from L. Benevolo, *The History of the City*

may start to understand what constitutes public space in the context of a post-civil-war society. First, wars are of different types. They can be either external, between one or more countries, or internal, within the same country. In a war between different countries, the enemy is clearly identifiable by each side of the conflict. It is the 'other,' the aggressive regime or people across one's border. At the end of such aggression, euphoria tends to bring people of the victorious country closer together with an exceptional willingness to sacrifice and rebuild the physical destruction and to heal the social wounds of war. This was the case in many European cities after both global wars, during which reconstruction brought people and governments closer to each other, with the sole objective of wiping out what the aggression inflicted on the country and on its cities. In this regard, looking at an image published in Leonardo Benevolo's book, *The History of the City*,[1] one can detect the euphoria in London immediately after the end of World War II. In it we see a British soldier changing his war outfit and assuming the role of a builder to reconstruct London based on plans prepared during the war (fig. 1). This image clearly asserts the will of a victorious nation to demonstrate its capacity to rebuild the physical destruction caused by its enemy.

However, this expression of solidarity and comradeship is quite different in the aftermath of a 'civil war.' By definition, a civil war is a violent conflict of a society with itself. Such armed civil conflicts rapidly eradicate the country's ruling institutions, disintegrate its prevailing social structure, fragment its cities' fabric, ruin its infrastruc-

Fig. 2. Lebanese fashion show on the ruins of the St. Georges Hotel

ture and built environment, bankrupt its economy, and physically split it into hostile enclaves. Thus, soon after the outburst of a civil war, a city becomes divided into districts, each dominated and ruled by an opposing ideological, ethnic, or religious armed power group. Fearing persecution, people generally relocate to whichever district of the city provides them with a sense of security. Soon after, what might have been a pluralistic city is transformed into a mosaic of human settlements based on religious affiliation, ethnicity, and/or political loyalty.

The end of such civil strife does not necessarily lead to an exceptional willingness for sacrifice by the war-torn society in the same manner that can be witnessed in cross-border wars. The process of healing has to go through a quite complex journey of political reconstruction, common reidentification, and social assimilation. Indeed, it could extend for many generations after the guns are put to rest. Having been victimized by their fellow citizens during the course of the war, and in order to combat the feeling of helplessness developed in the course of war, the fragmented post-civil-war era accelerates the restoration of the prewar 'normal' state which once governed all constituents, even if more fundamental, still controversial issues are not resolved. For example, an image that appeared in the *Boston Globe* in October of 1990 to announce the end of the Civil War in Lebanon was that of a fashion show organized on top of the ruins of the famed St. Georges Hotel (fig. 2), as if life would just go on where it stopped some twenty years earlier.

The difference between the two announcements is acute. On the one hand one can sense a public acceptance of war and an official call for assuming responsibility to remedy its impacts. On the other, the *Boston Globe* photo demonstrates an insistence on forgetting the war, as if announcing to the rest of the world that it did not even occur. These two images raise questions about the reasons why different societies deal with the aftermath of war in such diametrically opposite ways.

In a cross-border conflict against an outside aggressor, like the case of London after World War II, the victorious society emerged with a stronger feeling of unity and sense of purpose to reconstruct what the outside enemy had destroyed. However, a fragmented, post-civil-war society, such as Leba-

non's, that resorted to carrying arms to defend religious, cultural, and political identities, has emerged after its civil strife more fragmented. Effectively, it has so far been unable to rally its dispersed citizenry around a common or similar purpose. Clearly, this situation raises a postwar challenge for planners about how to understand public space, particularly if reintegration is to be pursued.

Neutral Space, Public Space

The violent and abrupt split in the social and physical fabric of a city due to civil strife has its own spatial logic. In order to claim control over the new territory, combating factions rapidly establish lines of demarcation to delineate their area of control. These instantaneous borders are not haphazard. They tend to trace boundaries that may have been socially, ethnically, or religiously present but not necessarily physically marked in the fabric of the city. The new physical boundaries, such as avenues, streets, and spaces, contrary to their role as elements of the public realm, acquire a strategic military importance as buffers and borders preventing people from interacting (fig. 3). Such was the case in Beirut during the Civil War. After some years of fighting, the city was split into two enclaves, each controlled by different militias. The 'Demarcating Line,' better known as the 'Green Line,' bisected the city (fig. 4). Christian militias assumed control over the eastern section of Beirut, which was predominantly a Christian sector before the war, while the western section of the city fell under the control of Muslim, leftist, and Palestinian militias.

Fig. 3. Roads transformed into buffers

Fig. 4. Militia fighter looking onto the Green Line

In between the two segments, the Demarcating Line extended from the center of the historic core of the city in the north, to the adjacent hilly slopes to the south (fig. 5). It traced the alignment of wide roads and public spaces that provided fighters with comfortable physical distances, sufficient to defend their respective communities from military infringements. From Martyrs' Square, Beirut's foremost public space, to the Damascus Road and the pine forest in the south, the Demarcating Line established itself as the 'neutral zone' between the combating sectors in the divided city. For quite a while, the Demarcating Line was the only space bisecting and combining the divided city at the same time.

At this stage, one can argue that for space to be truly 'public,' specifically in the context of a post-civil-war urban environment, it should posses a high degree of 'neutrality.' As a spatial quality, neutrality allows the general public to feel equal. It is an attribute of space that allows for "diversity and unity, intimacy and distance, and to allow groups to mix but not necessarily combine" as described by Samir Khalaf in his book *Beirut Reclaimed*.[2] Such qualities prevail in

those urban spaces and elements of the public realm that do not fall under the immediate dominance of any subgroup. Urbanistically, these spaces are generally located in areas that form borders between different communities, rather than within any one of them.

Given their geographic location, these spaces embody two contradictory attributes. On the one hand, they are a separator or a buffer between rival communities, while at the same time, they are their meeting place.

Fig. 6. The Central District, from Martyrs' Square to the Bay of St. Georges, created a buffer between the adjacent communities

Fig. 5. The Demarcating Line bisecting Beirut

Charged with these contradictory attributes, such spaces acquire an intrinsic power to resist the hegemony of any one group over another. They provide the opportunity to be used and abused equally by all and make all feel they are truly in a neutral public space.

Along these lines, one may argue that the Beirut Central District (BCD) as a whole, together with the Demarcation Line, is the most neutral space in postwar Beirut. Unlike most of the other areas in the city that have witnessed a densification of people of the same religious affiliation, the equal exis-

Fig. 7. Fighters along Damascus Road

Fig. 8. Public scene in Beirut

tence of all denominations in the Central District and around the Demarcation Line neutralizes their influence over space. It is not a coincidence then that the Central District, the historic core of Beirut, was first systematically looted by fighters from both sides and then transformed into Beirut's prime battlefield. This district, that used to be the common space for all Lebanese before the war, became a buffer space between them during the war (fig. 6). And since it was not hegemonized by any religious subgroup prior to the eruption of war, it was naturally destined to become their battlefield. The BCD provided a space, some 500 meters wide, between what soon became known as Eastern Beirut and Western Beirut.

The physical condition of the Demarcation Line which extends south of the Central District was different, however, in that its being the main north-south artery passing through the city enabled it to be a line-buffer rather than a district-buffer between the combating communities on each side (fig. 7). Given that this road always separated religiously distinct neighborhoods, fighters immediately established this relatively wide artery as the new border to protect their neighborhoods. Buildings along both sides of the Demarcation Line were gradually destroyed until they became almost totally ruined after twenty years of fighting. Quasi-normal life in the surrounding neighborhoods immediately behind this border, however, continued (fig. 8).

The disappearance of the Central District from the daily life of the citizens of Beirut left the city without a center for some twenty years. What was previously a monocentric

Fig. 9. Ruined infrastructure

city became transformed to a multicentric configuration, even if this shift was not planned. Such a transformation helped the city survive the war and its residents to con-

tinue their lives. Some government offices were split into two, one in each half of Beirut. The same was done to some universities, schools, and businesses. This transformation did not resolve the question of public space. Even though each side of Beirut had some open spaces, none of them catered to the community at large. By virtue of their location, these open spaces serviced either the Christian or the Muslim communities, depending on where the space was located.

Given this fact, it was no surprise when in 1991 the first postwar government, in an attempt to jump-start national recovery and reconciliation, asked the Council for Development and Reconstruction (CDR) to draw up plans for rebuilding the Central District. It was clearly understood that the reconstruction of the center of the city was not only an economic necessity, but also a public requirement, since it would provide turf for social and political interaction among Lebanese on geographically 'neutral' grounds.

Similar to postwar conditions in other cities, decision makers of the period faced a set of unusual constraints that demanded an unusual approach. After years of fighting, Beirut's center, the vibrant commercial, financial, and administrative hub of the country was left in a state of overwhelming destruction and devastation. Much of the physical environment and infrastructure was ruined beyond repair (fig. 9). Distinctive historic and turn-of-the-century buildings were damaged (figs. 10 and 11). In addition, the presence of squatters in several areas, and the extreme fragmentation and entanglement of property rights involving tenants and lease holders, rendered the decisions on how and when to start reconstruction almost

Fig. 10. Ruined buildings in the Beirut Central District

Fig. 11.
Ruined buildings in the
Beirut Central District

an impossibility. Added to this seemingly intractable situation, there was a need to solve major environmental problems caused by garbage dumping into Normandy Bay, located on the northern seaside of the Central District.

These complex problems could not have been resolved by individual efforts, nor through piecemeal reconstruction efforts. Given the dilapidated state of the Lebanese government and its institutions after the war, it was seen by those in authority as best

Fig. 12. Master plan of the Beirut Central District

the vehicle for the financing and implementation of the development and reconstruction of the Central District. In effect, Solidere was established within the framework of Lebanese laws regulating the creation of joint stock real estate holding companies specifically aimed at the reconstruction of war-torn areas in Lebanon. The company gained a capital base with the contributions in kind of the BCD property right holders, and cash subscriptions of eligible investors following a public offering. The private real estate holding company was vested with several responsibilities, among them to implement the officially approved master plan for the Central District, which governed, in turn, the provision of all public spaces (fig. 12).

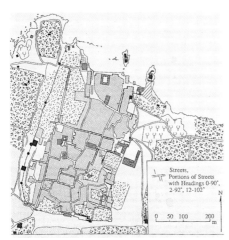

Fig. 13. Plan of medieval Beirut

Fig. 14. Street in medieval Beirut

to resort to private sector dynamics in order to spearhead and manage the difficult task of reconstruction. A holistic approach to planning, financing, and administration was proposed, based on a set of legislative measures which facilitated the creation of a private joint stock corporation – Solidere – as

Space in the Central District

Historically, the medieval walled city of Beirut did not embody squares and urban spaces as might be described today (fig. 13). Like most Arab cities, the Beiruti prime public space was the street (fig. 14). Some *sahats*, small informal and unplanned

city that introduced the notion of planned open space as a reflection of political authority. The Grand Serail building, built in 1853, with its size, imposing location, and surrounding gardens, inaugurated a new urbanistic era in the city," states Davie.

Some twenty years later, the Ottomans introduced a vast program of reforms to

Fig. 15. The gardens on Martyrs' Square during the Ottoman period

spaces, existed near the city gates, like Sahat al-Dirka, Sahat al-Saray, and so on. Public activities were also associated with economic activities of the souks, the *khans* (bakeries), and *hammams*. In an unpublished study about public spaces in the Beirut Central District, sociologist May Davie[3] observes that, unlike medieval Beirut, public spaces were neither introduced nor used by the local political powers for military parades. Instead, she argues that in the pre-Ottoman era, Beiruti political authority was expressed by "building useful infrastructure such as souks, khans, fountains, schools or religious buildings," very much in line with the mercantile mentality of the city's inhabitants. "It was the Ottomans' rule over the

modernize their cities, called *Tanzimat*. Beirut benefited from these planning measures, especially in providing planned public spaces and road improvements. The medieval urban fabric went through some transformation to reflect the image of the Empire and its authority. Among the most noticeable public spaces introduced to the city were Burj Square (later known as Martyrs' Square), located outside the eastern edge of the walled city, and the improvement and planting of some leftover spaces (figs. 15, 16, and 17).

With the collapse of the Ottoman Empire, and its replacement by the French Mandate, the French planners continued the transformation of medieval Beirut through estab-

Fig. 16. Martyrs' Square
in 1972

Fig. 17. Martyrs' Square
in 1981

Fig. 18. Place de l'Etoile

Fig. 19. The Corniche of Beirut

lishing a clear and direct association between space and political authority. On top of the medieval fabric of the city center, a mini Place de l'Etoile was planned and constructed "as a showcase of France in the Levant." This new plan shifted the center of political attention from Martyrs' Square to the new Place de l'Etoile (fig. 18). In the same period, that is from 1919, the district currently known as the Foch-Allenby District replaced the medieval fabric and was built in accordance with new models of architecture introduced by Deschamps and Destrée, two French engineers. Consequently, all new buildings in this district were mandated to follow the aesthetics of the new traditional style introduced by the colonial powers. This 'cleansing' of the medieval city continued until 1943, during which lower classes were forced to relocate.

Perhaps the most successful public space in Beirut that was initiated by the Ottomans and continued during the French as well as the independence and postwar planning eras is the construction of the seaside promenade known as the Corniche (fig. 19). The original seafront promenade project was initiated in 1885. The plan called for building a seaside promenade from the Manara area to the historic core, of which parts were never built. The seaside promenade provided Beirutis with a vast public space, accessible to all. In 1934, the Corniche was lit and nightlife emerged, especially along Avenue des Français, where it was flanked on both sides by nightclubs.

The abandonment, due to fighting, of the Central District with all its spaces and activities and its disappearance from the daily life of the Lebanese since the mid '70s polarized public life in the city (fig. 20). Though some open spaces existed in the various neighborhoods, they did not fulfill the desired public role of intercommunal mixing. One exception is still the Corniche, which falls at the fringe of the city rather than within any of its socially polar segments.

For this reason and from their outset, the different plans forwarded as the basis for the reconstruction of the Central District, even since the early '70s, gave priority to the re-creation of the center's public role as a mediator among all Lebanese. Different plans handled this notion differently, however. In 1992, and after the governmental decision to establish private real estate holding companies to spearhead reconstruction, a concept tailored to this approach was forwarded by the Lebanese consulting office of Dar al-Handasah. Similar to the strategies

The first concept forwarded by Dar al-Handasah under the leadership of former prime minister Henry Eddeh was based on a formal spatial configuration of three axes terminated by monuments, very much in line with *beaux-arts* urban design principles (figs. 21 and 22). The plan was criticized from an urban-architectural point of view as being too monumental, and as not preserving enough of the memory of the city. Amongst the principal spatial ideas for-

Fig. 20. Aerial view of Beirut Central District

used in the postwar reconstruction of some European cities, the destruction was seen by the planners of the period as an unprecedented opportunity to introduce radically modernizing changes to the urban fabric on a scale that had been almost impossible before.

warded in the plan were the creation of three north-south axes, the establishment of a major government center, and the transformation of the landfill into an island. After a series of public debates, criticism, and discussions primarily questioning the monumentality of the concept, as well as its

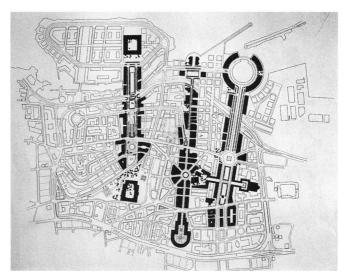

Fig. 21. Master plan for the Beirut Central District by Henry Eddeh

Fig. 22. Model for the Beirut Central District by Henry Eddeh

'surgical approach,' transforming the urban morphology and eradicating a number of older buildings, even though many of these are still in a ruinous state, a revised plan was forwarded which was much more in tune with preserving the memory of the city as well as allowing for new development.

Public Spaces in the New City Center

The new planning framework favored the preservation of some buildings and maintained most of the original street layouts and widths. It also proposed a system of open spaces and promenades with the

Fig. 23. Proposal for the new Corniche in the Beirut Central District

intention of preserving the city's memory, as well as providing ample public space for intercommunal mixing. One driving spatial principle in the updated planning framework was the provision of a network of open spaces. Given their location within the geographically and religiously neutral Central District, these spaces had the opportunity to serve the public at large and provide badly needed space for religious and social interaction.

The planning framework called for the creation of three different levels of public space. The first was a city-wide space network attracting people from all over Beirut. The second was formed by a series of public open spaces around the theme of heritage trails strategically located to form centers for districts and links across them. And the third level of space concerned local residential neighborhoods, such as pedestrian passages and

Fig. 24. The souks of Beirut

inner-block courtyards for the use of nearby residents.

The city-wide open spaces were planned to provide badly needed breathing and inter-communal mixing spaces for people from all over the city. Most notable is the extension of the Corniche of Beirut alongside the reclaimed edge, which will tie the renewed city center with the existing leisure-time and social promenade of the Beirut Corniche (fig. 23). This sixty-meter extension will itself be the largest piece of infrastructure in the central district constructed on top of a one-kilo-meter-long and twenty-five-meter-deep concrete wall, designed to withstand the severest storm conditions which might occur every 100 years.

The waterfront park is another example of city-wide public open space that will provide leisure and entertainment amenities for all people. Located at the edge of the Corniche, this 70,000-square-meter park, the second largest park in Greater Beirut, is seen as a natural extension to the kind of intercommunal mixing made possible on the Corniche. The park is expected to top the remains of the landfill forming the site, and will be isolated from the city proper by cut-off walls to ensure that no leftover gases will infiltrate into surrounding building basements.

The second level of open spaces relates to districts and to the preservation of the city's memory. The new city center has been subdivided into planning districts in conformity with their desired uses and/or existing character. Each planning district is equipped with appropriately scaled public open spaces in order to establish clear, animated, and legible centers. For instance, to mark entry

to the city, a gateway park is planned as a ceremonial introduction. Another example is the provision of a public open space, opposite the reconstructed *khan*, that will be transformed into a department store, similar to traditional provision of space alongside areas of intense economic activity. The planning framework also calls for the rejuvenation of public life along streets and in tradi-

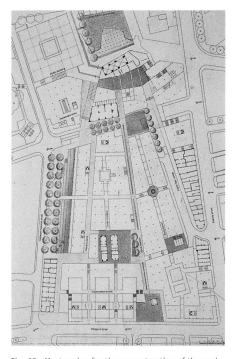

Fig. 25. Master plan for the reconstruction of the souks

tional bazaars. To that end, all the narrow streets in the conservation zone will be transformed into pedestrian areas, especially alongside the reconstructed souks of Beirut, to enhance the opportunity for traditional public life (figs. 24 and 25).

In an attempt to provide spaces that relate to the city's memory, the planning

Fig. 26. Looking down on the Roman baths at the base of Serail Hill

Fig. 27. View of the
Roman baths

framework establishes networks of public space within urban areas along the old traces of the waterfront edge. For instance, the 'Old Shoreline Walk,' as it will be called, ties the Corniche back to the old port, as well as tracing the alignment of the Ottoman port jetty. By maintaining elements of its history, such themed public spaces will contribute to an understanding of the evolution of the city.

As mentioned, the third level of public spaces ensures that city blocks, especially for residential purposes, will have semi-public inner courtyards linked to surrounding areas by an intricate web of through-block pedestrian connections. Markets will also be reintroduced into the residential areas in order to allow and encourage use by street vendors. Altogether, the Central District will contain more than thirty local squares.

Perhaps the most exciting and challenging form of public space that is emerging in the city are the sites of archaeological discoveries. Paradoxically, it is also the most recent form of public space. As a city that has existed for more than 5,000 years, Beirut's Central District is currently the world's largest urban archaeological excavation site. Findings from the Bronze, Phoenician, Roman, Byzantine, Mamluk, and Ottoman eras have been discovered in numerous locations in the city center. While it is impossible to preserve all discoveries on their original sites, numerous opportunities are being provided to enrich the public character of the Central District by integrating archaeology into the redevelopment process. These glimpses of the past can be seen as traces, alongside restored buildings as well as fragments of spaces, that collectively establish a sophisticated interpretation of the past rather than a literal recollection. Problems of archaeological interpretation and integration are among the most complex challenges that the construction of the public realm of Beirut will face in the coming years. Some easy solutions for integrating archaeological

Fig. 28. Roman baths at the foot of Serail Hill

Fig. 29. Prewar bank notes

and West, is now living through one of its most severe identity crises. The post-civil-war society has not come to terms with the problems that originally caused armed conflict. Differences in identity between religious groups have not been resolved. More-

finds into public spaces have already been implemented. The reconstruction of the garden of the Roman bath in the Beirut Central District, for instance, was the first to be achieved in 1997 (figs. 26, 27, and 28). After the restoration of the discovered Roman bath, a public garden inspired by Roman gardens was designed. Aromatic plants in amphorae, waterfalls, and mosaics were then used to animate surrounding sites. While such solutions seem to be simple to achieve, the sheer scale and extent of the discoveries necessitates a more complex approach.

Public Space as the
Infrastructure of Tolerance

The city of Beirut, which has always prided itself as being a bridge between East

over, such identity crises are perhaps made most visible through the failure of the first postwar government to identify symbols capable of representing all Lebanese to be used on new editions of the local currency (fig. 29). 'Neutral' geometrical shapes that cannot be associated with any religious or political subgroup replaced archaeological monuments that once represented all Lebanese.

On the popular culture level, this East-West identity amalgamation is portrayed in the advertisement of the recently opened Hard Rock Cafe, in which the popular figure of Abou al-Abed, once a legend of tradition, is also going through much the same transformation (fig. 30). In one hand he is hold-

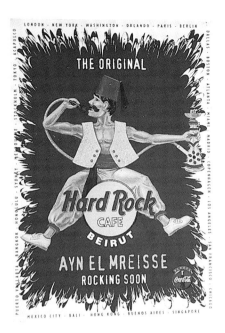

Fig. 30. Abou el Abed as symbol of the Hard Rock Cafe, Beirut

ing an *argile* (water pipe), one of the icons of Beiruti tradition, and in the other a microphone, thus literally having a foot on each side of the globe.

So What Is It That We Are Witnessing Here?

On the one hand, a deliberate attempt at the level of government is being made to avoid references to any common identity in Lebanon, perhaps to avoid an explosive

confrontation. On the other, there is a popular tendency to express the identity of a society hanging onto its roots while also embracing the new icons of Western civilization. In this political and cultural milieu, a new city center is being rebuilt, a project that could prove to be one of the most important laboratories for contemporary architecture and public open space design. For the postwar society to negotiate its differences and explore the physical and spatial context that will best accommodate and dilute these differences, the neutral grounds of the city center provide the best possibility for a fresh, new beginning. The public spaces of the city center are well suited for such explorations, for they allow the postwar society to come back and to interact without trespassing on one another's turf. In short, they have the potential of providing the right infrastructure for the emergence of a pluralist society in Beirut.

Notes

1. L. Benevolo, *The History of the City* (Cambridge, Mass.: MIT Press, 1988), p. 932, fig. 1405–60.
2. S. Khalaf, *Beirut Reclaimed* (Beirut: Dar An-Nahar, 1993), pp. 153–61.
3. M. Davie, *The History and Evolution of Public Spaces in Beirut Central District* (unpublished report prepared for Solidere, 1997).

Beirut Sublime

by
Rodolphe el-Khoury

"The city I am talking about offers this precious paradox: it does possess a center, but this center is empty." The city is Tokyo and the statement is Roland Barthes'. I quote it from his quasi-utopian account of Japan in *Empire of Signs*. I say utopian because Barthes does not approach the Orient as a reality that can be contrasted historically and politically to the West, but rather as a reserve of features whose inventive manipulation allows him to entertain the idea of an unprecedented symbolic system: the center of the European city is always full, it is the site of truth, where the values of civilizations are condensed. In Tokyo, where the urban traffic is forced into a perpetual detour around the imperial residence, and in the visible form of invisibility that conceals the indifferent monarch, the 'sacred nothing,' Barthes can entertain the notion of a voided center, a city where "the system of the imaginary is spread circularly, by detours and returns the length of an empty subject."[1]

Barthes' utopia may well have been realized in Beirut, quite fittingly in a city which has historically negotiated – and frustrated – the extremes of Orientalist fantasy. In Beirut's city center, where once the busiest and densest structures stood, now lies an empty field. For the last few years it has attracted crowds of curious Beirutis and held the attention of international media. Visitors

to the city center have yet to exhaust their fascination with this dusty field. Some are supposedly interested in the ancient artifacts that archaeologists and bulldozers have recently found. Others are interested in the development of the Central Business District; they come to survey what PR slogans have promoted as the largest construction site in the world. In fact, Beirut's BCD project is dwarfed by dozens of other developments across the globe. Do not be fooled by the subterfuge: their curiosity for the excavated past and the speculative future is an alibi for a morbid fixation on the scene of the absent center.

The combined effects of thoroughly destructive warfare and equally uprooting reformulations of property law and zoning ordinances – namely, the forces of capital – have created a *tabula rasa* at the very heart of the city. This cleared ground has no discernible physical differentiation: all traces of streets and building masses are now erased. Also obliterated are the property lines, zoning envelopes, and other invisible but no less 'real' demarcations which customarily determine or inflect urban morphologies. The homogeneity and superficial neutrality of this clear slate may have been compromised when the archaeological strata were exposed in the recent surveys. But the excavations finally participated, perhaps most effectively, in the systematic erasure of modern Beirut by challenging the primacy of the surface, eventually replacing one ground with several others: by the time the survey is complete, the valuable artifacts collected, and the trenches filled up, the new ground will be artificial, and therefore arbitrary, abstract, and more vacant still (fig. 1).

Keeping in mind that the war period saw more building construction than actual destruction, and if reconstruction entails the systematic deployment of efforts and resources in the transformation of Beirut, we may then argue that the most radical if not substantial project in this process has already been realized in the 'deconstruction' of the center. By 'deconstruction' I mean literally a systematic dismantling of pre-existing structures (physical, political, and legal); 'deconstruction' also refers to the

symbolic assault on the plenitude of the center. To go downtown, or to the city center, Barthes reminds us, is "to encounter the social 'truth,' to participate in the proud plenitude of 'reality.'"[2] This ritual persists in Beirut's city center but only in its inverted form. In today's Beirut, we go downtown to encounter another truth in the spectacle of a sublime emptiness.

The ritual engagement with the center, be it the positive participation in logos or the negative but still gratifying encounter with the sublime, may be altogether lost once this site is reclaimed for development. In fact, Beirut has survived for twenty-two years without its downtown and its centrifugal energy and is not about to waste its momentum, despite the efforts of planners, legislators, and investors. So no matter what we build on the site, be it the developer's

Fig. 1. The souks area after archaeological excavations

fantasy of a miniature Manhattan where enclaves of wired office buildings will rival the inscrutability of Tokyo's walled precinct, or the nostalgic reconstruction of a vanished historical district where simulation can only hasten cultural degradation, losses will linger on and indifference will grow.

But as long as this *terrain vague* persists in its vagueness, vacancy, and vagrancy,[3] our Beirut could very well be Roland Barthes' Tokyo: we may see in the emptiness of the evacuated center the possibility of difference, of mutation, of a revolution in the propriety of symbolic systems. At the site of Beirut's sacrificial immolation, we may recognize an opportunity for the remorseless detournement of a negative yet liberating violence.

Beirut is dead; long live Beirut.

Notes

1. R. Barthes, *Empire of Signs*, Richard Howard, trans. (New York: Hill and Wang, 1982), pp. 30–32.
2. Ibid., p. 30.
3. See I. de Solá Morales, "Terrain Vague," in *Quaderns*.

The Souks of Beirut

by
Rafael Moneo

I went to Beirut in February 1996, after having been approached by Solidere,[1] to design the souks of the city, the main bazaars that were destroyed during the war. It was impossible for me to go to Beirut and not accept the proposal I had received. I was impressed by the city, the extent of the area to be rebuilt in the center, and I understood very quickly the importance of the project for the reconstruction of the city center and for the city as a whole. It was quite a challenging job for an architect. Moreover, the dramatic excavation in the ground that is there today was already dug when I arrived in Beirut, a token of the eagerness of the Beirutis and the client to develop this project quickly. The excavation, which was to be filled with four floors of parking underneath the souks, offered evidence of the changing conditions of retail trade, and the need to access the city center by car. While Beirut's size remains modest, when compared with American or European cities, its dependence on the car is quite similar.

An international ideas competition had been held for the general area of the souks, and three winners with very different ideas were selected. A master plan was then drawn up by the Lebanese architect Jad Tabet, who proposed to maintain the alignments of the main prewar souks, to add more open space, and to integrate the archaeological finds on this site into the design.

Archaeological evidence shows that the site has served as the commercial and sometimes residential center of the city since the early Phoenician settlement and then through Hellenic, Roman, Byzantine, Arab, Mamluk, and finally Ottoman and French periods. The site also enjoys a strategic location in the center of the city as the meeting place of goods and people coming from the adjacent port and from the city. Given the topographic conditions of the site, it is also the intersection of lower, coastal Beirut and the more elevated business and residential areas of the city to the south. The recent expansion of the city toward the landfill to the north will no doubt further enhance this strategic location, even if it will diminish the link with the port and the sea. In the postwar context of Beirut, the souks will also serve as a meeting place for the country's different communities.

The charge for the project concerning the souks of Beirut entailed finding an architectural solution that revitalizes the familiar character of a souk while accommodating contemporary needs of shopping and retail. The main response to this charge has been to provide an architectural framework that does not interfere with retail trade but that is enriched by the activity and variety typical of a souk. The general urban layout reinforces the relationship of the souks with the surrounding context by connecting the roads

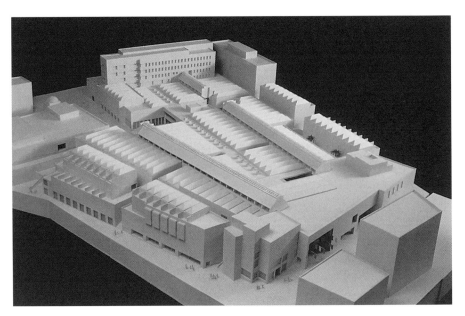

Fig. 1. View of model looking southeast

with the souks. As such, the souks retain their prewar openness to the city's pedestrian traffic, a quality that has always distinguished the Beirut souks from the self-contained character of other souks such as those of Aleppo and Istanbul (fig. 1).

Programmatically, the main body of the project accommodates the traditional souks which are complemented by modern retail needs such as larger stores, a department store, a supermarket, and increased vehicular access. Housing is integrated into the project at the western and eastern edges, bringing residential life back to the center of the city. Office facilities and restaurants are also added at the southern and northern edges of the project respectively.

The plan, as stipulated by Tabet's master plan, maintains the main souks in their prewar location and re-creates their respective sizes and roles (figs. 2 and 3). Open spaces are introduced both as a spatial relief within the souks and as links between the souks and abutting areas of the Beirut Central District. Archaeological finds are also preserved *in situ,* wherever required, and integrated into the design of the project.

In section, the souks operate on two levels (fig. 4). At the lower level, they follow the topography of the site descending from Weygand to Trablous Street. At the upper level, they connect directly to Weygand Street and remain horizontal throughout. The two levels are then connected at several key circulation points.

Volumetrically, the buildings at the perimeter of the site are higher than those in the middle, in order to meet the surrounding streets and neighborhoods each according to its own scale. The internal souk buildings have an average height of two floors (exclud-

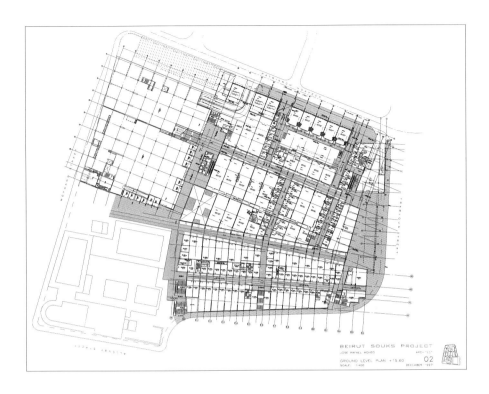

Figs. 2 and 3. Plan of the souks at lower ground level

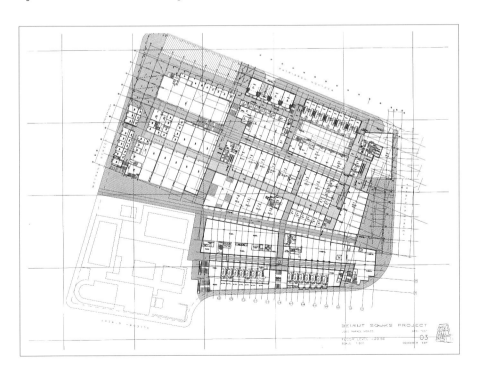

ing mezzanines), and they maintain a horizontal datum at the roof line, thus enhancing the experience of ascending and descending through the complex.

Architecturally, the skylights that shade and protect the main souks provide each larger shops and some that are smaller have mezzanines or basements. Restaurants occupy the northern edge of the souks and provide for animation in the area after hours.

Housing occupies the eastern and western edges and helps to increase the

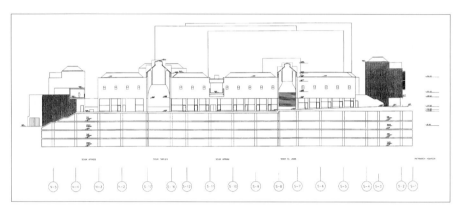

Fig. 4. Transversal section of the souks

with its distinct character without interfering with the retail activity at street level. The chevron pattern of yellow stone that clads the exterior facades stresses the joyful character of this unique place in the city center.

Program

The project consists of three main programmatic elements. They are: retail, housing, and office. The retail section is the largest and is laid out in a traditional manner. The major souks, al-Tawileh, al-Jamil, and al-Arwam, are lined with larger shops that satisfy modern retail criteria, whereas the smaller souks, Ayyass, Sayyour, Boustros, Arwad, and al-Franj, maintain the scale of retail in a traditional manner. Most of the

project's liveliness. The housing units are two-stories high and start above the level of the souks, but with access from within the souk area itself. The thirty-six units average about 100 square meters each. Finally, the office component of the program is confined to a five-story building along Weygand Street even though many of the retail areas, particularly the upper levels, could also serve as office space.

Site Perimeter

The main entrance to the souks from the business center of the city is located along Weygand Street (fig. 5). Here, the strong slope along Weygand provides the advantage of connecting to the souks at two levels. In effect, all the souks running south to north start at Weygand Street.

The edge of Weygand Street is defined by two structures. The first consists of a one-story row of shops, thus bringing the souks to the main street. This building then aligns

ing area are provided along this road, but they are integrated within the building volumes. In order to enhance the pedestrian activity on Patriarch Hoayeck Street, shops at ground level are set back from the street creating wider sidewalks. Along its length,

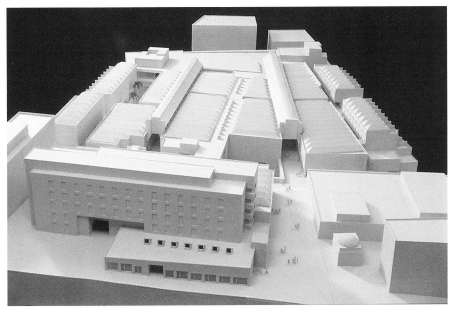

Fig. 5. View of model looking north with Weygand Street in the foreground

with the northern edge of Weygand Street and runs between Weygand and Souk al-Franj. It also acts as the gateway to Souk al-Arwam. The second is a five-floor office building that defines the northern face of Souk al-Franj, but extends further to Bab Idriss. This building acts as the gateway to Souk al-Jamil.

Patriarch Hoayeck Street serves as the main north-south vehicular connector to the souks from the residential area of Wadi Abou-Jmil and the Etoile district. In response, two entrances and exits to the park-

four entry points connect this street to the souks.

Trablous Street creates an edge between the upper and lower souk areas, along which the north-south souks converge. It also acts as the extension of the Avenue des Français, the main boulevard of the hotel district into the souks. Given these conditions, a large covered space is located along the street at the bottom of the souks in order to mark their convergence and to define a large portico. The covered space is animated by the activity surrounding it both inside and out-

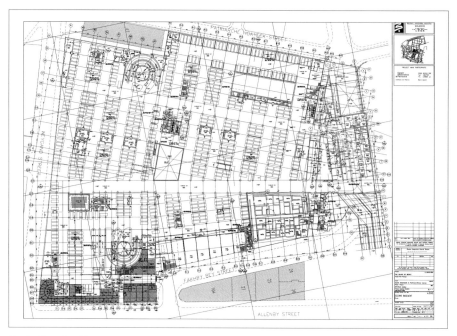

Fig. 6. Plan of parking area

side, namely the connection with the department store and the public stair leading to Khan Antoun Bey Square, the mosque, the restaurants around the mosque, and the cinema complex, as well as to the Ajami Restaurant building and the vertical circulation of the parking.

Fakhry Bey Street forms an edge between the souks and the restored Foch-Allenby area. While shops and restaurants align this facade, the street is conceived of as external to the project. It is linked to the level of the souks by three public stairs, two of which connect directly with public passages to the Foch-Allenby area. Above the shops are residential units which are accessible from Souk Ayyass. The northern end of Fakhry Bey Street features an entrance to the archaeological ruins under Souk Ayyass, and a pedestrian link between the cinema and parking.

Parking is an integral part of the new souks (fig. 6). The 2,000-car capacity emphasizes the importance of the automobile in the daily life of postwar Beirut. The design of the parking area benefits from the sloping condition, exposing the different parking levels to the surrounding streets. The direct entrances along Allenby Street, the archaeological sites, and the use of natural lighting through the light court and other points help to provide an above-ground aspect to the underground structure.

The main circulation of both vehicles and pedestrians follows the system provided by the souks above and, as such, connects the different levels of the city with the souks by providing direct entrance from Allenby at two levels, and from Patriarch Hoayeck Street. It also provides for traffic circulation that reflects the hierarchy of the above-ground souks and makes the passages running below Souks al-Tawileh and al-Jamil the main circulation lanes in the parking area. In addition, the locations of vehicular access points are positioned in accordance with the main traffic scheme proposed in the master plan of the Beirut Central District.

al-Arwam Square and the northern end of Souk al-Jamil. Two secondary connections are also provided by a ramp entrance on Fakhry Bey Street at the Ajami Restaurant, connecting directly to the second level and to a vertical core. Within the parking area, the cars move along the axes of Souk al-Tawileh and Souk al-Jamil in six-meter-wide

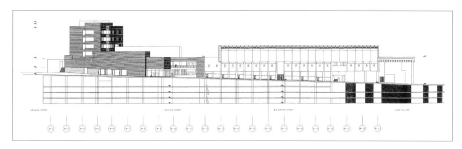

Fig. 7. Longitudinal section through Souk al-Tawileh

Parking is accessed at the four corners of the site. Two southern entrances and exits are entered through circular double ramps. One is located along Allenby Street, whereas the exit point is directed to Fakhry Bey Square in order to relieve traffic from Allenby and to link with a pick-up point on the square. The other is located along Patriarch Hoayeck Street, behind the Sabbagh Building, and is the only point of access that links to the first basement level of the parking area. Two northern entrances, one from Allenby Street and the other from Patriarch Hoayeck Street, are linked together underground in a large ramp system that acts as the main entrance to the parking area and reflects the primacy of the covered plaza above.

Pedestrian access to the parking area is located at two main points: the light court at

lanes, with a main drop-off point at the light court off Souk al-Tawileh. The grid of the parking area is for the most part 8.4 by 8.4 meters.

The Souks

The north-south souks comprise the main historical souks of the city, namely al-Jamil, al-Arwam, al-Tawileh, and Ayyass. They start along Weygand Street at different altitudes, ranging from 20.5 to 17.5 meters above sea level, and all converge toward the covered space on Trablous Street at about 12 meters above sea level. The fan-shaped layout in plan emphasizes this sectional convergence.

The buildings that flank the souks maintain a height of 26 meters and, given the downward slope, these buildings exaggerate the experience of ascent and descent through the complex. Specifically, the primacy of Souk al-Tawileh is reflected in its width (8.4 meters) and length (about 200 meters from Weygand Street to Trablous Street) (fig. 7). It is also reflected in the souk's important extremities (Ibn Iraq Square and Ajami Square), and in its continuity with Riad el-Solh Street and the banking district of the city. The major feature of Souk al-Tawileh is Arwam Square, which incorporates the light court and the pedestrian circulation of the parking area (fig. 8). Also of importance are connections to the upper-level souks, the covered space at Ajami Square, and a skylit, naturally ventilated cover. All the shops along Souk al-Tawileh have mezzanines or ancillary spaces

Fig. 8. View of Arwam Square showing the parking patio

above street level. Shop areas at street level range from about 65 to 170 square meters, increasing in size from Ajami to Arwam Square.

Second in the overall hierarchy, Souk al-Jamil is six meters wide and connects Bab Idriss Square, through the office building on Weygand Street, to the covered space on Ajami Square to the north (fig. 9). Souk al-Jamil is organized along the model of modern malls, anchored between a large supermarket and store on the southern end and a department store on the northern end. The main features along Souk al-Jamil are the lobby of the office building, Arwam Square, located about halfway through the souk, large shops (ranging from 80 to 200 square meters), a pedestrian circulation core both to parking and to the upper level souks at the northern end, and a distinct skylight structure for shade and protection from rain.

Souk Ayyass is 4.5 meters wide and extends from the jewelry souk off Weygand Street to the Ajami Restaurant on Trablous Street. Souk Ayyass is characterized by smaller shops (ranging from 20 to 80 square meters); Intabli Fountain and Square; Ajami Restaurant, a famous prewar landmark at the northern end of the souk; the recently uncovered Perso-Phoenician archaeological site under its northern entrances leading to the residences on the upper levels; and a multipurpose hall on the upper level at the northwestern end connected to Ajami Restaurant.

Souk al-Arwam is the internal spine of the second level of the overall souks area, between Souks al-Tawileh and al-Jamil. It is 4.5 meters wide and links up with Weygand Street at a level of 20.5 meters above the street, leading through an office building and ending at a large store on the northern side.

The east-west souks are generally narrower and less continuous than the north-south souks. They are lined with smaller

over it. The main pedestrian access to parking and to the upper souks area is located at Arwam Square.

Boustros Street is the 3.5-meter-wide extension of the stair from Fakhry Bey Street to Intabli Square on Souk Ayyass. It contin-

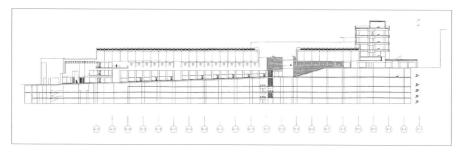

Fig. 9. Longitudinal section through Souk al-Jamil

shops, each averaging about 18 square meters in area. They act as connectors among the souks and between the souks area and the street network outside. These souks are covered at intervals, particularly at their entrances. Specifically, Souk al-Franj brings retail activity all the way to Weygand Street, enforcing the continuity between the Beirut Central District and the souks. It maintains the level of the entrance to Souk al-Jamil and then connects to Souk al-Tawileh by a staircase. Souk al-Franj is slightly skewed away from Weygand Street, pushing the office building back and enlarging Bab Idriss Square.

Souk Sayyour extends the exclusively pedestrian Al-Moutran Street, in the eastern business district, through the souks in a six-meter-wide uncovered passage. It starts at the top of Fakhry Bey Square and crosses through all the major souks, with the exception of Souk al-Arwam which bridges

ues to Souk al-Jamil and then breaks to connect with Patriarch Hoayeck Street. It incorporates access to the service areas of the souks and is mostly covered. Finally, Arwad Street is also 3.5 meters wide, stretching between Souk al-Tawileh and Patriarch Hoayeck Street, crossing through Souk al-Jamil at its northernmost tip, and ending at the tip of Souk al-Tawileh.

Main Open Spaces

The open spaces in the souks are understood as transitions and connections in an otherwise continuous pedestrian road network. The main public spaces, as identified by the master plan, are Ibn Iraq Square, Bab Idriss Square, and the covered space at Ajami Square. Ibn Iraq Square acts as the main entrance from Weygand Street to the overall area of the souks. It is flanked by the jewelry

Fig. 10. Study model of
Souk al-Tawileh

souks and Ibn Iraq Shrine on one side and by
the supermarket, office building, and Souk
al-Franj on the other. It connects Riad al-
Solh and Weygand Streets with the souks and
acts as a funnel, both in plan and in section,
from Weygand Street to Souk al-Tawileh.

Bab Idriss Square is the most elevated
point of the souks, and maintains its traditional role as the southwestern gate to the
complex. This role is further enhanced by the

change in width and direction that Weygand
Street undergoes to the west past Bab Idriss.
For this purpose, Bab Idriss Square is en-
larged from its prewar footprint specifically
to accommodate for the change in street layout and traffic circulation. Finally, as the
convergence place of the north-south souks,
the covered space at Ajami Square acquires a
strong presence in the overall circulation
layout. In particular, it serves as the entry

point to the souks from the lower city. In addition, its exterior wall provides a much needed definition to Trablous Street, which is otherwise composed of a series of disparate buildings.

Architectural Character

The architectural character of the souks is not meant to interfere with retail activity, nor to restrict shop owners from defining the identity of their stores. Therefore, the character of the souks is determined to a great extent by the nature of the covers which provide diffused lighting and enhanced scale. Furthermore, each of the major covered souks has a distinct cover which is derived from its dimensions and structural system. These covers consist of skylights that diffuse direct sunlight both to the souks and to the upper levels of shops, while also protecting shoppers from rain and allowing fresh air to circulate (fig. 10).

The upper facades of the souks are finished in stucco, whereas at street level, the shop fronts are defined by a flexible module of store shutters and windows. Columns and bare surfaces are protected by special sheets. In addition, the souks are paved with concrete, with the edges of the two wider souks (al-Tawileh and al-Jamil) made of slanting stone berms (about two meters wide) that mediate between the sloping souks and the stepped shop slabs.

The main exterior facades of the souks are clad with yellow stone, enhancing their connection with the city center. The chevron pattern of cladding, as mentioned before, deliberately conveys a joyful image to the city. This overall exterior treatment is differentiated from street to street by features that underline particular programs, such as bay windows to mark housing, horizontal stone cladding for the office building, and different stone colors and patterns for the more monumental northern facade of the souks. In all, the souk buildings create a generic, background framework that, nevertheless, acquires a level of specificity in response to surrounding urban environments. In this sense, and while determined to a large extent by the architecture, the character of the souks remains open to specific retail and shopping activities.

Note

1. The Lebanese Company for the Development and Reconstruction of the Beirut Central District.

Section Six
Prospects and a Vision for Urban Beirut

The Age of Physical Reconstruction

by
Hashim Sarkis and Peter G. Rowe

Chroniclers and observers of contemporary Lebanon often refer to the last seven years as 'The Age of Reconstruction.' Obviously, this label has been chosen not only because of the magnitude of development and reconstruction projects, but also because of the prominence of these projects in the public interest, on political agendas, and in the assignment of economic priorities. Magazine kiosks in Beirut abound with new periodicals and economic reports on the state of reconstruction. Speculative builders working around the city center carry the impact of reconstruction to inner-city neighborhoods. European consultants, from real estate marketing specialists to salesmen of fire security devices, constitute the first postwar wave of tourists to the country. The daily life of the city is punctuated by highway inaugurations and foundation laying ceremonies. Moreover, one discerns a general sense of excitement among the citizens, despite a high level of disorientation created by the constant reorganization of traffic and extension of construction deadlines within the city.

Critics of the reconstruction activity and its support policies often lament the fact that it is distracting public attention from the need to institute new social programs and to restructure the administration. Physical reconstruction, so the common criticism goes, has been favored over social reconstruction. This form of criticism, however well justified, has in turn distracted the public debate from an assessment of the quality of physical reconstruction. Even when a particular project, such as a new highway or the city center, is mentioned in a newspaper article or in a public debate, the discussion frequently centers on its financial and administrative aspects, with very little significance attached to its design attributes. While at no point in Lebanon's history has the public been as aware of its claims to the built environment as it is today, these claims have yet to be fully elaborated in design terms.

The aim of these concluding remarks is to extract from the foregoing essays major concerns relating to the design aspects of reconstruction, and to present these in the form of themes that could help guide a design-related debate on the reconstruction process itself. The aim is not only to focus on the physical attributes, nor simply to introduce design criticism, albeit much needed, but also to show that it is possible to derive the social implications of a project from a discussion of its design characteristics. In other words, the aim is to complement discussions that set social concerns against actual building and to show how, through the choices they make at the drawing table, architects and urban planners can take part in defining the political culture of reconstruction.

Design and the 'Big Picture'

Questions of design are not limited to buildings and cities. They can even be posited at the scale of the surrounding territory. Lebanon's recent history, observed the late Albert Hourani, is characterized by the transformation of an "agrarian republic" into "an extended city-state – a metropolis with its hinterland."[1] Ever since the Welfare State period (1958–1970), legislators and planners have tried to reverse the hegemony of Beirut over the hinterland, proposing plans and projects to revitalize the regions outside the metropolitan area in order to slow down the incessant waves of rural migration and to spare Beirut from over-congestion. These plans have focused primarily on the need to distribute resources, services, and job locations evenly among the regions, primarily to attain a balanced demographic redistribution. At certain instances, addenda about the physical planning were featured in these plans, a recent example being the Recovery Plan of 1992 commissioned by the Council for Development and Reconstruction and prepared by Bechtel in association with Dar

al-Handasah. These studies have been, for the most part, restricted to identifying suitable locations for planned public utilities and proposing road and infrastructure networks on a national scale.

Hourani's observation, if interpreted spatially, suggests that it is possible to conceive of Lebanon as a city-state, as a single extended territory which could be grasped and accordingly planned as a region. Rarely is it possible, let alone desirable, to implement regional planning at a national scale. Regional planning involves, among other operations, immense coordination efforts bringing together different local governments and constituencies, and converging their often conflicting interests. Yet paradoxically, in the case of Beirut and Lebanon, the only way actually to reverse the negative consequences of this expansive city would be by studying the physical impact of Beirut's growth on the whole territory and by proposing a physical plan that regulates the interaction between the city and the countryside. As it is used today, regional planning stops at setting the boundaries of the metropolitan region of Beirut and coordinating between the different reconstruction projects surrounding the city. As such, it has been more a case of metropolitan planning looking again at the hinterland from the standpoint of Beirut. For example, the Schéma Directeur of 1986 dissociates the villages surrounding Beirut from their regional affinities and links them to the continuous urban network. Similarly, both the Ecochard (1963) and the IAURIF (1986) plans failed to conceive of a regional entity. The problem is most visible in the way each of these plans defines the boundaries of metropolitan Beirut, turning neighboring villages and secondary centers into peripheral areas of the city and subjecting them to the same laws and principles of building. This, in turn, effectively effaces the distinct features of these areas and their connection with the hinterland. Also, such distinctions in zoning and density will necessarily fail if not enhanced by sensual dimensions with sufficient impact on human experience.[2] Despite the fact that there exists no political entity that administers the affairs of metropolitan Beirut, such metropolitan thinking prevails in the planning and execution of public projects.

The more important benefits of regional planning, namely of preserving building diversity and enhancing it; of creating breaks and boundaries between the different towns and cities, rather than melting them into one single metropolis; of providing clear orientation for movement between places and not just building highways; and of using the natural setting to enhance adjacent settlements, have yet to be addressed. When such issues as environmental protection and local governance have risen to the top of public priorities, a regional planning policy will be both possible and necessary. Moreover, although metropolitan planning requires a very strong centralized authority, the implementation of a regional planning strategy could well be delegated to the powers of local municipal governments and to local groups. Typically, most concerns in regional planning emerge from local groups wishing to preserve a river basin or protect the heritage of some district that requires action across the jurisdictions of local governments and other governmental agencies.

At the level of the central government, especially considering the responsibilities of planning authorities outlined in Assem Salam's essay, it is not impossible to imagine an advisory organization, within the Council of Development and Reconstruction, whose role it would be to develop the physical planning parameters of a recovery plan, and to encourage local governments to articulate their distinct local features within the 'big picture.' Such a welcome approach would almost certainly reinforce the articulation of local traits within a national framework.

Design at the Interface

If the first theme concerns the relation among different scales of the built environment, the second is oriented more toward coordinating among different forms of spatial order and control. Specifically, it concerns the interface between urban planning and architecture, and in this regard the experience of the '50s and '60s, as recounted by Marlène Ghorayeb, Assem Salam, Hashim Sarkis, and Jad Tabet. This history reflects the impossibility of planning implementation beyond a limited and the often delayed building of infrastructure beyond a partial enforcement of zoning and building codes. Still, the '50s and '60s represented a period of consonance between planners and architects, occasionally leading to well-articulated codes and well-defined buildings. During this period, architects of individual buildings in certain areas like the Corniche, Badaro, and Riad al-Solh Street were able to imagine the larger context in which they were located. Unfortunately, however, these successful cases did not pervade other areas of the city.

Today, this rift is visible not only at the level of the means of implementation, since many planners are pulling further away from physical planning and moving toward policy and economic approaches, but also in the fact that many planners of metropolitan Beirut are actively working against further new development. A first form of interface, then, would be to look for ways in which the highly justifiable approach of planners is made compatible with a development culture that propels the reconstruction economy, does social good, and gives architects jobs. For example, planners should work more forcefully to instigate policies that encourage the much needed rehabilitation of old city quarters and the upgrading of existing buildings. Such an approach would certainly generate a new market for architects and would also curb an almost total reliance on new development. Other examples are being proposed by preservationists who are calling for laws involving, for instance, the transfer of development rights in order to safeguard architectural heritage.

One form of mediation between planning and architecture, introduced by the planners of Beirut's city center and by other large-scale developments, has been the use of urban design parameters as a way of translating building codes and zoning regulations into more specific building practices. Urban design guidelines regulate alternatives for massing buildings, street alignments, and points of access, and, as such, help link individual buildings with the overall framework of a plan. In general, however, and because these areas have been either created from scratch, like Linord and Elisar described by Joumana Ghandour Atallah and Mona Harb el-Kak, or strongly tied to a preservation policy, as explained by Angus Gavin in the case of the BCD, the potential of such guidelines has not been fully explored.

By the same token, if the project of the Beirut Central District has managed to introduce urban design parameters as the interface between overall planning and individual buildings, the evolution of the project from the initial plan, as set by Dar al-Handasah and Henri Eddeh, to the master plan being implemented by Solidere shows a weakening of the overall character of the neighborhoods, streets, and blocks. Despite the overdetermined nature of the first (Eddeh) plan, with its polemical contextualism, it tended to be urbanistically stronger than the second project, which defers the issues of character almost solely to the architecture. As such, the urban design of the city center awaits further articulation, either on a district-by-district basis, such as that prescribed in Kabbani's and Gavin's essays, or by depending on the architects of individual buildings. It is still too early to judge whether the work of the architects will succeed in giving a stronger articulation to these plans, but the current urban attitude of new buildings, again as illustrated by Kabbani, promises a difficult path ahead.

The responsibility of this interface to mediate between urban design and architecture becomes all the more visible with large, block-like buildings typical of the new city center. For the most part, the experience of building such projects in Lebanon, like the Gefinor Center by Victor Gruen in Ras Beirut and the Starco Center by Ador et Julliard in the city center have been confined to an internal composition of three or more buildings around a semi-public space without much regard for the surrounding street network. More recent examples of such large-scale developments, or 'centers' as they are often called in the suburbs and in new quarters like Verdun, promise a further fragmentation of streets into self-contained blocks. An alternative approach to internally-oriented designs is provided by the souks project of Rafael Moneo. What is most relevant about this project is the way that the architecture responds to both the overall armature of the city's streets and to the idiosyncrasies which mark the presence of individual spaces. In effect, the identifiable features of the project are not created by the whim of the architect, but by contingencies in the street layout, by topography, and by history. Even though it is a commercial project, the souks provide public spaces at the crucial links between the souks and the city, and do not confine them to the interior of the block. Given the size of the project and the nature of its activity, the architect rightly chooses to subdue matters of architectural expression, allowing variety to be created by the retail activity itself. Thus the architecture not only becomes an armature for commerce, but also for establishing connections with the context without losing either its commercial viability or its discerning character.

Designing New Public Spaces and Building Types

The introduction of urban design as an interface in the reconstruction process has made available a new tool for the design and improvement of public spaces. Even if the presence of public plazas may not be a guarantee for public life, the articulation of street intersections, divisions between neighborhoods, and funnels for traffic are devices that inadvertently create open spaces in the city and require design consideration. Most of the public plazas in Beirut have either developed from leftover pockets of empty land or around traffic exchange points. The main public squares of the city center, Riad al-Solh Square and Martyrs' Square, as illustrated by the historical research of Jens Hanssen and Angus Gavin, are rather clear examples of public use slowly transforming leftover spaces into plazas. While Riad al-Solh Square has, for the most part, kept its prewar delineation, despite the way that the United Nations building has turned its side to the plaza and reduced its potential liveliness, it is the design of Martyrs' Square that promises to be a major challenge for today's city planners. It is also an important example to study since it would, no doubt, be emulated everywhere in the country, even if the final result was less than successful.

At present, Beirutis experience a different Martyrs' Square every other week, especially given the regular rerouting of traffic in the city center and the new exhibition space constructed at the edge of the square. It is as though the traffic engineers and the planners have joined the citizens in rehearsing

Fig. 1. Martyrs' Square
before the war

different possible scenarios for the future of the square before they cast it, so to speak, in concrete. Prewar Martyrs' Square centered movement in the city (fig. 1). It was at once a transportation hub, a commemorative space, and an entertainment center. The present plans have not only extended the square to the sea, but have also 'bracketed' this area off for further study, given its importance and the new archaeological finds at the square's northern end. Yet the exposure of the sea, archaeology, and a few religious monuments around the square will no doubt transform its past multiplicity of meanings into a more specific, symbolic space. Furthermore, urban designers should come to the rescue of this space by re-creating a variety of uses both as a means to its success as an urban space and also to

guarantee that it will be used by a diversity of groups. If symbolic spaces have proliferated throughout the city during the war and have, in some ways, preserved some aspects of public life, more inclusive public spaces are urgently needed to guarantee the success of postwar reconstruction.

As is often the case, the discussions of public space in Beirut today are coupled with the call for more parks and greenery in the city. While both are valid issues, they need to be separated, as the use of greenery as such could well compromise the vitality of some places, in addition to glossing over the absence of large recreational parks in the city. Even though the Schéma Directeur, Linord, and Elisar frameworks have provided for open spaces and for parks, the recent revisions of these plans have compromised much of the projected open spaces. Furthermore, the quality of these spaces, as described by Joumana Ghandour Atallah and by Mona Harb el-Kak, along with their implementation strategies, need to be revised if they are to be realized at all.

The task of mediating between large-scale planning and the local setting is not restricted to the designers of large-scale urban projects, or of public spaces, but should be shared by the architects of small buildings as well. One of the more fundamental tools for establishing such an extension architecturally emerged theoretically in the 1970s in the form of building 'types.' This term refers to the way in which buildings share common organizational traits, whether geometric or spatial, and that these traits necessarily transcend use and style in order to achieve continuity with the city and its evolutionary pattern of development.[3] Thus typological concerns are necessarily urban in orientation. Indeed, many cities are associated with particular building types that have defined the character of certain neighborhoods. In Beirut, for instance, the prevailing type of building has been the apartment building. In fact, this type has proven ubiquitous and adaptable to a variety of uses but, almost without exception, the architects of Beirut have failed to provide solutions that appropriately integrate apartment buildings into the surrounding context and into the difficult conditions of topography and the exigencies of multiple use. The architects of new buildings that punctuate the skyline of Beirut, for example, have ventured to test new layouts for apartments, new building technologies, and new material finishes, but they have, for the most part, shied away from testing new links between buildings and the urban context (fig. 2). Moreover they have returned to bankrupt modern types for multiple-use functions and

Fig. 2. View of postwar construction in Ras-Beirut

for offices and schools. Recent public programs for new schools and university buildings, for instance, have promoted the idea of typological innovation but, so far, type has only been used by architects in the familiar, expedient manner.

Heritage and Style

In spite of some progress, this call for "urbanization of the architecture of reconstruction" still cannot address all the issues and debates taking place in Beirut today concerning the formal articulation of new architecture. Indeed, two such debates will illustrate this dilemma. First, what attitude should be adopted toward existing buildings? Reconstruction and the speculative development around it have led to the bulldozing of old buildings both in the city center and in surrounding areas. Understandably, such acts of destruction have been resisted by groups of concerned citizens which, on a few well-organized occasions, have succeeded in saving some buildings from destruction. Newspapers have come out in support of preservation campaigns, dedicating whole pages on a daily basis to safeguarding old buildings, so much so that the threat of the disappearance of the architectural heritage of Beirut pervades every article in these pages. Specifically, though, the campaign has focused mostly on the preservation of actual buildings and raises issues very similar to those raised around inner-city development in the United States and Europe after World War II, namely: which buildings should be preserved? What financial means should be used for

their protection and management? And, how do we avoid the 'museumification' of old buildings? Clearly such debate turns on different criteria and, as outlined in the essay of Farès el-Dahdah, positions are taken without much reflection on the ideological bases and physical consequences of these attitudes.

At the other extreme, and in some areas of the city center, new buildings set in specific preserved contexts are being guided by very strict criteria about materials, style, motif, etc. This, in effect, transforms preservation strategy into design guidelines while ignoring, in some cases, the existing typological and urban considerations of the same areas. However, through due process, what is also evolving, both in the city center and elsewhere, is a debate about the need to preserve the urban configuration of neighborhoods, as in the case of Gemmayzeh described by Samir Khalaf, and not just the individual buildings. This provides an interpretation of the issue of preservation that is better linked to the impact of old buildings on their inhabitants, rather than in terms of architectural merit.

Archaeology, as explained by Helen Sader and Farès el-Dahdah, has also been the subject of the politics and controversies of preservation. It has also succeeded in drawing the attention of international agencies to help set the terms of preservation and to protect certain classified sites. Here again, the debate has yet to find the right terms for shifting from questions of preservation to questions of integration within the urban context.

The second debate concerns the style in which to build. In areas of the city center, for example, preservation policies have been extended into stylistic guidelines dictating what should be built around preserved areas. Such an extension is bound to face problems when the areas to be built are completely new and, thus, devoid of recognizable stylistic references, and when the programmatic and building size issues become distinct from the contextual projects. Most positions today are polarized around a highly traditionalist approach, theorized in the early '70s by such figures as Rifaat Chadirji and Hassan Fathi, and an ultramodern approach exemplified by architects such as Pierre el-Khoury. The present scene also contains some leftovers of postmodernism which have settled into a kind of tame contextualism. The existing palette of styles and accompanying variations, whether confused or deliberate, is still fluctuating between representing and paying for what was destroyed on the one hand, and perpetuating another nostalgia, namely that toward modern architecture, on the other. For in as much as the old evokes authenticity, the modern is still indelibly stamped on the image of Beirut during the 'good old days.' The current spectrum of styles may be very broad, but it is not sufficiently deep. Third terms that do not only relate to these styles, but acquire enough authority to establish a presence in architectural production at large, should begin to emerge and to generate more associative, and less literal references. In other words, the age of reconstruction deserves its own formal elaboration.

Historical and Future Implications

Once again, the building activity and the writing of the history of the age of reconstruction meet, but this time in the present. Furthermore, as well might be the case, this present period is burdened with the responsibility of rewriting and rethinking past epochs, and is undertaken with a strong emphasis on dealing with current architectural and political questions. As Michael Hays observes, it is the most valid form of history. Effectively, the biases for the present help set comparative agendas with the past more productively. The importance of these tasks is that neither the past nor the recent history of the built environment has been properly written, and that recent archival research, as well as physical and archaeological evidence, have come to represent a welcome rigor, challenging prejudices and correcting inaccuracies.

To establish the issues and problems that confront planners and architects today leads one back genealogically to different epochs in city history, but mainly to the grounds upon which its institutions and infrastructure were built. If they were built at least partly during the period of the Welfare State, the fact that they no longer carry the ambitions of the politics of that time should be indication enough that the physical environment needs to be dissociated from the political discourse that wills it, although not from political discourse altogether. The foregoing themes illustrate, we think, how one can move from architecture as an illustration of social and cultural inquiries to architecture as an constitutive act. Moreover, if the chroniclers and critics of the age of reconstruction, and eventually its historians, accept this understanding of the physical environment, then the terms of criticism and discussion could be guided from within the physical process and, therefore, the terms of design would no longer be seen as exclusive to the social reconstruction process. After all, the political implications of design do not precede it and are not only to be found within it, but are also present in the very act of selecting a style or of building in a clearly specific manner. Perhaps if we pay more attention to the design aspects of the built environment we would be able to show how the social and the physical forms of reconstruction are inextricably intertwined.

Notes

1. A. Hourani, "Ideologies of the Mountain and the City," in Roger Owen, ed., *Essays on the Crisis in Lebanon* (London: Ithaca Press, 1976), pp. 33–41.
2. See for instance K. Lynch, *Managing the Sense of a Region* (Cambridge, Mass.: MIT Press, 1976).
3. A. Vidler, "The Third Typology," *Oppositions 7*, Winter 1976, pp. 1–4.

From the Geography of Fear to a Geography of Hope

by
H.E. Ghassan Tuéni

This monster of a city, or *city-region*, is united in form, but pregnant with contradictions. It is marked with the scars of successive wars, visible in its diversified and inconsistent frontiers: bordered to the north, so far, by Kaslik, to the south by Sidon, and extending east as far as Aley, Beit-Mery, and Bikfaya.

Uninterrupted, disorderly and haphazard constructions have brought together Furn al-Shubbak, Shiyyah, Ain al-Remmaneh, Burj al-Brajneh, Uzai, Shwayfat, Aramoun, Bshamoun, Hazimeh, Baabda, Yarzeh, Sin al-Fil, Mansouriyyet al-Metn, Mkalles, Ain Saadeh, Fanar, Rabièh, Naccash, Kornet Shahwan, Deek al-Mehdi, Zalka, Jal al-Dib, Burj Hammoud, Dora, and others in the maze of places that I might have forgotten. Even while the war was going on, we were building surreptitiously, often by night. Indeed, we managed to build (a credit to our resilience and resourcefulness, as some are inclined to say) more square meters of home and office space than we have destroyed. Until recently, the places I mentioned and those I didn't, where buildings sprang up overnight, all were localities, villages, and small towns enjoying a modicum of self-sufficiency, some content with being suburbs of the capital. Others became slums harboring revolt and violence. The rich and privileged who moved there took shelter in their own exclusive 'bubbles' of country clubs, *park-townlet* preserves which now punctuate our landscape.

This whole area – may we not call it 'region-city?' – bathes in total chaos, where the industrial, commercial, and residential intermix with residues of agricultural economy. Deregulated by the uncertainties of its future, as well as by hasty developers, it is an insult to urbanization. It also violates the most elementary conservation policy. It may be interesting to remember here that as far back as 1961, a prime minister with vision, Saeb Salam, solemnly proclaimed the creation of 'Greater Beirut,' whose sole ambition was to extend the city to Khaldeh, Furn al-Shubbak, and Burj Hammoud, borrowing from vague urban studies that suggested such a move. The project and the man both were bullied by 'confessionalists.' Instead, ruthless and savage developments were creating what soon became the theaters of the wars that have followed ever since.

The fundamental difference between the two 'Greater Beiruts' is worth noting here. The first was the culmination of a peaceful phenomenon of *conversion* toward the city, started over a century ago in the mid 1800s, under the dual impetus of trade and politics. Relatively slow at the outset, this largely spontaneous process gathered momentum after 1860, then rapidly growing after World War I, culminated in the city of the post-

World War II era, particularly between the 1950s and 1960s.

The second 'Greater Beirut' phenomenon is but a distressing atomization and fragmentation of city life and city structures. Under the effects of the successive wars, as people were fleeing Beirut, they were promptly replaced by other deportees; at first slowly and in limited waves, then nervously, in panic, and thereafter in the most dramatic conditions. Business had to follow, reinvented at every stage. First improvising new souks with the same old names, then inventing and investing in new hometowns, many of which rapidly boomed, whereas others were content to survive sporadic hours of glory. Schools, colleges, hospitals, and even improvised institutions of higher learning all followed.

The country was not only splintered; offensive forms and patterns of social life, some of which (*including* casinos, nightclubs, and precarious tourist hotels) mushroomed here and there. Even in times of acute warfare, this strange, unreal life was booming, reinforced by a thriving and pathological 'war economy' which carried every form of the illicit, the obscene, and the mischievous.

The tragic paradox is that while the city was being killed, when it did not commit suicide, its offshoots were inheriting its characteristics, positive and negative alike.

A form of resilience, indeed, bereft of morality, rarely matched in recent history, and which some ascribed, not without a strange sense of pride, to the 'earthly' character of the Lebanese. This became visible not only in their proverbial determination to survive but to live as best they could, not hesitating at times to display scandalously the surprising wealth acquired by warlords and their clientele on all sides of all the fences, with no exception whatsoever.

Going beyond *judgments of value*, let us now ask: where would we stand if we were to examine the future of the present Greater Beirut?

What recommendations? And for what reconstruction? Reconstruction cannot and should not be debated as an abstract problem, as concepts to be proposed in the vacuum of unknown communities, composed of unknown citizens, and managed by still more unknown authorities. We find the Lebanese divided into two categories: the 'do's' and the 'do not's.'

Confronted with ideas, schemes, or blueprints, they suddenly rise, as if in some mythical agora, to talk endlessly and to get lost in giant debates. We find them gladly accepting to divide, over and over again, into five constant categories, of which none can be convinced by any.

First: *The Fatalists.*
To them, the Beirutis are and have always been so ... and so is Lebanon. It is the curse of History!

They love to indulge in doomsday scenarios, the least dramatic of which is that the war has not really ended. So why waste our time, more efforts, and all the monies that we do not have?

Second: *The Pessimists.*
".... So, what can we do?" they ask.

Are we not all engaged in strangling Beirut? We *should* save it. But what about the *others*?

Nobody will, nobody can ... least of all the government!

And if so, none better will come to power. The whole ruling class is rotten.

We should keep trying, but the Lebanese are unruly people.... They don't want to be governed, they don't want to be educated.

We're comfortable, and joyfully sliding down into a terrible state of underdevelopment.

Conclusion: we have the City we deserve.

But good luck to you – they say – if you want to change it.

Third: *The Optimists.*
Never discouraged, nor discourageable, they are always ready to jump to a drawing board.

Not only are they inclined to look at the rosy side of things, they picture things in that way, even though they are black: Streets are cleaner now, so there's progress. Buildings are erected, but unsold? So what!... Can't we wait?

Patience is the motto, even if we do not fill our patiently earned time with any action.

But we're always eagerly hoping, and moving, even if we have nowhere to move to.

Fourth: *The Nostalgics.*
Beirut will return.... So wait, they say. Don't touch *my* past, my history, lest you spoil it. Is it already gone?... Be patient with the past.

The streets are there, clean them. The souks, my God – you, not the war, are destroying them.

Was it all a dream, a nightmare?

Okay for reconstruction.

But do you really think reconstruction will be stronger than war? And triumph?

Fifth: *The Pragmatists.*
To them, reality is 'touchable,' or it is not reality.

You speak to them of men, of liberty unpredictable, or ideas and ideals? Okay, but what about stones and iron and cement? And infrastructures? Be careful on infrastructures. Are they not 'more real'?

Livability is what life commands. Blueprints for the future? Maybe not, but plans, plans, plans, tested by figures and hard-core realities.

The only concession: if the city does not create life, so what? Let us live, but live practically... then life will re-create the city, and maybe change people and land alike.

The Human Imperative

Beirut is today a *collage* of cities and townlets. It should become a harmonious megalopolis of microcommunities. Each community is to retain its identity, its own culture, from the pristine garden towns to industrial zones and patches of farming areas and greenhouses. Even the present Beirut should not alter its diversity. On the contrary, diversity should be enhanced going beyond mere coexistence into 'conviviality.' Hence a region in a city, to avoid present suffocation, with new zones and zoning regulations. New systems of 'interaction' and communication. The haphazardly built patrician 'country clubs' should multiply and evolve into open spaces for cultural promotion, social exchange, and dialogue, to which not only the *chic*, but the underprivileged and marginalized suburbs must have easy access.

Fig. 1. Rebuilding an infrastructure around the city center

The Environmental Imperative

A 'state of emergency' must be proclaimed to save the natural environment, the landscape, from perpetual as well as temporary destruction: concerted efforts must be made to preserve *'environmental human rights,'* with ample citizens' participation to correct present government abuses of clean air, healthy water, waste disposal management, etc.

The first measure: the 'Fakhreddine approach,' i.e., a forest belt around the present city. A salvation of nature: every green area, however large and wherever it is, should be considered a sacred heritage, and proclaimed *non edificandi*. Every community or town must be compelled to build playgrounds and establish parks and open areas. Town squares must be preserved as pedes-

trian havens. Trees should be planted to shade the roads and streets, using sidewalks where they exist, building new ones where they don't.

Voluntary groups, students, and disaffected youths, must be mobilized. Even our fairly idle army must be made to contribute systematically, as has sporadically been the case.

We should be saving the shoreline, or rather what is left of it, particularly the former Jnah beaches, the old *'mudawar'* area of East Beirut, and the new Jdaydeh reclaimed land. Force 'Linord,' if implemented, and other development projects, not to build high-rises on the seafront, but instead civilized sea-parks and public swimming facilities should be created. Open access to salvaged, as yet undeveloped shorelines north of Jounieh and south of Khaldeh.

The Socio-Economic Imperative

First and foremost, what's needed is a comprehensive, phased policy to bridge the natural gaps between city and periphery. Periphery should be *'civitasized*,' not to say civilized, to prevent the 'slumming' of Beirut. We must prevent cheap labor towns from choking the city. Remember the 'misery belt' of the 1960s which became the red belt, or 'fire belt' of the 1970s and its role in provoking the Civil War.

A political solution to the security problem of the Palestinian camps must be found with an economic dimension to it. Neither a geographic class war nor a political class war should be allowed to happen again. We should avoid sowing further the seeds of a new civil war between the city's microcommunities and the mini-towns of the periphery.

Extrovert expansion, resulting from introvert progress and development, must not generate socio-economic conflicts. The industrial belt must be carefully reconsidered. Industrial zones should gradually be transferred to areas well beyond the city limits, ensuring appropriate transport and harbor facilities.

The 'transnational city' must return to Beirut. No viable alternative in the region has succeeded in replacing Lebanon's capital in twenty-five years of trial and error. Using Max Weber's definition, Beirut must return as a 'massive communications switchboard.' Far from us is the idea of seeking to re-create the Levantine city that was a mere romantic curiosity for nineteenth-century Orientalists and travelers: 'the city as spectacle.' Yet, much of the legendary characteristics of the Alexandrine, Antiochian, and East Mediterranean harbor cities must be revived and developed to global dimensions.

Given the basic cultural infrastructure of international trade which the Lebanese have always easily acquired, their traditional, centennial fluency in multiple languages, plus their tested ingenuity in trade and discovery – given all this, the Lebanese have retained their letters of credit, notwithstanding the war years. Other East Mediterranean cities could not measure up in the interim. To this we must add, beyond classic 'cosmopolitanism,' the continued physical presence in Beirut and Lebanon of foreign communities, or communities of foreign descent which have maintained roots in their countries of origin, and can thus draw on resources there. This in itself is an important human channel of perpetual contact and renewal. It keeps Lebanon constantly on the alert, familiar with innovations and progress. In this context skills are developed and foreign labor is welcome. So are leaders of foreign corporations and institutions, as well as auxiliary and ancillary personnel.

We must all bear in mind, at all levels, that reconstruction can only be sustained if we expand the range of profitable private investments. Hence, the economic imperative must play, with its social implications, a regulatory role not only in reconstruction schemes but also in all fields of development, not excluding the urban planning of the future megalopolis.

The 'transitional city' is obviously not faultless. The difficulties sometimes created by the lack of management of what is called, in a derogatory manner, Third World people: the low-income population, mostly workers

Fig. 2. View of Beirut in the early '70s

and peddlers. But this should in no way be conducive to any xenophobia or limitations on the freedom of movement of persons and goods, as it is of paramount importance to the macroeconomy and possible cash-earning, export-oriented industries.

Should we forget, be it for a time, our old, now dormant, and probably *dépassé* share of the growing international tourist market? By all means not. But the rules of the game should change. Neighboring countries, friendly or otherwise, have already built circuits with greater attractions and facilities. To match this competition necessitates not only new or renovated hotels, but a comprehensive policy which goes from re-creating beaches to conserving natural wealth and restoring an internationally recognized heritage, its antique cities, and abandoned vestiges or monuments. The heritage cities must, in this context, coordinate efforts within a specialized intercity council.

A most positive feature cannot be denied: despite an absence of nearly a quarter of a century, Lebanon was able to attract, as soon as signs of health appeared again, the support of major international banks and investors. More significant perhaps is the eagerness of world artists to perform at festivals, although this is, as yet, uncertain.

The Cultural Imperative

In concluding his marvelous book *Beirut Reclaimed*, Samir Khalaf calls for the creation of new 'political culture,' a culture of tolerance which "demands, among other things, that every Lebanese today should change his perception of the 'other.'" "Only by so doing," he tells us, "can we begin to transform the geography of fear into genuine, but guarded forms of coexistence."

Surely Samir does not want us to stop at mere coexistence and to be guarded, which would be the case if this notion is to be understood as static and conducive to merely repairing the past or restoring it.

So let us but briefly talk about our cultural imperative existentially, and in a *dynamic* perspective looking beyond the 'geography of fear' to horizons of creativity, progress, and idealism. If war and the post-war consequences have led the Lebanese, often wittingly, into 'collective amnesia,' our first task, within reconstruction, is to open the gates to the past, old and new. Yet in doing so we should be selective. We should be armed with reason, critical, but also with respect and fervor. If our culture is in crisis, let us also remember that culture is the way to overcome the crisis and resolve it.

Catharsis should come first. But the objective should be to change Lebanon from within, while preserving its true soul, the ideals we have entertained over the centuries, the destiny that has been ours. Our 'passion to pacify the pathos' should not obliterate soul searching, nor harness our initiative to seek inventiveness in all arts, all letters, all sciences. So let us trust the process in which we have all been engaged, at times with great success, and without having ever allowed the most challenging dialectics to endanger the peace of our yet fragile civil society.

A caveat is in order here: let us beware of parochial complacency. Advocating the creation, in the center of town, and wherever welcome, of war monuments and museums should not transfigure Lebanon into a living memorial to war. Beyond cataloging the victims and catastrophes of the war, and engaging in some hero worshipping of dubious taste, let us orient our interest toward nurturing hopes for a peaceful future. The redemption of our cultural destiny can only come from entering fully the global avenues not only of information, but of partaking, or hoping to partake, in research and invention.

A transformation of our institutions of higher learning should be a major component of the city's reconstruction. The *campus* notion, dear to all of us, should be preserved and adopted not merely for students' welfare, but as the only suitable environment for academic serenity, peace of mind, dialogue, and love of ideas. Campus universities should be patterned on the American University in Beirut's experiment, which today stands as the one and only vibrant sanctuary attesting to distinguished heritage in this regard. For we should always remember that we are building for a new generation. They, better than us, and probably alone, can understand and implement the imperatives of a revival of land and country, a renaissance in all fields. They – the new generation – should be able to reinterpret culture, the culture of the future, in popular terms, not merely to express the national or collective memory, but to invent the ways and means that will heal society from the scars of war, the culture of the barricades, and the barricades' culture. Postwar society, all over Lebanon, will undoubtedly be and should be molded by the city's popular culture.

The Historic Imperative

The first question that comes to one's mind, hammered by so many and from so many angles, is the following: should Beirut or its center, even if deprived of life, become a museum-town? I think we are now nearing a realistic, though not universally accepted solution: Beirut is not Pompeii, but should seek its emulation, as far as humanly feasible, by approaching the models of both Athens and Rome, where one constantly wonders whether it is antiquity that inhabits the modern town, or the reverse. Equally important, nearer to us, let us look at such models as Grenada, Cordova, or Segovia – why not? – at France's friends, not Paris, but Avignon, Orange, and all of Provence.

The surprising fact, however, is that dealing with antiquity, particularly in Beirut's center, is a more complicated and forbidding exercise than rearranging Greek and Roman ruins. Beirut, we always knew, had both Greek and Roman ruins. What we

rediscovered, some with joy, others with surprise, and Solidere with initial dismay, is that our archaeological finds go as far back as the Bronze Age. These finds reveal an important Phoenician town, unsuspected; then a Persian presence, not to speak of the latter Hellenistic, Byzantine, medieval, and Mamluk vestiges; then nearer to present life, Lebanese Arab (Fakhreddine) ruins, and finally intact Ottoman monuments. Solidere could not, understandably, keep everything *in situ*, one civilization on top of the other: temples below churches, the *'decumanus maximus'* crossing from one square to another, with huge columns buried here and there, mosaics in the middle of vital streets, and last but not least, the arches of the probable Roman forum or basilica, and the School of Law, buried under modern landmarks.

Keeping all this *in situ* means chaos and paralysis. The golden rule devised is almost satisfactory to all as it is inspired from important cities which moved, for example, most of their mosaics from streets to adorn and embellish monuments and museums. Here and there, arches and columns must be testimonies to antique space and history. Museums, plural not singular, should be enriched, but important pieces should be incorporated into buildings being erected on their sites, and thus be given a new lease on life, let alone their original aesthetic contribution.

A few words now about the Beirut Museum, semi-destroyed, already 'overstuffed' and, incidentally, 'under-staffed' – and which cannot possibly, if we were to revise its obsolete museography, harbor all the treasures now unearthed. So, why one museum only? And why is it an incongruous mélange of disparate vestiges and artifacts?

Why not a museum for Phoenician to classical antiquity, another for Islamic art and jewelry, of which Beirut, incidentally, has one of the most important collections in the world; a Christian art, particularly Byzantine, museum, possibly in one of the churches; a medieval museum in the remnants of a Crusader monument, say 'the Castle of the Sea.' Let alone the museums reaching into modern concepts of education: a science museum, a zoological and botanical museum, an anthropological museum, a museum of modern art, a museum of modern history, a historical museum of the city of Beirut, etc. And last but not least, a reborn, modernized national library to house our now dispersed documents, archives, and manuscripts.

All this has to be said now and emphasized as a healthy counterbalance to the mounting, almost obsessional, yet not to be derided archaeological consciousness. History is not of archaeology alone; archaeology is but a witness, a didactic component of history, and an emblem for the future. Heritage, live heritage, is what counts most. It should be a source of pride reborn, a shield against real and imagined threats. The lessons of the past should be taught by every possible modern, electronic means, not excluding virtual reality displays. But more constantly present will be the role of landmarks, monuments, statues, squares, and streets renamed, opening to each and all the closed citadels of communal life, but also reminiscing the forgotten heroes and occulted events. Example? Who remembers still the forty martyrs hanged on Martyrs' Square,

whose fate, as a square, is now uncertain? Where is the castle of Fakhreddine in Beirut, and why not a statue? What, apart from present futilities, happened in Parliament Square?

And what was, not what will be, the Grand Serail, the Justice Palace (now CDR), and the *Sanaeh* buildings, now half a university and half a government house? And Unesco? And the first printing press (St. Georges'), and the oldest press building? And who, apart from Lamartine and de Gaulle, was living where, and when, and how? And the souks, of course, the history of houses and streets, etc.? Here the media should be called upon to play their finest historical role as messengers and gate-keepers, not only of today's news, but of the splendid heritage; a unique witness to our living past.

The Urban Imperative

'Urban wisdom' is what we need to restructure the Greater Beirut reality as a city-region. Not merely 'town-and-country' integrated urban design, but a mix of technicity, sociology, vision, and universal knowledge that is particularly culture oriented; 'historicism' and above all a readiness to consult and listen to the 'users,' the present inhabitants, as well as the future generations of Lebanese.

We should always remember that the city is not the stones, but stones built by men, for men's welfare and progress, and according to their rational design. Above all, let's overcome the skyscraper syndrome. We should limit the high-rises to business districts; avoid, if not prohibit, high-rise dwellings in rural areas and forest towns, such as Yarzeh, Fanar, Mansouriyyeh, Rabieh, etc. Protect and enhance village squares (e.g., Baabda). Balance all high-rises, including the city's, with broad green areas, dotted with one- or two-story public buildings and facilities, such as exhibition, theater, and concert halls. Encourage neighborhoods' character in and around the city center, as well as wherever they are in the city, particularly around churches, mosques, and as many landmark buildings as possible; or in areas where antique *quartiers* are or should be preserved, which is now the case in the Burj district, the former souks (the pedestrian area), and other localities being rebuilt or restored in Solidere's revised scheme – which incidentally, is a major departure from the initial, uncultured, and almost despotic version.

One also must pay tribute to initiatives following APSAD's which are materializing in major conservation decisions, as well as private schemes reclaiming old districts. We should stop all wild commercial housing projects in the vicinity of Beirut until a comprehensive master plan is drawn up and imposed giving priority to low-cost housing for young couples. Incentives may be given to *wakf* properties and community-owned broad lands. In the same vein, we must avoid, at all costs, building in the city a collection of ghost towns: giant, but economically inadequate centers soon to be 'squattered,' or to attract the wrong people to the wrong places. Here, a remark: I am told by the young upcoming architect Nabil Gholam that "most of the reconstruction energy in Beirut so far has been exercised in

the old-fashioned and rigid prewar framework." If there is any truth to this charge, recommendations must be addressed to the proper authorities, and violations examined before it is too late. In this perspective, a reassessment of the slaughterhouse and garbage disposal projects is long overdue. The danger to public health and the environment of such scandalous enterprises as Burj Hammoud must alert us all.

Similarly, the abnormal situation with all of its complexities of the so-called *dahia*, or the southern suburbs of Beirut, a conglomerate of shabby towns unique in their high density of basically poor, displaced groups, now an almost independent society, cannot remain beyond the law, a menace to social development and order. Bringing the area to an acceptable degree of normalcy is a very daunting task as it entails political dispositions that cannot be dealt with by Lebanon alone, independently of the regional context, much the same fate of the Palestinian camps. Yet middle- and long-term policies must be negotiated today if they are to be applicable tomorrow. In all cases, preserving the sovereignty of the state must go hand in hand with the public concern for health, environment, and urban development.

The Elisar development project seemed to be an excellent approach, but proved a poor beginning. The reasons for its so far unsuccessful implementation may depend, as is said, on financial implications of an embarrassing nature! But if neither Elisar nor the adjoining highway to South Lebanon are implemented, much of the future of the reconstruction of Beirut remains in jeopardy. Let us add that Elisar, if properly understood, should serve as a model for other neighborhoods. Such projects would mean a tremendous social betterment, and the opening of unexpected economic horizons.

Finally, a major observation which takes us from the urban to the political: we all know that free government is inversely proportional to the size of the community. So we should, by a system of multimunicipal consultations, neither take the megalopolis into an Orwellian 'Big Brother' society, nor continue the present process of municipal, hence political, disintegration.

Biographical Notes on the Authors

Freddie C. Baz is advisor to the chairman at Banque Audi Sal and managing director of Bankdata Financial Services WLL. Baz received his Ph.D. in economics at the Sorbonne in Paris. He started his banking career in Lebanon and pursued it in France before returning to his homeland to establish himself as an economic and financial consultant and to found his own company in 1986: Bankdata Financial Services WLL. Freddie Baz publishes *Bilanbanques*, an extensive annual reference book on the structural analysis of banks operating in Lebanon, and a yearly update of the Lebanese economy with facts and figures entitled "Ecochiffres." He is also the author of "The Banque Audi Quarterly Economic Report," since its inception in 1991. In July 1991, Freddie Baz joined Banque Audi Sal as advisor to the chairman responsible for planning and development. In March 1996, he became a member of the bank's board of directors.

Farès el-Dahdah is currently an assistant professor of architecture and the director of Graduate Studies at Rice University. He received his BFA and BArch from the Rhode Island School of Design, and his MAUD and DDes from the Harvard University Graduate School of Design. In 1994, he was the recipient of the Caudill Lectureship from Rice University's School of Architecture. His essays in architectural history and theory have been published in numerous journals such as *Assemblage, ANY, Casabella*, and in such publications as *Unprecedented Realism* and *Slow Space*.

Angus Gavin, MA, MAUD, RIBA, is urban planning advisor to the chairman of Solidere, the Lebanese Company for the Development and Reconstruction of the Beirut Central District. Before joining the company, Gavin was leader of the consulting team that prepared the Beirut Central Business District Master Plan. His previous experience in the Middle East has included the planning and implementation of new city and community projects, several involving large reclamation schemes in Saudi Arabia and a number of Gulf States, and the preparation of a historic district action plan for the center of Amman, Jordan. He has also been an urban planner and consultant to Turkey, Greece, West Africa, and the UK. Before moving to Beirut in 1992, he was with the London Docklands Development Corporation as head of urban design and a development manager in the Royal Docks Area. He was a professor at the University of Virginia, and also taught at the Bartlett School, University College London.

Joumana Ghandour Atallah is a practicing architect in Beirut, Lebanon. She received her BFA and BArch from the Rhode Island School of Design and her MA in architecture and urban design from the Harvard University Graduate School of Design, where she won the Urban Design Thesis Prize in 1990. Ghandour Atallah has since practiced architecture in New York and Beirut, and worked as an urban designer at Solidere between 1994 and 1996. She is a member of the newly revived committee for the Baalbeck Festival and the director of the Beirut activities of Plan B, Institute for Urban Design Studies in Lebanon and the Middle East.

Marlène Ghorayeb pursued her advanced studies in architecture in Paris where she currently works at the Laboratoire des Mutations Urbaines. Ghorayeb's dissertation on Michel Ecochard is considered a major contribution on overseas French modern architecture. She has published extensively on this and related topics.

Jens Hanssen is presently at St. Anthony's College, Oxford University, completing his Ph.D. in modern history. In 1996, he received a fellowship from DAAD, the German Foreign Exchange Service, to study at the Center for Behavioral Research at the American University of Beirut. His thesis is entitled, "The Effect of Ottoman Rule on Fin de Siècle Beirut: The Wilaya of Beirut, 1888–1914." Previously he received grants to study at Tübingen University (Islamic studies, political studies), Alexandria University (Faculty of Arts: Arabic), and Durham University (Middle Eastern and Islamic studies).

Mona Harb el-Kak is an architect, urban planner, and research associate at CERMOC-

Beirut (Centre d'Etudes et de Recherches sur le Moyen-Orient Comtemporain). She is currently pursuing a Ph.D. in political science at Montpellier University, France, and focusing on a research project entitled, "Urban Services and Political Spaces: Actors and Stakes of the Reconstruction Process in Southern Beirut."

K. Michael Hays, BArch, MArch, Ph.D., AM (hon), is professor of architectural theory at the Harvard University Graduate School of Design. Hays is the founding editor of *Assemblage*. His published work focuses on ideological issues in the history of the avant-garde and on current debates in the field of critical theory. His book, *Modernism and the Posthumanist Subject*, examines productivist architecture and its mass cultural reception. Hays has served as lecturer and chairman of the program in the history and theory of architecture at Princeton University, and as assistant professor at the Rhode Island School of Design.

Oussama R. Kabbani received his BArch degree with distinction in 1985 from Beirut Arab University, and his MA in urban design from the Harvard Graduate School of Design in 1988. He was awarded the Harvard Graduate School of Design Urban Design Thesis Prize for the class of 1988. Between 1988 and 1992 he practiced urban planning and design with the Boston Redevelopment Authority and was a member of the team awarded a *Progressive Architecture* citation and an AIA Urban Design Award of Excellence for the Central Artery in Boston. Kabbani joined Solidere, the Lebanese Company for Development and Reconstruction of

Beirut Central District, during its formative stage in 1992 to review the master plan for postwar reconstruction in Beirut. In 1994, he assumed the role of town planning department manager, and in 1997 he was appointed head of the Urban Management Department at Solidere. He is the author of *Rebuilding Beirut*, published by the Center for Lebanese Studies.

Samir Khalaf, BA, MA, Ph.D., is professor of sociology and director of the Center for Behavioral Research at the American University of Beirut. The Center sponsors research and activities that are particularly related to the relationship between the reconstruction of the physical environment and the challenges of social reintegration. Since its revitalization under Khalaf's directorship, the Center has acted as a magnet for international scholars to Lebanon. Prior to his tenure at AUB, Khalaf was adjunct professor at Princeton University and visiting lecturer at MIT, where he organized the conference on the postwar reconstruction of Beirut in 1991 and coedited *Recovering Beirut* with Philip Khoury. He is the author of several books on the urban sociology of Beirut and the political culture of Lebanon, mainly *Lebanon's Predicament, Hamra of Beirut*, and *Beirut Reclaimed*. He is currently completing a publication on American missionaries in the East.

Rodolphe el-Khoury received a BArch from the Rhode Island School of Design, an MA from MIT, Program in History, Theory, and Criticism, and a Ph.D. in architectural history from Princeton University. His latest publications include a translation and criti-

cal edition of Jean François de Bastide's *The Little House: An Architectural Seduction* and *Architecture in Fashion*, a collaborative patchwork of essays and design projects. With Rodolfo Machado, he coauthored *Monolithic Architecture*, a catalogue for the exhibition they curated at the Heinz Architectural Center of the Carnegie Institute, Pittsburgh. El-Khoury started his independent architectural practice in Cambridge, Massachusetts, in January 1997; until 1986, he was a principal in the Boston firm Office da. El-Khoury is an assistant professor at Harvard's Department of Urban Planning and Design. He has taught previously at Columbia University and the School of Architecture at Louisiana State University. He has lectured at several institutions in the United States and abroad.

Rafael Moneo, Dipl. Arch, DArch, AM (hon), Josep Lluís Sert Professor of Architecture, was chairman of the Department of Architecture at Harvard University Graduate School of Design from 1985 to 1990 and now teaches in the design studio. Before joining the GSD, Moneo was a fellow at the Spanish Academy in Rome and taught in Barcelona and Madrid. His projects include the Bakinter Building in Madrid, Logroño Town Hall, the Museum of Roman Art in Mérida, the headquarters of Provisión Española and the San Pablo Airport in Seville, the transformation of Vellahermosa Palace in Madrid, the Pilar & Joan Miró Foundation in Palma de Mallorca, and the Davis Art Museum at Wellesley College. Moneo won the 1996 Pritzker Prize for architecture. He has been awarded the Gold Medal by the Spanish Government, the Arnold W. Brunner

Memorial Prize by the American Academy of Arts and Letters, the Prince of Viana Prize (Spain), and the Swedish Schock Prize on Visual Arts. He received his Dipl. Arch and DArch from the Madrid School of Architecture.

Nasser Rabbat (Ph.D. MIT, 1991) is associate professor at the History, Theory, and Criticism of Architecture Program, Department of Architecture, MIT. His main areas of interest are the history of Islamic architecture, medieval urban history, and nineteenth-century historiography. He recently published *The Citadel of Cairo: A New Interpretation of Royal Mamluk Architecture* (Leiden: E.J. Brill, 1995); "The Formation of the Neo-Mamluk Style in Modern Egypt" in *The Education of the Architect*: *Historiography, Urbanism and the Growth of Architectural Knowledge. Essays Presented to Stanford Anderson on his Sixty-Second Birthday*, edited by Martha Pollak (Cambridge, Mass.: MIT Press, 1997); and "Al-Azhar Mosque: An Architectural Chronicle of Cairo's History," *Muqarnas* 13 (1996). He is currently working on a book on the visual milieu of the counter-Crusade in Syria and Egypt in the twelfth to thirteenth centuries.

Peter G. Rowe is the Raymond Garbe Professor of Architecture and Urban Design at Harvard University, where he also serves as dean of the Graduate School of Design, a position he has held since 1992. Prior to joining the Harvard faculty in 1985, Rowe was director of the School of Architecture at Rice University and a senior member of several research organizations, including the Rice Center and the Southwest Center for Urban Research. The author of numerous articles, Rowe is also author of the following books: *Principles for Local Environmental Management* (Ballinger, 1978); *Design Thinking* (MIT, 1987); *Making the Middle Landscape* (MIT, 1991); *Modernity and Housing* (MIT, 1993); *Civic Realism* (MIT, 1997); and *Asia Modern* (Costa and Nolen, 1998). Rowe received a BArch from Melbourne University in Australia, an MArch in Urban Design from Rice University, and an AM (hon) from Harvard University.

Helen Sader is currently associate professor of archaeology in the Department of History and Archaeology at the American University of Beirut. She received an MA in archaeology from the American University of Beirut in 1979 and a Ph.D. in Assyriology and northwest Semitic epigraphy from the Eberhard-Kark University, Tübingen, Germany in 1984. She is scientific coordinator of the AUB-Tübingen archaeological excavations in downtown Beirut (site BEY 020). Her main publications are concerned with the history of the Aramaeans and Phoenician epigraphy and archaeology. Her recent publications include: "Nècropoles et tombes phéniciennes du Liban," *Cuadernos de Arqueologia Mediterránea* 1 in 1995, "Beirut BEY 020: Preliminary Report" on the 1995 excavations, with Uwe Finkbeiner, *"Bulletin d'Archéologie et d'Architecture Libanaises,"* volume 1, part 2 in 1997, and "Tell el Burak: An Unidentified City of Phoenician Sidon," *Festschrift Wolfgang Röllig*, Tübingen, in 1997.

Assem Salam is president of The Order of Engineers and Architects in Beirut, an elected position he has held since 1995. He received his architectural education at Cambridge University, England, and worked on the English new towns before returning to Lebanon to establish his own practice. His office is reputed for the design of such major public buildings as the Ministry of Tourism and the Serail of Sidon. He has also been in charge of the restoration of several architectural landmarks in Lebanon. Salam has served in several capacities on governmental planning agencies and he has taught at the American University of Beirut. He has lectured and published extensively on the reconstruction of Beirut.

Hashim Sarkis, BFA, BArch, MArch, Ph.D., is assistant professor of architecture at the Harvard Graduate School of Design, and teaches advanced urban design studio options and courses in politics and architecture. Sarkis is a founding member and programs director of Plan B, Institute for Urban Design Studies in Lebanon and the Middle East, a nonprofit organization concerned with postwar reconstruction. He practices architecture in the Middle East in collaboration with Hani Asfour. Sarkis has been a lecturer in MIT's Department of Architecture and a research fellow in MIT's Department of Urban Studies and Planning. He has taught design studios at RISD and Yale University and has been a visiting lecturer at the American University of Beirut. Through a Graham Foundation Grant, he is currently studying educational facilities in the United States. Sarkis is the author of several articles on architectural theory, urban planning, and Beirut architecture. He received his BArch and BFA from the Rhode Island School of Design, his MArch from the GSD, and his Ph.D. in architecture and political theory from Harvard University.

Jorge Silvetti studied architecture at the University of Buenos Aires and the University of California, Berkeley. Since 1975, he has taught at the Graduate School of Design, Harvard University, where he became chairman of the Department of Architecture in 1995. In total, Jorge Silvetti has received eight *Progressive Architecture* awards, several in collaboration with his partner Rodolfo Machado. Their firm Machado and Silvetti Associates has also received numerous awards, including an AIA National Honor Award, an AIA Brick in Architecture Award, three design awards from the New England Chapter of the AIA, and the first Award in Architecture given by the American Academy and Institute of Arts and Letters. Recent buildings and projects include a master plan and addition for the J. Paul Getty Villa in Malibu, a master plan, parking structure, and dormitory for Princeton University, a landmark tower and dormitory for the University of Cincinnati, a multi-use building for Seaside, Florida, and two pavilions in a park at the southern tip of Manhattan. Two monographs have been produced on the firm's work: *Buildings for Cities: Rodolfo Machado and Jorge Silvetti*, 1989, and *Unprecedented Realism: The Architecture of Machado and Silvetti,* 1985.

Jad Tabet is an architect who has run an established atelier in Paris with Sami Tabet since 1986. Since 1994, Tabet has been the leading master planner for the reconstruction of the souks of Beirut. He is currently in charge of several projects in Lebanon: a multimedia center and an office building in the Beirut Central District and a master plan for the Jezzine region (5,000 hectares) in southern Lebanon. In 1971, Tabet started his own practice in Beirut in association with Rahif Fayad. The firm undertook projects mainly in Lebanon, Yemen, and Saudi Arabia. Tabet received his diploma in architecture from the American University of Beirut in 1969. He taught architecture at the School of Architecture of Belleville (UP8) from 1992 to 1995, where he headed the "Atelier Beyrouth" postgraduate program. He has also taught and lectured at the Lebanese University, the American University of Beirut, the School of Architecture of Venice, the School of Architecture of Lyon, and the School of Architecture at MIT.

H.E. Ghassan Tuéni has been the publisher of *An-Nahar* since 1948. He was a member of the Lebanese parliament between 1951 and 1953. In 1970, Tuéni was vice-premier and Minister of Education and Information, and a cabinet member in 1975. He was Lebanon's permanent representative to the United Nations from 1977 to 1982. He is a member of the Board of Trustees of the American University of Beirut and a founding member of Balamand University in 1988, where he was president from 1990 to 1993 and is presently chancellor. He received an MA in political science from Harvard University in 1947. Tuéni writes regularly and has published several books on political conditions in Lebanon. Among his recent publications are, *Secret of the Trade and Other Secrets, Letters to President Sarkis,* and *The Republic on Vacation.*

Sources of illustrations and photographs:

All illustrations and photographs were provided courtesy of the authors, respectively, except in the following cases:

Wassek Adib: fig. 18, p. 99
Aga Khan Trust for Culture/Michel Ecochard: figs. 2–8, pp. 108–115; fig. 1, p. 127; fig. 1, p. 145
Ahmad Al-Assaad: figs. 3–4, p. 243; figs. 7–8, p. 245
Banque Audi Sal, Economic Analysis Unit: figs. 1–11, pp. 167–170
Richard Barnes: fig. 4, p. 72; fig. 1, p. 261
L. Benevolo, *The History of the City*, MIT Press, Cambridge, Mass., 1985, p. 932: fig. 1, p. 240
Ricardo Bofill: figs. 1–5, pp. 204–205
The Boston Globe, October 1990: fig. 2, p. 241
René Burri: fig. 9, p. 246
Constantinos Doxiadis Archives: fig. 2, p. 14; fig. 3, p. 152; figs. 1–10, pp. 187–195
Council for Development and Reconstruction: fig. 2, p. 130; figs. 11–12, pp. 197–198
Hans Curver: fig. 2, p. 27
Ferdinand Dagher: figs. 5–7, pp. 72–74

Dar al-Handasah: figs. 2–4, pp. 177–179; figs. 6–7, pp. 207–208
Michael Davie: fig. 13, p. 248
Fouad Debbas: fig. 1, p. 42; figs. 3–5, pp. 43–61; figs. 14–15, p. 248–249
Raymond Depardon: figs. 10–11, p. 247
Henri Eddeh: fig. 13, p. 95; figs. 21–22, p. 253
Pierre el-Khoury: fig. 14, p. 95; figs. 21–23, pp. 100–101
Linord: figs. 8–11, pp. 208–211
Pierre Nehmeh: figs. 16–17, pp. 97–98
Oscar Niemeyer Foundation: figs. 9–10, p. 76
Agnès Rousseau, DGA: fig. 10, p. 37
Assem Salam: figs. 24–26, pp. 102–103
Hashim Sarkis: fig. 3, p. 70; fig. 1, p. 107; fig. 9, p. 116; fig. 2, p. 281
Allen Sayegh: fig 2, p. 42
Solidere: fig. 1, p. 13; fig. 2, p. 145; figs. 1–16, pp. 217–232; fig. 12, p. 248; fig. 23, p. 254; fig. 1, p. 280; figs. 1–2, pp. 288–290
Jad Tabet: fig. 25, p. 255
Dimitri Trad: fig. 5, p. 88
André Wogenscky and Maurice Hindieh: fig. 15, p. 96

Front cover: Defense Ministry, André Wogenscky and
Maurice Hindieh, architects, 1965 (courtesy of the
architects)
Frontispiece: Photomontage of an urban renewal
project in the city center by Michel Ecochard, 1963
(Courtesy of Aga Khan Trust for Culture / Michel
Ecochard)

Back cover: ESCWA building proposal, courtesy of
Pierre el-Khoury; Building massing, plan of Saifi
Village, both courtesy of Solidere; Cité de la Mer,
entrance to plaza, courtesy of Pierre el-Khoury

Sources of illustrations and photographs: see page 303

Library of Congress Cataloging-in-Publication Data

Projecting Beirut--episodes in the construction and
reconstruction of a modern city / edited by Peter G.
Rowe and Hashim Sarkis.
            p.   c m.
            Includes bibliographical references.
            ISBN 3-7913-1938-8 (alk. paper)
            1. Architecture, Modern--20th century--
Lebanon--Beirut. 2. Architecture--Lebanon--Beirut.
3. City planning--Lebanon--Beirut--History--20th cen-
tury. 4. Urban renewal--Lebanon--Beirut. 5. Beirut
(Lebanon)--Buildings, structures, etc.
I. Rowe, Peter G.   II. Sarkis, Hashim.
NA1476.7.B45P76   1998
720 .95692'50904--dc21   98-11909 CIP

Manuscript edited by Claudine Weber-Hof

Prestel-Verlag, Mandlstrasse 26, D-80802 Munich
Tel.: (+ 49-89) 38 17 09-0, Fax: (+49-89) 38 17 09-35
and 16 West 22nd Street, New York, NY 10010 USA
Tel.: (212) 671 8199, Fax: (212) 627 9866

Prestel books are available worldwide.
Please contact your nearest bookseller
or write to either of the above addresses
for information concerning your
local distributor.

Design: Cilly Klotz
Lithography: Repro Ludwig, Zell am See
Printing: Biedermann, Parsdorf
Binding: Almesberger, Salzburg

Printed in Germany on acid-free paper

ISBN 3-7913-1938-8